Catholic Dogmatic Theology ⁺ A Synthesis

BOOK 1

Catholic Dogmatic Theology ✦ A Synthesis

BOOK 1, ON THE TRINITARIAN
MYSTERY OF GOD

JEAN-HERVÉ NICOLAS, OP

FOREWORD BY JOSEPH RATZINGER

FOREWORD TO THE ENGLISH EDITION
BY ARCHBISHOP ALLEN VIGNERON

TRANSLATED BY MATTHEW K. MINERD

The Catholic University of America Press
Washington, D.C.

Originally published as *Synthèse dogmatique: De la Trinité à la Trinité*, Paris, France © 1985, Beauchesne Editor. Toute demande concernant les droits de traduction, de reproduction, d'adaptation, en quelque langue que se soit, devra obligatoirement être adressé a Beauchesne Editeur, 7 Cité du Cardinal Lemoine 75005 Paris — France, Editeur de l'édition orignale.

Design and composition by Kachergis Book Design

Library of Congress Cataloging-in-Publication Data available from the Library of Congress

ISBN 978-0-8132-3439-7

Contents

———:———

Foreword to the English Edition   vii
by Archbishop Allen Vigneron

Translator's Preface   ix

Foreword to the Original Edition   xiii
by Cardinal Joseph Ratzinger

Preface to the Original Edition   xv

List of Abbreviations   xix

General Introduction   1

1. Introduction to The Mystery of One God   37
   in Three Persons

PART 1. THE MANIFESTATION OF THE
DIVINE PERSONS AND THE FAITH OF
THE CHURCH IN THE TRINITY

2. From One God to the Triune God   45

3. The Ways and Means for a Dogmatic Treatise   109
   on the Trinity

PART 2. THE DISTINCTION AND UNION OF
THOSE "BEING GOD" IN THE ONE GOD

4. The Processions in God   127

5. The Distinction of the Three Who Are One God   172

6. The Divine Persons   200

PART 3. CRITICAL REFLECTION ON
OUR KNOWLEDGE OF GOD

7. Reason, Revelation, and Theology in Our   283
   Knowledge of the Mystery

8. Knowledge of the Divine Persons in   309
   Their Singularity

PART 4. THE DIVINE PERSONS AT WORK
IN SALVATION HISTORY

9. From the Immanent Trinity to the   337
   Economic Trinity

10. Mission of a Divine Person   343

11. The Mission of the Word and of the Spirit   375

    Bibliography   397
    Index   407

Foreword to the English Edition

Archbishop Allen Vigneron

——————:——————

In guiding the work of the Second Vatican Council, St. John XXIII and St. Paul VI made it clear that this epochal event was not for the sake of the Church herself. As their successor Pope Francis might put it: the Council was not "self-referential." The aim of the Council was the renewal of the Church as the sacrament of Jesus Christ, the Light of the Nations—*Lumen gentium,* so that she would be the ever more effective instrument for sharing the Good News. The aim of the Council was to launch the Church once more out into the deep of evangelizing the world (cf. Lk 5:4).

The Council Fathers identified the renewal of theology as a necessary dimension of this more general project of renewal-for-mission. As part of that mandate they explicitly mentioned the role that the theological achievement of St. Thomas Aquinas ought to play in achieving this aim: "In order that they may illumine the mysteries of salvation as completely as possible, sshould learn to penetrate them more deeply with the help of speculation, under the guidance of St. Thomas, and to perceive their interconnections" (*Optatam totius,* 16).

As a bishop, charged, as I am, to do my part to fulfill the Great Commission "to make disciples of all nations" (Mt 28:19), I welcome the publication of the English translation of Fr. Nicolas's *Synthèse dogmatique,* since it makes readily available to students an effective instrument for Aquinas to guide them into a deeper understanding of the saving mysteries of the gospel. And as Cardinal Ratzinger affirms in his foreword to this work, Fr. Nicolas goes about his task of exploring the mind of Aquinas with the conviction that "revealed truths are not only truths. They are principles of life, conversion, and therefore also of preaching." Thus, the deeper penetration of gospel truth that students will achieve by joining with St. Thomas to think about them with the help of Fr. Nicolas will be a blessed resource for the Church on her mission to give an account for the hope that she offers the world in the name of Christ (cf. 1 Pt 3:15).

I first became acquainted with Fr. Nicolas's *Synthèse dogmatique* when I was engaged in teaching theology to seminarians. Since then I had looked for the day when this work would be available to English-speaking students in their own language. Through the considerable efforts of the translator, Dr. Matthew Minerd, with help of those he so generously acknowledges, I have the satisfaction of seeing my long-felt need for this resource met for the good of students and professors alike. To Dr. Minerd and his colleagues I offer my sincere thanks.

A key moment in my own theological studies was when a wise professor observed in passing, "To explain a profound mystery simply you must understand it profoundly." I have made this piece of advice an axiom for my study and for my teaching. I am confident that the appearance of Fr. Nicolas's *Synthèse dogmatique* in English will aid in that profound understanding which yields in students of theology the great good fruit of their being able to offer that clear and compelling explanation of the revealed mysteries which goes by the deceptive name of "simple."

Translator's Preface

————:————

This work represents the first portion of Fr. Nicolas's *Synthèse dogmatique*, a formidable pair of tomes which, in English, will presented as a series of separate thematic volumes. As Fr. Nicolas explains, *Synthèse dogmatique* is based upon a sequence of course lectures given over a number of decades. Because of these origins, his written French style can be a bit choppy at times, using formulations that are either fragmentary or idiosyncratic. The voice of the original classroom lecture texts is often obvious in the original French. Furthermore, as is particularly evident in the final volume of this series, Fr. Nicolas's own personal writing style (in contrast to his lecture-derived style) is *quite* wordy, often falling into sentences that are seventy to a hundred words in length, if not longer. In most cases, care has been taken to retain Fr. Nicolas's voice. However, upon consultation with Fr. Thomas-Joseph White, OP—to whom my work on this project owes a great debt—I decided it was best to err on the side of readability, for these texts are destined for use in the pedagogical formation of theologians. When slight stylistic modification was necessary, this generally required me to present a slightly more paratactic style than the more serpentine forms used by Fr. Nicolas. However, where there is a chance that I have added a nuance, I utilize square brackets (either for my added text or to provide the original language equivalent). Moreover, Fr. Nicolas frequently utilizes a non-standard style of quoting authors, setting off in block quotes even single lines of quotation. I have worked to stylistically integrate these quotations into a standard form conformed to the stylesheet of the Catholic University of America Press. On occasion, he expresses side comments or technical qualifications in small text as well. At the request of the Press's editors, these have been moved to footnote unless otherwise noted.

In Fr. Nicolas's original text, the footnotes were written in short-hand, referencing a single bibliography at the end of the lengthy volume. I have moved all bibliographical references to the footnotes for ease of reference. On occasion, I have had to note what appear to be mistakes by Fr. Nicolas in these notes.

In general, scriptural references have been taken from the Revised Standard Version of the Bible. Where contextual rhetorical concerns did not seem to allow this, I translated the text from the French provided by Fr. Nicolas. All such citations from the Revised Standard Version are marked in the scriptural citation. For example, if a direct citation has been taken from Romans 6:1, it is cited as Rom 6:1 (RSV).

All direct citations from Denzinger are taken from the English translation provided in the forty-third edition published by Ignatius Press. Where available, citations from contemporary non-French works have been taken from authorized translations with the relevant citation details being provided in the appropriate footnotes. Also, due to style concerns, slight alterations to footnote numbering were necessary. All French authors have been translated anew. Because Fr. Nicolas has made slight interpretive nuances to his citations from St. Thomas, I have chosen to translate from his own translation of the Angelic Doctor but have done so with an eye to the original and always with a literal approach to Fr. Nicolas's own rendering. The same holds for his occasional citations Patristic and Scholastic sources. On occasion, Fr. Nicolas makes slight additions to citations from St. Thomas in order to clarify the latter's point. He does so in parentheses, and I have chosen to retain this formatting, instead of the use of brackets, which otherwise indicate my own occasional slight additions or clarifications to the Fr. Nicolas's text.

Thanks go to Dr. Reinhard Hütter and, especially, Fr. Thomas Joseph White, OP, for their support in undertaking this project, as well as to Matthew Levering, who offered friendly encouragement through the long hours of working on this volume in conjunction with future portions of Fr. Nicolas's text. Likewise, gratitude is owed to the Thomistic Institute (and a kind donor) for providing funds for the overall project of translating Fr. Nicolas's *Synthèse dogmatique*. Also, a generous reviewer helped me in the development of my craft as a translator; for this I am deeply appreciative. Finally, thanks are owed to all those persons involved in the editorial process without whom this volume would have been significantly more deficient: John Martino for his able and kind shepherding of the volume through the process of publication, David Dashiell for his indispensable copy-editing work, and to the design and marketing team for creating so beautiful a volume, by so profound a Thomist theologian.

This translation is dedicated to the eternal repose of the soul of Archabbot Paul Maher, OSB.

Foreword to the Original Edition

Cardinal Joseph Ratzinger

—————— : ——————

Ours is an age of hyper-specialization. Even in theology, publications stretch out beyond the horizon, making it increasingly difficult for one to grasp, in a single glance, the whole of theology. Hence, contemporary overviews of dogmatic theology are most often collective works by a number of authors. Certainly, such volumes contain profound treatments of particular topics; however, the connections between their various parts remain only extrinsic. Now, given that (according to Hegel's expression) "the Truth is the Whole," contemporary theological culture gives rise to something more problematic than merely didactic and pedagogical concerns: it compromises the very task of theology in what is essential to it. To this end, recall that Irenaeus of Lyon laid the foundation for Catholic theology, in the proper sense of the word, establishing it upon "the primordial system" (*Adv. Haer.* IV, 33, 8), upon what is fundamental for the unity of ecclesial life. This enabled him to perceive the unity of the Old and New Covenants, of the Creator and the Savior, of philosophy and faith, and what alone can constitute the distinctive character of theology.

Thus, for many reasons, the publication of Fr. Jean-Hervé Nicolas's dogmatic theology text, which matured over the course of many years of teaching, represents a theological event of great importance.

His choice on behalf of Thomism, which serves as his point of departure, is not based on St. Thomas's authority as such but, rather, on the latter's theological thought, which Fr. Nicolas receives by critically thinking it through anew. Above all else, the characteristic feature of such an approach to theology is its synthetic combination of historical knowledge and philosophical reflection. However, it also joins together the Church's teaching and critical reflection, as well as theory and practice. "Revealed truths," writes Fr. Nicolas, "are not only truths. They are principles of life, conversion, and therefore also of preaching." What strikes me in Fr. Nicolas's book is, above all, its sure erudition in exegesis and the history of dogmas. However, I am no less struck by something that is rarely encountered these days in pedagogical volumes of dogmatic theology: Fr. Nicolas's vigorous grasp of philosophical truths. This gives his book its depth and internal unity, and at the same time, makes his text compelling in a way that no more-or-less positivist organization of these various topics could be. The reader who allows himself to be guided by Fr. Nicolas will perceive that an authentically ecclesial theological outlook in no way impedes the power and openness of one's thought. On the contrary, it places our thought in profound agreement with the great thinkers of all ages, failing which all that remains is individual isolation and, ultimately, skepticism, depravation in want of the truth. May Fr. Nicolas's book help us to draw closer to this "unity in theology," without which theology, precisely as such, disintegrates. Thus, I hope that this text will be broadly received by many open-minded readers.

Rome, Feast of the Exaltation of the Cross [1984/5]

Preface to the Original Edition

———— : ————

Can a dogmatic synthesis be proposed today, faced as we are with many problems that have been raised in the field of theology? Can we do so, faced as we are, with grave doubts concerning positions that once seemed certain, as well as doubts concerning fundamental points, doubts that have not yet been overcome and brought under control?

The course in dogmatic theology from which this work emerged was indeed conceived as being such a synthesis, though one intended for the formation of young theologians. It was not concerned with dispensing them from the effort of entering in their own turn into these discussions and from expanding their own outlook concerning these matters, whether by welcoming new openings when they are justified and fruitful, or by rejecting them (though wisely and not without having measured what is at stake in the discussion, and also not without having attempted to find a response to the questions that gave birth to it, by clarifying and deepening past responses to these questions). In short, the goal of this work was to assure that they received a basic formation. On the basis of such a formation, they would be able to critique the new solutions in an intelligent manner, in light of the principles of theology. Likewise, they would be able to judge how far one can proceed along new pathways, along with what sort of renewals are needed for the former ways to be able to rejoin and connect new achievements to the origins of faith, thus integrating the new achievements into theology, all the while eliminating those proposals that ultimately cannot be integrated into theology in this way—but to do so in full awareness of what is at stake. Does not the introduction to any branch of knowledge begin with such a formation?

It was in no way expected that this course would be proposed (outside the already rather extended circle of students who followed upon each other for thirty years in pursuing the course, revised each time at the end of the cycle of three years that the course covered) to the larger circle of those who are interested in the study of theology, a circle of people that is increasingly expansive today: laypersons, religious men and women, priests, and candidates for the priesthood. Others desired that this course be published, and their arguments led me to write this text, a decision that is perhaps foolhardy, though not thoughtless.

Such a project could not have been brought to its completion without the encouragement I received from colleagues, former students, and friends. I cannot name them all. However, how could I not express my recognition by name to the person who first had the idea for the enterprise and who expended such energy in its implementation? Without him, it would doubtlessly not have been started and, in any case, could not have come to fruition. I refer to my confrere and friend, Fr. Christoph Schönborn, who was my colleague at the Faculty of Theology in Fribourg, where he taught Dogmatics in German.

I must also express my gratitude to the Council of the University of Fribourg, to the Conference of German bishops, to the Conference of Swiss bishops, to the Archbishop of Cologne, to my confreres and friends of the Dominican community of the Albertinum in Fribourg, and to the Dominican Community of Saint-André in Cologne. They graciously provided the financial assistance without which this project could not have been realized. I warmly thank them for their quite generous contributions and for the encouragement that it gives me.

Recognition is also owed to my former assistant, Fr. Juan Gutierrez Gonzales of the Missionaries of the Holy Spirit in Mexico, who aided me so efficaciously in the arduous work that was required in converting the notes distributed as a record for students into a manuscript prepared for publication. I likewise owe a debt of gratitude to the devoted collaborators who took on the task of copying out my text, carrying out this task to its conclusion. Their work began with an original text that was quite difficult to decipher, and they performed their task with much labor and intelligence.

His Eminence, Cardinal Ratzinger, the Prefect of the Congregation for the Doctrine of the Faith, has kindly agreed to write the foreword for this work. I am extremely sensitive to the great honor that he has shown me in so doing, not only on account of the lofty offices that he exercises in the Church's governance, but also, perhaps even more so, on account of the great renown as a theologian that he has acquired through the course of a long and fruitful career of teaching and writing. What he has written in his preface is doubtlessly more laudatory than this book deserves. Nonetheless, even if I must recognize that there is a great distance separating the realized work from the intention that was originally pursued, how could I not be pleased to see that my project was understood and approved in its essentials by a theologian of his merit? For this I wish to express my deep and abiding gratitude.

This book is fraternally dedicated to all of my former students at Saint-Maximin and Fribourg. Without them, this text would not have been written.

Abbreviations

—————:—————

D.-Sch.	Denzinger, *Enchiridion Symbolorum*
De pot.	Thomas Aquinas, *Quaestiones disputate De potentia*
De ver.	Thomas Aquinas, *Quaestiones disputate De veritate*
FC	*La foi catholique: textes doctrinaux du magistre de l'église,* ed. and trans. G. Dumiege
In Ioan.	Thomas Aquinas, *Expositio in Evangelium Ioannis*
In Meta.	Thomas Aquinas, *Sententia super Metaphysicam*
In Sent.	Thomas Aquinas, *Scriptum super libros Sententiarum*
PG	Patrologia Graeca
PL	Patrologia Latina
SC	Sources chrétiennes
SCG	Thomas Aquinas, *Summa contra gentiles*
ST	Thomas Aquinas, *Summa theologiae*

General Introduction

———— : ————

What I present here under the title "A Dogmatic Synthesis"—a title which some will believe to be ambitious—is the course in dogmatic theology that I taught at the Faculty of Theology at the University of Fribourg for a period of twenty-five years and, before that, for seven years at the Studium of the Dominican Province of Toulouse.

At each repetition of the cycle of studies (four years at the start, three later on) the course text was corrected and supplemented. In this volume, I present the final state of the text, that of my final cycle of teaching at Fribourg, reworked one last time and slightly modified in view of publication.

It is an ambitious project and a formidable challenge to publish a dogmatic theology at a time when preferences are given in theology to studies that are specialized, sometimes very erudite (more erudite than is humanly possible for a general dogmatic theology), profound, and often directly related to the most burning questions pertaining to current events of the ecclesial order and even those of the social or political orders. In the current state of theological studies, many today doubt the possibility of constructing a synthesis gathering together and unifying all the various subjects that together form dogmatic theology into a coherent whole, each being treated *in itself*, according to its proper requirements, though as integrated into the primordial subject of theology, God such as He has revealed Himself, and not apart and *for itself*.[1]

---

1. Marie-Rosaire Gagnebet, "La nature de la théologie spéculative," *Revue thomiste* 44 (1948): 213–255, 645–674.

1

Insistent, friendly requests, as well as numerous and valuable contributors (valuable not only for the indispensable financial support that they provided, but also—and perhaps above all—by the confidence that they have shown in this undertaking) encouraged me to take up the challenge and attempt to prove the possibility of such an enterprise, just as one proves the existence of movement by walking.

However, before undertaking this demonstration (at my own risk), I feel that I must set forth the conception of theology that commanded all my teaching and the path that I traced in carrying it out.

I. A PARTICULAR IDEA OF THEOLOGY

Theology is a science. That is, it is a form of knowledge aiming at objective certitude. By its nature, every science is the work of man and of reason—a difficult and lengthy work. It is so lengthy that a single human lifetime is insufficient for it to be brought to its completion. Every science is slowly fashioned, through the long effort of generations, and the generation that receives a given science from the preceding generations will leave it behind to the next generation unfinished and forever in the midst of being accomplished. Every science is the never-definitive terminus of a never-accomplished investigation. Moreover, he who today enters into the worksite cannot content himself with reaping the fruits of the investigation in progress. He must, on his own behalf, take it up anew for himself. Certainly, he does not do this by starting over as though nothing had been accomplished before he existed. Rather, he remakes this intellectual journey by personally reproducing the efforts undertaken by his predecessors, though not without critiquing them, all so that he might make their results his own. This is how things must be because achieving scientific knowledge is not merely a matter of knowing only what others have discovered regarding some given object. We must retrieve it for ourselves, under their guidance, so that we may not merely know the conclusions reached by others but may know the reasons for those conclusions. We must make these reasons our own, as though we had discovered them ourselves.

Such is the case for theology as well. It is a work of human reason that is the fruit of an investigation that is at once collective and personal. However, theology is a unique sort of science, for the object of its investigation is supra-rational. Reason, by its own means, cannot know that which is in question in theology (i.e., its "subject," according to scholastic terminology). Theology's concern is with God in His mystery, in His difference, in His intimate nature. Its subject is God giving Himself to man, in Christ, by the Holy Spirit, God the Savior. And it is likewise concerned with man, called to divinization, man who has been saved (This is only known through revelation coming from God and received by man. In other words, it is only known through faith. All of this means that the subject of theology (i.e., its primordial subject, along with the multiplicity of secondary subjects into which it projects itself—e.g., man who has fallen and has been saved, the Church, the sacraments, and so forth....) can become an object for reason only if reason believes and to the degree that it abides under the influence of faith.

What a paradoxical situation! Theology is a science, the fruit of a rational investigation, practiced with full intellectual rigor, establishing conclusions with certitude founded upon necessary reasons. And nonetheless, this investigation is concerned with an object that reason does not control. Reason has neither immediate nor mediate evidence for this object. Reason holds it as being true with complete certitude, though it does not see it and does not know why it is true. Its certitude comes from elsewhere. In what concerns the reasons for believing, they come from the motives of credibility, though they essentially come from the action of the Spirit, who comes from On High, like revelation itself.[2]

2. On the nature of theology and its methods, one can consult, as regards the general sense of our remarks, Yves-Marie Congar, "Théologie," *Dictionnaire de théologie catholique*, ed. Vacant et al., vol. 15, 341–502; Marie-Rosaire Gagnebet, "La nature de la théologie spéculative," *Revue thomiste* 44 (1948): 213–255, 645–674; Michel Labourdette, "La théologie intelligence de la foi," *Revue Thomiste* 46 (1946): 5–44; Karl Rahner, "Essai d'une esquisse de Dogmatique," in *Ecrits théologiques* IV, 9–50. In a quite different sense, antithetical to our "idea of theology" exposited here, see Claude Geffré, "La théologie, science de la foi," *Encyclopédia Universalis*, vol. 15, 1087–1091; "La mort comme nécessité et comme liberté," *Vie Spirituelle* 492 (1963): 264–280.

Therefore, what is the nature of theological investigation? Let us first see what it cannot be.

1. Theological Investigations Cannot Demonstrate the Truths of Faith

Faith is not demonstrated. *Apologetics*, which is a part of theology (and constitutes an important chapter of what is called "fundamental theology"), investigates *the reasons for believing*, discussing and excluding the reasons for not believing, reasons that the unbeliever opposes to the believer (and that the believer himself is tempted to raise for himself, for unbelief remains in him as something overcome but never wholly vanquished). Dogmatic theology necessarily presupposes faith and therefore cannot place faith into question in any way. Faith is not (and indeed cannot be) the result of a rational investigation, even if reason has its place in the movement that leads a man from unbelief to faith under the action of the Spirit. This is so because although the act of faith itself is an act of reason (indeed, a reasonable act), it can only be made if reason renounces its own truth criteria. Reason thus opens itself up to a truth that exceeds it, a truth that was already secretly and dynamically present at the beginning of the movement that resulted in conversion: "You would not seek me if you had not already found me." At the decisive moment when man becomes a believer, he is mysteriously certain that this truth comes from on high, from "the Father of lights." On the basis of pure non-faith, even were it merely a form of methodological doubt, a purely rational process could only arrive at non-faith, for faith is indemonstrable.

Faith does not depend in any manner on theology, but theological investigation intrinsically depends on faith.

2. Theological Investigation Cannot Be Conceived of as Being an Effort to Reinterpret the Truths of Faith

The effort of interpretation is not exercised on a brute intelligible datum that would itself be free from all interpretation. The intelligible as such exists only in the intellect. Every statement is the fruit of elaboration by whoever utters it (even when this statement itself refers to the teaching of another person), provoking an elaboration by whoever intellectually receives it in his intellect and accepts it. This elaboration is interpretive.

However, this does not mean that whosoever receives and transmits a teaching gives it, merely because he reflects on it and tries to understand it, a new meaning in relation to the meaning that the master himself wished to give to the ensemble of statements in which he expressed his thought. Certainly, this meaning can be discussed, and this will lead to a number of interpretations. However, the point of reference and criterion of verification for each of them is the author's published text. Moreover, yes, we can have debates about the author's ideas. However, in that case, we are not concerned merely with interpreting his thought but, rather, with discussing his own interpretation either of an anterior text or, quite simply, of the object about which he speaks.

Therefore, if every intelligible statement is interpretive, a fundamental interpretation must exist for every object upon which the intellect exercises its activity, an interpretation that is recognized as being true for all. Here, the concern is to discover, not to reinterpret. In the purely rational order, these so-called fundamental interpretations are the first principles in which every intellect immediately knows being and expresses it. Furthermore, in each science, there are the first principles of this science, those in which its object is recognized and grasped.

If the ensemble of intelligible statements to which a theologian adheres by faith comes from God through revelation, he must be clear about the ultimate reference point to which all the interpretations of these statements are related so that they may be judged. This reference point is the Infinite Divine Truth, the Truth that is God. And in this case, there is no interpretation but, rather, perfect transparency: the Logos, the Word subsistent in God, is God with the Father who speaks, like Him, about the same and identical, con-

substantial Godhead. However, this is concerned with a reference
point that is wholly transcendent and inaccessible. God is revealed
to man by the prophets and the apostles, themselves instructed by
Him who is the Incarnate Word, Christ. This revelation is made with
human words, expressed in human concepts and images. Likewise,
it is made with deeds and events. However, as we will see, these are
accompanied by words that give the latter their meaning at the same
time as the deeds and events illustrate the words.

A first and fundamental interpretation occurs in the passage
from the Infinite, Divine Truth, who is simple and transparent, to a
multitude of partial statements, making use of means of knowledge
that are disproportionate and opaque. It occurs in the mind of the
prophet and, at its source, in the human mind of Jesus Christ, who
saw this Truth immediately (a point we will discuss in Christology) and translated it, so to speak, into human ideas, images, words,
and actions. The perfect rectitude of this interpretation of the Infinite Truth is assured by the living continuity, in Jesus's humanity,
between His human thought (which is submitted to the conditions
of man's earthly existence and communicable to men through words
belonging to their language and actions subject to their experience),
and His vision of the Divine Essence. The latter is not interpretive
since it is immediate and since the created intellect does not there
grasp the Divine Truth but, instead, is grasped by it: "No one has
ever seen God. The Unique Son, who is turned toward the bosom of
the Father, was the revelation [of God]."[3]

On the other hand, neither the prophets, nor the apostles, when
they lived upon the earth and transmitted to men the revelation that
had come from Jesus Christ (or that was to come from Him, if we are
speaking about Israel's prophets), shared in this immediate vision of
the Divine Truth, which was the Incarnate Word's singular prerogative. Their preaching consisted in an interpretation of Christ's teaching (we speak now only of the apostles), and this is clear enough

3. Jn 1:18. Taken from the text found in translation in Ignace de La Potterie, *La vérité
dans Saint Jean*, vol. 1 (Rome: Biblical Institute Press, 1977), 228.

in the notable differences found in how they present this teaching, something that exegetes detect. How would it be possible for the theologian to verify the truth of what they said and wrote by making reference to the very teaching and actions of Christ, given that the theologian knows about these latter only by way of what has been said and written about them? Faith, and therefore theology, would lose all certitude and would thus become impossible if we did not have the particular assistance of the Holy Spirit bestowed upon those who were the purely human conduits of revelation, namely, the apostles and their immediate collaborators, speaking in their name. This is the charism of revelation, which the believer recognizes in the very act by which he adheres to revelation: "First of all you must understand this, that no prophecy of scripture is a matter of one's own interpretation, because no prophecy ever came by the impulse of man, but men moved by the Holy Spirit spoke from God."[4]

However, we have access to the apostolic teaching only through the writings that they left behind for us. An interpretive activity is obviously involved in the reading of these writings (above all the discernment of the books that transmit this teaching to us), and this activity leads to a number of interpretations. They all refer to this oral and written preaching (at least those that intend to be properly theological, i.e., that recognize the divine origin of the apostles' preaching and its conformity with Christ's own teaching). However, how could that oral and written preaching serve as the criterion of an interpretation's truth if we know it only by means of these books and, therefore, by means of the interpretation that they give us? Here again, faith, as well as theology, is impossible if there is not a fundamental interpretation to which the theologian can refer with certitude.

This makes clear the necessary role played by the Church. She is the living tradition by which the contemporary believer is connected back to the apostolic preaching and receives the testimony of the apostles, authentically reported and actualized. Through her, the

4. 2 Pt 1:20–21 (RSV).

believer's faith can be referred to the Infinite and Simple Truth that has been made known to the world by Christ. In a famous text, St. Thomas writes that: "The act of faith does not terminate in the statement in which it is expressed but, rather, in the very reality to which the statement refers."[5] The proposition's relationship to reality would be problematic and would always need to be left in question if the relay of an incontestable interpretation between the teaching of the apostles and our faith today did not exist.

In order for the interpretation given by the Church concerning the apostolic tradition to be objectively incontestable, she must be able to count on the assistance of the Holy Spirit. She has counted on this assistance from her beginnings, from that first sketching of the ecumenical councils that was the assembly of the apostles and the elders (perhaps the assembly of the brothers with them as well) in Jerusalem, the decisions of which were thus declared: "For it has seemed good to the Holy Spirit and to us to lay upon you...."[6] Through the course of the ages, she has not ceased to rely upon this assistance. She does not first and principally rely on it as upon a prerogative claimed for herself, but rather, relies on it through the very act of teaching, from which faith is born into the world. It is on her testimony that one believes. That is, it is on her testimony that one receives what she teaches as being the Word [*Parole*] of God. By this very act of faith, one welcomes the Word and recognizes the Church as the bearer of the Word. She herself relies on this intimate certitude of the Spirit's assistance, not only to teach with authority, but also, secondarily, to condemn those interpretations of the apostles' teaching that she judges to be false. Discussions and clarifications come only afterwards, requiring her to explain the awareness that she has always had of her infallibility, not to prove it.

However, what is meant when it is said that the Church is assisted by the Holy Spirit so that, at each moment of history, she may transmit to the world the authentic teaching of the apostles?

5. *ST* II-II, q. 1, a. 1, ad. 2.
6. Acts 15:28 (RSV).

The Holy Spirit, given to the Church, communicates Himself in the Church to all her members. Does He not assist each member so as to make each one recognize God's Word [*Parole*] and to place each member in relation with the apostles' testimony?

There can be no doubt that, according to the expression of the Second Vatican Council, laypersons are "made sharers in the priestly, prophetical, and kingly functions of Christ."[7] As regards the prophetic function, this is traditionally translated by the recognition that the People of God have "infallibility in the act of faith" (*infallibilitas in credendo*). However, this obviously does not mean that each member of the People of God, taken separately, would enjoy such an infallibility that each believer by himself could permissibly rely on his own conscience so that he might enunciate what he believes, presumptuously opposing his personal faith to the Church's own (an assertion which is proclaimed all too frequently in various quarters). There is (and can be) only one faith, for there is only one Divine Truth: God Himself, revealed to the world by Jesus Christ. This one faith is the Church's faith. Doubtlessly, it is the faith of all the People of God, but the People of God is [made up of] all the baptized gathered under the guidance of the sole Shepherd, Jesus Christ, the invisible Shepherd who directs his flock by means of the visible shepherds, who are chosen by Him from the midst of the people and who themselves also remain members of His people, thus being subject to His guidance. The particular assistance of the Holy Spirit sent by Christ to His shepherds makes them the authoritative interpreters of the faith of the People of God. This assistance goes so far as to assure that they have infallibility for all those decisions whose object is the faith itself in Jesus Christ, without which none can be saved.

Certainly, this raises a grave and difficult problem, namely, the necessary submission of the Church to her Lord—for it is upon the Word [*Parole*] of Jesus Christ that we believe and not otherwise. We will address this in Ecclesiology. Here, let us only say that this prob-

7. Vatican Council II, *Lumen Gentium*, November 21, 1964, 31.

lem cannot be resolved by having recourse to exegesis, history, and theological reflection when such recourse is made in a spirit of dictating these resolutions to the shepherds of the Church or of rejecting the resolutions that they have made. Of course, such recourse is certainly legitimate when it is undertaken for the sake of illuminating the decisions that must be made by the shepherds. Nonetheless, if the Church were to allow herself to be dictated to in the aforementioned manner, she would not submit herself to her Lord but, instead, to her theologians and her exegetes. Nonetheless, it is to her, the Church, that the Holy Spirit's assistance—which is the key for arriving at the true resolution to this problem—was promised, and theologians benefit from this assistance only to the degree that they are in communion with the whole Church, by the intermediary of her shepherds.

Moreover, what criterion could the theologian use in order to render decisions that would claim to bind the entire People of God and to exempt them from the shepherds' teaching (both the teaching of past shepherds, as well as of that of contemporary ones to the degree that they assure the heritage of their predecessors)? People speak of reinterpreting dogmas in function of the needs and aspirations of contemporary man, in function of the understanding that he has of himself. We must first ask ourselves who this contemporary man is and whether he has sufficient unity so that the faith that would supposedly respond to his contemporary needs and aspirations would indeed be one and the same for all men of the same generation. Otherwise, if contemporary man is multiplied—according to cultures and political choices, according to historical circumstances (which most certainly do not affect different men's mentalities in a similar manner), and also according to the weight of the very history of which both are inheritors—would we thus need to admit that the Word of God, on which faith is founded, is multiple? It is one, and faith can only be one: "One Lord, one faith, one baptism"[8]— one, not only for each generation, but in all eras.

8. Eph 4:5.

The Word of God is addressed to each and every man. In each man and in each woman, it reaches a point that is more profound than all the differences of culture, than those of social situation and political choice, as well as those of historical and temporal circumstances, reaching a point shared in by all: on the one hand, the opening to God by which man is made in the image of God and called to divinization, as well as, on the other, the point in man that is affected by sin, by which he is turned away in rejection of this calling and has entered into the region of dissimilitude. By welcoming this Word, the believer, indeed, all believers, are formed into one body, the body of Christ. In every case and in all eras, this does not take place without a wrenching conversion of heart and of mind [*esprit*] on account of the situation of sin wherein man ever finds himself, from whence he comes to faith, maintains himself in it, and makes progress in it. It is utterly illusory to think that one could present revealed truth to man today in such a way that he would be on equal footing with it, thus doing away with the need for conversion. Alas, this need for conversion is evidenced well enough by the great number of men and women who today, on account of their cultural, social, or political standpoints, reject the Word of God itself, refusing to submit themselves to it as a whole and not merely with regard to this or that point of content or this or that expression of the Word of God transmitted by the Church. The theologian who is most concerned with speaking to the men of his era and who is most disposed to interpret the truths of the faith in such a way as to bring them closer to him, knows well that he runs into this dismissal in the great majority of men (and will ever run into it): "Christ cannot be anything but a scandal for all the ages of history on account of the fundamental opposition that exists between His Spirit and the spirit of this world."[9]

The expression "a reinterpretation of the faith" is equivocal. We will see that, in a way, theology can be called an interpretation of the

9. von Balthasar, 35. [Tr. note: The particular reference is unknown. This reference does not follow Fr. Nicolas's short-hand style correctly. It refers to pagination that cannot be found in the relevant entry in the bibliography at the end of the full volume.]

faith. However, as we have already discussed, it can be an interpretation only by ceaselessly referring to the fundamental interpretation of the faith, namely the Church's teaching. Without this reference, theology would not be an *interpretation*, but rather, would be an *invention*, and no man has in himself the means for inventing and for finding the truth about God. The Word became incarnate for our sake in order to speak this truth, and nobody can know it and express it except by being instructed by Him. This teaching comes to us through the Church. To speak about "reinterpretation" is to evoke the idea of placing this fundamental interpretation in question, and if this is what one means, the theologian, in so doing, manifestly exceeds his power and cannot fail to go astray. However, if the term "reinterpretation" expresses the task of questioning the way that the revealed teaching has been understood and presented in the past, all the while taking care that this teaching itself (as the Church has transmitted it and continues to transmit it) remains unquestionable, then, yes, we can speak legitimately about reinterpretation. The theologian is a human being in a particular situation, and he speaks, directly at least, to men who themselves exist in a particular situation. Determinate cultural orientations and determinate historical circumstances can orient reflection about revealed truth and bring new aspects of it to light. In this way, it can respond to man's various and sundry preoccupations, as well as to new questions. However, we cannot allow these new aspects to render obsolete what the Church has believed and taught in the past. For example, Chalcedon's formula [concerning the two natures and single personality of Christ] is far from expressing the whole mystery of Christ. However, it is inconceivable that theological reflection today could bring to light aspects of the mystery that would be incompatible with it and would lead to the rejection of it by this or that segment of the People of God.

3. The Investigation into the "Intelligibility of Faith"

Faith is the welcoming of the Word of God, and God speaks to man in order to teach him. Yes, God speaks to man in order to call

Him. Indeed, this is the principal end of God's communication to man. However, in order to call man, He reveals Himself to him, as well as His designs, making His ways known and also revealing man to himself. To believe is to receive this teaching. Faith is knowledge. Yes, it is indeed more than that, for if God instructs man in order to call him to Himself, man can truly allow himself to be instructed only by responding to this call, by going to the Father through Christ, under the impulse of the Spirit, according to the ways that are indicated for him. However, faith is first of all a kind of knowledge, and it would be nothing if it were not that. Indeed, how could man go to God if he did not know the Father, the Son, and the Spirit, as well as the Incarnation of the Son who came to instruct him and to save him? How could he do so if he did not know himself as fallen through sin and reconciled by grace? The salvation that has been proclaimed to us is not an indeterminate salvation. Indeed, what would an indeterminate salvation even be? What has been proclaimed to us is salvation through the sacrifice and resurrection of Jesus Christ, the Son of God, sent by the Father, having become a man, sending us the Spirit so that He may bring us back to the Father through Him.[10]

If faith is knowledge, its content is an ensemble of truths. There is one doctrine of faith. It is composed of assertions about what is the case—about what God is, about the Incarnation of the Son and the Redemption, about the sending of the Spirit, and about the Church raised up and animated by Him. These assertions are true. That is, they are conformed to what the things to which they refer are in themselves, independent of what they represent for man.

It is quite clear that these assertions also have a meaning for man, since the Word of God is addressed to man and since the salvation

10. Of course, for those to whom it has not been given to receive the teaching of Christ and of the apostles, salvation is possible by implicit faith. See Jean-Hervé Nicolas, "Universalité de la mediation du Christ et salut de ceux qui ne connaissent pas le Christ," in *Acta del Congressso internazionale Tommaso d'Aquino nel suo settimo centenario*, vol. 4 (Napoli: 1976), 261–273. However, a dogmatic theology can be founded only upon explicit faith.

that they speak of is man's salvation, carried out by God. May God have a meaning for man! This is the least one can say! He is, Himself, man's ultimate meaning. However, what He is in Himself is anterior to the human existence to which He gives meaning. Likewise, the assertions of faith, which are related to what He is and to what He wills, have their truth in themselves, even were this truth never to appear with evidence and would forever require faith in order to be known. But their true meaning only appears when their truth is recognized through the act of faith, and this meaning is disengaged slowly to the degree that faith is intensified, arousing an ever-firmer adherence of mind and reflection.

Hence, this truth, as well as all the partial truths that compose it without fragmenting it, enter into the believer's intellectual universe and must find their place therein—not without sometimes provoking painful ruptures in it, purifying it and reforming it. Questions emerge, arising from the very assertions of faith. Faced with such questions, one cannot avoid asking oneself how faith's assertions cohere with each other, as well as with the fundamental certitudes from which reason could not release itself without destroying itself: the first principles of natural reason, above all the principle of identity and its logical face, the principle of non-contradiction. The intellect cannot in any way hold two contradictory assertions together at the same time. It could only utter them one after another and pass successively back and forth between them. How then can one avoid asking oneself what it means to say that the Father has a Son and that there also is a Spirit in God, that they are really distinct and yet that they are only one God? How can one avoid asking oneself what can be meant by faith's assertion that Jesus Christ is the Eternal Word, God, and that He is also (indeed, fully) a man? How is one to understand the fact that, through the sacrifice of His life, He saved man who fell through sin and the fact that He obtained for him the grace of salvation? And how many other questions are aroused, often one after another, in reason by revealed doctrine as it penetrates into reason through the act of faith!

Theological investigations look to find a response to these questions so that the internal coherence of revealed doctrine and its profound agreement with reason may become apparent, without prejudice to that doctrine's transcendence. From the moment that the Word of God is a teaching, faith, which is the adherence to this teaching by the human intellect and by reason, naturally induces the need to understand what is said. It induces the need to understand what it means and to understand it with its reason (i.e., by ordering the various assertions in relation to each other, as well as in relation to other rational certitudes according to the order of reasons).

This need for understanding is the principle of theological investigation. It is implied in the first act of faith, that of the prophet who receives revelation and who, already, understands it in his own way, transmitting it such as he has understood it. This explains how one can speak of the theology of this or that sacred author. However, as we saw above, this first rational elaboration is brought about under the inspiration of the Holy Spirit, who assures and guarantees perfect conformity between the truth in God and the prophet's comprehension as well as his speech in which the truth is found (obviously in a manner that is partial, though in no way falsified). One need not speak here about a kind of revealed theology, for theology is always, as such, a work of human reason. We only mean to speak of a theology that is divinely guaranteed and whose results express what God wished to teach mankind through the prophet. In this theology, the truth that he speaks comes forth without any error, though partially. Hence, it is not surprising that different writers speak differently, although not contradictorily, concerning the same subject so that, in the end, the same divine truth concerning a given mystery is presented in different, though converging, manners by many authors. Thus, we can speak of the "Christology of Paul," the "Christology of John," that of Luke, and so forth. In these various Christologies, one and the same Christ is considered from different and complementary perspectives.

At the wellspring of theology there is, more immediately still, the interpretation of the apostolic teaching performed by the Church from her beginning and continued throughout all the ages under the protection and guarantee of the Holy Spirit's assistance, preserving her from error in the transmission of the apostolic doctrine and stimulating her interiorly, stimulating her pastors, her theologians, and all the faithful ever to pursue investigation into the revealed truth, which is too profound and too vast to be completely known and understood before the end of time. Nevertheless, the Holy Spirit's assistance guarantees only the pastors against error, and then, only in the acts by which they authoritatively speak the faith of the People of God to them. The immense effort of theologians' investigations, undertaken in her and by her, humanly preparing for such decisions, is not placed immediately under the Holy Spirit's guarantee. Instead, it has such a guarantee by the mediation of this teaching of the Church to which it must ever be referred, and when this reference is gravely deficient, such theological investigation finds its guarantee in the authoritative interventions of the pastors, who have the responsibility to ceaselessly recall the necessity of such a reference and to require it.

According to the classic formula, what theological investigations pursue in the Church and under her influence [*mouvance*] is the *intellectus fidei*, the understanding of what the Church teaches.

4. The Role of Philosophy in Such Investigations

To define theology as the investigation belonging to a form of knowledge concerned with the being of God and of the things of God is to take a side on behalf of a philosophical outlook holding that knowledge is concerned with knowing what things are, how they are, and why they are so. It is to put into force a philosophy of being. Through the ages, theology has indeed made use of different philosophies (Stoicism, Platonism and Neo-Platonism, Aristotelianism, and even nominalism). In the midst of their diversity, all of these had at least this common characteristic: they were philosophies of being. That is, they took the being of things as the measure of their truth.

Now, in modern times, Kant's Copernican revolution took place, preceded by Descartes's bias for holding that the criterion of truth is found in clear ideas, not the objective evidential character of being. Taking up this perspective, modern philosophy began to seek its measure for truth and objectivity no longer in the being of things to be known but, instead, in the knowing and thinking subject.

Such a perspective profoundly modifies the conception that one can form not only of theology but, first of all, of faith. The latter will no longer be conceived as being knowledge of God and of His designs and as an acceptance of a divine teaching concerning being (and man as well, though inasmuch as he also is a being, a creature made in the image of God, realizing the project of divinization, a project that is not elaborated by him but, instead is proposed to him). Rather, from this modern perspective, faith will tend to seem like a knowing subject's attitude toward the world, toward Christ, toward God, and so forth, all without necessarily implying determinate affirmations about what Christ is, about what God is, and ultimately, about His very existence. This will go so far that, at the limit, not only is the idea of a truth to be believed in abolished, but beyond that, the idea of Anyone whose words would be believed is abolished as well. In these circumstances, what will theology be if not a mere investigation into the meaning that the statements of faith can have for man, these statements no longer being related to the given being about which they speak but, rather, to the subject who utters them? "Christ is risen" will not be related to a real event concerning Jesus of Nazareth. Instead, the truth of this statement will consist in the meaning that it has for me. Moreover, it will be a meaning that can vary according to different stages of culture. Thus, one will assert that theology has an essentially mutable character, with new interpretations being substituted for older ones and abolishing them. (Thus, it will be said—and, indeed, it is said—that since Chalcedon's formula does not speak to the concerns of contemporary man, it can be abandoned.)

We have critiqued and ruled out this conception of faith and of theology. However, if engagement in theological investigations requires one to return to a philosophy of being, which many of our contemporaries regard as being passé, this is a hard and difficult sacrifice for a contemporary man. Many feel this difficulty. This is not the place to justify the philosophy of being and to show that, in reality, it is not as removed from the modern mind as it is thought to be and that it remains the necessary basis for all philosophical investigations in a hidden and, as it were, "embarrassing" manner. The only thing that must be said is that it is manifestly implied in all the enunciations of the faith. As Claude Tresmontant has shown, there is a metaphysics underlying revelation itself.[11] From the beginning, our *Credo* was composed of a series of ontological affirmations, and through the centuries, they have been understood in this way and also have been disputed and defended as though they were such. They indisputably had this ontological scope in Jesus's own teaching and in that of the apostles, as well as in the consciousness of the first Christians. One does not sacrifice one's life for a mental fiction. In these conditions, to refuse today to take them as such is to utterly cut oneself off from the beginnings of faith. Hence, the faith that one would like to substitute for true faith would have no foundation and would be purely arbitrary. It was the realization of this foundational realism of the formulas that express the faith that led, among others, Jacques Maritain to St. Thomas's philosophy of being as a consequence of his conversion.[12]

However, we are not suggesting that modern philosophy must be completely rejected. It is not an entirely true philosophy. However, it also is not an entirely false one, and the contemporary theologian can profit much from the immense philosophical effort undertaken in modern times. In particular, the discovery of the "[knowing and willing] subject" in philosophy is a precious acquisition. Indeed, it is a precious acquisition for theology itself, for the doctrine of faith is not an abstract system of relations among natures but, in fact, is

---

11. See Claude Tresmontant, *Les idées maîtresses de la métaphysique chrétienne* (Paris: Seuil 1962).

12. See Jacques Maritain, *La philosophie bergsonienne* (Paris: Téqui, 1948), xii–xiii.

the revelation and elicitation of personal relations between man and God. God is He who freely creates and who calls man. The Father is He who sends His Son, and the Son is He who gives His life in order to save man. Man is he who is called to believe and follow Christ and to be conformed to Him. As every existence implies an essence, this ensemble of interpersonal relations necessarily implies a system of ontological relations upon which it rests. To believe that the entire world, and especially man, proceeds from the free divine decision to create obviously presupposes that one believes in the real existence of a personal and free God. Likewise, to believe that the Father sent His Son to us through the Incarnation presupposes the real distinction in God between the Father and the Son, as well as the reality of the Hypostatic Union. However, a theology that would limit itself to the analysis of these ontological relations (a reproach that can be registered against theology in scholastic thought, at least in its period of decline) would indeed be insufficient and deceptive. It would be so not through excessive fidelity to the philosophy of being but, rather, because it was unfaithful to the requirements of such a philosophy, for the being that is to be attained here is the being of living persons and of interpersonal relations. Clearly, then, to this end, phenomenological investigations in particular open new and interesting pathways for theologians. Likewise, hermeneutic investigations will aid theology in usefully critiquing the formulas in which our faith was expressed at the beginning and then through the course of the ages, so that we may retrieve the same truths in a new cultural context. Theology's fidelity to the philosophy of being will not consist in the defense of this or that thesis (for, within the philosophy of being, every thesis can be critiqued). Rather, this fidelity will consist in a resolute inclination to refer all its statements and all its investigations to being (the being of God and the being of things, willed by God). Its resolute inclination will solely be to seek to know, in the domain of revealed mysteries, that which is, how it is, and why it is thus. It will be resolved to seek it with reason, on the basis of what revelation (received and transmitted by the

Church) tells us about these mysteries and what faith enables us to know about them. This rigorous attitude is what the philosophy of being demands of the theologian, and it is an attitude that can only extend his outlook as a believer, seeking after explanations.

II. A THEOLOGICAL PROJECT

The idea of theology that has just been presented to the reader is the one that presided over the elaboration of the course presented in this *Dogmatic Theology*. In what concerns the realization of this elaboration, the reader will himself recognize insufficiencies and perhaps will choose to concentrate upon them. Nonetheless, it falls to the author to state the limitations he has voluntarily placed upon his project and what he has wished to accomplish.

What is presented here can be summarized under the following headings.

1. A Theology Founded on Scripture and Tradition, but not a Biblical or Historical Theology

"Biblical theology" refers to the task of investigating into the theology of a sacred author, the doctrine of the Bible in general,[13] or that of the New Testament, concerning a given theme.[14] Obviously, it proceeds by performing a very exacting exegesis, but its ambition extends much further than mere exegesis. It is not only concerned with determining a text's exact meaning. Rather, biblical theology seeks to bring the texts closer to each other according to an internal coherence, so that one may draw forth the doctrine of the author or of the ensemble of authors. This is already a theological task, and it

13. For example, see François-Marie Braun, *Jean le théologien*, vols. I, II, III/1, and III/2 (Paris: Gabalda, 1959–1972).

14. For example, see Oscar Cullmann, *Christologie du Nouveau Testament* (Neuchâtel, CH: Delachaux et Niestlé, 1966). Also, Ignace de La Potterie, *La vérité dans Saint Jean*, vols. I–II (Rome: Biblical Institute Press, 1977); Ceslas Spicq, *AGAPÈ dans le Nouveau Testament, Analyse des textes*, vols. 1–3 (Paris: Gabalda, 1958–1959); Vincent Taylor, *La personne du Christ dans le Nouveau Testament* (Paris: Cerf, 1969).

is justified if one recognizes (as we have) that theology begins at the same level as revelation, in the mind [*esprit*] and writings of the inspired author. It is also justified if one recognizes that the principal author of the Bible is the Holy Spirit, a fact that enables one to bring together the texts of many different authors, considered from the perspective of the thought expressed therein.

This is not what we will seek to do here, since this effort is assured by the work of others. Besides, in addition to the special competence that this requires, engaging in such a biblical theology would prevent speculative theology from being devoted to its proper task.

We could also think of theology as being a study of the formation of the doctrine of faith taught today by considering its historical development through Church history, as expressed by her doctors and councils. We have also chosen to leave this to others, to whom it falls as a proper competence and task.

Obviously, this does not mean that the theologian could be disinterested in biblical sources and those drawn from tradition. The data on which he reflects are the things Scripture tells us about God and about the salvation that He offers and accomplishes in Jesus Christ, as the Church has received, understood, and taught since her beginning and through the course of the centuries. That is, reference to the revealed Divine Reality, which we have said was the essential characteristic of theological investigations, can only take place through the documents of Scripture and tradition.

How can we reconcile the need to refer to such documents with the fact that it is impossible for one to devote personal and deep study to them? Such a reconciliation is possible only by making use of specialists' works. This involves an obvious difficulty, namely the fact that the specialists do not always agree. If one is to take a position personally, would it not be necessary to undertake a new investigation into the problem? Nonetheless, one can appreciate the argumentation of a specialist without oneself being a specialist, and it is legitimate to trust researchers whose competence has been generally recognized. On the other hand, we do have the expression of the

Church's faith in the documents of the Magisterium, which express how the Church has received and understood the message communicated by the apostles. Certainly, this does not suffice for determining the meaning of this or that text or of this or that book, and this fact leaves an open field for research in biblical theology and in exegesis. Still, it indicates the general direction for this investigation, which, striven after today by the exegetes and historians of our time, using new means and renewed methods, takes over an effort going back to the Church's beginnings. It is clear that this effort will never come to an end, and if the beginning of the theologian's reflection on the data must wait for the latter to have been definitively brought up to date, theological reflection would never begin. This is not necessary, for as we see in the Patristic age, theological reflection is, in fact, contemporaneous with the Fathers' nascent exegesis and with their first attempts at biblical theology, which is barely distinguished from their exegetical activity. Having taken on a kind of autonomy in the ages following it, as the natural effect of a slow, corresponding development, it ever continues to be connected with them.

We will attempt to assure this connection by having recourse to the Church's exegetes and historians. Very often, in these cases, we will suggest that the reader should personally study the relevant documents for himself or herself.

2. A Theology Attentive to the Teachings of the Magisterium, Though Not Proceeding by Way of Authority

The determinations of the Magisterium (i.e., dogmatic formulas and authoritative teachings) are the fruit of exegetical investigations as well as of theological reflection. However, they are something completely different than the simple result of these investigations. They express the Church's faith, our faith (i.e., the Word of God such as the Church receives it, understands it, and communicates it to men). She does this *humanly*. That is, she does so by using human processes of investigation. However, she also does it *supernaturally*, that is, by controlling and discerning the results of these investigations, thanks to *the sense of the faith* that exists in her as the Spirit's gift, a sense which, at least in her major decisions, acts infallibly through the Holy Spirit's assistance.

Retracing human reason's journey through the development of doctrine represents an important aspect of the theologian's work. Starting with the very words of revelation, this journey has arrived at dogmatic formulas through the course of time. The theologian must come to see how these formulas, obviously without themselves being in Holy Scripture, nonetheless express for believing reason the same thing that is contained in Scripture and that was believed by the first community. Thus, for example, Scripture does not say that Jesus is a person in two natures, but it quite clearly says that He is the Word of God and, at the same time, that He is fully man. As we will see, this is what Chalcedon's formula expresses in terms that are more precise, without adding anything to them.

However, because dogmatic formulas find their ultimate and formal justification in the meaning of the Church's faith and in the Holy Spirit's assistance, they are also normative for theological investigations. They express the truths of faith on which the theologian reflects and from which his investigations cannot deviate without going astray.

To say they are normative does not mean that they dispense the theologian from undertaking his own investigations, as though he only had to repeat them. Rather, they illuminate such investigations and rule them as directive principles. After Chalcedon, and after the Second, Third, and Fourth Councils of Constantinople, there is still much to seek concerning Christ's being, His actions, His mediation, and so forth. (As Rahner once said, the Chalcedonian formula is not a *terminus* but, instead, a *point of departure*.)[15] However, if theological investigations arrive at a result that is incompatible with Chalcedon's formula (a result that, because of this incompatibility, would

15. See Karl Rahner, "Problèms actuels de christologie," in *Ecrits théologiques*, vol. 1 (Paris: Desclée de Brouwer, 1959), 117. Cf. Jacques Liébaert, *L'incarnation*, vol. 1, *Des origines à Chalcédoine* (Paris: Cerf, 1968).

imply the rejection of the Chalcedonian formula), this would be a sign that they have deviated and that he who has conducted such research (with the best faith in the world, with the most authentic faith) is warned by this fact that he must rectify his reasoning.

3. A Theology Proceeding by the Way of Reasoning and Methodically Making Use of Analogy

The human intellect is discursive by its very nature. It can proceed only by way of reasoning. Theological reasoning does not have the goal of discovering new truths on the basis of the truths of faith. It is indeed quite evident that the truths of faith contain everything that the believer needs to know concerning the things of God and that a supernatural truth that has not been in some way revealed could not be recognized as a certain truth by the power of reasoning alone. The truths of faith are the bearers of intelligibility, and theology aims at increasingly actualizing this intelligibility. This is so because the truth is one. It is God Himself, who is all Being, all Truth, and all Good. If this one truth is broken up by revelation into a number of distinct truths, this is because of the weakness and limitations proper to the human mind, which must multiply its conceptions (and, even more, its words) so that it may know and express what is, in itself, one. Its reflective effort essentially involves the retrieval of this transcendent unity of the Divine Truth by a rational organization of particular truths, making their interdependence and order come to light, illuminating one by another. Thus, the theologian will come to connect the Incarnation to the Trinity by means of the notion of the "mission of the Son." Likewise, he will connect the Sacrificial Redemption to the Incarnation by means of the notions of the inclusion of all men in Christ, satisfaction, and the priesthood. And such connections will be established throughout the various truths of faith. All of this activity does not quantitatively increase the number of truths to believe (and to live). Rather, it makes us penetrate more profoundly into our knowledge of these truths and brings us closer to the "whole and entire Truth."

Such reasoning necessarily makes use of *analogy*, for in order to reveal Himself to men, God necessarily made use of human words and human concepts. Such concepts have been elaborated on the basis of experience (which is concerned with the visible universe), and in first intentional knowledge, they express the being of created things. How can they be of use in enabling us to know Uncreated Reality? On the one hand, they do so in virtue of the creature's likeness to the Creator. On the other hand, they do so on the basis of the profound and mysterious kinship of the human intellect to the Divine Mind. However, to pass from created reality to the Uncreated Reality, these concepts must be submitted to analogical treatment, which is broken down into three inseparable, though distinct, movements. First, there is the *via causalitatis*, for creatures bear resemblance to God as to their cause. Second, there is the *via negativa*, for while creatures bear resemblance to the Creator, He does not resemble them—He is "wholly other." Finally, there is the *via eminentia*, for while He does not resemble them, this is not because He is lacking in the perfection that the intellect has discovered in those created things as a "pure perfection" (i.e., a perfection that does not include any limitation in itself). Rather, He does not resemble them, for that perfection exists in Him in a supereminent manner.[16] Therefore, analogy presupposes that one first disengages the precise point of resemblance from the limitations it undergoes in creatures. (Revelation indicates to us the path to be taken here.) Then, freed from its limitations, one projects this pure perfection to infinity. However, under no circumstances can this projection be brought about by means of a concept [formed solely by the first operation of the human intellect], for all concepts are limited and none can enclose the Uncreated Perfection. They are all "concepts of a creature," representing the perfection that they (intelligibly) contain, if not in a precise delimitation, at least as it is ordered to the ensemble of beings from which it has been abstracted and in which it is limited. Thus, the notion of goodness can indeed abstract from this or that form

16. See chapters three and five in this text.

of goodness, but it ever refers the mind to a subject in which good-ness will be, as it were, enclosed and constricted. It is solely through a judgment[, fashioned by the second operation of the intellect, and also enunciated at the terminus of the intellect's third operation, rea-soning,] that the intellect can transgress all limits. Attributing this perfection to the infinite subject, whose existence it knows about by the *via causalitatis*, it truly attains this infinite subject in its infinity by the act of affirmation, without ever being able to conceptually repre-sent it in its infinity in a concept.

Thus, take the concept of *person* as an example. God presents Himself in the Bible with the characteristics of a person: awareness, love, freedom, and independence. But we cannot think that this means that we must attribute to Him the limitations and imperfec-tions that are inseparable from created personality. It is only after a process of such purification and transcending that the concept of *person* could be used for knowledge of God, for knowledge of Three Distinct Ones [*Trois distincts*] who are but one God, as well as for knowledge of Christ. This concept, *person*, which aims at the myste-rious Divine Reality without enclosing Him within it, is transcended by and in the very judgment that attributes it to God, making Him known in a real, though partial, manner, as an object remaining in the distance. This concept, *person*, is not directly revealed. However, it is necessary so that we can understand what has been revealed to us.

This process is oriented to something more than more complete knowledge of a particular truth, aiming also at a *doctrinal synthesis* in which truths are illuminated by one another, each being interdepen-dent in its intelligibility within the whole. When such a synthesis is concretely realized by a theology or by a "school," we call it a "system." A system cannot coincide exactly with a *doctrinal synthesis*, which is an ever-sought objective ideal which will never be realized, for its in-accessible model is the transcendent, simple, and total Divine Truth. This means that a system is only an imperfect realization of the ide-al synthesis, one ever to be perfected, corrected, and supplemented.

However, this does not mean that one system could be indifferently substituted for another, whether on account of the change of an era (leading to a change of philosophical or scientific worldviews), or on account of the genius of a theologian creating a new system, as a new philosopher creates a new philosophy, or on account of the exercise of one's free choice among existing systems. Every theological system's common reference to the ideal synthesis (and, through it, to the Divine Truth known—imperfectly, but surely—through revelation) bestows upon them all a community that is as profound as is their diversity. (A doctrine that would not expressly refer itself to this revealed Truth would not be a theological system in the sense of theology spoken of here.) One's choice of a system is not (and cannot be) arbitrary. It is justified by the fact that one judges it to be more apt for providing reason with an account of the revealed truth and, consequently, by the fact that one judges it to be closer to the ideal synthesis. This does not in any way imply the naïve belief that this system would be theology brought to completion, henceforth excluding the possibility of any new investigations. Nor does it imply that all of its parts would be equally valid (that is, equally true). Nor does it imply, by consequence, that other systems would be totally false and must be rejected. On one and the same point, two contradictory statements cannot be true at the same time. However, a system is not false *as a system* merely because it contains false conclusions. Each system (at least every system that merits being taken into consideration) sketches out and organizes its synthesis around true principles, and a given system has the merit of placing its central principles in relief, though it sometimes attributes such a role to them that other, equally true principles are misunderstood. This is what unbalances its synthesis and is a cause of errors in its conclusions. A theological system is fully valid (even at its own particular level as an ever-developing system) only if it is truly capable of integrating all the truth found in other systems and is capable of eliminating its own errors. Moreover, one quickly perceives that theological systems are not monolithic blocs that are perfectly separated from one another. Their common dependence on the same revelation and their common effort toward the doctrinal synthesis that would express the Divine Truth perfectly (for believing reason) establishes a profound resemblance among them and leads them to undertake perpetual exchanges with each other.

Nevertheless, they are distinct, and theological pluralism is a fact. Let us only say that through all its effort, each theological system (as well as each theologian) aims to reduce this pluralism to unity, without fully succeeding in this task. This effort at reduction can indeed be expressly renounced by the theologian, and some profess that pluralism as such is good and ought to be maintained. Nonetheless, such an effort represents an inseparable aspect of theological investigation and the affirmations or denials to which it leads. Indeed, it is impossible to theologize without affirming and denying, and whoever simultaneously affirms that one statement is true and another false, affirms at the same time that everything that contradicts what he affirms (and that affirms what he denies) is false. On the other hand, a theological statement (a *theologoumenon*) is never isolated. It necessarily enters into an organized ensemble from which it receives its justification, meaning, and value. In short, it is part of a system. No theologian truly holds that the system that he adopts and that he constructs (for a system takes on a unique form in each person) is equivalent to every other system and can be indiscriminately replaced by any other whatsoever.[17]

4. A Deliberately Thomistic Theology

This is the spirit guiding my claim to be a Thomist. I do not think that St. Thomas has definitively resolved every problem (or even that he posed every one of them) such that theology would come to a halt with him. Nor do I think that all the solutions that he gave to the theological problems that arose for him are unchangeable. I am not disinterested in the problems that were posed after him, nor in

17. See Georges Cottier, "Difficultés d'une théologie de la liberation," in *Les Quatre Fleuves. Cahiers de la recherce et de réflexion religieuses*, vol. 2, (Paris: Seuil, 1974), 64–81; Jean-Hervé Nicolas, "La théologie et les théologiens," *Vie Spirituelle* (1960/62), 279–301.

the new ways that problems are posed today. I do not wish to isolate myself in any way from contemporary theological investigations and to ignore their preoccupations, concerns, and results. Nonetheless, I strive to take part in this investigation in continuity with St. Thomas's own line—even if this leads me to extend this line of investigation into new domains and, within these new domains, to raise problems that St. Thomas himself did not imagine. Indeed, I am committed to undertaking such investigations even if they lead me to find for such problems solutions that require the enlargement or even the modification of one or another of his conclusions. I compare these results to St. Thomas's master insights—even if this sometimes means that they must be enlarged so that these results can take up their place there. This methodological outlook does not proceed from an arbitrary choice, nor even from submission in the disciplinary order to the directives of the Church's Magisterium. Instead, it proceeds from the conviction that St. Thomas's theology is fundamentally true, that it is in vital agreement with revealed truth, and that it is the theology most capable of making that truth's intelligibility come to light as well as the one that is most capable for assuring the interiorization of it by reason without sacrificing its transcendence in any way. This choice likewise proceeds from the conviction that St. Thomas's theology is the theology most capable of integrating all the valid contributions made by other theologies. Granted, while it does not do so without itself being enlarged and adapted, it still can integrate these truths without in any way renouncing its organizing principle, method, and unity. Moreover, if this choice reflects a desire to follow the Church's directives, it is in the sense that I made this choice with confidence in these directives even before I was able to perceive and recognize the exceptional value of this theology. However, to the degree that I have grown in my knowledge of it, becoming increasingly accustomed to its ways and means, the reasons for choosing it became more apparent to me, and the Church's choice thus became a conscious and personal one.

In order for the reader to follow a course such as this one, he or she need not begin with a preferential acceptance of Thomism. St. Thomas himself did not ask his reader to be a Thomist. For his own part, he did not advance any conclusion that he did not himself strive to justify theologically—on the one hand by referring to the sources of revelation and, on the other, by reasoning through to such conclusions. My project intends to follow the same procedure, and I do not rely on St. Thomas's authority in order to advance this or that point, to take a given position, or to accept or refuse a given conclusion. Instead, I rely on St. Thomas's own theological reasoning or on that which has been inspired by him, though forever maintaining a critical eye.[18]

And I myself ask only to be "critiqued," not in my person—which, in any case, is pointless—but, rather, in my intellectual advances, in my taking of positions, and in my reasoning. I say that I wish to be "critiqued," which means that I wish to be "judged," that is, according to criteria that are reasonable and pertinent (i.e., in the present case, theological criteria). I have striven to set out such criteria in this introduction.

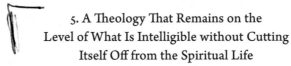

5. A Theology That Remains on the Level of What Is Intelligible without Cutting Itself Off from the Spiritual Life

Here we encounter another major difficulty involved in theological investigations such as I have described them. Revealed truths are not only truths. They are principles of life, of conversion, and therefore also of "preaching." Can one teach them while remaining solely on a merely intellectual level, solely concerning oneself with their intelligibility?

Thus, a common reproach registered against scholasticism is that is desiccated and desiccating, dissecting revealed truths and reducing them to dead abstractions. Generally speaking, Orthodox theologians strive to take up the theological perspective characteristic of the

18. See Jean-Hervé Nicolas, "Maintenir la place priviliégiée de saint Thomas dans un enseignement moderne de la théologie," *Seminarium* (1977/73), 878–897.

Patristic era. From this point of view, they mix together rational investigations, the testimony of spiritual experience, mystical elevations,
and pastoral exhortations. Therefore, they reproach Latin theology,
saying, "The Orthodox never separate theology from mysticism."[19]

Certainly, theology must not be separated from mysticism in the
theologian's own life. All his investigations aim at knowing more fully "the Father, the only true God, and Jesus Christ sent by Him,"* that
which is eternal life. Is scholastic theology's bias for remaining on the
level of intelligible relations opposed to that? (And we should add,
this bias is not limited to scholastic theology. Is it not that of modern
theology as well?) If one is profoundly convinced that it is precisely a question of knowing, in this way, God, who is personal, and that
these intelligible relations lead the mind to the interpersonal relations
in which they are realized, theological investigations will naturally lead
the theologian to living communion with God and Christ. Moreover,
theological investigations are themselves ordered to such a communion precisely on account of the fact that they cannot by themselves
know their object perfectly. Thus, theology tends to pass beyond itself
into *mystical theology or contemplation*. And although this represents
a different kind of knowledge, it nonetheless is a knowledge of God
Himself, the One and Triune God. If theological reflection as such
does not arrive at such mystical contemplation, it gives one the taste
and desire for it. If, under the pretense of rigor and fidelity to the nature of theology (which is a work of reason illuminated by faith), the
theologian refuses to give himself over to theology's impulse to pass
beyond itself, he in reality betrays theology by closing himself within
his investigations into the intelligibility of the faith, by blocking its dynamism, which stretches beyond itself toward mystical contemplation
here below and toward clear vision in the hereafter.[20]

---

19. See Myrrha Lot-Borodine, *La deification de l'homme* (Paris: Cerf, 1970), 143–189.
Vladimir Lossky, *Théologie mystique de l'Église d'Orient* (Paris: Aubier, 1944), 6–7; *Théologie negative et connaisance de Dieu chez Maître Eckhart* (Paris: Vrin, 1960), 43ff.

* Jn 17:3, my translation.

20. See Jean-Hervé Nicolas, *Dieu connue comme inconnu* (Paris: Desclée de Brouwer,
1966), ch. 7.

If theology is above all concerned with God as the Truth, its movement would be arrested if it forbade itself to go fully onward toward Infinite Love, for this Truth, who is God, is also Love. By the ways of knowledge, theology goes fully onward toward Love, but it is by love that the theologian, like every Christian, is united to Love beyond mere knowledge.

6. A Theology That Wishes to Be Present to the Temporal Existence of Men without Turning Aside from the Eternal Truth That Is Its Object

Thus, by its very nature, theology is ordered to eternal life. This life finds its consummation in the Beatific Vision, which is inaugurated and sketched out here below in contemplation and, already, in the stages of spiritual progress (that is, the progress of grace) that lead to it. But what about its insertion into men's temporal existence?

Many problems are raised today concerning this subject. Motivated by a most lively awareness of the social and political implications of revealed truth, as well as by the spiritual freedom that is the situation wherein grace places the man who accepts it (indeed, a freedom that is offered with grace to each person), many contemporary theologians look to introduce into the very movement of theological investigations the inflections, characteristics, and requirements of political freedom, social equality, cultural independence, and many other such things. Given that these requirements vary according to time and place (and thus, equally, according to social divisions), a whole host of theologies arises, tending not toward unity but, on the contrary, toward antagonistic relations, insofar as the human objectives in function of which they are conceived are themselves set in opposition to each other. Thus, *political theology* and *liberation theology* are spoken of, and classical theology is accused of being a "*classist*" theology....

This text cannot follow this path in any way, for it turns theology away from its object and proper task. Theology cannot be anything but unifying, for it is intrinsically dependent on faith, which unites men into one single body of Christ, beyond all their differences and temporal oppositions—believers, to the degree that they truly are such, as well as non-believers, for all are called to believe so that they may be saved. It is from this perspective that we presented theological pluralism above as a situation that is inevitable but provisional in itself, one that, above all, can be maintained only inasmuch as various theological systems have an intrinsic and deliberate ordination toward *Doctrina sacra*. This latter is the point where they coalesce, unifying them already as the pole toward which they converge, a pole that is ever placed before theologians' efforts.

This does not mean that theology must, or even could, cut itself off from the temporal lives of men. Man is a unified whole, and his movement toward the earthly objectives of his temporal action must be integrated into his movement toward his final end, by which he accomplishes (or fails to accomplish) his eternal destiny. To a certain degree, spiritual freedom is conditioned by temporal freedom. However, this conditioning only extends so far, for since spiritual freedom is the work of grace, it can be realized in the worst conditions of servitude. Christ upon His cross is at once man perfectly free and totally constrained. This also was the case for His martyrs, and throughout the entire history of grace, we encounter men and women who have found the loftiest spiritual freedom not only in the worst of conditions of servitude but, indeed, precisely through this servitude. Consider, for example, the shocking testimony of this freedom that we have been given by someone like Solzhenitsyn. However, this requires exceptional grace—although, it is more frequent perhaps than it is believed to be—and heroic fidelity. Many are crushed and, if by grace, they ultimately find spiritual freedom, this is because their wretchedness makes them into the poor who attract God's mercy. It is a grave duty, indeed a Christian duty, for Christians to strive to alter society's inhuman structures and change social and political relations between men so that they may "free the captives," inasmuch as this is possible. Theology discovers this duty without in any way being turned away from its own object: God who saves, and man who is saved. Theology discovers it, and without any doubt, it falls to the theologian to speak about it as well as to show to all people that although spiritual freedom can exist without temporal freedom, the former calls for the latter, reclaims it, and fights for it.

Nonetheless, temporal freedom is not man's salvation, and theology is the science of salvation. Its objective and primary task is investigation into the truth: the truth that is revealed, the truth that saves. Theology is no longer itself if, on the pretext of entering into the lives of men, it turns away from this truth, which is eminently man's life. The theologian, performing his work within in the Church, is beholden to this truth on behalf of all men. This course strives to realize such a theology, one that is all the more present to humanity who toils and fights in its temporal existence inasmuch as such a theology is more faithfully devoted to truths that are eternal.

7. A Theology That Voluntarily Restrains Itself to a Limited Field of Theological Investigations

Theology is one, through its subject (God in the mystery of His Being and of His Salvific Action) and through its object. This is the light under which this subject becomes an object, namely the light of reason instructed, elevated, and strengthened by faith. At this very lofty level, it is at once speculative and practical:

Due to their contemplation of Subsistent Life and Love, they (theology and the wisdom of grace) penetrate down into the most intimate depths of human life and of human interests. They are practical because in the light of the Uncreated Reality who reveals Himself, we likewise discover that human action finds its ultimate end beyond time in the vision of God and is guided along in accord with divine rules.[21]

Thus, the distinction that we make in theology between *dogmatic theology* and *moral theology* was unheard of by St. Thomas and his contemporaries. With a single movement of striking breadth and élan, the *Summa theologiae* treats of all revealed truths: those that are re-

21. Jacques Maritain, *Réflexions sur l'intelligence et sur sa vie proper* (Paris: Desclée de Brouwer, 1930), 126.

lated to divine realities (the mystery of God and the means of salvation), truths that are concerned with knowing such things as they are, as well as those revealed truths that pertain to human conduct, where it is a question of knowing them in order to "do" them. Theological problems, in the domain of speculative truth, as well as in that of practical truth, have become far too numerous and complex for one to reasonably dream of taking up anew such a synthesis, even under the aegis of St. Thomas. The course presented here is a course in dogmatic theology. However, the close connection, noted above, between the speculative and the practical in revealed truth is opposed to an overly strict partitioning. In many cases (e.g., as regards the *divine missions*, or as regards the *Redemption*, and likewise again as regards the *Church* and the *sacraments*), the "practical" dimension of theological knowledge will not fail to be apparent and indeed emphasized.

The field of dogmatic theology itself, taken in its entire breadth, would be far too vast as well. By the intractable requirements of the division of labor, theologians have been led to treat separately, under the title of "fundamental theology," the general problem of revelation, along with all the problems that it brings in its wake: the inerrancy of Scripture, the role of the Church's Magisterium, hermeneutics, and so forth. These problems are not given direct treatment in this Dogmatic Theology but are only treated when they are encountered in relation to some more particular problem and, even then, are given only rapid treatment.

Finally, the necessities befalling my teaching duties also led me to further narrow the field of dogmatic theology, even already so delimited. During my first period teaching dogmatic theology—at St. Maximin, as well as during my first years at Fribourg—over the course of four years, I covered all of the questions treated by St. Thomas in the first and in the third part of the *Summa theologiae*. When the chair of dogmatic theology was split apart at Fribourg, I left it to another professor to teach that which is improperly called "*de Deo uno*" (in reality, according to St. Thomas: "*ea quae ad essentiam Dei pertinent* [those things that pertain to God's essence]") as well as the sequence on creation (i.e., God's creative action, His governing action, and man). For the publication of this dogmatic theology text, I could not return to the former courses. After so many years, they would have needed to be entirely reworked.* Naturally, it was impossible to discuss "God according to the distinction of Persons" without speaking about the one essence, common to the Three Persons. It was also impossible to avoid the essential problems of theological anthropology, and for this reason, I could not fail to address them as well. However, they are not treated with the breadth that they deserve, and this places limitations on the scope of this Dogmatic Theology, which cannot present itself as being complete.

Thus limited and delimited, this "Dogmatic Synthesis" is comprised of three great parts: †

1. THE MYSTERY OF THE ONE GOD IN THREE PERSONS

2. THE INCARNATION OF THE WORD

3. THE CHURCH AND THE SACRAMENTS

---

* [Tr. note: Fr. Nicholas did eventually write a volume addressing some of these topics. It is the final volume in this series of English translations of his dogmatic synthesis.]

† [Tr. note: This first volume of the English edition includes all of "The Mystery of the One God in Three Persons." The subsequent parts will be published in multiple English volumes due to their length and clear divisions of content.]

1

Introduction to The Mystery of One God in Three Persons

Theology is the science of God. It is the science of God such as He has revealed Himself to man and as He is known by faith: God the Savior, who saved the world through Jesus Christ; God the Last End, in whom man must find his fulfillment; more profoundly still, God in His mystery, for man's salvation and beatitude are his vital participation in the mystery of God, eternal life, the Trinitarian life, proposed to him and given to him if he accepts it. We encounter a host of various "subjects" in theology. A great number of them belong to the created order. However, theology considers all these beings and events only inasmuch as they come from God and lead back to Him.[1]

The mystery of God, of the *Living God*, is the living and eternal communion of *Three who are Only One God*, the Father, the Son, and the Holy Spirit. Thus, to say that the "subject" of theology is God is the same as saying that the mystery of the Holy Trinity is at the heart of theology. This means not only that the study of the Trinity should hold the central place in theology, but even more, it means

[Tr. note: In Nicolas's organization of the text, this introduction begins "Part One: The Mystery of One God in Three Persons," whereas the prior "General Introduction" marks the introduction to the entire *Synthese Dogmatique*.]

1. See *ST* I, q. 1, a. 7.

that everything that is studied in theology is studied in function of the Trinity and in its light.

Moreover, although theology is a science, it is also much more than a science, in the sense that its ultimate finality is not mere knowledge but, instead, is the believer's personal union with the personal God whom the believer seeks to understand better by means of theological reflection. In its perfect form, this union, promised for the hereafter, is the Beatific Vision, overflowing in a totally self-giving and fruitful love. In its imperfect form, here below, this union is had through contemplation in faith and through love. Therefore, theology can only be understood as being intrinsically ordered to mystical contemplation and, beyond that, to the Beatific Vision, which is sketched out in mystical experience distantly yet authentically. The object of this Vision and that of our contemplation is God in His Triune personality, the Trinity.

Indeed, in a course in dogmatic theology, the mystery of the Trinity sometimes seems to be "superadded" to the Godhead, as though it were a sublime, but in some way accidental, property which we would not really need so as to understand God, whether in the economy of salvation or in Himself.[2] For example, St. Thomas does not say that the subject of theology is the Trinity but, instead, says that it is God. Certainly, in the treatise devoted to the Trinity, he says that God is the Trinity, but in what follows after this treatise, he continues to speak about "God" (following in this the example of all the theologians [preceding him], including the most esteemed of the Fathers of the Church).

An embarrassing paradox results from this fact. The treatise on the Trinity, which should be the heart of all theology and which should show the believer the loftiest and most profound object proposed to his contemplation, is in reality the most abstract and most

2. See the perhaps excessive observations, though ones calling for reflection, in Karl Rahner, "Quelques remarques sur le traité dogmatique 'De Trinitate,'" Ecrits théologiques VIII (Paris: Desclée de Brouwer, 1967). [Tr. note: Taken from Karl Rahner, "Remarks on the Dogmatic Treatise 'De Trinitate,'" in Theological Investigations, vol. 4 (More Recent Writings), trans. Kevin Smyth (Baltimore: Helicon, 1966), 99.]

foreign (at least in appearance) to Christian experience and like-wise is the most distant (always in appearance) from the "economy" or "salvation history." It constitutes "a system which makes one ask whether God has really revealed [to] us such far-fetched things in so obscure a way that it needs such complicated explanation."[3]

In order to avoid "isolating" the treatise on the Trinity, many theologians would like to reduce the theology of the mystery of the Trinity to the study of the manifestations of the Divine Persons with-in history, that is, to the theology of the divine missions. In such an account, we could only know the manifestations of the Divine Per-sons and of the Trinity. The term thus used for the Divine Persons inasmuch as They manifest themselves in history is "the Economic Trinity," and inasmuch as They are the very inwardness of God, the term thus used is "the Immanent Trinity." For some, the "Immanent Trinity" is what we know when we know the "Economic Trinity," whereas, for others, the "Immanent Trinity" is unknowable, for ac-cording to them, we can only know the "Economic Trinity."

This represents a seductive solution inasmuch as it wishes to en-close the effort of theological reflection within the strict limits of scriptural data. But is this not, in reality, to place theological reflec-tion itself, its value and its scope, in question? Would this not lead to theology being nothing other than exegesis, which would tend to abolish the effort of understanding the revealed data, an effort that began with the Church's own beginning in the inspired writings themselves, an effort that has never slackened off through the course of the centuries up to the present day?

Later on in this text, we will undertake a more thorough ex-amination of the problem of the relations between the "Economic Trinity" and the "Immanent Trinity." However, we can immediately note that the manifestation of the Divine Persons in their distinction (which is certainly the point of departure for every "Trinitarian spec-

---

3. See Rahner, "Quelques remarques," 135. [Tr. note: English taken from Karl Rahner, "Remarks on the Dogmatic Treatise 'De Trinitate,'" in *Theological Investigations*, vol. 4 (Baltimore: Helicon, 1966), 77–104.]

ulation") inevitably poses problems related to the inwardness of the Trinity. For example, how is one to reconcile the distinction of Three who are manifested distinctly as God in the New Testament with the manifestation of God as One, both in the Old Testament and in the New? If Jesus manifested Himself as the Son in God, as God Himself, how are we to understand the idea that a begetting would occur in the depths of the Godhead? How are we to understand the procession of the Holy Spirit? And so forth.... The manifestations of the Divine Persons are not clear by themselves, and they were accompanied by explanatory statements without which they would remain inscrutable for us. Moreover, their qualified witnesses, the apostles, who have reported to us Jesus's deeds and words, as well as the signs of the Spirit's presence and action, themselves referred us to the inwardness of the Immanent Trinity, as we will see in the first section of this treatise.

It is altogether impossible to do away with reflection on the inwardness of the Trinitarian mystery to the degree that we can know it by means of the revelation that we have received. Of course, this reflection will necessarily be difficult and of the loftiest sort of intellectuality. It must be abstract in the sense that it must submit the notions that it will use to a rigorously analogical treatment. Indeed, at the terminus of this analogical treatment, these notions will seem quite distant from their experiential origins (i.e., the notions of *generation*, of *intelligible conception*, of *love*, of *relation*, etc.). Nonetheless, through these very abstract and very intellectual means, the knowledge that we aim at—and that, if our effort is sufficiently successful, the knowledge that we obtain—is the most concrete, most existential, and most living knowledge that can be experienced—not only because the God thus known is *the Living God*, but above all because He is *living for me, the source of life*. For God's self-revelation is His Self-Giving[4]—fully in the perfect revelation of face-to-face vision, inchoately in faith, theology, and mystical experience. The mystical

---

4. See Jean-Hervé Nicolas, *Dieu connue comme inconnu* (Paris: Desclée de Brouwer, 1966), ch. 4.

experience to which notional theology is ordered (in the sense that the project of knowing God by believing reason is part of a vaster project that is inscribed in faith, namely, the project of knowing God inasmuch as He is knowable here below, a project that calls us to transcend all reasoning and all concepts)[5] is nothing other than each person's personal participation in the manifestation that each Person has made of Himself in salvation history. Thus, the loftiest speculations of Trinitarian theology have no other intention and no other meaning than that of leading the believer to know more fully the Father, the Son, and the Holy Spirit who are manifested and who manifest themselves in salvation history.

The solution to the paradox noted above consists not in excluding rational speculations, which are indispensable but, rather, from the beginning and throughout their elaboration, in keeping our eyes fixed on the concrete and living Reality whom these speculations aim to make known to us. If we cannot be limited to studying the missions of the Divine Persons (since these "sendings" of the Persons are not sufficiently self-explanatory), we must base ourselves on them as upon the place wherein the Trinity and the Church's faith were revealed so that we can then elevate ourselves to a consideration of the Divine Persons in the inwardness of the Divinity, the Immanent Trinity. In this way, we will elevate ourselves from the manifestation to Him who is manifested, then descending once more to the manifestations of the Divine Persons in salvation history, now illuminated by this knowledge of the Trinitarian mystery in itself, which they have rendered possible and which, in its own turn, explains them.

Our treatise's divisions will follow this plan. The first task will be the matter of discussion in part 1. The second task will occupy parts 2 and 3, one devoted to the search for some degree of theological knowledge concerning the Immanent Trinity and the other to the criticism of this knowledge. Finally, the third task will occupy part 4, which is devoted to the divine missions.

5. See Nicolas, *Dieu connue comme inconnu*, ch. 7.

PART 1

———— : ————

The Manifestation of the Divine Persons and the Faith of the Church in the Trinity

2

From One God to the Triune God

I. THE GOD OF THE PHILOSOPHERS
AND OF THE LEARNED

It is undeniable that philosophy has always been occupied with God—even if only to deny Him. In other words, there is a philosophical problem concerning God. What is the relation between such investigations and those that are undertaken by the theologian?

A. The Affirmation of God on the Basis
of Our Knowledge of the World

1. The Existence of God and His Attributes

Nevertheless, given that effects depend upon their cause, on the basis of such effects, we can come to know that God exists and can know of Him the attributes that belong necessarily to the first universal Cause who surpasses all these effects.[1]

This is the essence of the philosophical process that proceeds from the beings given to our experience to others being above our experience, with the former depending on the latter. Because of this dependence, we can have some knowledge of them, at least as regards their existence.

---

1. *ST* I, q. 12, a. 12, ad. 1.

At the end of this process, God is not attained directly as an object of knowledge. Instead, He is attained as the terminus of the universe's relation of total dependence upon the Necessary Being who is situated above every experience (whether totally or partially sensible) but who is necessary in order for the universe to be intelligible. The affirmation of God is implied in the affirmation of the being of things given to our experience, and the "proofs of the existence of God" only serve to develop this implication, making the mind pass from the implicit to the explicit:

It is true that the relation to the cause does not enter into the definition of the caused being. Nonetheless, it is implied in the constitutive elements of this defined thing. Given that a thing has being by participation, it follows that it is caused by another, meaning that a being of this kind cannot exist in any other way than as something caused by another ... However, from the moment that we realize that "to be caused" does not pertain to being precisely as such, we find that it is possible to discover that an Uncaused Being exists.[2]

To understand the full dimensions of this process, we must realize that the universe, whose very intelligibility thus hearkens to the Being who is situated above it in perfect transcendence, is not only the universe external to man, the universe of objects. It is also man's own universe, the universe of subjects.[3]

The divine attributes are discovered where two processes converge at infinity. One is *a posteriori*, ascending from created perfections (pure, or *simpliciter simplices*, perfections) to their infinite realization in God. In this ascent, we must observe the three classical rules of *causality*, *negation*, and *eminence*.[4] The other process is *a priori*, based on the affirmation of God as the Absolute Being, identical with Existence (*ipsum esse subsistens*), demonstrating that the properties of being exist in Him, each of them equally pushed to infinity:

2. *ST* I, q. 44, a. 1, ad. 1.

3. See Louis Bertrand Geiger, "Transcendance et subjectivité," in *Problèmes actuels de la connaissance de Dieu*, ed. Norbert A. Luyten (Fribourg: Éditions Universitaires, 1968), 73–92.

4. See *ST* I, q. 12, a. 12.

unity, which gives us immutability, eternity, and unicity; *aliquid* [something], which makes us see God as a Being at once perfectly determined, a "nature," and a Being who is infinite and distinct from the beings of the universe *ex ipsa sua separatione* [by virtue of His very separation];[5] "truth," which simultaneously gives us perfect intelligibility and intellectuality in pure act (subsistent thought);[6] "goodness," which gives us infinite appetibility and subsistent love.

However, the affirmation of God's existence stands at the beginning of both of these processes, and this affirmation is *a posteriori*. For this reason, the following point is of critical importance: *every judgment concerning God is a judgment of existence.* That is, every judgment concerning God is only a determination of the primordial judgment: God exists. This likewise holds true for sacred theology and for faith itself. The affirmation of God's existence is not only the starting point in theology. It is implied as the presupposition and condition for every theological judgment.[7]

2. The Knowability of God

{2} The paradox of the affirmation of God's existence (as much for the philosophical affirmation as for faith's affirmation, as well as for the theological affirmation of His existence) is that God can only be affirmed as existing beyond the universe, "outside" of it, and therefore beyond knowledge. God can be known only as unknown.[8]

Many modern thinkers draw an argument from this, saying that God is not "known" but, rather, is only "aimed at."[9] This claim conceals an equivocation, for if God is "aimed at," one performs such aiming by means of the intellect and by means of one of its acts, an

5. St. Thomas, *De Ente et Essentia*, 4.26.

6. *ST* I, q. 14, a. 1; q. 19, a. 1; q. 20.

7. See Jean-Hervé Nicolas, *Dieu connue comme inconnu* (Paris: Desclée de Brouwer, 1966).

8. St. Thomas, *In Boetium de Trinitate*, prol., q. 1, a. 2, ad. 1.

9. See Henri Duméry, *Critique et religion* (Paris: Sedes, 1957), 193ff; *Le problème de Dieu en philosophie de la religion* (Paris: Desclée de Brouwer, 1957); Edward Schillebeeckx, "La notion de vérité et la tolerance," in *La liberté religieuse, exigence spirituelle et problème politique*, 113–153 (Paris: Centurion, 1965); and many others.

act of knowledge. What, therefore, is the object of this act? What is it that is known by this act if not God?

Other interpreters of St. Thomas insist on the numerous statements made by this doctor who says (or seems to say) that man can know only the fact of God's existence without knowing what He is.[10] However, can one know a being that exists without knowing what it is? And did not St. Thomas, who is marshalled in support of this claim, spend all his life seeking to know God and to express something about what He is? If such a conception of our knowledge of God were true, it would destroy the very possibility of theology and even of revelation, for revelation is a teaching and theology is an assimilation of this teaching by reason. How could God Himself teach man truths that human reason would be radically incapable of knowing?[11] When St. Thomas says that we can know of God "*quia est*," not "*quid est*" ["that He is," not "what He is"], he means that we do not know the divine attributes on the basis of His essence. (In other words, we do not know them quidditatively.) However, on the other hand, he does mean that we know His essence imperfectly and partially on the basis of the judgment of existence (discussed above) concerning these attributes.[12]

God is knowable by man "on the basis [of our knowledge of] creatures." This is not to be understood simplistically as meaning that human reason could pass from knowledge of creatures to knowledge of God, as though He were a new object, reached by means of new concepts. Instead, it is to be understood as meaning that, on account of participation (which is itself founded on God's universal and complete causality), creatures resemble God. And while they resemble Him only in a very deficient manner, they do truly resem-

10. See Étienne Gilson, *Le thomisme, introduction à la philosophie de Saint Thomas d'Aquin*, 5th ed. (Paris: Vrin, 1945), ch. 5.

11. See the discussion in Nicolas, *Dieu connue comme inconnu*, ch. 2; Maurie Corvez, "Le problème de dieu," *Revue Thomiste* 67 (1967): 95–104.

12. See St. Thomas, *In Boethium De Trinitate*, q. 6, a. 3; *In Dionysius, De divinis nominibus*, ch. 7, lect. 4; *ST* I, q. 12. [Tr. note: The citation for the commentary on Pseudo-Dionysius's *De divinis nominibus* reads "ch. 7, 1, IV." Based on the content it appears that this was an incorrect rendering of "l. IV."]

ble Him in such a way that God can be known in them as in a mirror. There is no concept representing God directly. (God is infinite,
noetically as well as ontologically, and therefore cannot be enclosed
within a concept. He is perfectly simple, and therefore, there cannot
be a concept that would "represent" one part of God that would hy-
pothetically be limited and circumscribable.) All the concepts that
we use in knowing God re-present created perfections—or, rather,
they re-present the perfections that we find in creatures (though,
they themselves do imitate the perfections of the Uncreated). We
are assured of this imitation by the fact of God's causality of finite beings, a fact that imposes itself upon us, as well as by the requirements
of this causal fact ([for,] "every agent assimilates its effect to itself"*).
On account of this imitation, we are rationally justified in attributing
these perfections to God by means of a judgment obeying the three
rules of causality, negation, and eminence. By means of these rules,
this judgment uses these concepts, making them transcend their limitations in such a manner that, in the act of this judgment and by its
power, they really enable us to know what God is, albeit imperfectly.
It is on the static level of representation (in the first act of the intellect) that these concepts remain "concepts of creatures." Dynamically, in the act of judgment, they attain the Divine Perfection Itself.[13]

Thus, we pass from the possibility of knowing God (a possibility recognized abstractly and *a priori*) to the fact of this knowledge.
We will discover the conditions for the possibility of knowledge of
God, its value and its limits, on the basis of the fact of this knowledge, which is imposed on us when we perceive the necessity of affirming God as the first cause and ultimate explanation of the world
given to our experience.

---

* [Tr. note: He is rendering the Thomistic principle *omne agens agit simi sibile*.]
13. See Nicolas, *Dieu connue comme inconnu*, chs. 2 and 3. [Tr. note: Fr. Nicolas
cross-references what appears to be the incorrect reference, namely, an article in *Revue
Thomiste*. See "L'unité d'être dans le Christ selon S. Thomas d'Aquin," *Revue thomiste* 65
(1965): 229–60.]

B. "Natural Theology" Contested

{3} What is the relationship between this knowledge of God solely by the ways of reason (i.e., "natural theology") and properly theological knowledge of God, which has divine revelation and faith as its source? The Catholic doctrine concerning this point, something set forth at the First Vatican Council, holds that natural theology is the foundation for supernatural theology, with the latter for its own part preserving the former from errors and deviations: "Not only can there be no conflict between faith and reason, they also support each other since right reason demonstrates the foundations of faith and, illuminated by its light, pursues the science of divine things."[14]

This doctrine had already been elaborated by scholastic theologians, with natural theology playing the role of providing "*praeambula fidei*."[15] Indeed, St. Thomas founds his theological synthesis on a rational demonstration of God's Existence (*ST* I, q. 2) and of the rationally-knowable divine attributes.

This outlook was brilliantly brought into question by Karl Barth, and in light of his criticisms, the rejection of "natural theology" seems to have become a commonplace in Protestant theology, to such a point that this rejection has become a seemingly self-evident point of departure.[16] Moreover, many people believe that this rejection is decisively supported by modern philosophy's profound tendency to consider the problem of God as something of no interest to philosophy. More recently, Maurice Clavel[17] brilliantly rejected every intrusion of metaphysics into faith on the grounds that Kant definitively made clear the failure of metaphysics and sounded its death-knell, thus liberating true faith from every form of philosophical contamination.

14. Vatican Council I, *Dei Filius* IV, no. 3019 (April 24, 1870) (D-Sch, no. 3019).

15. See St. Thomas, *In Boetium de Trinitate*, q. 2, a.3, and in many other places.

16. See Gabriel Widmer, "Sens et non-sens des énoncés théologiques," *Revue des sciences philosophiques et théologiques* 51 (1967): 644–65; Gabriel Widmer, "Intelligibilité et incompréhensibilité de Dieu," *Revue de théologie et de philosophie* 18 (1968): 145–62.

17. See Maurice Clavel, *Ce qu je crois* (Paris: Grasset, 1975).

1. The Barthian Rejection of Natural Theology

{4} This rejection is fundamental in Barth and is therefore found in numerous places within his oeuvre. He set it forth and justified it in particular celebrated pages of his *Church Dogmatics*.[18]

Barth provides two reasons, which he sets forth at length, for his impassioned rejection of the doctrine of Vatican I. The first is that to divide the knowability of God in two (God naturally knowable on the basis of creation, then knowable in His mystery through revelation) necessarily leads us to divide up God Himself (even if we do not intend to do so), separating God the Creator from God the Savior, a separation that renders revelation useless. The second reason for his rejection, which he presents as being the most decisive one, is that natural theology would claim to understand a being and essence of God anterior to the God who is revealed in the event of revelation. This assertion is his famous denial of the *analogia entis*, understood as meaning that God and man would be, independent of grace and of sin, encompassed within the universal notion of being. Thus, "God would be knowable without God, that is, without any particular divine intervention." Such a God is an "idol":

> Our primary contradiction is not of the "natural theology" of the *Vaticanum* as such. This is only a self-evident consequence of our initial contradiction of its concept of God. We reject this because it is a construct which obviously derives from an attempt to unite Yahweh with Baal, the trine God of Holy Scripture with the concept of being of Aristotelian and Stoic philosophy.[19]

---

18. See Karl Barth, *Dogmatique* (Genève: Labor et Fides, 1953–1970), II, 62–127. For a discussion of Barth's position, see: Henri Bouillard, *Karl Barth*, vols. 1, 2, and 3 (Paris: Aubier, 1957); Henri Bouillard, "Le refus de la théologie naturelle dans la théologie protestante contemporaine," *L'existence de Dieu* (Tournai: Casterman, 1961), 95–108; Henry Chavannes, *L'analogie entre Dieu et le monde selon saint Thomas d'Aquin et selon K. Barth* (Paris: Cerf, 1969), 207–80.

19. Barth, *Dogmatique*, II, 83. [Tr. note: Taken from Karl Barth, *Church Dogmatics*, vol. 2.1, trans. T.H.L. Parker et al., ed. G.W. Bromiley and T.F. Torrance (Edinburgh: T & T Clark, 1957), 84.]

Next, he carefully and critically studies the reasons adduced in justification of natural theology, reasons that are so strong that they remain "perennial" despite all the refutations to which natural theology has been subjected, indeed so strong that it was able to become one of the buttresses of Christian theology "already in post-apostolic Christianity," then throughout the entire history of the Church and "up to the thought of the Reformers." The first of these reasons is that, in fact, men through the course of history (and by many paths) have arrived at some knowledge of God without revelation. Barth factually concedes all of this. However, he all the while strongly reaffirms that such a God is only an idol, one of the idols that Scripture prohibits us from formally identifying with the true God.[20] The second reason adduced in justification of natural theology would be pedagogical in nature and also related to "the care of souls." Here, one would be concerned with finding a middle ground, a basis for common discussion with a still-unbelieving world. To this, Barth responds that, prior to the acceptance of revelation, no decision point exists which would be a fitting intermediary decision-point whither a man might be brought so as to prepare him for faith:

> When a man stands in the decision of faith or unbelief, he has not arrived at this position from any of the pre-decisions which are possible to him apart from God's revelation. But—and this is a very different thing—the real God Himself has come to him.[21]

On the basis of this fact, he disputes, quite rightly, the pedagogical value of such a process, which would deceive the interlocutor by concealing from him what faith really demands of him. Finally, the third reason adduced in support of natural theology rests on the numerous scriptural testimonies that seem to lead us to admit the existence of natural theology, and Barth begins by openly recognizing the weight of these testimonies.[22] However, he does this in order to

20. See Barth, *Dogmatique*, II, 85–86.
21. Barth, *Dogmatique*, II, 92. [Tr. note: Taken from Barth, *Church Dogmatics*, vol. 2.1, 91.]
22. See Barth, *Dogmatique*, II, 98.

then contest that Scripture really has this meaning, something that it could not do without contradicting itself. His assertion is contradicted by Lackmann, who concludes: "The Barthian conception admitting only a single revelation is contradicted by the entire tradition, even the Calvinist tradition."[23]

On the whole, Chavannes insightfully argues that Barth's virulent critique of the Catholic position contains a considerable number of misunderstandings, especially in his criticisms registered against the idea of natural theology in St. Thomas.[24]

It still remains the case that Barth denies the possibility and validity of natural theology as opposed to the revelation of God in Jesus Christ, the sole way that is open to man for knowledge of the True God.[25]

2. The Exclusion of the Problem of God by Contemporary Philosophy

{5} The outcome of a meditation conducted on the basis of this datum (namely, that God is of interest to the philosopher only to the degree that the Divine is presented as a property of metaphysics) is inevitable. There can only be a purification of being through the elimination of every contamination due to the intrusion of the notion of God. Therefore, it is natural that from Hegel through Nietzsche and today, in the philosophy of Martin Heidegger, one tends to consider methodological atheism to be a necessary condition for the progress of metaphysical reflection. In it, God is inevitably absorbed by being or is methodologically set out of consideration.[26]

23. See Max Lackmann, *Vom Geheimnis der Schöpfung. Die Geschichte der Exegese von Römer 1, 18–23; 2, 14–16 und Acta 14, 15–17; 17, 22–29 vom 2. Jahrhundert bis zum Beginn der Orthodoxie* (Stuttgart: 1952).

24. See Chavannes, *L'analogie entre Dieu et le monde selon saint Thomas d'Aquin et selon K. Barth.*

25. In the opposite direction, in Orthodox theology, see Pangiotis N. Trembelas, *Dogmatique de l'Église orthodoxe catholique*, vol. 1 (Paris: Desclée de Brouwer, 1957), 168–97.

26. Étienne Gilson, "L'être et Dieu," *Revue Thomiste* 62 (1962): 187; Dominique De Petter, "Le caractère métaphysique de la preuve de l'existence de Dieu et la pensée contemporaine," in *L'existence de Dieu* (Paris: Casterman, 1961), 167–80.

This methodological non-consideration of God finds a remarkable expression in Merleau-Ponty's inaugural Discourse at the Collège de France.[27]

It is also true that certain tendencies in contemporary philosophy lead it to be expressly atheist (as in Sartre, who judges the idea of God to be contradictory, and in Merleau-Ponty also, in the end). However, even where it is not precluded that philosophy prepares for and renders possible an eventual encounter with God (as in Heidegger), it remains the case that the discovery and affirmation of God is not a work of philosophy itself.[28]

In other words, from such a perspective, "natural theology" is impossible, for it is nothing if it is not philosophical (or at least susceptible to being conducted in a philosophical form).[29] This is manifestly the meaning of the expressions used by Vatican I: "By the light of natural reason"; "that which is in the divine realities does not of itself escape human reason."[30]

3. The Meaning and Necessity of "Natural Theology"

{6} Certainly, we must recognize that God is not, and cannot be, a philosophical object like other objects. He can be affirmed only as being beyond all objects, though as the necessary source of their intelligibility. This is the paradox of the affirmation of God that we recalled earlier.

It is also certain that the necessity of this affirmation of God finds its setting and justification in a philosophy of being that is quite different from contemporary philosophy in its inspiration and presuppositions. This is not the place to justify this primordial grasp of being, which is contingent in its existential realizations (beings) and necessary in its essential requirements (the properties of being,

27. See Maurice Merleau-Ponty, *Eloge de la philosophie* (Paris: Gallimard, 1965), 52–56.
28. See Henri Birault, "De l'être, du divin et des dieux chez Heidegger," in *L'existence de Dieu* (Paris: Casterman, 1961), 49–76.
29. See St. Thomas, *In Meta.*, prol.; *In Boethium De Trinitate*, q. 5, a. 4.
30. Vatican Council I, *Dei Filius* II, nos. 3004–3005.

essences, and the factual necessity of existence). The necessity that it postulates can only be assured by its ontological dependence on the Necessary Being. This Necessary Being is beyond the universe, as well as beyond what the human mind can grasp. Nonetheless, It must be affirmed as the real cause and condition of the intelligibility of the beings that make up this universe which is offered to the mind's grasp.

a) The Necessity of Natural Theology for Faith Itself

{7} Not only does natural knowledge of God not contradict the knowledge had through faith and is not rendered void by it, but it is also the case that such natural knowledge is necessarily presupposed by faith. The rejection of such natural knowledge would render faith impossible (in a sense that will be specified below).[31]

Indeed, faith is an acceptance of the Word [*Parole*] of God concerning God and concerning man in his relationship with God. Therefore, it cannot represent an absolute beginning of knowledge. It presupposes at least some kind of knowledge about what the word "God" means and also some kind of knowledge about what the word "man" means (i.e., knowledge about the fact that man is open to the transcendent).

However, we must press on further still. Faith presupposes knowledge of this God as transcending man, as a distinct Being, who has His existence in Himself and is not a simple projection of man's aspirations, a creation of his subjectivity. Indeed, I cannot receive Scripture as revelation, as the "Word of God," without admitting, by the same fact, that God is "external" to man,[32] capable of speaking to him, of manifesting Himself, and of teaching him something new in comparison to what he knows by himself and of himself.

It is in no way [immediately] evident that Scripture is the Word

---

31. See Claude Geffré, "Théologie naturelle et revelation dans la connaissance de Dieu un," in *L'existence de Dieu* (Paris: Casterman, 1961), 297–318.
32. "External": Not in a spatial sense, obviously, but in the metaphysical sense: alterity.

of God, and this affirmation itself is meaningless if God does not exist independent of man's thoughts and aspirations. What it tells us about God and about man in his relationship with God necessarily presupposes this existence of God "in Himself":

> This is why, as a Catholic, I am convinced that appealing to a particular revelation is impossible and meaningless if ... man, by relying upon human powers and without appealing to a particular revelation, is not capable of justifying the existence of a personal God on the basis of his human experience.[33]

b) A Response to Barth's Objections

{8} It is not true that "natural theology" would render revelation useless, substituting reason's efforts for the gracious gift of God, "in such a manner that God would be knowable without God," thus leading to a false god, an "idol" that would be exclusively different than Yahweh. This natural knowledge of God cannot by itself lead to God the Savior, for salvation depends on God's absolutely free initiative, which cannot be known by the playing out of rational and *a priori* necessity. Natural theology has meaning for salvation as a preparation for the reception of revelation. A natural preparation? Yes, in the sense that man has in him, in his nature, the real capacity to be prepared in this manner. No, if one means that natural theology is not, by this fact, graciously bestowed by God. Reason, in fact, is a gift from God, and its own light comes from God as well: the Word who came into the world through the Incarnation, in order to save man, is "the light, the true light that illuminates all men."[34] Moreover, the divine action of revealing Himself—of giving Himself in revealing Himself—begins with the creation of man "in God's image." Hence, there is no question of attaining an existence and essence of God "anterior to God who is revealed in the event of revelation," except in the sense that creation—which is an act of God!—is anterior to the

---

33. Edward Schillebeeckx, "En quête du Dieu vivant," in *Approches théologiques 2: Dieu et l'homme* (Bruxelles: 1965), 59–60.

34. Jn 1:9, my translation (Minerd).

event of revelation. It is anterior, but ordered to it, and already takes part in it as its preparation:

Therefore, belief is a gift of self to God in which we only abandon ourselves to the interior divine invitation. But this gift is not an unjustified act, a jump into the dark, since we first have acquired, on the basis of our experience and natural evidences, certitude concerning the existence of a personal God.[35]

On the other hand, God is not divided up by us admitting that God, who is one and infinitely simple, can be known only partially, for we are not here speaking of a direct form of knowledge that would be concerned with God as with an immediate object. Certainly, He is simple as an object. Rather, we are here speaking of an indirect form of knowledge, concerned with created beings in their various relations to their Creator. Creatures resemble God enough that I am able to form some idea for myself concerning Him on the basis of them. However, He does not resemble anything,[36] and the Barthian expression is indeed acceptable: the Wholly-Other. God is known as not having parts, but He is only partially known, that is, inasmuch as creatures resemble Him. The successive parts belong to our knowledge of God, for our knowledge is what is complex and progressive, forever imperfect and forever perfectible. Hence, the way remains open for a revelation by which God would enrich and bring to completion the knowledge that man can obtain about Him on the basis of creatures by making known His "mystery" (i.e., that in which He is infinitely dissimilar from creatures, a mystery that, consequently, cannot be known on the basis of creatures).

Does this mean that natural knowledge of God is prior to acceptance of the Word of God through faith, meaning that one would need to begin by acquiring such knowledge? In no way is this necessary, for that would unduly rule out the possibility of faith, not only for the mass of people who cannot (or who do not wish to) acquire

---

35. Schillebeeckx, "En quête du Dieu vivant," 65.
36. See *ST* I, q. 4, a. 3.

such knowledge, but also for a great number of those for whom philosophy—in which they have been formed or which they have deliberately chosen—partially or totally excludes this knowledge. The truth of faith "objectively" presupposes and implies these truths, meaning that the believer holds them through the same act of faith by which he adheres to a properly supernatural mystery. In believing that God is Triune and that He has spoken to men, he believes that God exists, and in believing that baptism has made us children of God and has prepared us for eternal life, he believes that the soul is immortal.

These natural truths are also part of revelation, for God in His mercy did not wish to leave men to suffer from the risks and difficulties inherent in their own groping and easily-aberrant investigations.[37] Therefore, they are themselves an object of faith, at least for those who have not acquired them in some manner through a rigorous philosophical process of reasoning. However, they are not distinct objects of faith but, rather, as was said earlier, are part of the object of faith that is the mystery of God, in Himself and in His communication to men. From this perspective, we can admit that, even for the person who, otherwise, has philosophically established them, they fall under faith as well, for he too cannot make an act of faith in the mystery of God without affirming, by this same act, the truths presupposed by the act of faith. This is why the numerous demonstrations of a purely philosophical appearance encountered in the *Summa theologiae* (in particular those that compose the majority of the treatise called "*De Deo uno*") are an integral part of the unified process of theological reasoning (understanding "theology" as referring to sacred theology). When the theologian "proves" the existence of God, he speaks of the one, unique God, who reveals Himself as Triune, and the divine attributes that he discovers by way of deduction or induction are the attributes of a God who is Triune.[38]

---

37. See *SCG*, 1.4; *ST* I, q.1, a. 1; II-II, q. 2, a. 4.
38. See Nicolas, *Dieu connue comme inconnu*, 290–92 and n. 69; Claude Tresmontant,

Therefore, in order to believe, and in order to theologically reflect on his faith, it is in no way necessary for one to have philosophically demonstrated the truths that make up "natural theology." In
this sense, we can admit with Trembelas[39] that faith is necessary in
order for the believer to be perfectly certain of the natural truths
that provide faith with its foundation. Nonetheless, the same author
recognizes that, "He who believes in the existence of God can be
certain that his faith rests on solid bases and can be rationally justified." This indicates that the uncertainty and hesitation that more or
less befall the demonstrations and affirmations of natural theology
do not come from a deficiency in these affirmations' objective certitude. Rather, this comes from the conditions of the knowing subject. (Man's sinful situation obviously must be included among these
conditions. We can understand Barth's teaching on this point, without, for all that, accepting his radical pessimism concerning the abil-
ities of human reason for knowing God by its own means.)

What would be inconceivable, ultimately rendering supernatural faith and sacred theology impossible, is the claim that certain
knowledge of God's existence and of His attributes would be impossible for man. Were that the case, faith would be a decision imposed
upon reason (for the act of faith is an act of intellectual knowledge,
and therefore, for man, an act of reason) and simultaneously would
be a decision that reason would be forced to disavow as something
foreign to its proper activity and unable to be integrated by it. Coming back to what we said earlier, let us say that one does not pass in a
necessary manner from abstract knowledge concerning the possibility of knowing God (nor, moreover, from the rational knowledge of
God) to the acceptance of His Word [*Parole*] and the new forms of
knowledge that this brings with it. However, the very act of accepting the Word [*Parole*] of God is a recognition (at least implicitly) not

Les idées maîtresses de la métaphysique chrétienne (Paris: Seuil 1962). [Tr. note: Again, Fr.
Nicolas seems to wrongly cite the article in the same manner as above.]
    39. See *Dogmatique de l'Église orthodoxe catholique*, vol. 1, 185–88.

only of His existence and of His attributes, but also of the possibility of the fact that reason can know God.

Ratzinger has shown that the first Christians, faced with the deliberate separation in the ancients between the "God of the philosophers" (Being) corresponding to the search for the truth and the mythical gods of religion who were taken for granted and accepted by all (including by the philosophers) as a rule for life, opted deliberately for the truth and against the gods of religion. This choice led to them being accused of being atheists:

> The Christian faith opted, we have seen, against the gods of the various religions and in favor of the God of the philosophers, that is, against the myth of custom and in favor of the truth of Being itself and nothing else. Hence, the accusation made against the early Church that her adherents were atheists.[40]

However, the Christians profoundly transformed the God of the philosophers by recognizing that this principle of all beings is the "God of men":

> So, in this sense, there is the experience that the God of the philosophers is quite different from what the philosophers had thought Him to be, though He does not thereby cease to be what they had discovered; that one only comes to know him properly when one realizes that he, the real truth and ground of all Being, is at one and the same time the God of faith, the God of men.[41]

Likewise, Cazelles observes:

> If you wish to distinguish the true God from the false gods, philosophy has its rights, which it can assert. Studying human thought, its processes and its conditions, the human quest for the True God (and, therefore for the truth about God) cannot abstract from the God of the philosophers or from the truth of philosophies, even if the philosophical schools did not wish to name God in the course of their search for the truth. Nonetheless, the God of the Bible, all the while assuming the attributes of the God of

40. Joseph Ratzinger, *La foi chrétienne hier et aujourd'hui* (Paris: Mame, 1969), 84. [Tr. note: Taken from Joseph Ratzinger, *Introduction to Christianity*, trans. J. R. Foster (San Francisco: Ignatius Press, 2004), 142.]

41. Ratzinger, *La foi chrétienne hier et aujourd'hui*, 144.

the philosophers or of the truth of the philosophers, presents Himself to
man in a different manner, offering him something more. This is what the
Pascalian adage expresses. It is what historical inquiry, with all the resources of modern discoveries, shows as well.[42]

{9} *Conclusion:* "The God of Abraham, the God of Isaac, the
God of Jacob, not of the philosophers and of the learned."[43] If the
God of the philosophers and of the learned was different from the
"living God," if He were an "idol," as Barth says, it would be impossible for man to accept the revelation made to Abraham, Isaac, and
Jacob, for man can only receive it by means of the same reason that
is at work in science and philosophy. But, quite obviously, through
such revelation, his reason learns many things about this one God
that it could not reach by solely philosophical efforts:

Contrary to the Pascalian position, the Christian paradox does not require
the revealed God not to be the God of the philosophers. The Christian
mystery is paradoxical precisely because the God of love who is revealed
in it is the perfect and autonomous God presupposed by creation.[44]

II. THE GOD OF ISRAEL

A. The Monotheism of Israel

"On no point is late Judaism more unanimous than in its fidelity
to this credo: God is One."[45]

The monotheism of the patriarchs is a practical monotheism, not
a theological affirmation of God's unicity and of the non-existence of
local gods. However, if the God who revealed Himself to Abraham
manifests a kind of affinity with the great God "El," the chief of the
Canaanite pantheon, we can also say:

He is so closely and personally connected to the semi-nomadic clan of the
patriarchs that they honor Him alone and that the other gods are practi-

42. Henri Cazelles, "Le Dieu d'Abraham," *Les Quatre Fleuves. Cahiers de la recherce et
de réflexion religieuses* 6 (1976): 5.
43. Pascal, *Memorial.*
44. Marie-Joseph Le Guillou, *Le mystère du Père* (Paris: Fayard, 1973), 119.
45. Hermann Kleinknecht, "Dieu (1968)," *Dictionnarie biblique* (Genève: Labor et
Fides), 73.

cally non-existent for them. The patriarchal religion consists essentially in their personal and exclusive connection with this God, who is conceived of as a universal sovereign. Quite clearly, the God who revealed Himself had as His first end *this monotheism of action and of life.*[46]

It seems that Moses's teaching did not expressly involve the denial of the existence of other gods. Rather, it seems to have involved only the prohibition of honoring or serving them. "You shall have no other gods before me."* Yahweh is the God of the Covenant. He becomes the God of Israel, and Israel becomes His people.

This "jealousy" of the God of Moses is a unique trait in the midst of ancient religions, which were very tolerant. For Israel, there is only (and can only be) one God, without it being expressly declared that the "gods" of the other peoples are non-existent:

So in this commandment declaring the zeal of [Y]ahweh, Israel was told two things: [Y]ahweh's turning towards her—of this Hosea speaks in terms of the passion of a lover—but at the same time his threat, in case she should only yield to him with a divided heart. This intolerant claim to exclusive worship is something unique in the history of religion, for in antiquity the cults were on easy terms with one another and left devotees a free hand to ensure a blessing for themselves from other gods as well ... The most concise definition of the demands which [Y]ahweh's zeal laid upon Israel is given in Deuteronomy—Israel is to be "perfect" with [Y]ahweh.[47]

Thus, the first commandment did not imply a formally monotheistic faith during this first period, which extends to the age of the kings.[48] Yahweh rejects only the worship of other gods, who are supposed as being real but powerless to save Israel.

Nonetheless, it is relatively just to speak of the appearance of a

---

46. Alfons Deissler, "La revelation de Dieu dans l'Ancien Testament," in *Mysterium Salutis. Dogmatique de l'histoire du salut*, vol. 5 (Paris: Cerf, 1970), 320.

* Ex 20:3 (RSV).

47. Gerhard von Rad, *Théologie de l'Ancien Testament*, vols. 1 and 2 (Genève: Labor et Fides, 1967), 184. See Dt 18:13 [Tr. note: Taken from Gerhard von Rad, *Old Testament Theology*, vol. 1, *The Theology of Israel's Historical Traditions*, trans. D. M. G. Stalker (New York: Harper & Row, 1962), 208.]

48. See von Rad, *Théologie de l'Ancien Testament*, vols. 1 and 2, 186.

form of monotheism in Israel, for we have a number of sufficient testimonies of a practical, as well as theoretical, monotheism dating from much later in Israel. However, describing this appearance of monotheism is a thorny issue.

The role of the prophets had been to fight vigorously against the permanent temptation to render worship to foreign gods, a temptation to which the people and its leaders often succumbed. When the great Assyrian kings extended their hand over Palestine, and even over Zion, the place where Yahweh dwelled, they found themselves faced with the problem of Yahweh's seeming weakness and powerlessness before this power and before the gods that protected it. Thus, one notes that in Amos and Isaiah the gods of the nations are not even named, being treated as being non-existent: "But as is perfectly clear, [Isaiah's] view of history leaves no place whatsoever for the gods of other nations or any functions they might exercise."[49]

It seems that during the Exile the reflection of an elite concerning Israel's vocation, undertaken in light of the terrible and disconcerting trial, led the Israelites to theological monotheism. Second Isaiah is the distinguished testimony of this reflection. "I am the LORD, and there is no other, besides me there is no God."[50] "They (the pagans) shall come over in chains and bow down to you. They will make supplication to you, saying: 'God is with you only, and there is no other, no god besides him.' Truly, thou art a God who hidest thyself, O God of Israel, the Savior."[51] The formulas in which this faith is expressed are found throughout this book (for example, 43:10–11; 43:6–9, etc.)

Following the Exile, Israel comes to profess this strict monotheism, which is expressed in many ways, for example in the wisdom literature (Wis 9:1–15). This not presented as though it were a truth obtained by a process of philosophical reason, nor, doubtlessly,

---

49. von Rad, *Théologie de l'Ancien Testament*, vols. 1 and 2, 187. [Tr. note: Taken from von Rad, *Old Testament Theology*, 212.]

50. Is 45:5 (RSV).

51. Is 45:14–15 (RSV).

through a new revelation, but rather, through a definitive awareness of the revelation of Sinai, a revelation whose means (or whose channel) was the community's religious experience of God's presence, conduct, and sovereignty over the people.

B. The "Personality" of God in the Old Testament

The God of Israel is not a personified force of nature. He is a "someone" who speaks, listens, and wills. His relations with His people arise from a free decision, from a choice, and they essentially take place in the form of a permanent dialogue. This is expressed in a strongly anthropomorphic form in the Bible. God *speaks*.* He "listens."† He "sees."‡ He "whistles." ("In that day the LORD will whistle for the fly which is at the sources of the streams of Egypt, and for the bee which is in the land of Assyria.")§ One speaks of His "eyes," His "feet," and so forth. His behavior is often described with extremely realistic images (for example, in Is 63:1–3).

In late Judaism, there were reactions against this anthropomorphism. The Septuagint arbitrarily changes the text in order to avoid attributing repentance or anger to God. Such changes represent the introduction of philosophical notions into the interpretation of the Bible, as well as into theology, in such a way as to assure the principle that God suffices unto Himself and is perfectly immutable:

Nevertheless, in all these battles and all these movements, Hellenistic Judaism has in no way abandoned its faith in a personal God. Josephus furnishes for us an example of the fact. It is true that he speaks about the God of the Old Testament in as cultivated a manner as is possible ... He is also convinced that God suffices unto Himself. But he is persuaded that this ideal finds itself realized in the Old-Testament doctrine of God, and the God of whom he speaks is the living God of his fathers, despite His often-strange appearance.[52]

---

* Gn 1:3.
† Ex 16:12.
‡ Gn 6:12.
§ Is 7:18 (RSV).
52. Kleinknecht, "Dieu," 99.

Likewise, the rabbis interpreted the biblical anthropomorphisms as being manners of speaking that are adapted to man's imagination. Nonetheless:

Faith in a personal God was in no way diminished by such declarations and restrictions. The great rabbis were men who were diligent in prayer … And that is not all. The rabbis conceived of the personal character of God more radically than anyone before. What is proper to God is neither divine wisdom, nor divine justice. What is ultimate and essential is God's will, irrational to the point of being arbitrary, absolutely contingent in its decrees.[53]

The designation "the living God," which is also found frequently in the form of the oath, "Long live God [*vive Dieu*]," is also a remarkable expression of faith in a personal God.[54] In the various usages of this expression, there is something common: the vivacity and power of His reactions, whether in order to save or to punish. The living God does not remain inert. He sees. He hears. He acts. He is "the living God and the everlasting King. At his wrath the earth quakes, and the nations cannot endure his indignation."[55]

We will see that the extension of the notion of "person" to God raises difficulties in both the philosophical and theological orders (precisely because of the dogma of the Trinity of "Divine Persons"). There can be no doubt, however, that Israel understood God as someone who can be "spoken to," someone with whom we indeed speak and who wills with a will that is all-powerful but also free, a will that can be bent through prayer. In brief, there can be no doubt that Israel understood God as a personal being. If this faith was expressed for a long time in a very anthropomorphic manner, with God being represented "in the image of man,"[56] the purification of this anthropomorphism through a more elaborated and more

53. Kleinknecht, "Dieu," 100.
54. Jacques Guillet, "Le titre biblique de Dieu vivant," in *L'homme devant Dieu, Mélanges offerts au P. H. de Lubac*, vol. 1 (Paris: Aubier, 1963), 11–23.
55. Jer 10:10 (RSV).
56. See Frank Michaeli, *Dieu à l'image de l'homme*, (Neuchâtel, CH: Delachaux et Niestlé, 1949).

demanding religious and rational reflection did not jeopardize this conception of God:

The great movement of opposition against anthropomorphism seized the Jewish world as it had seized the Greek world. But, the end result was radically different. In the Greek world, even the idea of a personal God seemed to remain part of an anthropomorphic mentality that would need to be left behind. Here, in the Jewish world, on the other hand, the Jewish people maintained the distinction between an anthropomorphic conception of God and faith in a personal God, a distinction that imposed itself ever more clearly upon the mind. God is not similar to man, but He is a God who wills, who speaks, and who listens.[57]

C. The Attributes of God

One obviously does not find in the Bible any sort of deduction (nor even a methodical enumeration) of God's attributes. Nonetheless, He is recognized as having certain characteristics, ones that make Him different from all the beings in this world and from all the gods.

1. Transcendence

{12} If Yahweh is experienced and known from start to finish as the "God of Israel," this does not preclude the recognition and affirmation of His dominion over all peoples and over all history, as well as His elevation above the world:

Yahweh is the powerful God, the living God who intervenes and acts here-below, without however, being tied to a determinate place. The gods of paganism were tied to the determinate places to which their efficacy generally was limited. There was the god of a given spring, of a given tree, he who healed a given sickness, at a given place, etc. Yahweh is the one God, omnipresent and universally sovereign. It is possible that at the time of the Exodus only monolatric affirmations were expressly recognized and that doctrinal monotheism appeared only much latter as an explicit theology. Nevertheless, the very *fact* of the liberation from Egypt "in manu forti," by His strong arm, and that of the Exodus intensely show that God reveals Himself and acts everywhere.[58]

57. Kleinknecht, "*Dieu*," 100.
58. Yves-Marie Congar, *Le mystère du Temple*, 1st part (Paris: Cerf, 1957), 29–30.

If God lives in the tent of meeting, then later on in the temple, if He lives above all in His people, whom He has chosen, He is also and simultaneously in heaven. He acts in time, but He is above time. This transcendence is expressed by the imagery of Thick Clouds and by that of Glory.[59] This is the teaching intended by the creation accounts. It is magnificently proclaimed in Deutero-Isaiah: "Who has performed and done this, calling the generations from the beginning? I, the LORD, the first, and with the last; I am He."[60] And, in the Psalms:

"O my God," I say, "take me not hence in the midst of my days, thou whose years endure throughout all generations!" Of old thou didst lay the foundation of the earth, and the heavens are the work of thy hands. They will perish, but thou dost endure; they will all wear out like a garment. Thou changest them like raiment, and they pass away; but thou art the same, and thy years have no end.[61]

Another important testimony to this conception of Yahweh's transcendence is found in the remarkable prohibition against representing Him by means of images.[62] The reason for this prohibition remains mysterious. The only reason given in the Bible (and, even then, at a late stage, quite obviously at a time when this prohibition was universally admitted) is that God does not show Himself in the theophany on Mount Horeb but, instead, is only heard.[63] In this text, Yahweh's transcendence over all the beings in this universe, including celestial bodies, is presented as the meaning of this prohibition:

Beware lest you act corruptly by making a graven image for yourselves, in the form of any figure ... the likeness of any beast that is on the earth ... And beware lest you lift up your eyes to heaven, and when you see the sun and the moon and the stars, all the host of heaven, you be drawn away and worship them and serve them, things which the LORD your God has allotted to all the peoples under the whole heaven.[64]

59. Congar, Le mystère du Temple, 1st part, 24–25.
60. Is 41:4 (RSV).
61. Ps 102:24–27 (RSV).
62. See von Rad, Théologie de l'Ancien Testament, 188–193.
63. See Dt 4:9–20.
64. Dt 4:16–19 (RSV).

The famous diatribes of Deutero-Isaiah against idols[65] place the idol's total dependence upon man (it is the work of his hands, made out of materials that are at are at his disposal) in violent contrast to Yahweh's sovereign domination over all things, over men and nations:

It is he who sits above the circle of the earth, and its inhabitants are like grasshoppers ... who brings princes to naught, and makes the rulers of the earth as nothing.... To whom then will you compare me, that I should be like him? says the Holy One.... The LORD is the everlasting God, the Creator of the ends of the earth. He does not faint or grow weary, his understanding is unsearchable.[66]

If representations of Yahweh are rigorously forbidden in cultural [*sic*] practices (and doubtlessly from the beginning),[67] this is so, at least in part, in order to prevent one from claiming to enclose God's saving power within an object, which would enable one to appropriate it. If God is present in His temple and if the believer can find Him there, this does not mean that He would be enclosed in it. He is always and everywhere above all things, transcendent.

Another biblical notion that expresses Yahweh's transcendence is that of "holiness." It means, above all, God's Infinite Majesty, His elevation above all others: "Who is like thee, O LORD, among the gods? Who is like thee, majestic in holiness, terrible in glorious deeds, doing wonders?"[68] It calls for adoration, worship, and obedience on the part of man. It inspires fear and, at the same time, confidence: "I will not execute my fierce anger, ... for I am God and not man, the Holy One in your midst."[69]

Yahweh "sanctifies" His people by His presence, meaning that He sacralizes them, separating them from the other nations, making them participate in His majesty in some manner, thus making it their own. In this, there is a lived conjunction between transcendence and immanence.

---

65. See Is 40:15–21; 44:9–21.
66. Is 40:22, 23, 25, and 28 (RSV).
67. See von Rad, *Théologie de l'Ancien Testament*, 190.
68. Ex 15:11 (RSV).
69. Hos 11:9 (RSV).

In turn, the people must "sanctify" the name of Yahweh. That is, they must declare His glory through worship. However, this worship cannot be merely external. It must express obedience to the Law, faith.

For this reason, the Holy God, the "Holy One," is the "Hidden God," the God whom we must believe and obey: "But the LORD of hosts, him you shall regard as holy; let him be your fear, and let him be your dread."[70]

2. Omnipotence and Lordship

{13} God's omnipotence is placed in high relief by the story of creation. In His rejection of Job's protestation against Him, God appeals to His action as Creator and Orderer of the world. This power is made manifest in all of Israel's history, whether in God's deliverance of His people from their servitude to the Egyptians and then from invaders, or in His punishing it, using other nations, whom He holds in His hands, doing with them what He wills. He is the Lord of history.

3. Wisdom and Justice

{14} Despite His omnipotence, He is not a blind tyrant. He is intelligent, wise, and just. Thus, Job, confounded, is not only crushed by His power but is also speechless before His wisdom:

I know that Thou canst do all things, and that no purpose of thine can be thwarted. "Who is this that hides counsel without knowledge?" Therefore, I have uttered what I did not understand, things too wonderful for me, which I did not know. "Hear, and I will speak; I will question you, and you declare to me." I had heard of thee by the hearing of the ear, but now my eye sees thee; therefore, I despise myself, and repent in dust and ashes.[71]

In the most ancient texts, His power is itself recognized in terms of His knowledge of all things, including future things and the secrets of hearts.

70. Is 8:13 (RSV).
71. Jb 42:2–6 (RSV).

In Deutero-Isaiah, this power of knowing the future is a sign showing that He is the only God: "Tell us what is to come hereafter, that we may know that you are gods";[72] "I am God, and there is none like me, declaring the end from the beginning and from ancient times things not yet done."[73] Thus, it is a question of knowledge and power being combined. What God announced is brought about because He Himself makes it happen.

This wisdom of God is magnified in the so-called wisdom books, in which, wisdom is presented in a personified form. This personification poses particular problems concerning whether or not they represent the first revelation of the mystery of the Trinity.

D. Can One Speak of a Revelation of the Trinity in the Old Testament?

1. Data Pertaining to the Question

If the true God, who is revealed to Israel, is a Trinity, [it seems that we must say with Rahner:]

The Old Testament must be understood to contain a genuine secret pre-history of the Trinity. And this pre-history—which no one can totally deny—no longer gives the impression of dealing with antique concepts (which without a doubt have this long history) which are suddenly used in the New Testament, and still more in early Church history, to make assertions utterly remote from their genuine contents.[74]

It would therefore be a question of "[placing] in relief the unity of the doctrine of the Trinity, in itself and in the economy of salvation."[75]

If we must note a progression and preparatory phase in the rev-

---

72. Is 41:23 (RSV).

73. Is 46:9–10 (RSV).

74. Rahner, "Quelques remarques sur le traité dogmatique 'De Trinitate,'" in *Ecrits théologiques* VIII (Paris: Desclée de Brouwer, 1967), 137. [Tr. note: Taken from Rahner, *Theological Investigations*, vol. 4, 100.]

75. Rahner, "Quelques remarques," 137. [Tr. note: Translated from the French, as the matching text in the aforementioned English translation is formulated grammatically in a way that does not fit well into Fr. Nicolas's narrative.]

elation of this fundamental truth, a truth that is monotheism itself,
how can we avoid thinking that the tremendous revelation of the
Trinitarian mystery had its own preparation? Moreover, given that
the entire Old Testament is a preparation for the New, the latter can
only be understood as representing the culminating point of the former.[76]

At the same time, however, exegetes and historians studying
Israel do not admit today (as the ancients did) even an inchoative
knowledge of (and an inchoative faith in) the Trinitarian mystery in
the Old Testament:

> The mystery of the Trinity is not revealed in the Old Testament. Men be-
> came aware of it only through the sending of the Son, having entered in
> person into human history through His Incarnation, and then through the
> sending of the Spirit, promised by the Son and sent conjointly by the Fa-
> ther and the Son from the time of Pentecost. Therefore, there is no need to
> search for any expression of Trinitarian theology whatsoever in the literal
> sense of the biblical texts before the Gospels.[77]

As regards the personification of wisdom, Chrysostome Larcher
provides an inventory of exegetes' opinions,[78] the majority of whom
reject the idea that a Divine Person is involved here.[79] According to
Larcher himself, this would indeed be a divine Person, namely the
very person of Yahweh.

2. Attempts at Reconciliation

{16} After having shown that, in the sapiential books, Wisdom
is more than an abstraction, a divine being, but instead is a fictive
personification of the divine action, Fr. Braun establishes that St.
John, especially in the Prologue to his Gospel, identified Christ with

76. See Raphael Schulte, "La preparation de la révélation trinitaire," in *Mysterium Salutis. Dogmatique de l'histoire du salut*, vol. 5 (Paris: Cerf, 1970), 71–79.

77. Pierre Grelot, *Sens chrétien de l'Ancien Testament Esquisse d'un traité dogmatique* (Paris: 1962), 466.

78. Chrysostome Larcher, Études sur le livre de la Sagesse (Paris: Gabalda, 1968), 398–410.

79. Excluding the authors cited on 400, n.2.

this divine being, likewise attributing a distinct personality to it. He cites this admirable passage from Origen: "The wine of Cana was still only water when we once drew from it, but the water became wine when Jesus had transformed it through His advent; for in truth, before Jesus, Scripture was water, but following upon His advent, it has become wine."[80]

André Feuillet attributes this identification to St. Paul.[81] Likewise, Schulte thinks:

If in the Old Testament we can note, through each phase of salvation history, a preparation, elucidation, and progressive development of the revelation of God tending even to a clear knowledge of faith in God the Father, Son (Word) and Holy Spirit, in the sense of the New-Testament faith in the Trinity, this is possible only in light of the New Testament and thanks to a retrospective examination of the Old.[82]

Grelot himself appeals to the "full meaning"[83] [the *sensus plenior*] of the text.

Conversely, one can say, in conformity with Rahner's desire, that certain notions or images, whose Trinitarian meaning was indecipherable for the Old Testament authors as well as for their readers (even those most elevated in wisdom, those who were the most "inspired"), were utilized by the New Testament revelation. By means of such images, the New Testament revelation was thus able to be assimilated by minds that the Old Testament had prepared for this revelation, without them being aware of it.

3. Old Testament Notions That Were Preparatory for the Revelation of the Trinity

{17} What we do find in the Old Testament are the "mediations of God" by which one seeks to build a bridge between man and the

80. See François-Marie Braun, *Jean le théologien*, vols. I, II, III/1, and III/2 (Paris: Gabalda, 1959–1972), 115–35.
81. See André Feuillet, *Le Christ Sagesse de Dieu* (Paris: Gabalda, 1966), 37–58 and 74–80.
82. Schulte, "La preparation de la révélation trinitaire," 82.
83. Grelot, *Sens chrétien de l'Ancien Testament*, 466

transcendent and elusive God. They are "beings" that belong to God, through which God acts, beings that He sends to His People. The primary ones are *the Angel of Yahweh, the Word of God, the Wisdom of God, the Spirit of God.*

We can say that each of these are only manners of designating God. Simultaneously, however, this introduces the idea of a mediation which mysteriously announces that of Jesus Christ:

> If the *absolute* nearness of the God "who comes" is to be realized with regard to the covenant in which he really and truly imparts himself to his partner, then the dynamism of this historical process leaves only two courses open. Either the Word of God and the Spirit just disappear as created things, like many prophets and their many words, in face of the unsurpassable and overwhelming presence of God himself, which is now revealed as the secret object of all partnership with God at all times. Or these two "communications" remain, and are then at once revealed as being themselves truly divine, that is, as God himself, one with and distinct from God who is to be revealed, in a unity and distinction which therefore belong to God Himself.[84]

4. Conclusion

God revealed Himself to Israel and, through it, to the world as the Transcendent Being on whom the entire universe, as well as each being that composes it (and, most especially, man and his history) are wholly dependent. This is the primordial reason for adoration and worship. He is an eminently personal Being, a "Someone," who acts freely and whose action is inspired by a paternal solicitude for man, His creature. Thus, above all else, His relation of power and dominion over man is a personal relation of love. Man's love must respond to this love, so that the relation of dependence itself may be transformed into a relation of free and confident docility through such a response.

The revelation of the Trinity in the New Testament was prepared for by the affirmation of God's transcendence and by the lived sense

---

84. Rahner, "Quelques remarques," 137. [Tr. note: Taken from "Remarks on the Dogmatic Treatise 'De Trinitate'" in *Theological Investigations*, vol. 4, 100.]

of this transcendence, through the mysterious mediations destined to join this transcendence to God's presence to His people. These mediations were attributed to beings endowed with a personality that did not seem to be distinct from that of Yahweh, thus preparing the believer's mind for the recognition of distinct Persons in God. This revelation was not the revelation of God's personality, for God had already revealed Himself as a personal Being. *It was the revelation of the mysterious way that God is personal.* Through His presence and words, Jesus Christ revealed to us that Yahweh, the God of Israel, the God of the Universe, is one as a personal Being, but that He is also Triune, for His personal being embraces a threefold personality.

III. THE FATHER OF OUR LORD JESUS CHRIST

{19} Obviously, the mystery of the Trinity was not revealed in a didactic manner. Jesus Christ was present in the world, a man among men, "a human person,"[85] manifesting Himself through interpersonal relations, both with men and with God, whom He called His Father. They were interpersonal relations which obviously included a distinction between the Persons thus related to each other. However, note well that little by little He manifests Himself as being more than a man, manifesting Himself as being True God, and His relations with "God" are presented as being those *of the Son* with *the Father*, God like Him, One Unique God with Him. Hence, these interpersonal relations, appearing as ascending from the creature to God and descending from God to the creature, were revealed to us as first being situated in the intimacy of the Godhead as part of His mystery. Then, another Divine Person was revealed, sent by the Father and the Son, though in relation with them in the intimacy of the Godhead as well, constituting with the first two Persons the mystery of God, the secret of His Triune personality.

85. See Jean-Hervé Nicolas, *Les profondeurs de la grâce* (Paris: Beauchesne, 1969), 234–38.

A. The Revelation of the Son of God in Jesus

1. Jesus' Filial Awareness

{20} Jesus himself expressed His relations with God as being those of a son with his father. This is clear in texts that are certainly to be numbered among the earliest ones, especially those in which He invokes God by making use of formula, "Abba," a formula that is utterly unusual apart from the use He made of it. It is a child's way of addressing his father: "Christian faith has seen in His 'Abba' the word by which Jesus expressed His most intimate communion with God and the knowledge that He had a wholly unique filiation."[86] In many parables, He clearly presents Himself as the Son sent by the Father (especially in the parables of the vintners and, equally, in the parable of those who are invited to the wedding).

Of itself, this was not a novelty. Israel called Yahweh its Father, principally on account of the Covenant and as a consequence of the fact that it was His people. Thus, Isaiah: "The yearning of thy heart and thy compassion are withheld from me. For thou art our Father ... thou, O LORD, art our Father, our Redeemer from of old is thy name."[87] "Yet, O LORD, thou art our Father";[88] equally: "Do you thus requite the LORD, you foolish and senseless people? Is not he your father, who created you, who made you and established you?"[89] On account of His Providence, He is the Father of all men: "But it is thy providence, O Father, that steers its course."[90] He is especially the Father of the king[91] and of the Messiah: "He said to me, 'You are my son, today I have begotten you.'"[92]

Nonetheless, something utterly new is found in Jesus's self-iden-

---

86. Franz Joseph Schierse, "La revelation de la Trinité dans le Nouveau Testament," in *Mysterium Salutis. Dogmatique de l'histoire du salut*, vol. 5 (Paris: Cerf, 1970), 133.

87. Is 63:15–16 (RSV).

88. Is 64:8 (RSV).

89. Dt 32:6 (RSV).

90. Wis 14:3 (RSV).

91. See 2 Sm 7:14.

92. Ps 2:7 (RSV).

tification as the Son of God. He is *the Son*, in contrast to all others. Certainly, God is also the Father of the disciples, though not in the same way: "My Father and your Father."[93] The *Our Father* is a prayer for the disciples' use. Jesus did not make it His own. It is only after Easter that it becomes the *Lord's Prayer* and that the community addresses it to the Father through the intermediary of Christ. In the parable of the murdering vintners, He is "the son" in contrast to the prophets who were servants. "Then the owner of the vineyard said, 'What shall I do? I will send my beloved son.'"[94] Even the famous text about His ignorance concerning the Day of Judgment sets Jesus apart as the Son: "But of that day or that hour no one knows, not even the angels in heaven, nor the Son, but only the Father."[95] The uniqueness of this title, as well as its "exorbitant" character, are quite clear in the High Priest's question, "Are you the Christ, the Son of the Blessed?", and in Jesus's affirmative response, which provokes his condemnation.[96]

Finally, we must recall the famous text concerning the Son's knowledge of the Father, and the Father's knowledge of the Son:[97] "All things have been delivered to me by my Father; and no one knows the Son except the Father, and no one knows the Father except the Son and any one to whom the Son chooses to reveal him."[98]

What did this prerogative mean for Jesus, as far as we can learn from the texts [of the Gospels]?[99] Many texts show Jesus submitting Himself to the Father, praising Him, and serving Him. On the other hand, other texts show Him acting as God, "master of the Sabbath," forgiving sins, and speaking with authority to Satan. Theology will

---

93. Jn 20:17 (RSV).
94. Lk 20:13 (RSV).
95. Mk 13:32 (RSV); cf. Mt 24:36.
96. Mk 14:61–64 (RSV); cf. Mt 26:63–66.
97. See Schierse, "La revelation de la Trinité dans le Nouveau Testament" 151–57; Vincent Taylor, *La personne du Christ dans le Nouveau Testament* (Paris: Cerf, 1969), 165–66.
98. Mt 11:27 (RSV). Cf. Lk 10:22.
99. See Taylor, *La personne du Christ dans le Nouveau Testament*, 155–86.

reconcile these two opposed aspects of Jesus' personality by saying that the Incarnate Word remained what He was, God, equal to the Father as God, but having become man, and precisely as a man, He is inferior and submitted to the Father. Do the texts justify such an interpretation? With Taylor, we can say: "Jesus will always be a challenge to be accepted rather than a problem to resolve."* The same author adds that between the words of the Gospel related to Jesus's divine filiation and the tradition taken altogether, there is a relation that is "too close to not suggest that the Christ of the Gospel places us in the presence of a Divine Person." This enables him to conclude (after the examination of all the texts): "The awareness that Jesus had of his Divine filiation is the key that opens up for us the secret of His personality. It is expressed in His words and in His actions ... All these things draw their truth from the fact that He knows with certitude that He is the Son of God."

2. Divine Titles Attributed to Jesus

{21} We should generally give much more consideration to the by no means self-evident fact that after the death of Jesus the first Christians without hesitation transferred to him what the Old Testament says about God. This indicates that they had followed through to its final consequences the idea of the present lordship of Christ. The idea in Philippians 2:9ff that God has "more than exalted" Christ, given him his own name, and conferred upon him all his authority, must really have been a common factor in early Christian Faith.[100]

The decisive title, in this regard, is that of *Kurios*:

If we are to understand the origin and development of New Testament Christology, we must center our attention on the *Kyrios* title, just as the first Christians themselves placed it at the center of their confessions and

---

* [Tr. note: No citation provided by Fr. Nicolas for the quotes in this paragraph.]

100. Oscar Cullmann, *Christologie du Nouveau Testament* (Neuchâtel, CH: Delachaux et Niestlé, 1966), 203. [Tr. note: Taken from Oscar Cullmann, *The Christology of the New Testament*, rev. edition, trans. Shirley C. Guthrie and Charles A. M. Hall (Philadelphia: The Westminster Press, 1963), 235.]

from that center attempted to understand the other functions of Christ in the total Christ-event.[101]

The three texts of St. Paul in which the title "Kurios" is presented as expressing the confession of the primitive Christian faith are found in Philippians 2:11, Romans 10:9, and 1 Corinthians 12:13.[102] Against Bosset, who thinks that the attribution of the title "Kurios" to Christ could have occurred only in a Hellenizing environment, Cullmann shows that we must hold that it is something coming to us from the very first Christian community, the community in Jerusalem. The principal reason for this assertion is that this title is found in an Aramaic form in a liturgical formula that must be very ancient, given the fact that St. Paul uses it without translating it:[103] "Once he was given the 'name which is above every name,' God's own name ('Lord,' Adonai, Kyrios), then no limitations at all could be set for the transfer of divine attributes to him."[104] In the same way, He was given the titles of Savior and Judge.

3. The Affirmation of Jesus' Preexistence

{22} If the title "Kurios," in the full sense of the term, is given to Jesus only after His glorification, this does not mean that He would have "become God" after His resurrection, something unthinkable in the climate of monotheistic thought wherein the Christian preaching arose and developed. This is clear from the fact that Christ is recognized as "preexisting," that is, existing from all eternity in God before becoming a man.

101. Cullmann, Christologie du Nouveau Testament, 204. [Tr. note: Taken from Cullmann, The Christology of the New Testament, 236.]

102. See Lucien Cerfaux, Le Christ dans la théologie de saint Paul (Paris: Cerf, 1954), chs. 5–7; Cullmann, Christologie du Nouveau Testament, 176–205; Taylor, La personne du Christ dans le Nouveau Testament, 43–70.

103. See 1 Cor 16:22.

104. Cullmann, Christologie du Nouveau Testament, 204. [Tr. note: Taken from Cullmann, The Christology of the New Testament, 237.]

a) The Great Pauline Texts

{23} The two great Pauline texts relevant to this are Philippians 2:6–11[105] and Colossians 1:15–20.[106]

Whatever the exact interpretation of these difficult texts may be, they clearly express the idea that Christ's divine prerogatives ("the form of God," "equality with God," "image of the Invisible God") have always belonged to Him and that they were not accorded to Him in time. This can be connected to the saying reported by the fourth Gospel: "Before Abraham was, I am":[107] "I am", which evokes, deliberately, God's self-affirmations in the prophets: "And me, I am God, from eternity, I am He."[108]

b) St. John's Prologue

{24} The fourth Gospel opens with a famous passage in which the mystery of the Incarnation is solemnly proclaimed and announced. The text is concerned with Jesus of Nazareth. The Gospel will show us this man in action during His public life in Galilee and Judea. It will report His teachings to us. His passion and death will be recounted to us, and it will affirm for us His resurrection and His appearances to the disciples after His death.

Throughout all the innumerable commentaries that have been written upon it, and despite the often-important divergences among these ancient and modern commentators,[109] it is clear that the author of John's Prologue wanted to expressly say that this man was

---

105. See Cerfaux, *Le Christ dans la théologie de saint Paul*, 283–301; Cullmann, *Christologie du Nouveau Testament*, 150–56; Feuillet, *Le Christ Sagesse de Dieu*, 340–49; Taylor, *La personne du Christ dans le Nouveau Testament*, 71–87.

106. See Pierre Benoît, "Préexistence et incarnation," *Revue biblique* 77 (Paris, 1970): 5–29.

107. Jn 8:58 (RSV).

108. Is 43:13, my translation.

109. See Marie-Émile Boismard, *Le prologue de S. Jean* (Paris: Cerf, 1953); F.-M. Braun, *La Mère des fidèles* (Casterman, 1954), 22–26, 59–61, 175–78, 195, 209; Cullmann, *Christologie du Nouveau Testament*, 216–33; P. Lamarche, "Le prologue de S. Jean," *Recherches des sciences religieuses* 52 (1964): 497–537; Ignace de La Potterie, *La vérité dans Saint Jean*, vol. 1 (Rome: Biblical Institute Press, 1977), 117–41.

the Word, who from the beginning was in God and was God—that is, in the beginning spoken of in Genesis, when God created heaven and earth. This Word has become "flesh," that is, a man living at a given moment of time—specified by the coming and ministry of John the Baptist. It is clear that He existed before being a man. He existed with God (or, "turned toward God") and therefore distinct from God (*o Theos*). He was God (*Theos*). All things existed through Him. (He is not part of the created universe).

This represents a clear and deliberate affirmation of preexistence. He who appeared in the midst of men, who lived among them as a man, who spoke and acted as a man, and who died and rose again, is the "Unique Son coming from the Father," existing "in the bosom of the Father from all eternity."

The sacred author never explains how we are to understand this distinction between the Father and the Son in the intimate depths of the One God of the Bible together with the conjunction in Jesus Christ of eternal preexistence alongside His human existence which has a beginning in time. From her beginnings and throughout the course of her earthly pilgrimage, the Church will tirelessly strive to understand this. She will do so through a lengthy and difficult reflection that will never come to an end, one that is punctuated by discussions that are sometimes passionate and marked out by increasingly precise dogmatic definitions. These definitions will never fully satisfy the mind, but they will always be inflexibly faithful to the fundamental affirmation which they strive to understand, never allowing this fundamental affirmation to be placed into question. The theologian's task is to render an account of this reflection and to take part in it himself.

4. Christ Designated as God

{25} "'Jesus is the Son of God' is therefore certainly one of the most ancient *creedal statements* of the early Church."[110] This confes-

---

110. Cullmann, *Christologie du Nouveau Testament*, 252. [Tr. note: Taken from Cullman, *The Christology of the New Testament*, 290.]

sion is found in Acts 8:36–38, in the context of the primitive baptismal liturgy. It is also found in 1 John 2:23, 1 John 4:15, Hebrews 4:14, and Romans 1:3. (In the last text, St. Paul recites what is obviously a formalized confession of faith.)

Although the designation "Son of God" is much less frequent in St. Paul than is "Lord," he does, on many occasions, present Jesus as "the Unique Son of God"—Romans 8:32 (with an evocation of Abraham's sacrifice), and also Galatians 4:4. Christ is "the image of the invisible God" inasmuch as He is the Son, and because the Son represents the perfect image of the Father, Christians are destined "to be conformed to the image of his Son."* Likewise, Christians are called "into the fellowship of his Son, Jesus Christ our Lord."†

The title, "Son of God," stands at the center of the discussions Jesus had with the Jews, as reported by the fourth Gospel.

Note that this designation of the Son is placed into relation with the idea of suffering and submission. Concerning the latter, see especially 1 Corinthians 15:28.

The problem posed by this fact will be treated in Christology. For now, note that this idea of "submission" is counter-balanced by the attribution of the title of "God" to Jesus. In the fourth Gospel, there are two certain texts (John 1:1 and 20:28, which "frame the whole Gospel"),[111] and a disputed text (from the point of view of textual criticism since there are three possible readings for the text), namely, John 1:18. See the discussion in Cullmann, who defends the reading, "Only-begotten God."[112] There is a text in St. Paul that is remarkable but also disputed, namely Romans 9:5. On this point, the reader may refer to Cullman's discussion of the matter. He defends the interpretation that attributes to Christ the title, "God eternally blessed."[113] This is equally the position of the *Traduction Oecuménique de la Bible*,‡ as

---

* Col 1:15 (RSV); Rom 8:29 (RSV).

† 1 Cor 1:9 (RSV).

111. See Cullmann, *Christologie du Nouveau Testament*, 230–238.

112. See Cullmann, *Christologie du Nouveau Testament*, 260–269.

113. See Cullmann, *Christologie du Nouveau Testament*, 271–272.

‡ [Tr. note: Though not expressly stated, this likely refers to the *Traduction Oecuménique de la Bible*.]

expressed in its comments on this verse. Likewise, one should consult Taylor[114] who is opposed to this interpretation, as well as Cerfaux.[115] Other controverted text are Titus 2:13 and also 2 Peter 1:1, which contain the same pairing, "God and Savior, Jesus Christ."

Karl Rahner, who holds that this attribution of the title "God" to Christ is exceptional, nonetheless recognizes six texts which he believes to indubitably contain this attribution.[116]

B. God the Father

{26} "Son" and "father" are terms that are relative to one another. Far from it being the case that "later theology" holds that they are absolute terms, as Cerfaux strangely claims, this perception concerning their relative nature will generate the entire theology of the Trinity from its very beginning.[117] Who, according to Scripture, is the "Father of Our Lord Jesus Christ"? Doubtlessly, it is "God" (*o Theos*).[118] Therefore, a difficult problem stands before us: what is the relationship between the God who, according to the New Testament, sent "His Son," and the Creator God and Savior, the One God of the Old Testament?

1. The Claim That Yahweh Would Be the First Person of the Trinity

{27} Rahner's response is categorical. According to him, the Yahweh-God of the Old Testament is the Father of Christ. The personality of God (which as we have seen, is revealed in the Old Testament) is the personality that later will be revealed as the first Person of the Trinity.[119] Pierre Grelot holds a similar position.[120]

---

114. See Taylor, *La personne du Christ dans le Nouveau Testament*, 64–70.

115. See Cerfaux, *Le Christ dans la théologie de saint Paul*, 389–90.

116. See Karl Rahner, "Dieu dans le Nouveau Testament," *Ecrits théologiques* I (Paris: Desclée de Brouwer, 1959), 96.

117. Cerfaux, *Le Christ dans la théologie de saint Paul*, 336.

118. See Rahner, "Dieu dans le Nouveau Testament," 80–111; Cerfaux, *Le Christ dans la théologie de saint Paul*, 388.

119. See Rahner, "Dieu dans le Nouveau Testament," 47–48.

120. Pierre Grelot, "De son ventre couleront des sources d'eau vive," *Revue biblique* 66 (1959): 147–48.

This position is not purely exegetical inasmuch as it relies on a presupposed theological outlook, one that claims to be only completely realistic and in conformity with revelation. According to this background philosophical conception, the word "God," which designates the Godhead in its concrete realization (that which is God, *"hic Deus"*), can only be understood as referring to one of the Three Persons of the Holy Trinity, for Christian revelation holds that the Godhead is concretely (and, therefore, personally) realized only in the Father, in the Son, and in the Holy Spirit. This is a conception that sets itself in opposition to (more exactly, intends to set itself in opposition to) that of "scholastic theology" (supposedly the scholastic theology "of Cajetan") holding that *"hic Deus"* pertains to God considered as concrete, before one knows (or envisions) the distinction of Persons. In due time, we will examine the "Cajetannian" conception of the *subsistentia absoluta Dei* and will see that, first of all, Rahner is not exact in his presentation thereof, thus failing to do justice to Cajetan's true thought. In any case, he thinks that in this matter his thought rejoins what he calls "the Greek conception of the Trinity." We must respond to this by making a clarification. In the divine reality, in the inwardness of God, it is quite clear that "God, *hic Deus*" is the Father, the Son, and the Holy Spirit. In each of these three Persons one and the same infinite, indivisible Godhead is concretely realized. However, here, it is not a question of the inwardness of God but, rather, of the knowledge that we have of Him, whether through rational processes or through revelation. Now, when reason affirms that God exists, it cannot know that He is Triune, although it can know that He is personal. Up to the coming of Christ, when God reveals Himself to Israel, He reveals Himself as an eminently personal being, but not as Triune. His personality remained mysterious, and this mystery of the Divine Personality is what Jesus revealed to us by presenting Himself as "the Son," eternally distinct from the Father, issuing from Him and facing toward Him. Likewise, He made the mystery of this Personality known to us by revealing to us the Spirit as someone in God, Him also sent by God, that is, by the Father and the Son. Let us recall a fundamental principle: while God is infinitely simple in Himself, the knowledge that we have of Him is complex and progressive. "The One God" is in no way distinct from "the Triune God." However, man's knowledge of God as one (not only rational knowledge but also the knowledge revealed during the first phase of revelation) is distinct from man's knowledge of God as Triune. Such knowledge is distinct and dissociable. Man can know (and, in fact, has known) God as one before knowing Him as Triune. And in knowing God as one in this manner, he already knows Him as personal, without however, knowing His mysterious manner of being personal.

2. Yahweh Must Be the Three Persons Together

{28} One cannot purely and simply reject Rahner's position, for he takes up traditional insights which are also evoked by St. Thomas in *In ev. Joannis Lectura* 1:1,* though Rahner hardens them. However, in its exact form, it does not seem to be admissible for the following three reasons.

1° In the Old Testament, Yahweh is the One God. He is the only one who must be adored ("a jealous God"), the only one who is God. To say that He is the Father, inasmuch as the Father is distinct from the Son and from the Spirit, would lead one to assert that a fundamental contradiction exists between the monotheism of the Old Testament and the New Testament (which holds that the Son is God as well and distinct from Him while also holding that the Spirit is equally God and distinct from the Father and from the Son).[121] The Trinitarian mystery obviously cannot be understood outside the line of the strictest biblical monotheism.

2° A primordial and most ancient datum of Trinitarian theology is that the Father and the Son are correlatives (i.e., relative to one another), so that They are (according to the Aristotelian adage,

---

* no. 30, 5:7; no. 830, 8:2; no. 1161, 17:2; no. 2195.

121. See Marie-Joseph Le Guillou, Réflexions sur la théologie des Pères grecs en rapport avec le Filioque," in *L'Esprit Saint et l'Église* (Paris: Fayard, 1969), 190n10.

which was known and used by the most ancient Fathers) "simultaneous both in reality and in knowledge."[122] As we will see, by understanding that the Father cannot exist without the Son and that They
are coeternal, the Church would overcome the spontaneous (and
innocent) subordinationism of the first Trinitarian speculations undertaken in her. Hence, it is inconceivable that the Father, in His distinct personality, could have been revealed without the Son being revealed at the same time. Therefore, Yahweh is not a distinct Person
of the Trinity (He is the Triune God) revealing Himself as eminently
personal, though not yet revealing the mysterious way that His personality is realized in three distinct Persons who are together and inseparably the One God of the Covenant.

3° Finally, another traditional datum, which originates in the
fourth Gospel (Jn 1:14), is that the Father is unknowable for us and
that He is revealed by the Son. We will see that for certain ancient
Fathers (in the wake of Origen), the Father is said to be absolutely
unknowable (and not only in relation to man's earthly condition).
According to them, the mediation of the Son is always necessary so
that man can, indirectly, reach the Father. As we will see, this is excessive and cannot be held for the Eternal Word in relation to the
Beatific Vision hereafter. However, it is certainly true, scriptural, and
traditional as regards the Incarnate Word's role for man in his earthly condition. In his earthly existence, man can know the Father only
through the (Incarnate) Son.[123] Thus, we must rule out the idea that
the Father would have been known before the Son.

3. The Distinction of Persons Was Revealed on the Basis of
Yahweh's Personality

{29} But should we interpret the fact that the New Testament
(and after it, the symbols of the faith) attribute to the First Person
what the Old Testament says concerning Yahweh? We must always

---

122. *Simul re et cognitione.*
123. See Jn 1:18. For the exegesis of this text, see La Potterie, *La vérité dans Saint Jean,*
vol. 1, 211–39.

bear in mind that all of revelation necessarily uses words, images, and notions familiar to those to whom it is addressed. The revelation of the Trinity is addressed first to the Jews, that is, to men formed according to the Old Testament (and through them to the world: "Salvation comes from the Jews"). Hence, Jesus Christ could reveal Himself (and could be revealed) as the Son only by reference to Yahweh: God (*o Theos*, Yahweh) has sent His Son. This was a scandal for those who cried blasphemy. It was astonishing for others, who saw, little by little, the incommunicable prerogatives of Yahweh attributed to this Son (manifested as a distinct person, a human person first, then more than human, and at last divine): Judge, King, and so forth. In this way, God, in revealing Himself, was able to gradually bring to light the idea that He wishes to instill into them: *not that Yahweh has a Son but, rather, that Yahweh is a Father and a Son.*

Nevertheless, it remains the case that the Person of the Father is manifested through all the divine works reported in the Old Testament. (In this way, one can do justice to Rahner's insights.) This is not the same as saying that the Father's Person alone would perform them, nor that, *at this moment of revelation*, He could have been known in His distinction by their means. By revealing Himself as the one sent by the Father, the Son revealed the Father as being especially manifested through them. This can be understood only by means of the process of appropriation, which is quite controversial but, nonetheless, indispensable. We will examine this topic in due time.

C. The Spirit Sent by the Father and the Son

{30} If the mission of the Son in the form of a "human person" who has been seen and heard and who has entered into the network of interpersonal human relations (cf. 1 Jn 1:1) clearly manifests that it is a question of a distinct person, and if this "human person" reveals Himself as being divine (i.e., if this person is accepted through faith as being divine), then the only possibility is that He is a distinct person in God, distinct from another Person, the Father. The mission of the Spirit does not have the same clarity at first. Even if the Spirit who has been sent is "divine," it is not immediately obvious that He is "God," a someone who is God, a distinct Person in God.[124]

1. The Divinity of the Spirit Sent by God

a) In the Old Testament

{31} The Spirit of Yahweh plays a large role in the Old Testament. First, it is the principle of life, as though life consisted in a communication in the life that exists in God. God breathes "a breath of life" into the nostrils of the statue of clay.* Death is understood as being God's withdrawing of this principle. "My spirit shall not abide in man forever."[125] "If he should take back his spirit to himself, and gather to himself his breath, all flesh would perish together, and man would return to dust."[126] Thus, the Spirit is a sensible, though invisible and mysterious, force—as symbolized by wind. Life and death are mysterious.

The extraordinary effects accomplished by certain men under its influence are attributed to this mysterious force.†

In the case of prophecy, it is a question of a more "spiritual" effect, one that is more clearly divine. The prophet utters the Word [*Parole*] of God under the action of God's Spirit. He becomes, as it were, God's instrument and His intimate collaborator. (This already appeared symbolically in the light breeze that announced Yahweh's presence to Elijah and made him go out in order to receive his orders.)‡

The Spirit is the source of justice and holiness. It rests on the "branch that shoots out from the trunk of Jesse" (the Messiah) in Isaiah 11:2. Yahweh places it on His servant, who, on account of it, "will bring forth justice to the nations," and God delights in him:

---

124. See Hermann Kleinknecht, "Esprit," *Dictionnarie biblique* (Genève: Labor et Fides, 1968), 37–55.

* Gn 2:17.

125. Gn 6:3 (RSV).

126. Jb 34:14–15 (RSV).

† Cf. Judges 3:10, 14:6 and 9, 15:14.

‡ See 1 Kings 19:12ff.

"Behold my servant, whom I uphold, my chosen, in whom my soul delights; I have put my Spirit upon him, he will bring forth justice to the nations."[127]

The messianic times are characterized by the outpouring of the Spirit, bringing to the people, "all who call upon the name of the LORD,"[128] life, justice, openness to the Word of God, and finally the "knowledge of God": "I will not hide my face any more from them, when I pour out my Spirit upon the house of Israel, says the Lord GOD";[129] "And it shall come to pass afterward, that I will pour out my spirit on all flesh; your sons and your daughters shall prophesy, your old men shall dream dreams, and your young men shall see visions."[130]

The Spirit will transform hearts: "And I will give them one heart, and put a new spirit within them; I will take the stony heart out of their flesh and give them a heart of flesh, that they may walk in my statutes and keep my ordinances and obey them."[131]

Thus, the Spirit of God is sent to man as a principle of interior renewal and holiness, no longer only the principle of powerful actions, nor even of the marvels of the prophetic proclamation.

b) In the New Testament

{32} These traits are emphatically expressed in the New Testament, though in a new sense. The messianic times announced by the prophets have arrived. The Spirit is here.[132]

At Christ's Baptism, the Spirit rests on Jesus as it is announced that He is God's servant, and Jesus is expressly designated as Him with whom the Father is pleased.[133] Whereas the prophets were

---

127. Is 42:1 (RSV).
128. Jl 2:32 (RSV). [Tr. note: He cites Jl 3:4.]
129. Ez 39:29 (RSV).
130. Jl 2:28 (RSV). [Tr. note: He cites Jl 3:1.]
131. Ez 11:19–20 (RSV).
132. See Acts 2:14–36. La Potterie, *La vérité dans Saint Jean,* 2nd part, 281–471; André Feuillet, *Le mystère de l'amour divin dans la théologie johannique* (Paris: Gabalda, 1972), 53–82. Eduard Schweizer, "Esprit," in *Dictionnarie biblique,* 127–233 (Genève: Labor et Fides, 1971).
133. See Mt 3:17; Mk 1:11.

seized by the Spirit when they were already at the age of manhood, He is, Himself, dedicated by the Spirit from the time of His conception: "The Holy Spirit will come upon you … ; therefore the child to be born will be called holy."[134] This Spirit is not a foreign power that seizes Him and would make Him go outside of Himself. It is His own Spirit.

He promises the Spirit to the Church. After the Ascension, He Himself sends the Spirit. The Spirit produces in the Church the two sorts of effects noted earlier. On the one hand, there are miracles, prodigies, and external manifestations having an interior influence. On the other hand, there are the renewal of the heart, the pardoning of sins, and the bestowal of new life. "But the fruit of the Spirit is love, joy, peace, patience, kindness, goodness, faithfulness, gentleness, self-control; against such there is no law."[135]

However, is this "Spirit of God," who plays so decisive a role in salvation history, only a name used to designate God's saving and sanctifying action, or is it rather, like the Father and the Son, a distinct Person alongside them?

2. The Distinct Personality of the Holy Spirit

{33} As we have seen, the designation "Spirit of God" does not, of itself, impose the idea of a distinct person in God. The distinct personality of the Holy Spirit was revealed with, by, and in Christ.

By manifesting Himself in the form of a person, by being in dialogue with another Person in God (though a Divine Person as well), the Word reveals Himself as being a distinct personality and simultaneously reveals the distinct personality of the Father. By placing the Holy Spirit on the same line, in a sequential enumeration, next to the Father and the Son, the apostles introduced believers (and were themselves introduced) to the idea that the Holy Spirit is Himself a distinct Person. The means for the revelation of the Trinitarian mystery was found in the Trinitarian schema of the first Christian preaching.

134. Lk 1:35 (RSV).
135. Gal 5:22–23 (RSV).

This schema is found in the most ancient testimony of the apostolic kerygma, the first discourse of St. Peter: "Being therefore exalted at the right hand of God, and having received from the Father the promise of the Holy Spirit, he has poured out this which you see and hear."[136]

This schema is fundamental in St. Paul's preaching: see Romans 1:4, 15:16, and 15:30; 1 Corinthians 6:11ff and 12:4–6; 2 Corinthians 1:21 and 13:13; Philippians 2:1, and so forth. Likewise, see the summary of salvation history presented in Galatians 4:4–7 (RSV): "But when the time had fully come, God sent forth his Son, born of woman, born under the law, to redeem those who were under the law, so that we might receive adoption as sons. And because you are sons, God has sent the Spirit of his Son into our hearts, crying, 'Abba! Father!' So through God you are no longer a slave but a son, and if a son then an heir."

Through the systematic connection of the mission of the Son and the mission of the Spirit, as well as the pronounced distinction of these two missions, we are led and, indeed, required, to consider the second as also being the sending of someone by someone. It is the sending of someone who is God by someone who is God— and, at the same time, God does not cease to be proclaimed as being one! Thus, what in the Old Testament simply was a *personification* becomes, in the light of Christ, a *personalization*. Likewise, Wisdom, the "Word," appeared in Christ as a distinct Person.

The distinction of the mission of the Holy Spirit and its connection to the mission of Christ, upon which it follows, is also placed in great relief by St. John. See especially John 14:16–17 and 26.

The theologian does not seek (and does not claim) to find in the sacred text the express affirmation of the personal distinction between the Son and the Spirit. Moreover, all the while leaving the exegete the responsibility for his opinion, the theologian will not contest, from his own perspective, an affirmation such as this: "Paul is

136. Acts 2:33 (RSV).

very little concerned with the metaphysical question of the relations between God, Christ, and the Spirit."[137] What the theologian retains from exegetical analysis itself is the fact that Paul speaks of the Spirit as a Being distinct both from the Father and from the Son. And the theologian is astonished to read, in the same exegete, in one and the same passage, two seemingly contradictory assertions concerning Jesus: "Alongside Jesus, He (the Spirit) is only the other comforter, and one could be tempted to say that John did not reserve a place for the Spirit. In the Paraclete, it is Jesus Himself who comes (Jn 14:18), and nevertheless He is not identical with Jesus."[138]

Likewise, it must be added too that personal actions are attributed to the Spirit in John as well as in Paul and Acts. See Acts 13:2, 15:28, 20:23, 21:11, etc. Likewise, see 1 Corinthians 12:4–11; John 4. This obviously also leads to the discovery of the Holy Spirit as being a Person. Moreover, the closing of the first Gospel should not be overlooked.

D. Conclusion: The Primitive Faith in the Trinity

{34} Should we follow Taylor in saying that the Trinity is not expressly revealed?[139] Obviously, the formulas by which the Church gradually came to express and "define" her faith in the Trinity are not revealed. Indeed, the very term "Trinity" is not revealed. However, what is revealed, alongside the unequivocal reiteration of Israel's absolute monotheism, is the fact that the Father, the Son, and the Spirit are distinct from each other and that each is God. The "dogma of the Trinity" is only the elaboration of this datum, and one must hold that it is revealed in the sense that all the elements from which it is composed are revealed data. These data were the object of the primitive Church's faith. Moreover, gathered together and ordered in the dogma of the Trinity, they are the object of our faith. [With Fr. Benoît we can say:]

---

137. Schweizer, "Esprit," 199.
138. Schweizer, "Esprit," 218.
139. See Taylor, *La personne du Christ dans le Nouveau Testament,* 243ff.

In truth, the entire message of the New Testament is founded on faith in the concurrence of the three divine Persons in the accomplishment of salvation. And if it is true that the Father and the Spirit are ordinarily considered in function of the Son's work, it would be false to conclude that the latter is first in faith ... And if he (the believer of the first century) wished to express in a single formula his complete faith in the Divine Name, it is logical that he placed the Father before the Son as He who sent Him, handed Him over to death for our salvation, and then resurrected and exalted Him, and the Spirit after the Son as He who is sent to us from heaven by the resurrected Christ in order to continue in us His work of salvation.[140]

IV. THE ELABORATION OF THE
TRINITARIAN DOGMA

{35} The passage from the affirmations of primitive faith, such as they were transmitted to believers by those who bore God's revelation, to the dogma[s] in which they are composed into a coherent whole and formulated more distinctly, was brought about by and in the Church, utilizing the work of intellectual assimilation of the revealed teaching undertaken by theologians, reacting to the false steps and errors to which this work sometimes leads, taking up its results in the "definitions" that translate the revealed teaching for the believing intellect. The assistance of the Holy Spirit assures the exactitude of this "translation." That is, it assures that the "definitions" remain homogeneous with the primitive affirmations of faith. Moreover, through the course of history, such definitions can become ever-richer and ever-more-precise. However, this progress is not produced by the substitution of one definition for another. Rather, it is produced by enriching the definition which precedes the newly formulated one.

This progress is what we here call, "The Elaboration of the Trinitarian Dogma."

---

140. Pierre Benoît, "Les origines du symbole des apôtres," *Exégèse et Théologie*, vol. 2 (Paris: Cerf, 1961), 209.

A. The First Awareness of Trinitarian Dogma

1. The First Confessions of Faith in the Trinity

{36} The confession of the Father, the Son, and the Holy Spirit expresses the faith of Christians from the beginning. This confession is found in the most ancient baptismal liturgy, such as it is reported, for example, by the Didache and by St. Justin. It is also found in the writings of the first "Fathers," even if their attempts at theological explication appear gravely deficient in relation to what this confession implies (e.g., the full divinity of each of the Persons, their equality, their non-dependence, and so forth).

2. The Primitive Expressions of Faith in the Trinity:
Involuntary Subordinationism

{37} The first Christians who sought after an "explanation" for the faith did not manage to avoid a kind of subordinationism in their verbal expressions (and doubtlessly also in their conceptual expressions too). In this search for some explanation of the mystery, they did not yet have the necessary "conceptual tools" at their disposal, namely, the necessary common notions treated analogically and adjusted in order to discern and designate entirely new realities that are above every experience and every process of reasoning. Lacking these tools, they were not completely and sufficiently able to analogically pass beyond the realities of this world. They did not arrive at the idea of a "production" of a being from another (procession, origin) without any causality exercised by the one nor any dependence being asserted regarding the other, without succession and inferiority. For this reason, they were led to conceive of the Son as being caused by the Father within Himself, as the Idea who presides at creation and at the organization of the world, who also reveals the intimate being of the Father but whose "production" by God (*o Theos*, the Father) *seems* in their explanation to be the first phase of the work to be realized. As was said earlier, these same authors professed the perfect equality and eternity of the Son, and this fact forbids us from holding that they are guilty of a form of intentional and systematic subordination. Their intention was certain, but their explanation deficient, leading to a kind of incoherence in their thought and in their expressions.[141]

3. Heresies Contrary to Faith in the Trinity

{38} Indeed, in many cases, progress in the elaboration of dogma by the Church has been provoked by the heresies that came to light very early on. On the one hand, these heresies elicited affirmations of the true faith in more precise terms. On the other hand, they made clear the errors that were latent in the first explanations, leading theologians to push the investigations further, perfecting the "conceptual tools" necessary for expressing the revealed mystery.

Every mystery of the faith involves reconciling data infinitely in God, despite the fact that on the level of natural reason these data seem antinomic (because they are not reconcilable in the domain of experience). Thus, heresy consists in choosing one of these data and exploiting it, thereby sacrificing the other antinomic datum, so that reason may maintain its tranquility. In this way, a perfect rationalization is obtained, though at the expense of the mystery.

In the case before us, the antinomic data are, on the one hand, God's unity, a fundamental truth, and, on the other, the distinction and multiplicity of Those "Being God."* Thus, we have a double series of Trinitarian heresies.

First series: the divine unity is affirmed to the detriment of the Trinity of Those "Being God." Thus, in the history of dogma, we are

---

141. See Gustav Bardy, "La Trinité. La révélation du mystère: Écriture et Tradition," in *Dictionnaire de théologie catholique*, ed. Alfred Vacant, vol. 15, 1580–1702 (Paris: Letouzey & Ané, [1950]); Leslie William Barnard, "The Logos Theology of St. Justin Martyr," *Downside Review* 89 (1971): 132–41; Pierre-Thomas Camelot, "Le dogme de la Trinité. Origine et formation des formules dogmatiques," *Lumière et Vie* 30 (1956): 9–48; George Leonard Prestige, *Dieu dans la pensée patristique* (Paris: Aubier, 1955), chs. 6 and 7.

* [Tr. note: Fr. Nicolas will explain later this odd kind of expression, which he uses before he takes up the notion of "person" as applied to God. On occasion, in order to express plurality clearly, I have needed to make slight changes to the article used in English.]

confronted with *monarchianism*, which attributes divinity to the Father alone. Likewise, there is *modalism*, which reduces the distinction of Persons to the simple distinction of modes of acting and modes of God's manifestations. This had its avatar in the *patripassianism* that expressed a form of modalism by claiming that the Father (the only divine Person) was the one who became man and suffered under the name of the Word. The term "Sabellianism" is also given to modalism, based on the name of one of its instigators, Sabellius.

Second series: the trinity of Those "Being God" is affirmed to the detriment of unity. Here, we can place the systematic subordinationism whose most elaborated form is *Arianism*: the Word and the Holy Spirit, who are God's creatures, are themselves inferior "gods." However, this classification is contestable, for according to Arius the Word and the Holy Spirit were not truly God. One could therefore just as much consider his position as being a kind of monarchianism.

As for a multiplication of the Godhead into three "gods" who would be truly equal and independent from one another, we cannot say that this heresy was explicitly held, although it appears to be somewhat implicit in a text of Pope Dionysius.[142] As a latent error, more or less mixed in with commonly-held conceptions of the Trinity, it is perhaps not wholly absent from the common observations of the faithful.[143]

B. Search for an Explanation of the Unity of the Three Distinct Ones "Being God"

{39} The Trinitarian mystery can be approached from two different angles. On the one hand, one starts with God's unity and seeks to explain, from this perspective, the Trinity of Those "Being God." This is how the bent of Latin theology is commonly described. On

---

142. Heinrich Denzinger, *Enchiridion Symbolorum.*(San Francisco: Ignatius Press, 2021), 112–15, Gervais Dumiege, ed., *La foi catholique* (Paris: Editions de L'Orante, 1961), and 206–7 (hereafter D.-*Sch*; *FC*); Prestige, *Dieu dans la pensée patristique*, 236–37.

143. See Rahner, "Quelques remarques," 139–40.

the other hand, the other approach starts with the Trinity of Those "Being God" (given in the Scripture, doubtlessly, though the unity of God is also given) in order to attempt to explain, on its basis, God's unity. Following this approach, one looks to respond to this question: if there are three "Being God," how are there not three gods? The second approach was the first chronologically. Its development can be divided into two great phases.

1. The Unity of the Three "Being God" explained by the Origin of the Son and the Holy Spirit from the Father (ex patre)

{40} This is the primitive explanation. God revealed Himself as the principle of all created things. He then revealed Himself as the principle and origin of non-created "beings," dwelling in the depths of the Godhead, distinct but not separate from Him. In both cases, He is the unifying principle. In the second case, which is that of the Trinitarian mystery, "God" designates the Father. We have seen that this is the case at the very level of revelation and have also seen why this is so.[144]

The earliest systematizations of this outlook[145] are first found in Hippolytus,[146] though above all in Tertullian.[147]

This outlook was never abandoned by the Eastern Fathers, and it has its place in Latin theology. However, by itself, it remains insufficient for resolving the problem, for it does not, by itself, succeed at surpassing a simple unity of order, which is manifestly insufficient for safeguarding monotheism. This insufficiency quickly became apparent, and a more complete explanation of the unity in the Trinity needed to be elaborated.

144. See §29 above.
145. See Joseph Moingt, *La théologie trinitaire de Tertullien* (Paris: Aubier, 1965); Prestige, *Dieu dans la pensée patristique*, ch. 5; Leo Scheffczyk, "Histoire du dogme de la Trinité," in *Mysterium Salutis. Dogmatique de l'histoire du salut*, vol. 4, 211–302 (Paris: Cerf 1969)
146. See St. Hippolytus of Rome, *Contre les hérésies: Fragment. Étude et edition critique par Pierre Nautin* (Paris: Cerf, 1949).
147. See Tertullian, *Traité du baptême*, ed. and trans. François Refoulé and Maurice Drouzy, SC 35 (Paris: Cerf, 1953).

2. The Unity of the Three "Being God" Explained by the Unity of the Divine Substance (Ousia)

a) The Arian controversies[148]

{41} Arius, a priest of Alexandria (256–336) systematized subordinationism. According to Him, the Word is a creature, the first of all creatures, with whom God subsequently created the Holy Spirit first, and then, together with the latter, the whole universe. On account of this priority and supremacy over all "creatures," They are "God." However, They are both inferior to the Father, and the Holy Spirit is inferior to the Son.

Condemned first by Alexander, the patriarch of Alexandria, at the synod of 318, under the impetus of Athanasius, who at this time was a deacon of this Church, Arius's position aroused violent controversies throughout the East, culminating in the Council of Nicaea (325), where the perfect equality of the Three "Being God" was proclaimed, and where their unity was defined by means of the term and notion of "consubstantiality," which henceforth became "dogmatic." The controversies continued throughout the 4th century on the subject of the exact interpretation of this "definition," leading to the formula of St. Basil which at last provided its exact meaning, such as the Church always recognized it: "one substance in three hypostases."

b) Consubstantiality

{42} St. Athanasius, who was the very soul of the Council of Nicaea (and who then, having become the patriarch of Alexandria, became its defender and its principal interpreter) explained why this new term, which is not found in Scripture, had been introduced into the creedal statement of the faith.[149] It was a question of providing

---

148. See Éphrem Boularand, *L'hérésie d'Arius et la foi de Nicée*, vols. 1–2 (Paris: Letouzey, 1972–1973).

149. See St. Athanasius, *Epistola de Decretis Nicaenae Synodis*; PG 25, 415–476; Johannes Quasten, *Initiation aux Pères de l'Église*, vol. 3 (Paris: Cerf, 1962), 100.

precision regarding the Son's perfect identity with the Father in the Godhead. The term "very similar" became insufficient as soon as certain people wanted to interpret it as expressing a mere resemblance without identity. (This is how we use this expression when referring to our own experience of similar realities. Two distinct "beings" can resemble each other perfectly but cannot be identical.) Tertullian introduced the formula *"ex substantia Patris,"* which indicated that the Son had not been produced *"ex nihilo."* This formula was introduced into the creed, but a further point needed to be specified: given the indivisibility of the Divine Substance, the expression *"ex substantia Patris"* meant that the very substance of the Father was, on account of this "procession," the substance of the Son. The term "consubstantial" was employed to this end, even though in profane language this term meant nothing more than the sameness of matter from which many objects are made (pieces of gold, for example).

In Eastern theology, this term already had a long, rather complex, history.[150] It was first employed by the gnostics, was reclaimed by the great Alexandrians (especially by Origen), and was applied quite commonly to the Son. Indeed, in 160 the faithful of Alexandria had accused their bishop, the patriarch Dionysius, alongside Dionysius the bishop of Rome, with having denied that the Son was consubstantial to the Father. However, in his response, Pope Dionysius, all while blaming the patriarch, did not employ the term *"consubstantialis"* even once. (This proves that, contrary to the assertions of Harnack and Duchêne, it was not the West that made this terminology prevail at Nicaea—though, we should note that this position seems today to be generally abandoned. In contrast to the East, it was hardly known of in the West and was not in use there.) On the other hand, Sabellius and his disciples made use of this term in their doctrine, understanding *homoousios* as meaning the total identity of the Father and the Son, entailing the denial of every form of real distinction between them. [Following Boularand, we can say:]

---

150. See Boularand, *L'hérésie d'Arius et la foi de Nicée*, vol. 2, 337–53.

From these data, we can conclude that around the year 260 there were bishops and teachers [*maîtres*] who admitted the term *homoousios* for characterizing the Son and others who rejected or did not make use of it. The word was already, as it were, a sign of contradiction. It enabled one to discern truth from error. Nevertheless, orthodoxy did not use the term without some hesitation due to the fact that the party of Sabellius itself made use of it. The question was not yet posed concerning whether, in applying the term to the Father and the Son, one attributed to them a numerical unity or a specific unity of essence.[151]

Furthermore, after Nicaea, the "homoians" (the semi-Arians) argued against the term *homoousios*, stating that the term had been rejected by the Fathers of the Council of Antioch (in 262) which had condemned Paul of Samosata. The fact, recognized by the defenders of the faith of Nicaea (e.g., Hilary, Athanasius, and Basil, among others) is incontestable. However, already in the fourth century, the reasons for this condemnation were not clear. It was concerned with the term as it was employed by Paul of Samosata. However, in what sense did he employ it?[152]

In reality, Athanasius and the other defenders of Nicaean orthodoxy had certainly desired to preclude that the divine substance would be divided between the Father and the Son. In fact, they had affirmed, at the head of the creed, that God is one, that the Son is "of the substance of the Father," and that He is identical to Him in His nature. The divine substance is indivisible. If the term *homoousios* applies to it, this necessarily implies the numeric identity of the substance.[153]

Thus, whatever meaning this term, which is ambiguous of itself, had in Paul of Samosata and in his defenders (a meaning that had been condemned at Antioch), it took on its dogmatic meaning as being understood within the context of the Nicaean Creed and the authoritative explanations offered by the fourth century defenders of the faith.

151. Boularand, *L'hérésie d'Arius et la foi de Nicée*, 346.
152. See Boularand, *L'hérésie d'Arius et la foi de Nicée*, 347–352.
153. See Ignacio Ortiz de Urbina, *Nicée et Constantinople, Histoire des Conciles Oecuméniques*, ed. Gervais Dumeige (Paris: Éditions de l'Orante, 1963), 82.

c) One Substance, Three Hypostases

{43} The formula "One Substance, Three Hypostases" is St. Basil's. He had the great merit of definitively illuminating the definition of Nicaea, once and for all fixing the (theological) meaning of *ousia* and of *hypostasis*, which, in ordinary language, were synonyms, and which St. Athanasius, for example, did not distinguish.[154] It is equally the case that St. Gregory Nazianzen defended the dogma of the Trinity against the semi-Arians by means of this distinction.[155]

This formula, which became classic, gives the dogmatic notion of the term "consubstantiality" its content.

d) Application of These Notions to the Holy Spirit

{44} Theological reflection more slowly and more awkwardly came to exactly "situate" the Person of the Holy Spirit in the Godhead. Nonetheless, as we have seen, His divinity was affirmed in the professions of the primitive faith and then in an author as ancient as St. Irenaeus. St. Athanasius defends His divinity and His consubstantiality like that of the Word, and reports the condemnation of the "Macedonians," who denied it, at the Synod of Alexandria in 362. In his celebrated "Treatise on the Holy Spirit," St. Basil implicitly teaches the consubstantiality of the Holy Spirit, something obviously included in the formula "one *ousia*, three *hypostases*," since the *ousia* is the substance of the Godhead.[156] However, He avoids saying it expressly, though he clearly grants the divinity of the Holy Spirit (as he does in other places).[157] He avoids an express statement for what we might call a "tactical" reason, namely in order to prevent his

154. See Quasten, *Initiation aux Pères de l'Église*, vol. 3, 329–330.
155. See St. Gregory of Nazianzen, *Discours 27–31* (*Discours théologiques*), SC 250 (Paris: Cerf, 1978), 29; Maurice Jourjon, "Introduction" in St. Gregory of Nazianzen, *Discours théologiques: Discours 27–31*, ed. and trans. Paul Gallay, SC 250 (Paris: Cerf, 1979), 7–65.
156. See Basil of Caesarea, *Sur le Saint-Esprit*, trans. and ed. Benoît Pruche, SC 17bis (Paris: Cerf, 1968).
157. See Johannes Quasten, *Initiation aux Pères de l'Église*, vol. 2 (Paris: Cerf, 1956), 334.

adversaries from seizing on the formula and redirecting the discussion at hand to the question of knowing whether or not it is scriptural. However, on the testimony of his friend St. Gregory Nazianzen, he firmly professed in conversation[158] his conviction that the Holy Spirit is God. St. Gregory Nazianzen did not even have scruples concerning this matter: "What therefore? Is he consubstantial? Yes, for He is God."[159]

e) Three Who Act Together by One Activity

{45} Although the principle, "Everything that God does externally (through creation and in the created universe), is done together and indivisibly by the three persons" is scholastic in its formulation, its content goes back to the utmost antiquity.[160] It represents the extension of the formula "one substance in three hypostases" onto the level of activity [opération] and could be translated, "one single activity proceeding from three agents."

Nobody openly rejects this principle, for to attribute to one divine Person a work that would be done by Him alone, separately from the others, would be to attribute to Him a separate substance of his own. Indeed, a being acts on account of what it is.

A very strong tendency is taking shape today calling for a recognition of the unique role played by each Person in the work of salvation. This tendency, forever characteristic of the Eastern theology, is also present in the Latin theology of the great era (in St. Augustine and St. Thomas) but was too neglected and obscured in the years that followed. It was revived in the seventeenth century by Pétau and vigorously recovered in the nineteenth century by theologians like Scheeben and de Régnon.[161] However, both in Greek theolo-

---

158. See Quasten, Initiation aux Pères de l'Église, vol. 2, 332–33.
159. Gregory of Nazianzen, Discours 27–31 (Discours théologiques), 32, no. 10.
160. See Prestige, Dieu dans la pensée patristique, 216–22.
161. See Dénis Pétau, Dogmata theological Dion: Petavii (Paris: Vivès, 1865), vol. 3, 6; vol. 8, 4–6; vol. 10, 447; see Matthias-Joseph Scheeben, Les mystères du christianisme (Paris: Desclée de Brouwer, 1947), 173–82; see Théodore de Régnon, Études de théologie positive sur la Sainte Trinité, 4 vols. (Paris: Victor Retaux 1892–1898).

gians and Latin theologians, this tendency does not go without the risk of attributing to each divine Person a proper and distinct action in the work of salvation.[162] A sanctifying action is attributed to the Holy Spirit by groundlessly invoking the authority of the Greek Fathers,[163] and a governing action over humanity assumed by the Word is attributed to the latter.[164] This leads to a serious distortion of an insight that is very just and necessary in itself, one that we will attempt to highlight in the fourth section of this volume and in the second part of this Dogmatic Theology, namely the distortion leading to even the smallest infringement on the unity of [the divine] activity, which is an ancient and fundamental theme in Trinitarian theology.

C. The Search for an Explanation of the Distinction of Persons

1. The Appeal to Relative Opposition

{46} The first approach to the mystery, which would be that of Latin thinkers, consists in beginning with the divine unity and from there seeking to explain how the Persons are distinguished from each other.[165] Relation is the means and conceptual tool that serves for conceiving of this distinction in unity. St. Augustine made it the essential means for his Trinitarian theology.[166] In this Augustinian line, St. Thomas again added to the precision of this conceptu-

---

162. See Paul Galtier, *Le Saint-Esprit en nous d'après les Pères grecs* (Rome: Pontifica Universita Gregoriana, 1946).

163. See Myrrha Lot-Borodine, *La deification de l'homme* (Paris: Cerf, 1970), 222–27 and n. 40; Scheeben, *Les mystères du christianisme*, 173–82; Régnon, Études de théologie positive sur la Sainte Trinité, especially Et. XXVII [sic].

164. See Pietro Parente, *L'Io di Cristo* (Brescia: Morcelliana, 1955), 48. In the opposite direction, see Paul Galtier, "La conscience humaine du Christ. A propos de quelques publications récentes," *Gregorianum* 32 (1951): 525–68; Jean-Hervé Nicolas, "Chronique de théologie dogmatique," *Revue thomiste* 53 (1953): 415–31. [Tr. note: Fr. Nicolas cites his bibliographical entry for Pietro Parente, "Unità ontological e psicologica de l'Uomo-Dio," *Euntes docete* 5 (1952): 337–401. This does not make sense given the page number (namely, 48) he cites in this note.]

165. See Henri Barré, *Trinité que j'adore* (Paris: Lethielleux, 1965), ch. 1.

166. See St. Augustine, *La Trinité, Books I–VII*, Oeuvres de Saint Augustin (hereafter OESA) 15, trans. and ed. Marcellin Mellet and Pierre-Thomas Camelot, introduction by Ephraem Hendrickx (Paris: Desclée de Brouwer, 1955), bk. 5.

al means. However, well before this, the Greeks had seen that relation provides the only means for resolving this problem, which they
could not avoid posing to themselves and which they did not cease
to pose to themselves. They found that they had to ask how this distinction in unity is intelligible, both against those who denied the
unity [of the Persons] (Arians and semi-Arians) and against those
who, in the name of unity, denied [their] distinction (by means of
various forms of modalism). By considering the fact that the names
of the Father and the Son are relative terms, they were oriented toward the idea of a real distinction between two beings thus relatively opposed, without this distinction dividing and splitting up their
common substance.[167] This manner of distinguishing the Father and
the Son solely by means of relation was already opposed to Arius as
an admitted matter. It was then significantly developed by St. Basil in
his *Against Eunomius,* and then by St. Gregory Nazianzen: "The Father is neither a name of a substance, nor a name of an action. It is a
name of a relation."[168] It is remarkable that, at the beginning of his *De
trinitate,* St. Augustine takes up and continues the refutation of Eunomius, using the notion of relation for this task, following St. Basil.

{47} [169]

167. See Irénée Chevalier, *Saint Augustin et la pensée grecque. Les relations trinitaires*
(Fribourg: Librairie de l'Université 1940); André Malet, *Personne et Amour dans la théologie trinitaire de saint Thomas d'Aquin* (Paris: Vrin, 1956), 11–31.

168. See Gregory of Nazianzen, *Discours 27–31 (Discours théologiques),* disc. 29, no. 16.

169. N.B. The orthodox theologian Vladimir Lossky vigorously contests the truth
of the claim that for the Greek Fathers relation is constitutive of the Persons. According
to him, the relations are consecutive to the Persons who would be already constituted.
They are therefore distinguished according to something absolute. See Vladimir Lossky,
Théologie mystique de l'Église d'Orient (Paris: Aubier, 1944), ch. 3.
We will discuss below how this conception implies a contradiction. For what concerns the interpretation of the Greek Fathers of the fourth century, see Chevalier's work.
For now, we will note only the following. In order to establish his thesis, Lossky cites a
text from John Damascene, preceding it with this commentary: "St. John Damascene
expresses himself with no less precision in distinguishing the persons of the Holy Trinity
without submitting them to the category of relation." Now, the text in question indeed
does use the notion of relation: "we call Him (i.e., the Father) the Father of the Son.
With regard to the Son, we say that He proceeds from the Father and that He is the Son
of the Father. We also say that the Holy Spirit proceeds from the Father and we call Him
the Spirit of the Father. We do not say that He proceeds from the Son, but that He is the

2. The Notion of Perichoresis or of Circumincession

{48} This notion intends to express another aspect of relation, namely the fact that relatives as such, *precisely as relations*, are inseparable: each Person is in the other two; the other two are in Him. This consideration, which is founded on Scripture (the Father is in the Son, the Son is in the Father), did not escape the early Fathers. Nonetheless, it is not until the seventh century, in Maximus the Confessor, that one finds the term being used.[170]

D. Dogmatic Formulas

This long history of the dogma of the Trinity is punctuated with definitions by the Magisterium and with formulas of faith in which its results, to the degree that they are necessary for rectitude of faith, are collected.

1. The Creed of St. Gregory the Thaumaturge

{49} This creed represents a remarkable summary of the faith just before the Arian controversies, expressed by an immediate disciple of Origen.[171]

2. The Niceno-Constantinopolitan Creed[172]

{50} The Council of Nicaea, convoked in 325 by the emperor Constantine to put an end to the grave doctrinal conflict stirred up

---

Spirit of the Son." "Father of the Son," "Son of the Father," "Spirit of the Father," "Spirit of the Son." … These are characteristic expressions of relation. The proposition, "We do not say that the Spirit proceeds from the Son," pertains to the question of the procession of the Holy Spirit "*a Filio.*" We will speak about this matter in due time.

[Tr. note: This is an example of Fr. Nicolas's use of small text for side comments and technical qualifications. This format will be maintained, though placed in footnotes, as the reader will see here.]

170. See Prestige, *Dieu dans la pensée patristique*, ch. 19.

171. See Léon V. L. Froidevaux, "Le symbole de S. Grégoire le Thaumaturge," *Recherches des sciences religieuses* 19 (1929): 193–247; Quasten, *Initiation aux Pères de l'Église*, vol. 2, 150–51.

172. See Camelot, "Le dogme de la Trinité. Origine et formation des formules dogmatiques," 9–48; Ortiz de Urbina, *Nicée et Constantinople, Histoire des Conciles Oecuméniques.*

by Arius, first in the patriarchate of Alexandria, then in all the East, forever determined the Church's Trinitarian faith by affirming, in the clearest and most decisive manner, the equality of the Son with the Father (i.e., His full divinity and His eternal begetting by the Father). In order to radically exclude the quibbling of Arius and his partisans, it introduced the new term "consubstantial." This term will be at the center of violent battles during the entire fourth century. However, the Church will never compromise in her use of it, and from this time onward, she recognizes it to be the most exact expression of what she has believed from the beginning: the Son and the Father are, together, the same, identical substance, the substance of the Godhead.[173]

Like the ancient creeds, although the profession of faith of Nicaea clearly mentions the Holy Spirit on the same level as the Father and the Son ("We believe in one God, Father ... and in one Lord Jesus Christ, the only Son of God ... and in the Holy Spirit"), it does not express the doctrine concerning the Holy Spirit in an explicit manner. This explication will be the work of the fourth century (in particular, among the Cappadocians), and it will be made official by the Church at the First Council of Constantinople, in 381, which completed Nicaea's confession of faith.

The Niceno-Constantinopolitan Creed is the Church's common profession of faith, both for the Eastern Church and the Western Church, before all the schisms that—alas!—tore apart the *"catholica"* in a lasting manner. It will be held to be the supreme norm to which all later councils will refer themselves and the touchstone of orthodoxy. It will be the norm not only in what concerns the Trin-

173. As Henri-Irénée Marrou writes, the adoption of this word, for the maintenance of which harsh battles will soon be engaged in, marks a momentous date in the doctrinal history of Christianity. See *Nouvelle histoire de l'Eglise*, ed. J. Rogier, R. Aubert et M.D. Knowles, vol. 1 (Paris: Seuil, 1963), 293–94.

By thus inserting into the profession of faith a new term that is no longer of scriptural origin, but of scholarly origin, the Council of Nicaea, recognizing the fecundity of the properly theological effort undertaken in elucidating the revealed datum, sanctioned by the Council's own authority the progress brought about in the explanation of the content of the faith.

itarian mystery considered in itself but also for the other mysteries that it places under its influence. The mystery of the Redemptive Incarnation will be placed under the Trinitarian mystery, for it is expressly said that it is the eternal and consubstantial Son who became incarnate, who died, and was resurrected for our salvation, who was exalted, and who will come again to judge the world. Likewise, the mystery of the Church will be placed within this Trinitarian context, for she is presented in the creed as being the manifestation of the Spirit in the world. Finally, there is eschatology, with the announcement of Christ's return and of the world's judgment. Certainly, in the centuries to come, all the other Councils will pronounce their own precisions and condemnations. Nonetheless, they will do this only in order to explain and develop the teaching that the very first, most venerable, and most venerated Council, the paradigm for all the others, condensed into a formula that is so brief, rich, and moving in its sobriety. This creedal formula represents the imperishable fruit of its properly doctrinal activity. The greatest geniuses of thought in the Church have spent themselves (and innumerable books have been written) in order to defend this formula, to explain it and to give an account of it. It is the ever-active source and necessary point of reference for all this effort and all this literature.

3. The "Quicumque" Creed

{51} This creed seems to have appeared in the fifth century in southern Gaul. It presents a magnificent exposition of Trinitarian doctrine. Its inspiration is Augustinian in character, and the Church consecrated it by introducing it into the liturgy.

4. "In Deo Omnia Sunt Unum et Idem Ubi Non Obviat Relationis Oppositio"

{52} The notion of relative opposition appeared for the first time in an official text of the Magisterium at the 11th Council of Toledo in 675.[174] As we have seen, from very early on, it seemed to be the only

---

174. See D.-Sch., 525–33.

means that reason had for reconciling (by avoiding contradiction) the real distinction of the Three Persons with their consubstantial unity. It powerfully declared that the Persons are only distinguished by relation, whereas their nature or substance is one.[175]

It is in continuity with these propositions (Augustinian in their form, though connected by their content to the most ancient tradition) that St. Anselm will express the fundamental rule of Trinitarian theology in a celebrated adage, disengaged by him at the end of many centuries of reflection and discussion conducted under the impulse of the fundamental affirmation of the faith: *the Father is really distinct from the Son, they are really distinct from the Holy Spirit, and together they are the one God"; "in Deo omnia sunt unum et idem ubi non obviat relationis oppositio."* ("All the attributes that one affirms of God are in Him one and the same reality, except where a relative opposition intervenes.")[176]

Henceforth, this becomes a commonly received adage used by Catholic theologians, one that figures in an official document of the Magisterium for the first time at the Council of Ferrara-Florence (1439–1445), not in the form of a definition, but as an introduction to the profession of faith imposed upon the Copts and the Ethiopians.[177] Therefore, the Council's authority alone would not suffice for giving it the character of being a dogmatic formula. Nonetheless, the Church has recognized it as containing the outcome of her long effort expended in elucidating the mystery that she has believed from the beginning, recognizing it as the perfect expression of the Tradition. Will we go so far as to say that faith itself is engaged in the acceptance of this formula? It is situated at a level of interpretation far above that to which most believers are called. However, denial of the formula would be tantamount to rendering faith's affirmation of the Trinitarian mystery irrational and absurd. Indeed, if, because of their consubstantiality, the Divine Persons are not distinguished accord-

175. See D.-Sch., 528.
176. St. Anselm, *De processione Spiritus Sancti*, PL 158, 288c.
177. See D.-Sch., 1330.

ing to substance (as the Church confesses) and if They nonetheless are really distinct from each other (as the Church also and altogether confesses), They cannot be distinguished from each other as three absolutes but, instead, only as three relatives. Thus, with good reason, we can hold that St. Anselm's formula represents the expression of what the Church believes.

3

The Ways and Means for a Dogmatic Treatise on the Trinity

Before we begin our study of the intellect's faithful investigation into the Trinitarian mystery—a study that will involve great difficulties—we first must undertake a brief methodological introduction. First of all, we wish to show that the very abstract analyses which we will undertake, using all the resources of logic and of metaphysics, do not separate us from the eminently concrete reality that has been revealed to us. Moreover, we wish to protect ourselves, as is necessary, against the temptation of separating ourselves from this reality.

I. FROM THE ECONOMIC TRINITY
TO THE IMMANENT TRINITY

The expression "the Economic Trinity" is used to designate the Trinity as self-manifesting and self-giving in salvation history. This manifestation is above all brought about in Christ and, then, in all the manifestations of the Holy Spirit. Moreover, there are those manifestations of the Father that are brought about through Jesus Christ and the Holy Spirit present in and through the Church. Likewise, according to this terminology, the "Immanent Trinity" is the Trinity as It is in Itself, in eternity.

A. The Economic Trinity Is the Immanent Trinity

{53} This is the central thesis defended by Rahner.[1] It intends to express the idea that everything that we can know and say about the Immanent Trinity is first known and said about the Economic Trinity. We know the intra-Trinitarian relations by the relations that the Persons have with each other in salvation history and that are manifested there: "The 'Trinity' of the relationship of God to us in the order of the grace of Christ is nothing else than the reality of God as it is in itself: a 'Trinity of persons.'"[2]

Consequently, the point of the departure for the treatise [on the Trinity] must be: "The historical experience of salvation and grace which is given in Jesus and the Spirit of God working in us."[3] This is so because revelation has been made to us above all through the very gift of the divine realities (the reality of the Trinity, who has come to us), and only secondarily through propositions: "Both mysteries, that of our grace and that of God in Himself are the same fathomless mystery."[4]

At first, the identity of the Economic Trinity and the Immanent Trinity seems to be so obvious that the affirmation of this identity could seem to be a truism, especially when expressed in such terms and with such arguments. It is indeed clear that, if "the Economic Trinity" is not a meaningless expression, it can only mean the Trinity, the eternal Immanent Trinity, God, acting in the world and manifesting Himself for the salvation of men through this very action.

The insistence on proclaiming this obviousness calls for reflection, indeed, first of all, on the fact that God, in Himself, infinitely transcends every representation and every manifestation:

1. See Karl Rahner, "Quelques remarques sur le traité dogmatique 'De Trinitate,'" in *Ecrits théologiques* VIII (Paris: Desclée de Brouwer, 1967), 107–40.

2. Rahner, "Quelques remarques," 134. [Tr. note: Taken from Rahner, *Theological Investigations*, vol. 4, 98.]

3. Rahner, "Quelques remarques," 134. [Tr. note: Taken from Rahner, *Theological Investigations*, vol. 4, 99.]

4. Rahner, "Quelques remarques," 135. [Tr. note: Taken from Rahner, *Theological Investigations*, vol. 4, 98.]

I have not begun to think upon the Unity when the Trinity bathes me in its splendor. I have not begun to think upon the Trinity when the Unity seizes me again. When one of the Three is present to me, I think that He is all. As much as my eye is filled, so much does the surplus escape me; for in my mind, which is too limited to understand one alone, there no longer remains a place to be given to the surplus. When I unite the Three into one and the same thought, I see only one torch without being able to divide or analyze the unified light.[5]

Thus, there is infinitely more in the Immanent Trinity than in the Economic Trinity. The second observation calling for reflection, an observation that follows from the first and completes it, is that if the Economic Trinity and the Immanent Trinity coincide, it in no way follows that knowledge of the one coincides with knowledge of the other, as Rahner says (or seems to say): "And it is certainly correct to say that the doctrine of the Trinity cannot be adequately distinguished from the doctrine of the economy of salvation."[6] Thus, the Immanent Trinity manifests Itself in the Economic Trinity, but knowledge of the latter refers us back to the Immanent Trinity in order to know more of It, in order to know the Trinity (to the degree this is possible for the believing mind) such as It is in Itself.

It is perfectly just to say that God has not limited His self-revelation to words. Revelation is God giving Himself. The Trinity about whom He has spoken (and about whom the theologian tries to speak) is the Trinity given and present. In the [Beatific] Vision, there will be a perfect coincidence between the Word [*Parole*] that instructs and the experience of the reality about which it instructs, since the mind of the beatified person is filled by the very Godhead, the Three Persons, making them know God immediately in the light of the Logos and in the substantial touch of the Spirit. But here below this coincidence is not yet realized, however real may be the Gift that the Holy Spirit makes of Himself to the be-

5. St. Gregory of Nazianzen, *Orationes*, PG 35–36, or 42, PG 36, 476B (trans. Vladimir Lossky, *Théologie mystique de l'Église d'Orient* [Paris: Aubier, 1944], 45).
6. Rahner, "Quelques remarques," 121. [Tr. note: Taken from Rahner, *Theological Investigations*, vol. 4, 88.]

liever. The manifestation is brought about by created intermediaries, namely, Jesus' humanity, the signs of the Spirit, and the Church. And these signs are decipherable only thanks to the words that accompany them. If Jesus had not said that He is the Son of God, none of the marvels of His existence would have sufficed to make this existence known to those who witnessed this existence. The same holds for the Spirit. If Jesus Christ had not spoken of Him, if He were known only by the signs of His action, without any verbal explanation, He could not have been known as a distinct Person, as being God. Revelation necessarily involves propositions, and they are what instruct us. They must be made known to us, even if they are inseparable from the reality of which they speak (and even if they cannot be truly understood without some experience of these realities).

There are, in reality, two acts involved in the act of faith by which man receives revelation: the act of intellectual adherence to propositions (i.e., the cognitive aspect of faith); affective adherence (i.e., charity or the attraction of charity known as the "*pius credulitatis affectus*")[7] to the person who teaches (Jesus Christ) and to the Persons about whom He speaks to us (the Three). Faith must develop along these two lines, distinctly, but not separately. In the "cognitive" line, this progress leads to "notional theology." In the "affective" line, it leads to "mystical theology," a form of experiential knowledge. These two theologies are intimately interdependent. Nonetheless, the one cannot replace the other.[8]

Thus, Rahner writes, "The Trinity is not merely a reality to be expressed in purely doctrinal terms: it takes place in us, and does not first reach us in the form of statements communicated by revelation."[9] In saying this, he seems to confuse these two modes of knowing a supernatural reality. Notional theology, for which the entire treatise on the Trinity is obviously responsible (even those

7. See 2nd Council of Orange, can. 5 (D.-*Sch.*, no. 375).

8. See Jean-Hervé Nicolas, *Dieu connue comme inconnu* (Paris: Desclée de Brouwer, 1966), ch. VII.

9. Rahner, "Quelques remarques," 134–35. [Tr. note: Taken from Rahner, *Theological Investigations*, vol. 4, 98.]

parts requiring the greatest degree of apophatism), can only be be-lieving reason's reflection on the truths presented in propositions by the Church transmitting revelation. It is a reflection which deploys the procedures of reason, though they all tend toward knowledge of the realities spoken about in these propositions and offered to our experience. If the propositions in question are directly concerned with the Economic Trinity, they arouse questions that themselves are concerned with the Immanent Trinity. Thus, "Jesus is the Son of God sent by His Father," inevitably arouses the questions: "How are we to conceive that there is a Son in God? How is He distinct from the Father and yet the same God as Him, the one God? And so forth.... " On the other hand, knowledge through (mystical) experi-ence does not respond to questions. Instead, it assures the existential realism of the questions and the responses.

Thus, the notional knowledge of the Economic Trinity refers us to a notional knowledge of the Immanent Trinity. This latter, in turn, illuminates our knowledge of the Economic Trinity from on high. These two kinds of knowledge cannot be identified with each other, but neither can they be separated. This is the distinction used by the Greek Fathers when they distinguished *theology*, which is occupied with God in Himself, from the *economy*, which is occupied with the salvific work performed by the Three Persons and ultimately leading to contemplation of the Trinity.

B. The Problem of the Theological Treatise "*De Deo uno*"

In the same study, Rahner vigorously critiques the distinction between the treatise "*De Deo uno*" and the treatise "*De Deo trino*," a distinction going back to St. Thomas which was generally admit-ted from then on. According to Rahner, such a distinction leads to a splendidly isolated confinement of the treatise "*De Deo trino*," for in one's discussion about the One God, one has already said every-thing that we need to know about God. Thus, the Trinity of Persons is presented as though it were a problem to be solved, though one that is lacking in vital importance and inconsequential for the rest of theology. According to him, this division leads to the writing of a treatise about an "a-Trinitarian" God. In such a treatise, one proceeds in a wholly philosophical and abstract manner, forgetting that the God in question is "the Father of Jesus Christ."[10] Therefore, it would seem necessary, like the Bible and like the Greek Fathers, "to start from the one absolutely unoriginated God, who is still the Father, even when it is not yet known that he is the Begetter and Spirator, because he is known as the unoriginated hypostasis, who may not be thought of *positively* as 'absolute,' even when he is not yet known expressly as relative."[11]

The questions that this raises will be discussed later. For now, let us only recall, from the perspective of tradition, one point that most certainly was acquired in the great Trinitarian controversies of the third and fourth centuries: the Father, Son, and Holy Spirit can only be known together, the one through the two others. The idea that the Father could be known as a distinct Person without the Son being known as a distinct Person, as well as the Holy Spirit (though, to a lesser degree), is contrary to the tradition. We will see that it is not theologically defensible.

This is an irrelevant critique in relation to St. Thomas. He did not write a treatise "*De Deo uno*" followed by a treatise "*De Deo trino*." The God about whom St. Thomas speaks from the outset of the *Summa theologiae* is the God who is revealed as the God of the Covenant and as the Trinity. This treatise "*De Deo*" is what is distinguished into several parts. Every rational undertaking requires that the matter under consideration be divided up. The treatise "*De deo*" is divided into three parts: "concerning that which pertains to the essence of God," "concerning that which pertains to the distinction of Persons," and "concerning that which pertains to the movement of creatures proceeding from God."[12] The first part is in no way "philosophical

10. See Rahner, "Quelques remarques," 116.
11. Rahner, "Quelques remarques," 116. [Tr. note: Taken from Rahner, *Theological Investigations*, vol. 4, 84.]
12. St. Thomas, *ST* I, q. 2, prol.

and abstract," except as regards its means of knowing, which obviously are philosophical and abstract notions. But what one seeks to know is the concrete God of the Covenant and of salvation. This is not a treatise "*de divinitate una*," for, from the outset, St. Thomas establishes that in God we find no distinction between form and subject, nor between existence and being [*entre l'être et l'étant*].[13] But a grave point of dispute still remains between Rahner and the "Thomists." According to the latter, God exists in three Persons, but this God who exists in three Persons is one essence subsisting by Itself. Is this exact? Does this represent the thought and the very teaching of St. Thomas? We will examine this question later.

In truth, the treatise "De Deo uno" cannot be suppressed in a theological synthesis. The solution that Rahner advocates is to treat of the divine attributes as attributes of the Father and, next, to explain how the Father communicates the Divine Nature thus known, with its attributes, to the Son without being deprived of it and without dividing it, with the Father and the Son together communicating it to the Holy Spirit without dividing it further. Such a solution is a mere imaginary fiction. In the end, we would have the treatise "*De Deo uno*" with a simple alteration, namely that we would have the intention of speaking about the Father. But how would this intention be realized?

If it is expressed at the beginning, how can we speak about the Father without speaking about the Son whose Father He is? How can we speak about the "First Person" without saying that there are two other Persons? And this would require us to stop at this moment in order to speak about the distinction of the Persons. Would we not then need to continue by expositing what can be known about this Divine Nature that the Father communicates to the Son (and, then, the Father and the Son together to the Holy Spirit)? Hence, we would merely come to place the treatise "*De Deo uno*" after the "*De Deo trino*." The disadvantage to such an approach is obvious, for in

13. See *ST* I, q. 3.

order "to explain" the processions in a theological manner, we will see that we must call on intellection and love such as they exist in God. That is, we will need to call on operative attributes. It is logically preferable to speak about them first. In any case, it is not clear what advantage we would draw from speaking about them later on. Would it have the advantage of ensuring that we note well that we are concerned with the attributes and nature of the Trinitarian God? But this fact is present to anyone who enters St. Thomas's thought from the outset of the "*De Deo*" of the *Summa theologiae*. Moreover, it is clear that the Divine Nature that the Father communicates to the other two Persons is this Nature that is studied in the "*De Deo uno*," and this fact suffices to ward off the danger of "isolating" the treatise on the Trinity. It would be "isolated" only for the person who does not enter into the organic synthesis of the *Summa theologiae*, thus being rendered incapable of grasping the living connection between its parts. Such a spirit should not guide one's judgment of St. Thomas's synthesis.

A second hypothesis would have the theologian limit his consideration to the Person of the Father, without explicitly stating this fact (as in the Old Testament, for according to Rahner, Yahweh would be the Father without making this known to men). In this case, the structure and situation of the "*De Deo uno*" would both remain the same.

II. INTRODUCTION TO THE SO-CALLED PSYCHOLOGICAL WAY

This manner of explanation, which is that of St. Augustine (and after him the whole of Latin theology), is the path that we will follow. We must provide an explanation of it.

A. In What Does the "Psychological Way" Consist?

{55} St. Augustine explained his methodology in many places in the *De trinitate*.[14]

The principle of the method used here is the "principle of analogy," which enables one to rise from the image of God in creatures to the ineffable and sublime Divine Reality. It is founded on this fundamental datum of theological anthropology: man was made "in the image of God," and it is principally through his "mind," his *nous*, his *mens*, that he exists as God's image. Therefore, it is a question of seeking out in man's mind analogies capable of leading us to some understanding of the mystery of the divine life, which itself can only be a purely spiritual reality.

Is it exact to call this method "psychological"? The point of departure for the procedure is the "psyche," the human soul: consequently, we find St. Augustine undertaking profound and subtle psychological analyses at this point of departure, ones that will hardly ever be repeated thereafter. Nonetheless, the procedure itself is highly metaphysical. Still, in practice, we can preserve the established term, "psychological."

B. The Origins of the "Psychological" Way

{56} It is traditionally said that St. Augustine was the inventor of the psychological way of discussing the Trinity. Undoubtedly, he was the first to have systematized it, constructing his treatise deliberately in function of it. Likewise, he was the first person to have elaborated a theological explanation of the [procession of the] Holy Spirit by means of an analogy with man's act of love.

However, at least with regard to the procession of the Word, this way was indicated long before him. We have seen that the first at-

---

14. See St. Augustine, *La Trinité, Books I–VII*, OESA *15*, trans. and ed. Marcellin Mellet and Pierre-Thomas Camelot, introduction by Ephraem Hendrickx (Paris: Desclée de Brouwer, 1955); St. Augustine, *La Trinité, Books VIII–XV*, OESA *16*, trans. Paul Agaësse (Paris: Desclée de Brouwer, 1955). Especially see the latter, bk. 14, ch. 8.

tempts of Trinitarian theology sought out the point of departure for some understanding of the production of the Word in God by reflecting on the reality of the intelligible conception of a given work to be done.[15] In the *Adversus Praxean*, Tertullian expressed it in the form of an analogy. Moreover, among the works of St. Gregory of Nyssa,[16] there is a brief work, *"De eo quod sit ad imaginem Dei et ad similitudinem,"* in which the principle of this method is established with strength and insistence:

> If you wish to know God, first know yourself. It is by the make-up of your being, by its constitution, by what is within it, that you will know God. Return to yourself, look into your soul as into a mirror. Decipher its structure, and you will see yourself, like an image and likeness of God.[17]

Whatever may be the case regarding the contested attribution of this work to Gregory, this text is certainly dated earlier than St. Augustine's *De Trinitate*.[18]

C. Methodological Justification

{57} This way is conformed to the fundamental theological methodology, which consists in transposing to God the perfections that one discovers in creatures, "delicately" making use of the threefold procedure of causality, negation, and eminence, basing oneself on the knowledge that we have about man's mind in order to rise up to the Trinitarian life, which itself can only be spiritual. Indeed, in the universe given to our experience, man's mind is the only spiritual reality, the only spiritual life. And it is the Bible that assures us that man was made "in the image of God." Note that this biblical datum has often been interpreted as meaning that man, by the dominion that he exercises in the material universe, is a kind of image of the Sovereign God. However, on further reflection, it is clear that

---

15. See above, §37.
16. See PG 44, 1328–45.
17. PG 44, 1332A–B (trans. Penido).
18. Maurílio-Teixeira-Leite Penido, "Prélude grec à la théorie psychologique de la Trinité," *Revue Thomiste* 45 (1939): 665–74.

man is able to exercise this dominion on account of his intellect and will. These are the means by which he rules all the other beings of nature. Therefore, we are justified with interpreting this as meaning that man is made in the image of God first and foremost by his mind, without prejudice to the other form of resemblance through man's activity of ruling, which is more immediately obvious.

Clearly, this does not mean that this way of understanding the Trinitarian processions as an intelligible procession and a procession of love in God could be held to be something held *De fide*. Faith precedes theology and does not depend on it.

However, can one say, as many have said, that the psychological way would be one kind of interpretation placed alongside others for understanding these matters? Such a claim would imply too relativistic a conception of theological reasoning. Likewise, it would deny the obvious ambition of theological affirmations, namely, the ambition of reaching the Divine Reality, however imperfectly they may do so. If theological reasoning were relativistic along the aforementioned lines, it would be hardly more than a mental game, without any purchase upon reality. Theology would then be perfectly useless.

To justify such relativism, one would first need to come up with other options set in opposition to the psychological way. Likewise, one would need to set other explanations in opposition to those to which the psychological way leads, and such opposed explanations must be truly different from the psychological way and the explanations to which it leads. Next, these ways and explanations would need to be compared to the psychological way (and to the explanations that it procures), showing that they are equivalent. Such an equivalence is, in fact, impossible, for two opposed explanations cannot be true at the same time. At most they could be complementary, and if so, they would need to be united in a superior synthesis.

In fact, another theological explanation opposed to that provided by the psychological way does not exist. Instead, we find ourselves faced with a refusal to search for an explanation under the pretense of respecting the mystery and its transcendence:

Relation ... must be understood in an apophatic sense. Above all, it is a negation showing us that the Father is not the Son nor the Holy Spirit, that the Son is not [the Father nor the Holy Spirit] ... To envision it otherwise would be to submit the Trinity to an Aristotelian logical category, that of relation.[19]

Behold the outcome of such apophatism:

The revelation of the Holy Trinity is an initial fact, an absolute reality, a first datum that cannot be deduced, explained, or discovered on the basis of one's knowledge of another truth, for there is nothing that would be anterior to it. The apophatic thought that renounces any support finds its support in God, whose unknowability appears as a Trinity. Here, thought acquires an unshakeable stability, theology finds its foundation, and ignorance becomes knowledge.[20]

There are other hypotheses which have been attempted, but they have hardly resulted in extensive elaborations. For example, there is the sociological scheme. Likewise, there is the way following the exigencies of love (which, because it is reciprocal by its very nature, calls for a plurality of Persons). The grand initiator of this latter way was Richard of St. Victor in the twelfth century.[21] However, what Richard sought in the exigencies of love was the *raison d'être* for the processions, not their mode, nor an explanation of the distinction of the persons. We will see that this is a case of complementarity, not of opposition.

---

19. Vladimir Lossky, *Théologie mystique de l'Église d'Orient* (Paris: Aubier, 1944), 54.

20. Lossky, *Théologie mystique de l'Église d'Orient*, 62. N.B., Lossky's text is beautiful and provides much food for reflection. Nevertheless, we must first note that the critique registered against scholasticism's use of philosophy contains a falsehood, for never was it concerned with using philosophical truths as something having priority over revealed truths. However, the Divine Truth, which is absolutely primary, can be revealed, and we can reflect on it, though only by utilizing naturally known truths, which are subordinated to it all the while being known before it. On the other hand, throughout his study, we find an uncritical mélange of apophatism and cataphatism. Apophatism, by definition, is silent, and Lossky has a great deal to say about the Trinity. In these conditions, can one legitimately dismiss, root and branch, scholastic reason when it no longer seems agreeable, dispensing oneself from the need to refute it directly, all in the name of apophatism? The latter, pushed rigorously to its end, would render one mute. This is indeed the case within apophatic theology's own, proper domain, namely, mystical experience, properly speaking.

21. See Richard of St. Victor, *La Trinté*, SC 63 (Paris: Cerf, 1959).

D. Examination of the Critiques Registered
against the Psychological Way

{58} We will encounter particular difficulties as we consider the psychological way of explaining the Trinity. For example, how can we hold that such a procession is, in fact, a person? Likewise, we will face the impossibility of surpassing the "essential" concepts of knowledge and love in God, concepts by which we can attain only the essence that is common to the Three Persons, not each in His distinction.[22] However, there are also fundamental objections which, in fact, belong more to one's intellectual sensibility than to something reasoned out.

For some, the advantages of this way of explaining the Trinity come at the cost of "the renunciation of the perspectives of the economy of salvation and of the sense of mystery."[23] As a critique of St. Augustine, this claim is odd, for his treatise is animated by an ardent search for union with the Trinity.* The first three books speak of the Trinity's action in the New Testament and in the Old Testament, as well as in the world. The fourth book is dedicated entirely to the mission of the Word in the Incarnation, about which he speaks later on as well.† In book 14, he explains that "*Donum*" [Gift] is the Holy Spirit's proper name, for it pertains to Him to be given. As regards St. Thomas, *ST* I q. 43, which is dedicated to the missions of the Divine Persons (that is, to their manifestations in the economy of salvation), is an integral part of the treatise on the Trinity in the *Summa theologiae*. Its brevity is in no way a sign of insignificance. In these few questions he recalls and condenses the entire doctrine developed more amply in the *Scriptum*.[24] Moreover, in the small treatise

---

22. See Karl Rahner, "Le concept du mystère dans la théologie catholique," in *Ecrits théologiques* VIII (Paris: Desclée de Brouwer, 1967), 117–18.

23. See Leo Scheffczyk, "Histoire du dogme de la Trinité," in *Mysterium Salutis. Dogmatique de l'histoire du salut*, vol. 4 (Paris: Cerf 1969), 279–97.

* In particular, see *De trinitate*, bk. 8, chs. 4–10.

† See *De trinitate*, bk. 13, ch. 10ff.

24. See *In* I *Sent.*, d. 14 and d. 15.

on creation that immediately follows in the *Summa theologiae*, the very production of creatures is presented as being the prolongation of the of the intra-Trinitarian processions.[25] Finally, in the treatise on the Incarnation, we find ourselves faced with what is, to a large degree, a treatise on the relations between the Incarnate Word and His Father as an extension of the intra-Trinitarian relations between the Father and the Son.[26]

There is no *a priori* reason to believe that the psychological theory of the Trinity would divert the theologian from the economic aspect of the Trinitarian mystery. St. Augustine himself led the way by establishing the connection between the notions of mission and procession, and St. Thomas will take up and methodically develop this explanation provided by St. Augustine.

The other critique registered against the psychological way is that it cannot aid in explaining the interpersonal relations between the Divine Persons.[27] This is to forget that in God the ontological and the intentional (thought and love) are identical, so that the ontological relations founded on the processions are also interpersonal relations of thought and love.[28] This will also be discussed later on below.

III. THE GREEK AND LATIN CONCEPTIONS OF THE TRINITY

{59} It is commonly said that the Greeks and the Latins approach the mystery of the Trinity from two opposite directions, such that their conceptions of the Trinity are different and mutually irreducible to one another.

Régnon first proposed this now-classical interpretation of the facts:
Latin philosophy first of all envisions the nature in itself and proceeds

25. See *ST* I, q. 45, aa. 6–7.
26. See *ST* III, qq. 20–24.
27. See Henri Barré, *Trinité que j'adore* (Paris: Lethielleux, 1965).
28. See Jean-Hervé Nicolas, *Les profondeurs de la grâce* (Paris: Beauchesne, 1969).

to the supposit. Greek philosophy first of all envisions the supposit and then penetrates it so as to find the nature. The Latin thinker considers personality as a mode of the nature. The Greek thinker considers the nature as the content of the person. Here, we are confronted with two opposed orientations that erect concepts of the same reality upon different foundations.[29]

From the perspective of the philosophies used in the East and the West, this opposition is a pure fantasy. It suffices to recall that the philosophy of the Latins comes from Aristotle, who was a Greek, and this philosophy was rectified by revealed truths drawn from the Bible, the common source for the Latin and Greek Fathers.

From the perspective of Trinitarian theology, the schema drawn from the artificial opposition between the respective philosophies of the person and that of the nature is extremely simplistic. The Greeks would first of all consider the Three Persons in their distinction, and the Latins would base their reflections on the one nature. This is to forget that the Greeks founded their reflection on the Bible, which proclaims God's unity before speaking (in the New Testament) about the distinct Persons. In reality, for every theologian, the Three Persons together are the One God. He who considers the distinction of the Persons must at the same time consider the unity of the Nature, for the one, indivisible Divine Nature is what the Father communicates to the Son, and the Son and the Father to the Holy Spirit. He who considers the Nature must at the same time consider the distinction of Persons, for the one Nature subsists in three distinct Persons. No theology could privilege one of the two considerations to the detriment of the other without simultaneously distorting the consideration that he intends to privilege.

Prestige understands this opposition in an entirely different way.[30] According to him, it comes down to an opposition between "*persona*" and "*hypostasis*." Thus, the theology of the Greeks would

29. Théodore de Régnon, Études de théologie positive sur la Sainte Trinité, 4 vols. (Paris: Victor Retaux, 1892–1898), vol. 1, 433.

30. See George Leonard Prestige, *Dieu dans la pensée patristique* (Paris: Aubier, 1955), 200–205.

be much more metaphysical and that of the Latins much more personalist.

Thus, we have a contradictory pair of reproaches. This diversity indicates the artificiality of the very idea of a Latin concept of the Trinity and a Greek one. In truth, the fourth century was the great century of Trinitarian theology among the Greeks. If the Latin tradition begins already in the second century with Tertullian and in the fourth century includes the illustrious names of Marius Victorinus and St. Hilary, it took its full flight only with St. Augustine's *De Trinitate* in the fifth century.[31] While the influence of Victorinus's treatise is difficult to estimate, we can say:

[It] is only important to the exact degree that it exerted an influence upon St. Augustine, that is to say, fairly little.[32] St. Augustine's Trinitarian theology shaped that of the Latin Middle Ages, and St. Thomas's only prolongs and completes it. Therefore, it is not a question of parallel theologies, and less still of opposed ones. Instead, Latin theology followed in the footsteps of the theology of the Greeks without contradicting it in any way.[33]

---

31. See Tertullian, *Traité du baptême*, ed. and trans. François Refoulé and Maurice Drouzy, SC 35 (Paris: Cerf, 1953).

32. See Pierre Hadot, "Introduction" in Marius Victorinus, *Traités théologiques sur la Trinité*, SC 68 (Paris: Cerf, 1960), 84–88.

33. See Marie-Joseph Le Guillou, "Réflexions sur la théologie trinitaire," *Istina* (1972): 457–464.

PART 2

———— : ————

The Distinction and Union of Those "Being God" in the One God

4

The Processions in God

I. HOW CAN ONE CONCEIVE THE DIVINE PROCESSIONS?

A. Why Does One Speak of Processions in God?

{60} First of all, the term "procession" is a biblical term. The personal distinction of the Son, and then of the Holy Spirit, was revealed by means of this notion.

Certainly, what is thus spoken of here is the mission of the Son and of the Holy Spirit to men. For this reason, the biblical term "procession" pertains to the "economy," that is, to salvation history. However, we have seen that the "Economic Trinity" refers us onward to the "Immanent Trinity." The temporal procession manifests the Son's and the Spirit's characteristic of having Their origin in the Father.[1]

In the disputed questions *De Potentia*,[2] St. Thomas advances a philosophical account that underlies q. 27 of the *Summa theologiae*. We have seen that Trinitarian dogma is necessarily expressed by the notion of consubstantiality. That is, the Persons are affirmed as not being distinct with regard to their substance, and this necessarily implies—an implication recognized and set forth in the formu-

---

1. See §53 above.
2. See *De pot.*, q. 8, a. 1.

las of faith themselves—that their distinction is only relative. Now, every relation is founded either on quantity (equality or inequality; similitude or dissimilitude) or on action (the relation of cause to effect or of effect to cause). The first type of relation embraces static relations, the second type, dynamic ones. The first type must be excluded from the case of God. First of all, this exclusion is necessary because every kind of quantity must be excluded from God.[3] However, we can also enlarge the problem, for we can also analogically speak about the "virtual quantity" pertaining to the various degrees of being. In this way, we pass from the relation of equality (or inequality) to that of similitude (or dissimilitude),[4] which also is useful for beings as regards the comparison of their essences. However, precisely speaking, such "static relations" absolutely cannot be found in God, for it can only be found between distinct essences and implies that the correlatives are distinct from the perspective of their substances. Therefore, the only possible foundation remaining for relations in God is action. In the case of action, there is a mutual relationship between two termini, one of which proceeds from the other.

B. How to Conceive of a Procession in God

The reader should consult the following texts in St. Thomas: *ST* I, q. 27, a. 1, a very terse, almost schematic, text which must be illuminated by the profound text of SCG, bk. 4, ch. 11 and also *De veritate*, q. 4, aa. 1 and 2.

1. Intelligible Procession at the Level of the Human Intellect

In this first article, St. Thomas speaks about an intelligible procession. However, this is not because he wishes to speak about the first divine procession in what is proper to it. This will be the subject discussed in the second article. Instead, he speaks about an intelligible procession because observation of intellectual life can make the

---

3. See *De pot.*, q. 8, a. 1; *ST* I-II, q. 52.
4. See Aristotle, *Metaphysics*, bk. Δ, ch. 15 (1021a8–15); *In V Meta.*, lect. 17, no. 1005.

general phenomenon of spiritual (or, immanent) procession clear on the very level of our own experience.

a) The Presence of the Object in the Intellect through the Concept

{61} To know is to become the other inasmuch as it is other. This definition alone can account for the experience that we have of knowledge. It is a wholly personal and interior activity which is also ordered to the other and submitted to what this other is ([i.e., it has] objectivity).

Now, this "other" for the intellect is not only, nor firstly, an external being in its individuality. This "other" indeed exists in this individual being. However, it is also its prisoner. What I am referring to are the great ensembles, one intelligible form, realized in a host of concrete beings but ultimately not imprisoned by any of them. Above all, and first of all, I am referring to the universal intelligible form of being, realized in all beings. The intellect knows everything that it knows as a particular determination of this absolutely universal intelligible form's realization, in which and through which it attains everything that it knows. The intellect faces toward being, and this is what endows it with universality and opens it up onto the infinite.

However, this universality does not befall it on account of its own, proper entitative being [être d'existence]. According to their entitative existence (*esse*), both the intellect and the understood [thing] are particular beings (*entia*), each enclosed within its limits and external to one another. If the understood [thing] can, without ceasing to be itself, become interior to the intellect to the point of being identified with it (elsewhere, exteriority between beings is constituted by alterity), this can occur only on account of another kind of existence (*esse*) than entitative existence. This other kind of existence is called "intentional," for it does not make the thing exist in itself and for itself. Rather, by means of this intentional existence, the intellect interiorly reaches out toward the understood [thing], and the latter is borne into the intellect.

What remains identical is the essence, that by which the under-stood [thing] is what it is. However, this "essence" exists in the intel-lect, and the intellect exists as identical with it according to an im-material *esse intentionale*.[5]

This *esse intentionale* belongs to the operative order, for knowing is obviously an act, an activity [*opération*]. It arises from the intellect, for the intellect is the source of this activity. It is the *intelligere* itself. Simultaneously, it is the *intelligi*, since by it the understood [thing] exists in the intellect and is the intellect: *intentionis intellectae esse est ipsum intelligi*, which must be translated, "the *esse* according to which the known thing is in the intellect is [its] 'being known,' that is, the existence (*esse*) that the intellect confers upon it by its very act of in-tellection."[6]

Thus, just as the external thing receives from its various causes (and principally from the First Cause) the existence (*esse*) accord-ing to which it exists for itself in the extra-mental universe, so too, in order to exist in the mind as known, it receives intentional existence (*esse*) from the intellect, and this existence is intellection itself.

This is what makes abstraction possible, for the universal cannot exist in the extra-mental universe. The various ontological elements that constitute a particular being cannot exist apart from one anoth-er. However, decomposed by the mind and recomposed in a univer-sal, intelligible form, these elements can be objects of distinct acts of intellection and therefore can *exist in the mind* separately. Thus, one can consider animal life separately, whether philosophically or scien-tifically. The naturalist can speak in general about vertebrates, about this or that other class of animals, or about a living species, without considering the details of this or that individual.

This means that the intellect must itself produce its object, for this presence of the known within it can only be its own work. Cer-tainly, the [known] thing exercises an action on the intellect, through the intermediacy of perception and of the imagination. Nonetheless,

5. *De Ente et Essentia*, ch. 3.
6. *SCG*, bk. 4, ch. 11.

perception itself and imagination are activities of a knower, and still more is intellection such an activity. Prior to intellection, the other to be known is not yet known in act. The intellect can confer intentional existence (*esse*) on it by its act of intellection only by producing it within its intimate depths, as the receptive subject of this being, the intelligible in act. This does not involve the creation of an object, since the other to be known is that which exists in the extra-mental universe. However, this other exists in it as an object by means of the act of understanding. Fertilized by its own action exercised upon the sensible image and by elevating its content to the intelligible level (in the light of the agent intellect), the intellect, by its act of intellection and simultaneously as the necessary condition for its intellection, produces the other in its alterity within the interior depths of the intellect. This is the idea or concept, or, the mental word.[7]

b) The Fecundity of the Intellect

Should we hold (as some have) that the act of intellection consists in this very production [of the mental word]?[8] Such an assertion overlooks the fact that this production has its meaning and *raison d'être* only in the fact that it renders intellection possible, procuring its object for it. However, should we conversely say (like Scotus) that they are two distinct acts? Such an assertion overlooks the fact that the one is the intrinsic condition for the other (i.e., that it has reality only in it and with it). To distinguish them in this way would be akin to claiming that one could distinguish as two separate acts the production of a thing's essence and the conferral of existence upon this essence, whereas, on the contrary, the production of an essence can only mean that it is brought into existence. Thus, when the intellect produces the idea inside itself, it makes the thing

---

7. See Jacques Maritain, *Réflexions sur l'intelligence et sur sa vie proper* (Paris: Desclée de Brouwer, 1930); Jacques Maritain, *Distinguer pour unir ou Les degrés du savoir, Oeuvres completes*, vol. 4 (Fribourg-Paris: Éditions universitaires-Éditions Saint-Paul, 1983), appendix 2.

8. See Henri Paissac, *Théologie du Verbe: Augustin et Thomas* (Paris: Cerf, 1951).

exist (intentionally) as known, which obviously cannot be separated from the act of knowing. Therefore, the very act of intellection,
which consists essentially in being the other intentionally (and, simultaneously, in making the other exist in intellect), must also and
necessarily include the production of this other as intelligible in act.
Therefore, it requires the uttering [*prolation*] of the idea, the word.

Why *necessarily*? This necessity is clear from the fact that, initially, the intellect and the other to be known are ontologically distinct.
In order "to be" the other inasmuch as it is other, the human intellect must "become" the other. The intellect is "intelligent" in potency, and the other is "intelligible" in potency. The idea (i.e., the concept, the word) is the other having become intelligible in act, in the
depths of the intellect, the latter itself having come into act.

But what about the case of self-knowledge? It seems that this necessity no longer holds, given that ontological identity exists from
the outset.

Whatever may be the case for self-knowledge that a pure spirit
has of himself, man cannot know himself intellectually without passing through being, the first object of his intellect. Since the human
person is also bodily and material, he is not by himself something
that is intelligible in act. Therefore, self-knowledge also requires the
production of an idea in which the self is identified with itself, no
longer according to ontological identity (as is true for every being)
but, rather, intentionally, according to the operative and living identity that is proper to intellection. It is a new, much richer, way of being present to oneself.

Nonetheless, reflexive self-awareness does exist, through an experience of the self which tends toward immediacy (i.e., thus tending toward the suppression of the mediation of the idea). This
knowledge is realized on the basis of the reflexive knowledge included in every act of knowledge. (When I know a thing, I simultaneously know myself knowing this thing.) One's attention is then turned
from the other, which is the object of knowledge (and indeed is its
point of departure) in order to consider oneself who, now by means

of this reflexive knowledge, is the other. According to St. Thomas, this knowledge is purely "existential," an experience of one's own existence.[9] That is, it does not, of itself, include the uttering [*prolation*] of a distinct idea. However, it is not found in pure isolation, that is, separate from every other form of knowledge. If the intellect were to completely cease knowing something, it could not itself be known, for it would no longer be in act as a knower [*en acte de connaître*]. Moreover, as we noted earlier, this "something" can itself be known by passing through being. In that case, there is a combination of objective self-knowledge (with the production of an idea, that is, the idea that one forms concerning oneself) and existential knowledge. Thus, thanks to such existential knowledge, man's objective knowledge takes on the character of being a new presence of the self to the self.

The following point must be carefully noted. If, after undertaking a rigorous analysis, the idea is clearly necessary on account of the initial exteriority of the other to be known (even in the case of self-knowledge), one cannot ignore the fact that it manifests a fecundity that is proper to the intellect. Now, while the exteriority in question is obviously the sign of an imperfection (the disproportion between the intentional infinity of the intellect and its ontological finitude, whence comes the solely "virtual" character of its intentional infinity), fecundity does not of itself imply any imperfection. On the contrary, of itself, it is a sign of perfection: *bonum diffusivum sui*. And in what concerns the intellect and the production of the idea, this can be observed with ease. Consider the need to say to oneself what one is thinking and to express it, as well as the satisfaction experienced in so doing—whether through a work of art, oral or written discourse, or bodily expression.

Can this fecundity of the human intellect be separated from the ontological imperfection which, in our own experience, is connected to it? Or, does it have its own proper, positive value, one which

9. See *ST* I, q. 87, a. 1; *De ver.*, q. 10, a. 8; see Maritain, *Distinguer pour unir ou Les degrés du savoir*, appendix 5.

would enable it to be found above all imperfections? In the latter case, we find the basis for being able to ascend, by way of the analogical *viae* of causality, negation, and eminence, all the way to the transcendent fecundity found in God.

2. The Emanation of a Word in God

a) Transferring to God the Notion of an Intelligible Procession

{63} The principle of this transfer is stated by St. Thomas as being self-evident: "Whatever knows (intellectually), by the very fact that it knows, has something proceed within it, and this is the thing as conceived within it by virtue of intellection."[10] And in a more developed manner, he states:

Inasmuch as it is known, the (intellectually) known reality necessarily exists in the knower. Indeed, the very act of intellection consists in the intellect's apprehension of that which is known. For this reason, when our intellect knows itself, it is present to itself, not only inasmuch as it is really identical with itself, but also inasmuch as it is known. Therefore, it is necessary that God be present to Himself as the known is present to the intellect (by virtue of the act of intellection). However, the known that is present to the intellect is nothing other than the intelligible representation conceived by intellection, the word. Therefore, in knowing Himself, the Word is there in some manner as God-Known in the intimate depths of God-Knowing: as the concept of the stone is in the intellect the stone itself inasmuch as it is known.[11]

Nonetheless, there is a difficulty that we must face here. If the "stone inasmuch as it is known" must be "produced" within the intellect, this is because the "stone in its existential reality" is not, of itself, intelligible in act and present to the intellect. However, this is not the case for "God inasmuch as He is known." By His existence, His *Esse*, God is at once infinitely subsistent (*Ipsum Esse subsistens*) and infinitely intelligible (*Ipsa Species intelligibilis*).[12] On the other hand, He is, quite obviously, perfectly interior to Himself and to His intel-

10. *ST* I, q. 27, a. 1.
11. *SCG*, bk. 4, ch. 11.
12. See *ST* I, q. 14, a. 4.

lect. Why, therefore, would a "word" be necessary in order for Him to have self-knowledge? And when it comes to the knowledge of other things, this can only be an extension of this knowledge that He has of Himself.[13]

Indeed, St. Thomas in no way claims to apply to God an *a priori* necessity, drawn from the examination of our intellectual life, as is quite clear in the judgment that he himself pronounces concerning the binding force of his argument.[14] Indeed, he expressly rejects the value of such an *a priori*: "The comparison with our intellection provides a full and certain proof for the case of the divine intellection [as involving the Trinitarian processions], for we do not say that man and God are intelligent in a univocal manner." Therefore, in the texts that we are considering, if he speaks of a "necessity," this is because he is profoundly aware that God's Being is necessary and, for this reason, that every contingency must be excluded from what constitutes Him. Knowing *by faith* that there is an emanation at the heart of the Godhead, he knows at the same time and *by the same means* that this emanation is necessary. Therefore, despite the appearances due to the wording, the necessity involved here is an *a posteriori*, not *a priori* necessity.

Therefore, we find ourselves led to reason out these matters as follows. Since there are processions in God, we must think that these processions remain within the intimate depths of the Godhead and must be immanent. (Failing this, the terminus proceeding would be "outside of God" and would belong to the created sphere. This would not be a procession *in God*, but rather, would be something *outside of God*, the *processus creaturarum a Deo*.) Therefore, these processions are immanent. We find in our own mind the type and image of immanent processions, namely, the emanation of the word or concept in the intimate depths of the intellect. Setting aside its *raison d'être* drawn from the limits of our being and of our intellectual activity (a *raison d'être* linked to the conditions befalling the less-

13. See *ST* I, q. 14, aa. 5, 6, and following.
14. See *ST* I, q. 32, a. 1, ad. 2.

er analogate, which obviously cannot be transferred to God), a rigorous analysis of this emanation led us to see that it is the sign and expression of a secret property of the intellect.[15] For this reason, no contradiction is involved in transposing this intelligible emanation to God, considering this emanation solely as arising from the fecundity proper to the intellect.

However, an objection may be registered here. Given that God is infinitely elevated above every created being (intellectual ones just as much as all the others), one may argue that the immanent procession that we seek in Him could occur as an activity that wholly differs from intellectual activity.

We will examine this argument later, an argument pertaining to questions of methodology. For now, let us provide a brief response to it. What one can know about God by reason, and what is confirmed by revelation, is that God is sovereignly intelligent. We know by faith that there are immanent processions in Him. Based on what we know about immanent procession, we can legitimately conclude from this that intelligible emanation is also found in His intellectual activity in an infinite manner. Indeed, while the notion of intellectuality is not found univocally in Him, it is indeed found there analogically. Moreover, can we not refer to Scripture, which itself proposes the idea of an intelligible emanation (the *Logos*)? Likewise, can we not refer to the most ancient tradition, which looked in this direction for an explanation of the procession of a distinct Person in God? Yes, if not as begetting a certitude of faith, at least as being an invaluable indication given by faith to theological reflection.

b) From Co-Essentiality to Consubstantiality

{64} In human intellectual life, co-essentiality is the characteristic property of the intellectual word's relation both to the intellect and to the object [known]. Indeed, we have seen that the same, identical essence was realized in the extra-mental world as existing (i.e.,

15. See §61 above.

by a real existence) and in the intra-mental world for the known being, that is, in order that, in it, the intellect may intentionally be the
known.[16] Correctly understood, it is not a question of saying that the
complete essence of the real thing, with all its "existential" determinations, is present to the intellect by means of the idea. Rather, what
is present to the intellect by means of the idea is realized in the thing.
(Thus, in and by means of the idea of an animal, the intellect finds
itself presented with the same thing that is realized in all beings that
are endowed with animal life, abstraction being made from the differences in their realization. Co-essentiality concerns the relation of
the idea to that portion of reality which is known by means of it. It
is a relation of identity.

In the case of God's self-knowledge, the identification is complete, for God knows Himself wholly and entirely. There is absolute
coincidence between the essence of "God, in an act of intellection of
Himself" and that of "God, the object of this intellection." This is a
case of perfect co-essentiality.

Of itself, however, co-essentiality is not consubstantiality. Indeed,
the substance in which the essence is realized is that which is, that
which exercises the act of existence. In the extra-mental world, the
essence is a substance, but it is not ordinarily one in the intra-mental
world, where the essence does not exercise the act of existence.

However, in God, the act of existence is not distinguished from
the act of intellection (*intelligere*), nor, consequently, from the "being known in act" (*intelligi*). The *Pure Act of Existence* (*Ipsum Esse
subsistens*) is identical with the *Pure Act of Intellection*, for intellection
itself is reduced to being, and it can be distinguished from it only as
a given act of being is distinguished from another act of being. And
various acts of existence are distinguished from each other only on
account of the various potencies into which they are received.[17]

For this reason, at the summit of being and of intellection, at
infinity, the essence present to the intellect as known is not distin-

16. See §60 above.
17. See *ST* I, q. 14, aa. 1–4.

guished in any way from the realized essence, the essence-substance. Thus, at this summit, co-essentiality becomes consubstantiality. What the intellect "produces" is not a duplication of the substance of the known [thing]. The "product" is this very substance inasmuch as it is intellectually known: *Deus intellectus*.[18]

c) Consubstantiality and the Real Distinction of Consubstantials

{65} We are here at the tensest moment of these reflections. This "consubstantiality" would seem to eliminate every real distinction. But, in that case, the very idea of "production" would also be eliminated and thus, too, that of "procession," for it is contradictory to say that the same proceeds from the same. Now, we are left with the affirmation of procession by intelligible emanation. Therefore, one must recognize (that is, affirm, outside of every possible representation) that if the Divine Intellection, inasmuch as it is knowledge, occurs through the substantial identification of the knower and of the known, it also entails the uttering [*prolation*] of a terminus, which must be really distinct from that from which it proceeds, which nevertheless is identical to it with regard to substance.

This "terminus" of the uttering [*prolation*] exists in God. It is constituted by the unique Divine Substance. It could not be super-added to it: "Everything that is in God is God."[19] And it is necessary to speak similarly about its principle, from which it is really distinct, though not according to substance. Therefore, there are two "Being God," two "Being the One God."

We will need to speak in the same manner about every other terminus that would proceed in God according to another immanent procession (or processions).

C. Conclusion

{66} This entire undertaking is underpinned by this affirmation of faith: processions exist in God. This itself is an affirmation under-

18. See *SCG*, bk. 4, ch. 11.
19. *ST* I, q. 27, a. 3, ad. 2.

pinned by the revealed affirmation that God, in His unicity, is Father, Son, and Holy Spirit, by a dynamic communication of the very divinity of the Father to the Son and to the Holy Spirit. If this indivisible divinity is communicated, this can only take place in a complete manner, being identically the same in Him who communicates It and in Those to whom It is communicated. It is not communicated like three aspects of His personality, or of His actions. Rather, it is communicated as three distinct [ones] "Being God."* This theological position seeks to provide a form that is rigorous and compelling for the mind, developing the very first intuition of the believer faced with this object of faith: God proceeds in God, from God, like the *logos* from the intellect.

II. GENERATION IN GOD

What is expressly revealed is that there is a Father and a Son in God. Therefore, there is a generation: a begetter and a begotten.

A. From the Uttering [*Prolation*] of a Word to the Generation of a Son

1. A Production of Another Self

{67} On the level of our experience, the uttering [*prolation*] of a word (or, a concept) completely lacks the appearance of being a form of generation. But why? Essentially because the existence (the *esse*) conferred upon the *intentio intellecta* (the reality actually known, precisely as known) by the intellect through the act of intellection is not, as we have seen, entitative existence (*actus essendi*). This intentional existence makes neither the intellect nor the known reality exist a second time but, instead, is wholly ordered to entitative existence, which makes the known [thing] belong to the extra-mental

* [Tr. note: As noted earlier, this methodological scruple, which Fr. Nicolas will discuss later in the text, is slightly more flexible in French. In most cases, I have handled this through slight alterations to the articles used. However, here, the somewhat awkward "ones" was necessary.]

universe. To beget is to make another self exist with a real existence. That is, begetting brings into real existence a being similar to oneself, at least with regard to one's essence (or, nature), and nevertheless, this new being is other than the begetter. Two points are to be observed concerning the intellect's activity in making the known thing exist intentionally in the knowing self. On the one hand, this activity does not bestow real existence upon it. On the other hand, it does not make another self exist in this way, since most of the time the knower knows something other than itself, and if one does know oneself, one does so imperfectly and partially.

As we have seen, this is not the case for God. What God knows is Himself, and He does so perfectly. The *esse* that He bestows on the *intentio intellecta* in this transcendent intellection is not only an intentional existence but simultaneously is entitative existence, since, in Him, at this summit of actuality, the two kinds of existence merge into one. He is simultaneously a supreme actuality of existing and a supreme actuality of intellection and of being known:

As the very essence of God is identical with His intelligible representation (*species intelligibilis*), it necessarily follows that His intellection, by which His intelligible representation exists intentionally in the intellect, is identical with His being, by which His essence really exists in itself.[20] However, since in God being and knowing are wholly one, the known in Him is identical with the intellect that knows it. And because His intellect is identical to the known thing, in knowing Himself He indeed knows all other things, as was shown earlier [in SCG, bk. 1, chs. 1 and 49]. Let us conclude that in the knowledge that God has of Himself, there is an identity between the intellect, the known reality, and the word.[21]

As we have seen, if the intelligible procession in God is a procession of one "Being God," distinct from the "Being God" from whom He proceeds, though consubstantial with Him, we must recognize that this procession has the character of being an authentic generation and must see in this other "Being God" the Son spoken of in Scripture.

20. *ST* I, q. 14, a. 4.
21. *SCG*, bk. 4, ch. 11.

Now, we must carefully note that, in this ineffable and incomprehensible generation, the nature itself is not begotten. In other words, since the nature according to which the two are God is identically the same, it is not produced by generation. At this summit, at infinity, the idea of generation is realized in such a way as to confound our intellect. However, in the absolute character of its perfection, *to reproduce oneself* implies a generative production of *an other* who would simultaneously be *perfectly similar to oneself*. When it is God who is reproduced, the resemblance becomes identity, but there is a mystery here still: the alterity remains.

Hence, what is begotten is not the Godhead, which itself is eternal, immutable, and without principle. What is begotten is the "Being God" who precisely is God by this same divinity through which He from Whom He proceeds is God. Here was the crucial point in the debate with the Arians, who relied on the certain truth that the Godhead is neither begotten nor generable, in order to thereby deny that the begotten one could be God and, therefore, that the Son would be God in a proper sense. St. Thomas gives the following explanation concerning this matter:

Obviously, it would not be befitting to a first principle to proceed from a principle in such a way that said first principle would be external and different from that other principle. However, to proceed from a principle in such a way that it would remain perfectly immanent within it and in no way different from it is included in the very notion of a first principle. Indeed, when we say that the architect is the principle of the building, we include in him the conception that he has formed of the building (by which, precisely speaking, he is its principle). And if he were the first principle of this building, this conception would be, along with him, a first principle. Now, God, who is the first principle, bears the same sort of relationship to creatures that the artist does to the works that he produces.[22]

Note that in this response St. Thomas refers to the Word's role as the directive idea of creation. As we have seen, this was the earliest manner of approaching the mystery of the Second Person.[23] It

22. *ST* I, q. 27, a. 1, ad. 3.
23. See §37.

is in no way false, for it is scriptural: "Through Him all things were made." There was need only to ensure that one be aware that if the Word played this role in creation, He does so because, independent of this role, He was "with the Father" or "turned toward the Father" in eternity, as Scripture likewise says. This point came to clear expression through the long years of early speculation on the mystery, and St. Thomas obviously makes this connection clear as well, placing the conception of the Word in the depths of the Godhead.[24] Far from being a vain subtlety, this explanation represents the ultimate formulation of the Fathers' response to this argument opposed to the Catholic faith.[25]

2. Intellectual Fecundity and Natural Fecundity

{68} In the preceding section, the key that enabled us to undertake our analysis of the production of the concept was the claim that the intellect as such is fruitful. We will see that, in God, this fecundity coincides with the fecundity of a living nature, which has reproduction as its effect, something characteristic of living beings.

Is this a simple coincidence? In reality, the dissociation that we find between entitative and intentional existence arises solely from the limitations of created being and hence is inevitable for a created intellect. For this reason, the fecundity of the created intellect is not the same as the transmission of life. That is, this dissociation arises from its limitation in being and, likewise, from its limitation in intellectuality. In Pure Act, this dissociation necessarily disappears, for there, all actualities come together and coalesce.

Thus, the fecundity proper to the intellect is only one form of the fecundity of being. At the level of bodily living being, life realizes itself through biological reproduction, which, in man, coexists with intellectual fecundity without being confused with it. At the level of created pure spirits, it cannot exist in the form of biological

24. See §42.
25. See St. Gregory Nazianzen, *Discours 27–31* (*Discours théologiques*), SC 250 (Paris: Cerf, 1978), 29, 10–12.

reproduction for lack of the necessary bodily dimension. (The angel cannot receive being by generation, for it is a pure spirit. It can only be immediately created.) Likewise, it does not exist in the form of reproduction by intelligible procession, for it does not exist at the summit of actuality. In it, intentional and entitative existence remain necessarily distinct.

Obviously, this does not signify any inferiority, for if natural fecundity is a perfection by which man resembles God in a special way, its condition of realization, *in man*, is matter, from which he draws the bodily dimension of his being. Thus, *of itself*, intellectual fecundity is a likeness which has a closer proximity to the divine fecundity. Indeed, precisely because of this closer proximity, it does not lead to reproduction through the transmission of life, for in the spiritual sphere to which it belongs, the transmission of life requires infinite perfection.

Thus, we find anew the truth of the notion that man is made in God's image according to the part of him that is spiritual. At first sight, this consideration is deceiving, for the multiple "trinities" that, following St. Augustine, we can detect in the "*mens*" are in no manner trinities of persons, of being-men.

However, they make clear the spiritual fecundity that, in God— and in God alone—leads to the procession of distinct "Beings."

3. Generation in God and Freedom

{69} A profound question still remains, one that comes down to us from the Arian controversies: does the Son proceed from the Father *according to His will*? That is, does He proceed freely? But if this were so, He could have not proceeded and His being would depend on a choice that the Father could have not made. In other words, if He proceeds freely, He is contingent. Or, by contrast, does He proceed necessarily? However, if that is the case, then it seems that the Father undergoes a form of constraint and, therefore, is not God.[26]

---

26. Col 1:13 (RSV); see St. Gregory Nazianzen, *Discours*, 29, 6ff.

St. Paul says that, in relation to the Father, Christ is "His beloved Son."[27]

Here too, St. Thomas makes a decisive distinction.[28] The generation of the Son is an act of *nature* and therefore is presupposed for every act of freedom. However, at the same time, His generation is an act of intelligence and, therefore, of awareness, not of constraint. Hence, His generation is a voluntary act in the sense that the Divine Nature is entirely aware of itself, not received from elsewhere, acting in accord with an absolute spontaneity that does not precede awareness but is identical with it. It is an act *of nature* performed *in Agape*.

In the Middle Ages, there was a received adage: the procession of the Son occurs according to the mode of nature, and the procession of the Holy Spirit according to the mode of will. St. Thomas uses this schema in *In I Sent.*[29] It is founded on a fact drawn from our experience, namely, that generation is an activity "according to nature."

In what sense is this the case? In the sense that the nature is the "form" that determines this activity. That is, generation is an activity intrinsically ordered to the realization of the nature of the begetter in another subject. By contrast, artistic creation is determined by an idea conceived in a voluntary manner and likewise realized in a voluntary manner. Artistic creation is characteristically free. Since nature is one, natural activity is *"determinatum ad unum,"* whereas the artistic forms in the artist's mind and imagination are multiple. Thus, the artist is in the presence of a host of possible realities, none of which are imposed upon him. Their realization depends on a decision made by His will.

Nevertheless, is it not true that human generation also depends on a free decision by those who beget a child? Yes, and for two reasons: first, so that the act ordered to it may or may not be posited (freedom *quoad exercitium*); then (to the degree that the develop-

27. See Ceslas Spicq, *L'epître aux Hébreux*, vols. 1 and 2 (Paris: Gabalda, 1952), 101–8; in the contrary direction: *Traduction Oecuménique de la Bible, in loco*, note 0.
28. St. Thomas, *In I Sent.*, d. 6, q. 1, a.2; *ST* I, q. 41, a. 2.
29. Especially in d. 6, q. 3 and d. 13.

ments of biological science increase) so that, in such or such conditions, it tends to confer such or such characteristics upon the begotten child.

This is true, but this primarily comes from the fact human generation is contingent, indeed in two ways. It is contingent *quoad exercitium*, in the sense that although every human adult ordinarily is a begetter in first act; he can choose either to beget or not to beget. In other words, the action of begetting is contingent. Second, it is contingent *quoad specificationem*. Of course, it is not contingent in this manner with regard to specification properly speaking, for the begetters are ordered to communicate life according to their species. However, it is contingent *quoad specificationem* with regard to individual determinations (e.g., sex, individual characteristics, and so forth). The "determination *ad unum*" characteristic of natural activity leaves a fringe of indetermination on which the will can act, thanks to technical knowledge. However, it acts externally and indirectly, by choosing the desired conditions so that the act, having its efficacy in itself, may produce the result that one seeks. This is not the same way that things take place in artistic production, for in that case the work depends on the artist's will for its very structure.

The divine generation excludes every kind of contingency. First of all, it excludes every contingency *quoad exercitium*. God is Pure Act. The Divine Nature is not fruitful first in first act, passing then to the act of reproducing itself. In its very structure, it is fruitful in second act. Moreover, it excludes every contingency *quoad specificationem* up to the ultimate determination. The Divine Nature is the concrete universal, infinite, and perfectly determined, not leaving room for any fringe of indetermination. It is infinitely simple as well. Here, the *determinatio ad unum* characteristic of activity *secundum naturam* is perfect, so that the will has no sway over such an activity, for nature precedes the will. It might be said, however, that this priority is not real in God but, instead, is a "conceptual" priority (i.e., one established by our reason), given that God's nature is identical with His thought and willing. This is true, and nevertheless it is not vain to affirm this priority as well as its consequence—namely, the necessary character of what flows from nature (and from thought as well), in opposition to the freedom that belongs to the will and what depends on it. This is not vain because every affirmation related to God uses concepts that are drawn from creatures, concepts that intrinsically depend on one another according to an objective order.[30] What we must say is that this necessity is not "undergone" [(or, "suffered")] in any manner, for not only is it the necessity of God's very being, but moreover, this being is in no way received and in no way depends on another "being." "Its necessity does not depend on any cause external to it."[31]

As we will see, this is no less true for the second procession, which is also an activity of nature. This is the why St. Thomas, from the time when he wrote the *Summa contra gentiles*, renounces a dichotomy that had become classic, namely procession *secundum naturam* (= first procession) vs. procession *secundum voluntatem* (= second procession), substituting for this dichotomy two processions that are both *secundum naturam*: procession *secundum intellectum* and procession *secundum voluntatem*.[32] (Nevertheless, note in the *De potentia* his use of the distinction between *secundum naturam* and *naturaliter*, the first of which properly belongs to the first procession and the latter which belongs to both.)[33]

4. *The Only-Begotten*

{70} Consequently, there can be only one Son in God. The fact that He is "only-begotten" is a certain scriptural datum. It is also a first-order [*première*] requirement of theological reason, for multiplicity is always a sign of imperfection. If the "natural desire [*voeu*]" implied in the generative act, giving it its meaning (namely, *to reproduce oneself*), were perfectly realized in a single stroke, a second

---

30. See below, §148.
31. *In* I *Sent.*, d. 6, q. 1, a. 1.
32. *ST* I, q. 41, q. 2, ad. 3.
33. See *De pot.*, q. 10, a. 2, ad. 4.

generative act would have no meaning. Because this "desire" [*vœu*] is unrealized and unrealizable in the biological domain, especially in the human domain, it continues, of itself, to call for, arouse, and justify the generative act after one or many have already been performed successfully. The divine generation is an absolute perfection. It leaves no room for any multiplicity.

B. The Double Analogy That Leads the Mind to the Divine Generation

{71} Thus, we are in fact led to some degree of understanding concerning the divine generation by means of a double analogy.

The first is immediately proposed to us by revelation, namely *generation*, a reality that we have direct experience of. The Fathers of the Church ever recur to this as to the solid rock on which the faith braces itself: God has a Son, the Only-begotten, whom He begets in the intimate depths of Himself from all eternity, and who is God precisely because, through this ineffable generation, He holds from the Father the indivisible, unique Godhead.

Already in the *Scriptum*, St. Thomas thoroughly and systematically makes use of this analogy.[34] A generation exists in God, and we know about it through revelation. Generation pushed to the summit of perfection leads to consubstantiality. That is, it leads to the distinction of subjects (Beings) in the perfect unity of nature (Being God).

However, by itself, this analogy insufficiently illuminates faithful reason. By means of it, we can know nothing about the mode of this generation. The only generation that we know about in the domain of our experience is bodily, which necessarily consists in division and splitting, the production of the (individuated) nature itself in its new supposit. How can we here separate the *ratio analogata* (generation) from the conditions in which it is realized in the creature, conditions which seem to intrinsically belong to it? The ancient Fa-

---

34. *In* I *Sent.*, d. 4, q. 6, a. 12.

thers took refuge in the mystery. St. Gregory of Nazianzen said, "In silence, we must honor the generation of God."[35] Faith indeed first commands such an attitude, and it defends faith against reason's impieties, insofar as the latter has not succeeded in resolving its doubts (in the whole of the believing community or even in the individual believer). However, such an attitude can only be provisional. Believing reason needs to "understand," however little that it may be able to do so, and it cannot be satisfied with a prohibition against pushing its investigations further.

Here, the other analogy intervenes, that of the intelligible word. Not that it would have arrived late in the day! As we have seen, it was part of Christian awareness from the beginning. However, it is a fact that it had only been slightly elaborated before St. Augustine's writing. With the scholastics, and most especially with St. Thomas, the elaboration already begun and brought quite far by St. Augustine was pushed to its limits. However, let us not forget the quite original enterprise, one of powerful boldness, undertaken by Richard of St. Victor, who, basing himself on a first intuition that sees charity as being the absolute value and supreme principle, proposed a Trinitarian theology founded on the requirements of charity, which in God can only be infinite. He likewise insists somewhat on the analogy of generation: "Thus to produce from Himself a consubstantial person like unto Him will be His immutable will, in virtue of a reason that requires it. Without any doubt, for Him, to beget a Son will be to find all His delights in this Son Himself."[36] And he also insists on the analogy of the Word: "Only the Son is the Word, for He proceeds from the only One who is the origin of the manifestation of all truth."[37] He does not completely avoid the danger of making the two processions depend on the Father's freedom:

35. Gregory Nazianzen, Discours, 29, 8; cf. Georges-Matthieu de Durand, "Sa generation qui la racontera? Is. 53,8B: l'exégèse des Pères," Revue des sciences philosophiques et théologiques 53 (1969): 638–57.

36. Richard of St. Victor, La Trinté, SC 63 (Paris: Cerf, 1959), VI, 3.

37. Richard of St. Victor, La Trinté, VI, 12.

Behold what enables us to understand the nature and gravity of this lack of benevolence in the hypothesis: God would prefer to keep for Himself alone, like a miser, the richness of His plenitude, whereas He could at will communicate it to another and thus savor such an achievement of goodness, such a surfeit of delights. In these conditions, He would have been right to hide from the view of the angels and of other beings. He would have been right to feel shame at letting Himself be seen and at making Himself known, if He was lacking this point of goodness.[38]

We have seen the value of this analogy with the intelligible word but have also seen its limitations. How can we pass from the notion of an intelligible procession to that of the transmission of His Life to another subject? Thus, we must return to the other analogy that was, as it were, "released" by our recourse to the second but which again becomes necessary so that we may maintain the latter.

Therefore, these two analogies complete each other, thus preventing the "negative way" from leading to an impasse in which the denial would be asserted of the *ratio analogata* itself and not merely of the conditions falling to the lesser analogates.[39]

These two analogies, so two speak, direct believing reason's aim, placing the mystery of the divine generation at an infinite point toward which they converge.

III. THE SECOND PROCESSION

{72} In order to provide a theological explanation for the Trinitarian dogma, we have embarked along the way opened up by the so-called psychological analogy concerning the intellect's production of the mental word. This naturally turns us toward the second transposable immanent activity in God, namely love, so that we might thus find the rational means for procuring some degree of understanding concerning the second procession, namely, that of the Holy Spirit. (For the discussion of the validity of this process, see §78 below.)

38. Richard of St. Victor, *La Trinté*, III, 4.
39. Jean-Hervé Nicolas, *Dieu connue comme inconnu* (Paris: Desclée de Brouwer, 1966), 256–60.

Now, this "way" must lead to a true "procession" (that is, to a causality-free "production") in God, one having a really distinct ter-mimus (for, according what we know through faith, the Holy Spirit is a "Being God" who is really distinct from the Father and the Son). In order for this to be the case, we must discover an *operatum* (that is, something that is produced) when we look into the lesser analo-gate (that is, in the act of love that we experience in ourselves). In-deed, if in our case love as an activity is distinct from the will from which it proceeds, it is distinct from the will as second act is distinct from first act. That is, it is distinguished as *perfectio a perfectibili*. (The perfection that brings a perfectible being to its completion is dis-tinct from it.) Therefore, they are distinct as act is distinct from po-tency. God is Pure Act. There is no potentiality in Him. There is no distinction between first act (one's nature, or a faculty) and second act (activity [*opération*]). Just as we have seen that in Him *esse* and *intelligere* are identical with each other (and with His nature, as well as His intellect), likewise, by the same necessity, *amare* is identical with *esse*, *intelligere*, and His nature. Therefore, just as we needed to discover a production (i.e., an *operatum*) in addition to His very ac-tivity (i.e., intellection), in order for us to be able to find an analo-gy in our intellection which we could use for imagining something about the first procession, so too we must here discover, in this act of love, an *operatum*, an *immanent production*, in addition to the ac-tivity itself (i.e., love). (For all this, see St. Thomas, *De veritate*, q. 4, a.2, ad. 7. Note, however, that, in this text, St. Thomas disconcerting-ly denies that there is an "operatum" in the will after saying that such an "*operatum*" is needed for one to be able to speak of a real proces-sion. Let us merely note that in this work St. Thomas speaks about the Holy Spirit only indirectly. Moreover, in later works he affirms, on the contrary, that such an *operatum* exists in the will.)

Therefore, we are concerned with knowing whether the analysis of our act of love reveals the existence of an *operatum*.

A. The Immanent Procession in the Act of Love

1. The Problem

a) The Difficulty in St. Thomas's Own Texts

{73} Remarkably, when St. Thomas analyzes the act of human love apart and for its own sake, he does not speak about the production of a terminus. Nonetheless, he does speak about it with regard to the Trinity. Granted, he does not do so in the *Scriptum*, and he even seems to discount it in *De veritate*.[40] However, already in *De potentia*,[41] he does write that this production is a universal law of voluntary activity and makes the same point very clearly in the fourth book of the *Summa contra gentiles*,[42] as well as in the *Summa theologiae*.[43]

Following M. Penido, should this lead us to infer that this is not a philosophical truth?[44] Such a claim makes no sense, for there can be no doubt that in these texts St. Thomas is speaking about the activity of the will in general and that, in a very conscious manner, he uses an analogy with our volitional activity in order to explain the procession of the Holy Spirit. Therefore, we cannot deny that he thinks that the production of a terminus in volitional activity is an established fact. Moreover, in these texts, he furnishes the reason for this fact. Why does he not speak of it, at least expressly, when he directly considers a question of created volitional activity? We will attempt to explain why.

b) The Difficulty Involved the Matter Itself

{74} How can we justify this production of a terminus in the will? The great and capital objection is that such a terminus is utterly superfluous. Indeed, the terminus of the act of love is the thing in its existential reality, and it is not at all clear how or why this thing

---

40. See *De ver.*, q. 4, a. 2, ad. 7.
41. See *De pot.*, q. 9, a. 9.
42. See *SCG*, bk. 4, ch. 19.
43. See *ST* I, q. 27, a. 3; q. 37, a. 1.
44. See Maurílio-Teixeira-Leite Penido, "Gloses sur la procession d'amour dans la Trinité," *Ephemerides Theologicae Lovanienses* 14 (1937): 43

would need to be rendered present to the will by a "vicar" akin to the concept which renders the known thing present to the intellect only according to an intentional manner of existence.

Clearly, this objection attacks an overly strict parallelism between voluntary activity and intellectual activity, and such facile a parallelism should be rejected. However, the objectors believe that this rejection requires us to reject the existence of something equivalent to the word in what pertains to voluntary activity. Now, it is clear that if there is a terminus produced in voluntary activity, this terminus will play a completely different role than that played by the concept in knowledge.

2. "The Beloved Impressed within the Lover"

{75} Therefore, let us examine voluntary activity. First, let us recall the connection that exists between the intellect and the will. The will is the appetite corresponding to the wholly new manner of being that has the intellect as its principle. The act of love, which is the principle and source of every voluntary activity, derives from the act of knowledge, most especially from the *word* in which the knower is the known.

But there is a great difference between elicited love and natural love. The latter derives from the constitutive form of the subject (i.e., from its nature). Moreover, it derives from it in a necessary manner, for a being cannot fail to be attached to its being and tend toward its natural forms of growth. It is an undetermined tendency, in the sense that the subject's good can be present in various objects—and in the case of a knowing and free subject, it has the power of choosing among them. On the other hand, it is a determined tendency inasmuch as the subject's own good is the reason for each of these objects being desired and pursued. Now, the good of the subject is proportioned to the form by which it is determined in its being. By contrast, elicited love does not derive necessarily from the form intentionally possessed in the intellect (or in the sense[s])—obviously, one does not love everything that one knows.

Pursuing this common-sense remark further, let us note that while the intentional being with which the thing is clad in the mind leaves the thing untouched and self-identical in its essence and form, it does, however, strip it of its goodness by substituting itself for the thing's real being, its existence in the extra-mental universe. This is the case because, as the adage goes, "the good exists in things." Goodness is connected to the real existence of the thing. That which cannot have real existence is deprived of every form of goodness. "Mathematical entities are not good," the ancients said, and while the essence of things is good, it is so in its existential realizations, not inasmuch as it exists in the intellect that knows it by means of the concept. This is the profound reason that explains why elicited love is not (and cannot be) provoked merely by the intentional existence of the known thing in the mind. This also enables us to see quite clearly that an interior terminus of the act of love is needed.

In fact, love is a tendency and a union—a tendential union. This union, which is affective, must be carefully distinguished from the effective grasp. The former can exist without the latter (i.e., in the case wherein the beloved being is outside the reach of the lover). However, even when they are realized together, they remain different from each other. It is not by love that the lover grasps one's beloved. It is by one's gaze. It is by a gesture of one's hands. It is by (experiential) knowledge.

And this makes clear the sophism involved in saying that since the object of love is the thing in its existential reality, there is no need for this thing to be rendered present to the will by something other than itself, for the real presence of the thing neither is required for love, nor does it suffice for explaining it. Since affective union formally differs from effective union, it must be assured in different way.

This is so because the law that we encountered for intellectual activity [opération] is at play here again. No activity is conceivable without the object's presence to the agent [opérant] (since the object is constitutive of the activity). In the case of a transitive activity (which is exercised in the world external to the agent [agent], the real world), real presence is required. No sculptor can sculpt without having before himself the matter on which he acts, the wood or the wax that he sculpts! In the case of immanent activity, which is brought about in the internal world of the agent, the intentional universe, the known or loved object must likewise be present to the agent, though with an interior, spiritual, and intentional presence. Thus, it is clear that, in order to assure the affective union in which love consists, the will must produce within itself an *affective* substitute for the beloved thing or being. This is the explanation furnished by St. Thomas: "By virtue of the love by which one loves any given reality, the beloved is impressed, if one can speak thus, within the lover, and it is on account of this 'impression' that the beloved is said to be present to the lover, as the known is said to be present to the knower."[45]

3. Comparison between This "Impression" and the Word

{76} However, the role of this terminus will be completely different from that of the concept. It in no way involves a representation, or a "likeness," of the thing loved. We cannot love what we do not know, and at the origin of this love there is obviously a more or less exact likeness of the beloved being. However, this likeness is assured by intellectual activity, not by the act of love itself, since the intellectual activity is prior to it. Here, we have something completely different, namely a tendency toward the beloved thing as toward my good. I can love only what is good for me, and mere intelligible likeness cannot make the known thing be my own good. Given that such an appetite is undetermined, it no longer is a merely natural appetite. Nonetheless, the tendency must be directed toward something determinate. *Love itself* is what brings this about. The thing becomes my good, and from the moment that I love it, it exists in me as *my good.*

45. See *ST* I, q. 37, a. 1. Likewise, see *ST* I, q. 19, a. 1; q. 20, aa. 1–2; I-II, q. 26, aa. 1–2; *SCG*, bk. 4, ch.19; Jean-Hervé Nicolas, "Amour de soi, amour de Dieu, amour des autres" *Revue thomiste* 56 (1956): 6–21.

What does it mean to say, "To exist in me as my good?" The good is being inasmuch as it is "appetible." What makes up a being's goodness is, first of all, its nature and all the ontological determinations that complete the nature. Likewise, the goodness of a being is also brought about by the ontological determinations not yet possessed but to be possessed, and in the final analysis, it is brought about by the End [sic], the ultimate perfection of this being. However, these ontological determinations to be possessed are already the given being's good from the moment that it is oriented toward them by love, that is, from the moment that it is affectively united to them. And, in spiritual beings, it is not only a question of ontological determinations to be possessed, but also and above all of other spiritual beings with whom one enters into communion, by a spiritual extension of one's own being. This spiritual self-extension is analogous to what is obtained through intellectual activity, though in an utterly different manner, for such spiritual existence is communion in the good. Here, we have two beings who are one in the order of good because their good is common, pursued in common so as to be possessed in common.

In the order of natural appetition, an ontological determination does not need to become the good of the desiring being. It is naturally the good of the desiring being by the fact that it is ontologically its natural complement. This means that the desiring being is by nature, by its ontological constitution, proportioned and adapted to it. This is not the case in advance for an elicited appetite, above all for a voluntary appetite. Nevertheless, love can be elicited only if this proportioning, this *coaptatio*, exists, for without it, the beloved being would be foreign to the lover, wholly unrelated to it in the order of the good. It becomes its good by being loved by it. Therefore, this *coaptatio* is produced in the lover in virtue of this love. This is the production of the beloved in the intimate depths of the lover, a production that is necessarily included in the act of loving.

This makes clear the radical difference between the mental concept and the "reality produced by love." The latter does not stand

at the terminus of the act of love, as the concept stands at the terminus of the act of understanding.* Instead, it stands *at its beginning* [à
son principe]. And the "reality produced by love" is in it in the same
way that there is an intimate proportioning and orientation toward
the end found at the beginning of every movement. This is what is
meant when it is presented as being a "weight," a "vital motion," and
an "impulse."

Whereas, in relation to intellection, the speaking of the concept
is *a consequence* of intellection, in relation to love, the production of
this reality (namely, the production of the *impressio*) is something
antecedent. I can love this thing or this being only if I make it be
my good, and *to make it be my good* means, quite precisely, to vitally adapt myself to it by an act emanating from me, as every being is
naturally adapted to its natural good. This act emanating from me
is productive of something. It produces the beloved thing, not in its
existential reality, not in its own goodness, but rather, inasmuch as
it is good for me, the object of my love. However, if it is the object
of my love, I cannot fail to love it, just as no being can rid itself of its
natural inclination toward its own good. It is therefore impossible,
not only that love would occur without the production of this intimate reality, but even that it would be distinguished from it as one
act from another. The act of love is itself at once an affective union
with the beloved being and productive of this beloved being as the
object of love, though from two different perspectives.

And this explains well enough why so little is said about this production when the act of love is philosophically analyzed. Indeed,
on the one hand, in order to detect it, very attentive reflection is required, whereas the concept offers itself to consideration as soon
as one reflects on intellectual activity. On the other hand, it offers
very little interest philosophically, since what this reality does is the

---

* [Tr. note: That is, as the *terminus in quo*, in which the known is grasped. Though
the distinction between the *species impressa intelligibilis* (*principium quo*) and the *species
expressa intelligibilis* (*terminus in quo*) is clearer in later Thomists, the claim that the concept or "expressed species" is the terminus *in quo* of intellection can be found, for example, in texts like *De potentia*, q. 9, a. 5c.]

same as what love does, though thanks to it. This is why, as St. Thomas himself noted (*ST* I, q. 37, a. 1), all the names that are used for designating it, as well as the very word "love," touch on the act of love. Hence, only one further step needs to be taken for one to say that it is purely and simply identical with the act of love, a step that Penido took all too quickly. However, upon more attentive reflection, it is clear that the one is distinct from the other, not as another act, but as a distinct and irreducible aspect of love itself. And the result of this production is an *operatum* that is really distinct from the agent [*opérant*], the lover, all the while remaining perfectly immanent within him. Let us add a precision: this *operatum* that is the *principle* of the act of love inasmuch as the latter is an affective union with the beloved is the *terminus* of the same act of love inasmuch as it is productive.[46]

B. The Immanent Procession in the Act of Love in God

{77} If it is true that in our own psychology the act of love involves, in the depths of the lover, the production of a reality that is the beloved being affectively present, we can thus understand how the Holy Spirit in God can be conceived of as being the fruit of the act of love.

1. The Mystery of the Second Procession

{78} Indeed, God loves Himself perfectly, just as He knows Himself perfectly. In knowing Himself He "produces," within His intimate depths, another self, God as known. Recall, however, an identity exists between God knowing and God known. That is, the knowing "*Being God*" is distinct from the known "*Being God*" only in the fact that the one proceeds from the other. Now, similarly, in loving Himself He produces, in His intimate depths, God as loved, again, identical with regard to the Godhead, the distinction existing

---

46. For a greater development of this analysis of the act of love, see Nicolas, "Amour de soi, amour de Dieu, amour des autres," 5–42.

only between the *beloved "Being God"* and the *loving "Being God."*
The mystery is the same as what we saw in the case of the first
procession. Given that God beloved is ontologically present (with a
perfect presence of identity) to God loving, it is impossible to see *a
priori* why the act of love must necessarily produce its object. Nonetheless, this necessity exists, for everything that is in God is necessary, with the absolute necessity of His Being. We know this necessity *a posteriori* by the revelation of the second procession. And, just
as the production of the intelligible word in us enabled us to detect
a singular fecundity in the intellect, a fecundity that is not thence-
forth impossible to affirm of God, so too the analysis of our act of
love has detected another fecundity in it, which we transpose to God
in the same way.

Nevertheless, an additional difficulty comes from the fact that
although Scripture itself, as well as early tradition, invited us to look
into our intellectual life for the analogy that could provide us with
a kind of entrance into the mystery of the first procession, it is only
later, with St. Augustine, that there arose this idea of looking into
our act of love in order to find the created analogy for the second
procession.

Still, there is a verse of Scripture that unquestionably establishes
the connection between the Holy Spirit and God's love: "God's love
[for us?][47] has been poured into our hearts through the Holy Spirit
which has been given to us."[48] Likewise, we must add the way our filial spirit is connected to the Holy Spirit: "For you did not receive the
spirit of slavery to fall back into fear, but you have received the spirit
of sonship. When we cry, 'Abba! Father!'"[49] As regards the primitive
tradition, no one disputes that it connected the believer's sanctification to the Holy Spirit, which again shows His intimate connection with love. Therefore, one cannot purely and simply say that the
idea of explaining the second procession by the intimate emanation

47. See *Traduction Oecuménique de la Bible, in loco,* note e.
48. Rom 5:5 (RSV).
49. Rom 8:15 (RSV). See also 1 Jn 3:24; 4:2, 13.

proper to love is an Augustinian invention. Yes, it is an invention in that it seeks the analogy apt for helping us know something about the second procession by turning to our experience of the act of love. However, Scripture and tradition pointed in the direction of the path to be taken by theological reflection.

On the other hand, this very reflection, by itself, could verify its own worth. Every spiritual being has these two, intimately connected activities, namely, intellection and love. The disjunction that we notice between the two (i.e., the fact that one can know a being without loving it and conversely that one can love a being more and differently than how it is known) comes from the limits of intellection and love as they are found in us. In Pure Act, there is perfect coincidence between the object of intellection and the object of love. God is infinitely loveable for God, and He knows Himself to be infinitely loveable. Hence, there cannot be any doubt that, in God, the act of love of itself immediately follows on His perfect self-knowledge. (Of course, this consecutive character of love in relation to self-knowledge belongs to our manner of conceiving, for in reality, love is identical to self-knowledge in the transcendence of Pure Act.) Given that this self-knowledge is expressed in the procession of the Word, one can think (since revelation assures us that there is a second procession) that self-love is also expressed in the procession proper to love, according to which the beloved exists in the lover (in himself) in a new way.

2. Consubstantiality

{79} Inasmuch as the divine love is an immanent activity consisting in affective union with the beloved being, it is totally identical with the lover when it is realized in Him who is Pure Act. From this perspective, this cannot be the reason for a real distinction. Love is an essential attribute. However, inasmuch as it is the production of a terminus, it requires the distinction between the productive principle and the terminus produced, as we already saw in the case of the Word. But this distinction exists without any diversity, for this terminus is the beloved being inasmuch as it is present affectively and operatively. Now, God loves Himself totally. By His essence, He is wholly present to Himself. Therefore, no other distinction will remain, other than that of the produced terminus and the productive principle. It is not an affective substitute for the Divine Nature. The Divine Nature itself is what constitutes this terminus, as it constitutes its principle. And as the Divine Nature subsists by itself, this terminus in which the unique nature is realized must be one "Being God" and must be distinguished from His principle as one divine subject is [distinct] from another divine subject in the identity of the same nature possessed in common.

3. The Naturality of the Second Procession

Like the first procession, the second is *secundum naturam*. If its principle is indeed the will, it is the will inasmuch as it is identical with the Divine Nature.[50]

{80} From what we have said, it follows that what is communicated in this procession is the very nature of God, His Life.

Whence, the question arises: how is this communication not a kind of generation? This is a question that the Church Fathers already encountered in their own era. In response, they held forth this certitude of faith: the Son is the Only-begotten. We have seen that this was also a certitude established by theological reasoning.[51]

St. Augustine encountered this problem and did not find the solution for it.[52] He too ultimately relies on faith in it. St. Thomas gives the following reason for it.[53] If, in fact, on account of the conditions proper to the Divine Love (i.e., the identity of the beloved and the lover), this procession is, like the first procession, a vital communication of the living nature, it remains the case that, of itself, the *impressio rei amatae in amante* is not the likeness and image of the beloved

---

50. See *ST* I, q. 41, a. 2, ad. 3.
51. See §67 above.
52. See Augustine, *La Trinité*, XV, XXVII, no. 50.
53. See *ST* I, q. 27, a. 4.

being. Therefore, this procession is not, of itself, productive of a likeness, of an image. It is something other than generation.

In God alone, beyond everything that we can conceive, we find this other manner of communicating Life, a superabundant manifestation of the divine fecundity, more distant still from our conceptions because it has no equivalent in our experience:

> It is because of the imperfection of the created will that the nature of the lover cannot communicate itself, for what proceeds by the mode of the will, namely love (meaning, here, a terminus produced by the act of love), is not a subsistent hypostasis, as is the case in the Godhead. It is therefore on account of the perfection proper to the Divine Nature that it is communicated not only through an act of nature, but also through an act of will, which is the adherence of love.[54]

In this language, we see the classical dichotomy which St. Thomas had to abandon later on: *per modum naturae, per modum voluntatis.*[55] According to the terminology used in the *Summa theologiae,* which is certainly better than that found in the *Scriptum,* one should say: "It is on account of the perfection of the Divine Nature that it is communicated both by way of intellection and by way of willing."

We have seen that, in order to approach the mystery of the first procession, we made use of two complementary analogies alternatively: generation and intelligible emanation. The equivalent of the first analogy is not available to help us reach the second. How are we to replace it? The analogy between love's emanation and intelligible emanation can lead us to pursue the analogy of the love's emanation up to the point where, at infinity, it is a communication of the Divine Nature to a distinct "Being God." In order to affirm this, our only experiential support is found by reflecting on generation, this latter being considered, through a final effort of purification, solely as a transmission of the living nature to a distinct living being, without taking into consideration what is specific to generation, namely the projection of another self vis-à-vis one's own self.

54. *In* I *Sent.,* d. 13, q. 1, a. 2, ad. 2.
55. See §69 above.

C. Exclusion of Every Other Procession

Scripture only speaks about two processions in God, and this would be a sufficient reason for not seeking out another. However, the necessity for this exclusion can also be explained through theological reasoning.

1. No Other Immanent Procession Is Conceivable

{81} As we have seen, the divine processions can only be situated in the order of immanent activities [*opérations*]. Perhaps, it will be said, one could try to imagine in God an activity that would be neither transitive nor immanent. However, this is purely fantastical and meaningless. No conceivable middle can be found between the two types of activity. If an activity exists, it is indeed necessary that the typical *actualization* in which activity consists have either the patient or the agent itself as the subject of that activity, for it is unintelligible to speak of actualization without any subject being actualized. If this subject is external to the agent, it can only be that upon which its action is exercised, the patient, and in this case, the activity "passes" (*transit*) from the agent to the patient. If this subject is the agent itself, we have a case of immanent activity in its most general sense, by which the agent gives to itself a "super-existence," by which it "is" (or "becomes") its object. Immanent activity is *unitive* by its very nature, for it consists in operatively "being" its object, not in "making" its object.

We know of two kinds of immanent activity: *intellection* and *love*. Here, we exclude sensation as a form of immanent activity, since it cannot be transposed to God, given that it includes, in its very nature, bodily action and passion.

Can we conceive of another kind of pure immanent activity?[56] Let us note first of all that we could not conceive of it on the basis of any data drawn from our experience.

However, we must go further. On the basis of the data drawn

---

56. "Pure": namely, without any exteriority, purely interior to the agent. See *SCG*, bk. 4, ch. 11.

from our experience, we can affirm that no other pure immanent activity is possible.

Indeed, a totally immanent activity is a purely spiritual activity. *Spirit* is obviously the superior form of *being*, and to say that God is the Perfect Being is the same thing as saying that He is Perfect Spirit. In other words, it is as absurd to say that God could be something superior to spirit as it would be to say that He could be something superior to being and other.

Now, *intellection* and *love* adequately divide the notion of spiritual activity. Indeed, spiritual activity is that which has being in all its universality as its object. There are two ways (and only two) by which being in all its universality can be an object. On the one hand, it can be an object *according to essence*. In that case, it is a question of an activity that consists in the agent [*opérant*] drawing the being to it, into it. On the other hand, there is an activity consisting in the agent [*agent*] going toward the being, tending toward it. In other words, our only two options are intellection and love.

Indeed, among all the actions and activities that Scripture attributes to God, only intellection and love are (analogically) transposable to God. Indeed, all the others (anger, sadness, regret, desire, and so forth) include a bodily datum in their very notion, which prevents us from giving them anything more than a metaphorical meaning (which does not at all mean that they would be meaningless).[57] For its part, the attribute of "power" (creative, governing, and redeeming efficacy) can only be understood as being an aspect of intellection and of love.[58]

2. The Trinitarian Circle

{82} A master insight of St. Thomas's pneumatology is that spiritual activities [*opérations*] constitute a circle. By the intellect, the mind draws things into its immanence by stripping them of their existentiality. By love, it goes back to them in their reality.

57. See Nicolas, *Dieu connue comme inconnu*, 161–69 and 245–50.
58. See *ST* I, q. 20, aa. 1 and 2; q. 25, aa. 1 and 2.

However, this circle is clearer in self-knowledge and self-love, for this movement of flow and re-flow happens within the being itself.

Finally, the circle is perfect in God, where Essence, Idea, and Good are rigorously identical, and where, nevertheless, the revelation of the Trinitarian mystery enables us to know that, in the immobility of Pure Act, there is this flow and re-flow of knowledge and love: "When someone knows himself and loves himself, he is present to himself not only by a real identity, but also as the known is present to the knower and as the beloved is present to the lover."[59] That is, he is present by intentional identity, according to a twofold intentionality, that of knowledge and that of love:

Both in God and in us, there is a circularity in the activities of the intellect and the will, for the will comes back to what was the point of departure of intellection (the thing in its existential reality). The difference is that, in us, the circle is closed on what is external to us, since the good acts on the intellect (that knows it), and the intellect acts on the will (by presenting it with the good that provokes it to will). Thus, the will is borne by desire and love toward the good, which is external to the (knowing and willing) subject. By contrast, in God, the circle is closed within the intimate depths of Himself. (It is perfect interiority.) For, in knowing Himself, God conceives His Word in the intimate depths of Himself, and the Word is equally the Idea by which He knows all that He knows, since it is in knowing Himself that He knows all things. And it is from this conception of the Word that He proceeds to the love of all things and of Himself ... After that, this circle is closed, and nothing can be added, so that there cannot be a third procession in the immanence of the Divine Nature. There can only be the procession of creatures outside of God.[60]

This opens up another path for us to approach the mystery, namely, that of *self-presence*. By infinitely knowing and loving Himself through a perfectly simple act, God is present to Himself in three ways: as being, as thought, and as loved. This infinitely real, threefold presence is realized in three hypostases, each of whom is the One God, without there being anything really distinct between them. We will need to ask ourselves how this distinction is intelligible.

59. *ST* I, q. 37, a. 1.
60. *De pot.*, q. 9, a. 9.

IV. "ESSENTIAL" ACTS AND "NOTIONAL" ACTS

{83} When theology loses sight of this scriptural connexion (that is: the relation of the intra-divine processions to man inasmuch as the Three Persons reveal themselves in a personal communication), the Augustinian speculation on the Trinity is inevitably brought up against the well-known difficulty which always seems to render futile this marvelously profound type of speculation. One begins with a concept of knowledge and love taken from natural philosophy and uses it to develop a notion of the word and of the "weight" of love; but after applying these speculative concepts to the Trinity one has to admit that they do not work: for the good reason that knowledge and love remain 'essential' concepts. One cannot and may not evolve a "personal," "notional" concept of the word and of the weight of love on the basis of human experience. For then the Word of knowledge and the Spirit of love would demand that a Word and a Spirit should proceed from them, again as persons.[61]

This difficulty is redoubtable and calls for examination. It can be summarized as follows. The Divine Intellection and His Love are identical with the substance of God and therefore are common to the "Three Being God." If our reasoning on this matter is correct (namely, "Whoever knows speaks a word.... Whoever loves produces in himself a presence of the beloved being"), how does it not apply to the Word and the Spirit, leading to an indefinite series of emanations of other Words and Spirits in God?

First, let us note that the remedy proposed by Rahner is hardly efficacious. In what way does the consideration of the "economic" manifestation of the Divine Intellection and of His Love provide me with illumination regarding the intra-divine processions? First of all, who can say with certitude that he has the "experience" of such a manifestation and that this experience is concerned with the "Three Distinct Ones Being God" [*trois Étant Dieu distincts*] and not only

61. Rahner, "Quelques remarques sur le traité dogmatique 'De Trinitate,'" in *Écrits théologiques* VIII (Paris: Desclée de Brouwer, 1967), 118. [Tr. note: Taken from Rahner, *Theological Investigations*, vol. 4, 86.]

with [the One] God? Mystical experience, even in its loftiest manifestations, could not provide this assurance if it were not itself illuminated and instructed by the word of revelation. This Word does not resolve the problem of the "Three Being God" at all. Instead, it raises it for reason.

Thus, if the difficulty in question (presented, in fact, as an impossibility) were truly "inevitable," we would not need to speak about the "marvelous profundity" of Augustinian speculation but, rather, we would need to reject it. And what other explanation has been proposed up to now?

The difficulty is not "inevitable," even though it is redoubtable, requiring careful and close attention in order to be resolved. (St. Thomas expressly considered it.)[62]

The Divine Intellection is an infinitely simple act which is identical with the Divine Substance. However, in its infinite simplicity, it includes a "saying," which brings with it a real distinction between the "sayer" and the "said," for one does not proceed from oneself. The "said" is identical with the sayer as regards the substance, and therefore as regards the intellect. The "said" is "God inasmuch as He is known." However, in God, at the summit of actuality, there is complete identity between "God known" and "God knowing," the Divine Essence being at once the Subsistent Intelligible (Subsistent Idea) and Subsistent Being. Therefore, the distinction determined by the "saying" implied in the intellection is a distinction between the "Being God saying" the known and the "Being God said" by Him, not a distinction between the Godhead (i.e., the Divine Essence) known and the knowing Godhead:

As the Divine Intellect is not only always in act but indeed is Pure Act, it necessarily follows that the substance of the Divine Intellect is identical with intellection itself, which is the act of the intellect. As regards the being of the word interiorly conceived, what we have called the "intentio intellecta," the known thing inasmuch as it is present intentionally to the intellect, it is the *being known* of the thing. And therefore, the being of the

62. See *SCG*, bk. 2, ch. 26; *De pot.* q. 9, a. 9; *ST I*, q. 27, a. 5, ad. 3.

Divine Word is identical with that of the Divine Intellect and therefore with that of God since He is identical with His intellect.[63]

Therefore, if the diction is truly an action, identical with the divine intellection, the "being said" in no way expresses a "passion" that the Word "would undergo." And no more is this the case for "being spirated." In no way can we say that the Word and the Spirit are the effects of the Father. Their being is the Infinite Being, Pure Act, which the Father communicates to them without losing them. They hold it from Him. They do not receive it, for it is Unreceived Being.[64] How can we conceive this distinction of subsistents (of Beings) in this perfect identity of substance? We have already indicated that the most ancient tradition looked to resolve this question by means of the notion of relative opposition. We will need to elaborate this explanation later on.

What we said about intellection holds good for love. The essential love, identical with the Divine Substance, is common to the Three. However, it includes a "spiration" (corresponding to the "diction") which establishes a real distinction between the "Being God Spirating" and the "Being God Spirated," within the identical substance of the Godhead.

It is therefore false to say that the psychological theory would imply the impossible scenario that, in "understanding" and in "loving," the Word and the Spirit would, in their own turn, need to "speak a word," which would be a Divine Person, and "spirate a spirit," which would itself also be a Divine Person and so forth *ad infinitum*. For the divine "intellection" is perfectly one, as is the "love" as well. Therefore, the "diction" and "spiration" which are identical with the intellection and love are "one." That is, at the heart of the identical intellection and the unique love in God, the diction distinguishes the "speaker" and the "spoken," and the "spiration" distinguishes the "spirating" and the "spirated." Thus, only the first "Being God" is "the say-

63. See *SCG*, bk. 4, ch. 11.
64. See *ST* I, q. 27, a. 2, ad. 3.

er," the second is "said," the first and the second together (we will see why) are the "spirating," and the third is the "spirated." All of this is so without us needing to imagine a second, then a third, etc., diction or spiration, the saying of which would be the Word and the Spirit, etc.

There is another question to be faced. What are we referring to when we say, "In knowing Himself, God produces a Word"? If we say, as Rahner wishes, that we are referring to the first "Being God," we will find ourselves engaged in inextricable difficulties, for the divine intellection is common to the Three. But if we say that it is the Trinity, there is another difficulty, for only the first of the Three "says the Word." The solution can only be found by shifting the *suppositio* of the term "God."[65] In the first phrase ("God in knowing Himself"), "God" designates the personal, subsistent God, that is, in fact, the three "Being God" taken together, for at this moment of reason's reflection, we do not yet know whether God is Tri-Personal. The second phrase ("produces a Word") marks the next step. God (implied) then designates the first "Being God," who appears as distinct only as the principle of the Word, who also is God. This could be expressed more clearly by saying that the Divine Intellection includes a "diction" that distinguishes a "Being God" saying from a "Being God" said, the intellection itself being common to the two. And the same holds for spiration. We will see, however, in due time, that spiration appears only at the end of a third step, following on the second and presupposing it (and, consequently, presupposing the distinction of the first two "Being God").

V. CONCLUSION OF THE CHAPTER

{84} A key idea in this theology of the processions is that of "fecundity." The Divine Nature is fruitful, although God cannot be "made." In other words, the revealed mystery of the processions opens up before us the perspective of a wholly interior fecundity.

---

65. In Aristotelico-Thomist logic, one calls "supposition" the relation of the uttered word to the reality that, in the proposition where this word is used, it designates.

Thus, we come to see that this marvelous fecundity is the infinite realization of the Good's property of being self-diffusive. On the one hand, it would seem that this property must be excluded in the case of God, since, in our experience, it occurs only by means of efficient causality. The good diffuses itself by provoking the agent to act—"the causality of the end consists in being loved and desired"[66]—and by communicating to the patient the good that is in it, in virtue of this principle:

It is better that the good conferred to a being be common to many rather than belonging exclusively to it, for (as Aristotle says) a good common to many is always "more divine" ([i.e.,] of a superior worth) than the good proper to one alone. But it is by passing from itself to others that the good conferred on one alone becomes common to many, and this can be so only if the good communicates its goodness to others by its own, proper action.[67]

Now, while God communicates something of His goodness to creatures (and, here, the principle of the diffusivity of the good has its role to play, although with the qualification we here have a wholly free communication, so that God is infinitely good, independent of creation, whether or not it exists), the Infinite Goodness is incommunicable in what is proper to it, for it cannot be caused, and causality is the means by which a good being communicates its goodness. On the other hand, how can we admit that this property (namely, "to be self-diffusive"), which most certainly is rooted in the formal notion of the good, is not found in the transcendent realization of this "notion," indeed to an infinite degree (i.e., to such a degree that the "Being God," in whom the Infinite Goodness of the Godhead subsists, would communicate it to other Beings, who will be, in turn, "Those Being God")? But how would they be so if their goodness were caused, if it depended on another for it to be or not be granted to them and if, for this reason, it was contingent (and, hence, limited) in them?

66. *De ver.*, q. 22, a. 2.
67. *SCG*, bk. 3, ch. 69.

Here, we find ourselves faced with an *aporia*. Someone like Richard of St. Victor freed himself a little too quickly from it by finding the "necessary reasons" for the Trinitarian mystery in God's infinite love (another name for the diffusivity of the Infinite Good).[68] St. Thomas objects against this Victorine interpretation precisely that we cannot hold that there is an *a priori* necessity requiring the Infinite Good to communicate Itself in Its Infinity.[69] Actually, on the contrary, this seems impossible at first sight.

The revelation of the Trinitarian mystery brings believing reason the solution to this *aporia*. By itself alone, reason indeed had been unable to find it, and it fulfills reason's expectations only by first disconcerting it. It makes known to us the communications of the Infinite Good at the intimate depths of the Godhead. They are real communications, for He who communicates is different from Him to whom the communication is made. Moreover, they are infinite communications, for the Good communicated to the other is the undivided, undiminished Godhead Itself, identical in Him who communicates and in Those to whom it is communicated.

Nonetheless, some have argued that St. Thomas did not use the principle *bonum diffusum sui* in Trinitarian theology.[70] More exactly, some claim that he made use of it in the first part of his career (principally in the *De potentia*), abandoning this outlook later on.[71]

Without entering into the difficult question about how the *Summa theologiae*'s treatise [on God] compares with St. Thomas's discussion in the *De potentia*, we must note that such a claim must be nuanced. It is certain that St. Thomas does not seem to utilize the principle of the diffusivity of the good in the *Summa theologiae*. Given that it was standard fare for theologians in his day to make use of it (under the influence of [Ps.-]Dionysius) and given that he himself

---

68. See Richard of St. Victor, *La Trinté*, III, 2–6; Gaston Salet, "Introduction," *Richard de Saint-Victor, La Trinité* SC 63 (Paris: Cerf, 1959), 37–45.

69. See *ST* I, q. 32, a. 1, ad. 2.

70. See Paul Vanier, *Théologie trinitaire chez saint Thomas d'Aquin. L'acte notionnel selon Saint Thomas* (Paris: Vrin, 1952).

71. See *De pot.*, q. 2, a. 1.

utilizes it in his earlier works, this omission cannot be unintentional. However, in the *Summa theologiae* he constantly appeals to the notion of the "communication of the Divine Nature,"[72] and this expresses the same idea: one's own good is enhanced when it is made common to many.

It is possible that St. Thomas feared that the evocation of the principle of the diffusivity of the good might suggest that this communication of the Divine Nature occurs by way of efficient causality. Or, indeed, perhaps he feared that it would give the impression that one could demonstrate the Trinitarian mystery *a priori* by means of this principle (as Richard of St. Victor seems to have done).

In any case, what we have seen up to this point is related to the ontological communication of the Divine Nature and, hence, can give the impression of a purely natural communication. Later on, we will see that this ontological communication provides the foundation for an interpersonal communication, a "communion." Moreover, we will see that they are, in reality, identical, for in God the "natural" and the "personal" are identical. However, the personal communication would be unintelligible without the ontological communication, for nothing can dispense us from asking ourselves, "How do these Persons who marvelously inter-communicate exist, and do They exist distinctly?

72. See *ST* I, q. 27, a. 2, ad. 3; q. 30, a. 2, ad. 4; q. 34, a. 2; q. 41, a. 3 and a. 4, ad. 3.

5

The Distinction of the Three
Who Are One God

{85} The study of the divine processions leads to a paradox. On the one hand, each of Those "Being God" proceeding from another is really distinct from that other, for it is a contradiction in terms to say that one proceeds from oneself. On the other hand, each is consubstantial with the other two. That is, they are not distinct from the others according to substance. Therefore, they seemingly cannot be distinguished. It is as though consubstantiality were implied by the divine procession and simultaneously abolished by it.

Clearly, this antinomy would seem to be insurmountable for reason alone. That is, a purely rational study of the possibility of transferring the notion of immanent procession to God would end in failure, for such a transposition would seem to involve an impossibility, thus destroying itself. If reason persists in attempting to resolve this antinomy, it does so because the antinomy is imposed on it by faith. There are real processions in God. There are Those "Being God" at the terminus of these processions, which are simultaneously consubstantial and yet really distinct from each other.

We have seen that from the beginning of theological investigations into this issue, there was an orientation toward holding that "relation" provides the key to this antinomy.[1] It gradually became clear that this notion was indispensable for articulating the Catholic faith against the deviations of heresy, and it entered into dogmatic formulation in the form that St. Anselm[2] had given to the elucidation provided by St. Augustine, who on this point prolonged the reflections of the Cappadocians and their predecessors: "*In Deo omnia sunt unum ubi non obviat relationis oppositio.*"[3]

We must first rationally justify this necessity: why can the distinction of Those "Being God" only be relative? Then, we must see how the aforementioned antinomy can be resolved by means of the notion of relative distinction.

I. THE DISTINCTION
OF THREE "BEING GOD" CAN
ONLY BE RELATIVE

We must first see how beings (*entia*) are distinguished from each other in general. In other words, what makes two beings distinct?

A. The Metaphysical Problem of
the Distinction of Beings

{86} The distinction of beings, as such, consists in alterity. The one is not the other and for this reason cannot be combined in the same realization. They are numbered. [*Ils font nombre.*]

A first form of the distinction of beings which is immediately present in our experience consists in spatial non-coincidence, the fact that two beings are mutually external to one another. It is obvious that, of itself, this alterity comes solely from matter, even if spatial alterity most often masks a more profound alterity arising from form. In any case, given that God is purely spiritual, spatial alterity

1. See §46 above.
2. See St. Anselm, *De processione Spiritus Sancti*, PL 158, ch. 1.
3. See §52 above.

quite clearly cannot provide us with any assistance for discovering the nature of the alterity existing among those "Being God."

Another form of distinction is that which is found between different parts of a being: between form and matter, between a body's various members, etc. Such a distinction is real, in the sense that these parts, in the whole in which they are realized, cannot coincide with each other: one is not the other. However, it is not a distinction between two beings since it involves the parts of a single being. In any case, this distinction still cannot be of use for distinguishing Those "Being God," for God is infinitely simple. He does not have parts. The whole divinity must be affirmed of Each One "Being God."

Another form of distinction is that which the intellect establishes between two aspects of a given reality. This is a so-called conceptual distinction. It is said to be "conceptual" because it is the distinction between two or more concepts, all in relation to the same reality, considered from various perspectives—for example, the distinction between rationality and animality in man. The human mind must establish these distinctions because it cannot grasp the entire intelligibility of an object in a single concept. However, through the act of judgment it retrieves the unity of being that it had thus divided ideally. Such distinctions are certainly found in our knowledge of God. The Divine Reality is something absolutely simple, but we can only attain It by means of a multitude of concepts (e.g., immensity, eternity, goodness, intellectuality, love, freedom, and so forth) that partially and deficiently express what the Divine Reality is in Itself. However, can they be of use for helping us to explain the distinction of the Three "Being God"?

It is crucial to see that, in what concerns those "Being God," recourse to a merely conceptual distinction is vain. This is the temptation to which Abelard seems to have yielded. According to him, the Three "Being God" designate three concepts which revelation uses for describing the perfection of the Sovereign Good. What is thus revealed to us are the three properties of the Sovereign Good:

power, wisdom, and benevolence.[4] According to such an outlook, which in fact merely represents a resurgence of Sabellianism (an unconscious resurgence, no doubt), the Father, Son, and Spirit whom Scripture designates for us and describes for us (through their activity) as three really distinct Beings (though together constituting the One God) would only be three aspects of the Godhead, distinct from each other only by human reason. However, it is not clear why, from this outlook, these three divine attributes would be "hypostases." In any case, the Trinitarian dogma affirms the real distinction of the Three "Being God" *in God Himself* and not only in the manifestations of God in this world, nor in our mind. The Father is *another* "Being God" than the Son and the Spirit; the Son is another "Being God" than the Holy Spirit.

To try to render account of these data of faith, we therefore must ask, "What does alterity consist in? Whence does it come about that two or more beings are different, each in relation to the others?"

B. The Notion of Opposition

{87} Alterity (and the multiplicity that it begets) is reduced to opposition.[5] Opposition is found between two beings every time the concept of one excludes the other: "*Opposita sunt quorum unum de sui ratione habet negationem alterius.*"[6] Indeed, in a realist conception of knowledge, the concept expresses what the thing is. The opposed concept, being excluded by the first, expresses what this same subject is not and, therefore, expresses that it is *other and really distinct* from the subject to which this opposed concept can be attributed: "In whatever form they take, opposites have this in common, namely, that it is impossible for them to exist together in the same being."[7] On the other hand, there is no opposition (and, therefore, neither is there necessarily alterity of subject) if one of the concepts only abstracts

---

4. See Hyacinthe-François Dondaine, "Notes doctrinales thomistes," in *Saint Thomas d'Aquin. Somme théologique, La Trinité*, vol. 2 (Paris: Cerf, [1946]), 411–12.

5. Aristotle, *Metaphysics*, A, 4; Δ, 10; *In V Meta.*, 12 and *In X Meta.*, 6.

6. *In X Meta.*, no. 2041.

7. *In X Meta.*, no. 2041.

from the other. For example, there is neither opposition, nor necessary alterity, between rational being and animal being. These two characteristics can be found in the same being or subject (e.g., man) or in separate beings (e.g., man and beast). When they are separate, alterity does not arise from opposition between these two concepts but, rather, from the opposition between two other concepts that are incompatible with each other, namely rationality and irrationality. This observation is of great importance for explaining how the divine attributes, whose concepts are opposed in creatures, are realized in God in a unique perfection. Thus, the concept of *potential intellect* is opposed to that of *potential will* so that they can only be realized as distinct parts of a single person. In contrast, the concept of *intellect as such* is not opposed to that of *will as such*, and thus it is conceivable (only in God, in Pure Act) that intellect and will are identical.

Consequently, in order to discover how and why two beings are really distinct, I must look into how and why one's concept expresses not only what the subject to which it is related is but also what it is not, that is, precisely what the concept of the other expresses.

C. The Four Kinds of Opposition

{88} The fundamental opposition, that which is grasped in the same intuition by which being is grasped, is contradiction. The positing of a being bears with it, immediately, the exclusion of its negation. For example, *homo* immediately excludes *non-homo*.

Here, recall that the ontological and the conceptual coincide at this level of the intuition of being. The principle of non-contradiction (i.e., I cannot affirm and deny simultaneously, from the same perspective, the same predicate of the same subject) is only the logical face, turned toward the intra-mental, of the principle of identity (i.e., every being is what it is), which, itself, is turned toward the extra-mental.

If there are many kinds of opposition, this is because the principle of non-contradiction can be at play on different ontological and conceptual levels.

At the level of being itself, it is *pure contradiction*. The contradictory concept does not have its own proper content. It is a pure and simple exclusion of the content of the opposed concept. It says nothing about what the other subject is. Rather, it only designates that every subject to which it applies is necessarily distinct from the subject to which the first applies. Every subject that I can truly call a *non-man* is necessarily distinct from every subject that I can truly call a *man*. This is an immediate judgment, an intellectual intuition.

If we now fix our consideration on a particular being, supposing that two concepts can be applied to it, contradiction will occur in an attenuated manner if one of the two concepts expresses a quality or form that this subject can have, while the other concept expresses the negation of this quality. Such is the case for the concepts of *seeing* and *blind*, each in relation to an animal capable of seeing. This is *privative opposition*. It only occurs in relation to a determined being and does so with regard to its goodness. A hump upon the back is something positive, but nobody will say that its absence in a man is a privation! For a man, "to be a hunchback" is a privation, the privation of his normal physical structure, even if, from the perspective of being, this privation arises from an addition ... an excess.

Next, we can consider two beings that are distinct with regard to their essence—and here we are faced with the metaphysical problem of the plurality of beings. In this case, the concept expressing one of these essences excludes the concept expressing the other essence. This is *contrariety*.

How does this come about? Two distinct essences can indeed have common elements. Such is the case for generic elements. Thus, man and animal have animality in common. But the determining, characteristic element (i.e., the specific difference) is proper to each. The presence of the one excludes the presence of the other in virtue of the principle of contradiction. Man's characteristic way of being an animal (i.e., rationality) is distinct, not only from the characteristic way in which animality is realized in different species, but also from what all animals have in common. We designate this by a negation, which makes the intervention of the contradiction obvious here: irrationality.

Thus, even though the opposition of contrariety is found between concepts expressing the positive intelligible content of two beings, it also is itself reduced to the opposition of contradiction. This is the case because the distinction of beings and their plurality is drawn from within the fundamental unity of being. Each essence is a partial realization of being, lacking the value of being that is also realized in other beings, though enclosed there, in the others, within other limits. All these beings are distinguished from each other by the different and graduated manner in which the unique value of being is limited in each one. Hence, it is impossible for two essences to be at the same level of ontological perfection, for in that case, they would be confused with each other. Essences are like numbers, said Aristotle. As a given number is unique and necessarily larger than those that come before it and smaller than all those that come after it, so too an essence is ontologically more perfect than those that are before it and less perfect than those that come after it. Therefore, a privation is found at the heart of contrariety, which, as we have seen, includes a contradiction.

In these three kinds of opposition, contradiction has played such a role that each given concept included at least the partial negation of the other (or of the others), which is the very definition of opposition. Moreover, contradiction is present because one of the subjects to which the opposed concepts are respectively related involves a positive ontological value that the other does not have: the negation, which belongs to the intra-mental order, has a corresponding an ontological deficiency [*manque*] in reality.

A fourth kind of opposition exists, and it does not imply this ontological deficiency. In this opposition, one concept includes the negation of another, without the subjects to which these two are related necessarily lacking [*manque*] what the other has. This kind of opposition is *relative opposition*.

Relation is a mode of being that qualifies a being, its subject, not in itself, but in relation to another. It is expressed (in an obviously descriptive manner since it is a first genus, which therefore cannot be defined) as *pros ti, ad aliquid,* "toward something." Thus, *in its very definition,* it implies a distinction between the two termini: the subject referred and the terminus to which it is referred. Here again we find contradiction. It would be contradictory for the referred subject to be identical with the terminus to which it is referred. However, of itself, the relative concept expressing the subject inasmuch as it is referred does not indicate that the referred termini are each this or that—*this* involving the negation of *that.* Instead, it only indicates that the one is not the other.[8]

D. Only Relative Opposition
Can Respect the Consubstantiality
of Those "Being God"

{89} This conclusion clearly springs from the very analysis of the four kinds of opposition.

First, if, as we have seen, the first three kinds of opposition imply ontological inequality between the opposed beings—so that B is other than A only by being ontologically inferior to it—they can in no way serve to explain the alterity of those "Being God," each in relation to the others, since each of these is God like the other two. Together, they are the same God, Infinite Being. Every gradation is obviously excluded. One can easily show that each of these three kinds of opposition is inapplicable to Those "Being God."

This is not the case for the fourth kind of opposition, which implies no ontological inequality.

This can also be shown by considering consubstantiality in itself (and no longer in its consequence, namely, ontological equality). Indeed, in the three first kinds of opposition, each concept expresses *what* the subject to which it is applied is and *what* it is not, as well as what the subject whose alterity is thus manifested precisely is. The

8. See Aristotle, *Categories,* ch. 7; *Metaphysics,* Δ, ch. 15; *In* V *Meta.,* lect. 17; *ST* I, q. 13, a. 7; q. 20, aa. 1 and 2; *De pot.,* q. 8, a. 1.

alterity of subject (or of supposits) therefore appears as following on the alterity of essences that are realized in them. If S1 is other than S2, this is because the essence of one (expressed by concept A) is other than the essence of the other (expressed by concept B). Thus, these three kinds of opposition are incompatible with the consubstantiality of opposed subjects.

Of itself, relative opposition is not incompatible with the consubstantiality of the relative [subjects] since the relative concepts indicate nothing of their essence but rather, only indicate that the one is not the other. Therefore, if one can conceive of an alterity that would consist only in relative opposition, to the exclusion of every other kind of opposition, it could be realized at the heart of consubstantiality itself. This is precisely what we are looking for.

In any case, no other way is open to reflection on the mystery of the Three Consubstantial and Distinct Ones "Being God":

This distinction (of Three Being God) cannot be taken from what is absolute in them: for everything that is attributed to God absolutely (that is, as expressing the divine absolute) designates the Divine Essence, so that such an attribution (which would be concerned with one Divine Person to the exclusion of the others) would distinguish the Persons according to the Essence, which is Arius's heresy. Therefore, it remains that the distinction between the Divine Persons can only be taken from what is relative in them.[9]

On the other hand, Vladimir Lossky refuses to recognize that the distinction of the Three "Being God" is purely relative.[10] Thus, he speaks of "the initial antinomy of absolute identity and of the no less absolute diversity that exists in God." However, this would not be an antinomy. It would be a contradiction, and in order to accept it one cannot take refuge in faith. We believe with our reason, and contradiction is inassimilable for reason. Reason cannot accept the possibility of contradictories being simultaneously realized, as is in-

9. *De pot.*, q. 8, a. 1.
10. Vladimir Lossky, "La procession du Saint-Esprit dans la doctrine trinitaire orthodoxe," in *A l'image et à la resemblance de Dieu* (Paris: Aubier, 1967), 75–76.

dicated by the formula, "Three distinct absolutes together constituting a unique and infinitely simple Absolute."

II. RELATIVE OPPOSITION IN GOD

Therefore, to explain the distinction of Those "Being God," our only option is to call upon relative opposition. We must first examine what a pure opposition is or could be. Next, we must see how we can conceive that such an opposition is realized *in divinis*. Finally, we must see how its realization assures the distinction of those "Being God," who are consubstantial.

A. Pure Relative Opposition

1. Every Opposition Necessarily Comes To Its Completion in a Relative Opposition

{90} We have seen that opposition explains and expresses alterity. Now, in the end, alterity is a relation, for pure and simple diversity is inconceivable and impossible, just like pure multiplicity. However profoundly "other" two subjects could be, they have something in common: being. Therefore, they have a connection with one another, a relation: a relation of likeness that is more or less perfect but that will never arrive at identity. Therefore, in the end, alterity is a relation of likeness founded on what many beings have in common and at the same time on the proper form that this common characteristic takes on in each of these beings. In short, alterity only exists between two beings belonging to one and the same order and distinguished from each other within this order.[11]

11. N.B., One could object here concerning the creature's alterity in relation to God, which is the extreme case of alterity: God is the Wholly Other One. This is the reason why every relation of God to creatures is necessarily a rationate relation, a relation that is only conceptual. However, this does not mean that the alterity of the creature would be only conceptual. The creature is "other" in relation to God because its own essence and all its ontological perfections are a limited (and therefore partial) likeness of the infinite and simple Divine Perfection. It is therefore wholly ordered to God by a real relation (which, in the end, is what its dependence upon the Creator is) as to its Exemplar. If

A first observation follows from this, namely, that the first three kinds of opposition imply the fourth. Therefore, it cannot be ignored when referring to the other three. Conversely, *of itself*, relative opposition neither implies nor entails another opposition. Let us make an exception, however, for it does imply the opposition of contradiction in the sense that it would be contradictory for one of the correlatives to be identical to the other, since the alterity of the one in regard to the other is part of the definition of each. For example, it is contradictory for a father to be identical to the son of whom he is said to be the father. However, this is not a contradiction implying that one of the correlatives would be contradictory to the other and be its negation. Indeed, rather, each is a positive term.

2. In Our Experience, Every Relative Opposition Presupposes Another Opposition

{91} It is clear that, in our experience, relative beings are distinct from each other not only by their relative opposition but also by their substance as well. A father and a son are two distinct individuals, each having his own substance. If one can justly speak of a relation between the various members of a body, it is then a question of several substantial parts and therefore, practically speaking (for our present purposes), of several substances, even if, in reality, it is a single substance that is composed of several quantitatively distinct parts.

The reason for this is that "relative being" can be only an accidental mode. The referred subject cannot be constituted by the relation. It is what it is by what it is substantially and by its other absolute at-

---

God, on account of His transcendence, is the Wholly Other One in relation to the creature, it itself is not "wholly other" in relation to God.

One could also register an objection concerning the opposition of pure contradiction, for in that case, one of the terms is purely negative, whereas relation requires that the referred [subject] and the terminus to which it is referred are two beings. However, in response to this objection, one must say that contradiction is a distinct opposition only in the conceptual order. In the real order, where the alterity is situated, it is, rather, the principle of other oppositions. This being is "other" in relation to that other because it would be contradictory that they be identical.

tributes. It is only then and *in addition* that it has a relation to other beings. These latter themselves are equally what they are by their substance, and they are termini of the relation *in addition* [to being what they are by their substance]. (Moreover, they themselves are referred to the first by a co-relation, which doubles the first relation in the opposite direction.) Hence, the alterity that the relation brings with it affects the subject in its substance. Just as the substantial subject is what is referred by the relation, so too the substantial subject is what is other.

Nevertheless, the relation itself is not what determines the substantial alterity. It is determined in this way by another, presupposed opposition. If the father and the son are substantially distinct, this substantial distinction does not come from the fact that they are relative. Instead, it comes from the fact that they are "contrary" within the common essence, each having his own, concrete substance, with what is proper to the one (individual characteristics) excluding that which is proper to the other.

Conversely, the alterity characteristic of relative opposition is not replaced and abolished by this opposition from which substantial alterity arises, although it is masked by it. A father and a son are not distinguished only as individuals of the same species, but equally because, quite precisely, the one is the father of the other and because it is a contradiction in terms for one to be his own father or his own son. *Of themselves,* opposed relations distinguish relatives as such (i.e., as correlatives) and not the substances in which these relatives subsist. (Let us say, according to the terminology that is required in Trinitarian theology: they are distinct *inasmuch as they are hypostases,* not *according to ousia.*) If these substances are opposed and therefore distinct, this is not on account of the relations.

3. What a Pure Relative Opposition Would Be

{92} Thus, *ideally,* relative opposition could suffice for assuring alterity between two beings in the case wherein no other opposition would be found between them. But in this case, this alterity could not pertain to their substance. They would simultaneously be consubstantial and other.

But what would this require? It would require that the relative being, the *ad aliud*, not be an accidental mode super-added to a substantial being. What is referred would need to not be a distinct subject from the relation by which it is referred. Instead, *the relation would need to be its own subject*. Indeed, then the referred being would be the relation itself, no longer the substance. The relations themselves (since every relation calls for a co-relation) would be other [in relation to each other] because they would be opposed [to each other], though this would introduce no substantial alterity.

Such relations would be "subsistent" (as one says that in God, Goodness is subsistent, Understanding is subsistent, and so forth).

Is this conceivable?

B. Subsistent Relation

1. Relation and Subsistence

{93} Generally speaking, *to subsist is to be real*, to have existence in the extra-mental universe and not only in the intra-mental universe by means of a concept. As is well known, there are two manners of subsisting. On the one hand, something can subsist *in se*, by being the subject that exists, the supposit. This is what is proper to substance. On the other hand, something can subsist *in alio* by being the ontological determination of a subject, of a substance. This characterizes accidents. To ask oneself if a relation can subsist, and how it does (i.e., *in se* or *in alio*), is to look into whether it has a place in the real, extra-mental world.

a) Not Every Relation Is Real

{94} Factually speaking, relation at first comes to light as an act of mind rather than as a reality external to the mind. The intellect's activity consists in reconciling objects, in "comparing" them, in separating them, in brief, in putting them into relation with one another. (It is a wholly different affair to say that intellection would be this and this alone! No, all this immense rational work tends toward something else, namely, grasping what the thing is in its reality, by way of intentional identification. However, intellection indeed arrives at this end by creating relations among its objects.)

Nevertheless, most often relations are not deprived of objective consistency. The mind does not arbitrarily place its objects in such or such a relation with one another. The genus is encompassing in relation to the species, not the reverse. (A given species—even if one takes this term in its most general sense, as does the biologist in his classifications—is in one genus and not in another. Structuralism seeks out the relations which exist among the parts of the object that it considers and does not invent them.)

This objective consistency comes from the essence. By its essence, a thing is what it is, as it is and not otherwise. By its essence, it imposes itself on the intellect, and the intellect submits itself to it at the same moment that it dominates it, making it its own, making it enter into it.

Subsistence belongs to the order of existence. Consequently, to say that a relation can have objective consistency, an essence, without for all that belonging to the real world, is to say that it is, or can be, an essence without an existence, having being (and, if one wishes, reality) only in the mind, for the mind, and by the mind.

At first there is nothing unique in this fact. We can imagine things that exist only in our imagination. We conceive of objects that, at least in the purity that abstraction confers on them, do not exist—for example, a "mathematical entity," a "universal." This is true, but the difference is immense. Whatever may be the essence that I consider, with the exception of relation, I am ever faced with the essence of something that is or could be, even if, in reality, it exists only as one element of reality, isolated in my mind by abstraction. In all these cases, the essence is conceived as ordered to existence either *in se* or *in alio*.

This is not the case for relation, and relation is unique in this fact. It is not necessarily conceived as the essence of that which exists. Indeed, we have seen that what is characteristic to it is the fact that it does not express what the subject to which it is attributed is in itself, but only expresses its relation to another thing. Now, clearly, this relation can quite well be established by an act of the intellect. It is possible for it to exist only through this act, that is, only in the mind and with a purely intentional existence.

Therefore, relation presents this paradoxical character: it is an essence that is indifferent, *of itself*, to being able to exist or not.

b) There Are Real Relations

{95} This unique character of relation presents a great temptation to conclude that relation is not and cannot be anything but an act of the mind, placing objects in relation within the mind itself, relations that are simultaneously objective and existing only for the mind.

Two grave reasons are opposed to this conclusion, requiring us to reject this temptation, however natural it may be.

The first is that the real, extra-mental universe is not simply made up of a disorganized multitude of beings, which reason alone would order on its own behalf. On the contrary, reason tries to retrieve the real order. At the level of the [natural] sciences, this order is [expressed in] the classification of things. At the level of the human sciences, this order is [expressed in] the interpersonal order which makes up various societies and which exists (at least partially) outside of him, in men themselves and in things, even if this is the work of man. (Thus the "rights of man" are not a mere mental fabrication.) At the level of metaphysics, we speak of the interrelated order of beings with each other and of the universe to God without which the plurality of beings would be pure multiplicity, which is unthinkable and impossible. Thus, therefore, I do not fully know a being if I know only what it is in itself. I must also know its relations with other beings. Therefore, these relations are part of its reality.

The second grave reason [attesting to the existence of real relations] is that this objective consistency that we have recognized in the relation that the mind establishes among its objects would be unintelligible if these relations were truly pure mental fabrications, for in that case, reason would be submitted, quite rigorously, to what, on this hypothesis, would only be its own work, kneeling in an act of idolatry before the work of its own hands. If the relation established by reason can be truly objective, this is because it is established on the model of real relations, imitating within the mind the external order of things to which the intellect is naturally submitted. And if such a relation is established in this manner, this does not come about through a vain mimicry. It is as an "artificial" procedure—do not forget that logic is an art—for the sake of rejoining the real order.

This point can be made clear if we analyze the process of classification. The zoologist's or botanist's classifications are artificial in the sense that the classified beings are organized in the scientist's mind and in his cabinets. However, this reproduces the relation of filiation, which is real. It is real first of all on the level of the individual, for it is real for this animal to have been begotten by this other. This relationship is real, even if nobody is ever consciously aware of it and even if nobody ever considers the biological likenesses resulting from this kinship. Then, moreover, it is real on the vaster level of the origin of species. These classifications statically (and artificially) represent the dynamic (and real) order of the origin of living forms and of their evolution. As regards the logician's classification of genera and of species, this artificially expresses the real relations of likeness and unlikeness that exist among individuals in which the species are realized.

Therefore, the objective consistency of the intra-mental order, which itself is assured by the so-called relations "of reason," is assured by the real order, consisting in real relations among beings. ("Relations of reason" [or, "rationate relations"] are those that are created by reason. A being of reason is precisely the essence that we spoke of as lacking an ordination to real existence: "a being of reason is that which only has objective being,* in the intellect.")

* [Tr. note: According to the terminology of the Thomist school, as well as other traditional *scholae*, objective existence is the mode of existence belonging to the known as known. For the purposes of this book, it may be understood as being equivalent to "intentional existence."]

c) The *ad* and the *in* of Real Relation

{96} Substance is defined as that which exists in itself, *in se*. Quality is defined as a particular ontological mode of substance, and so forth. As soon as the essence of relation does not include this relationship to real existence (which, in contrast, every other essence includes), the concept that only expresses the essence of relation does not suffice for conceiving of it as being real. It only designates that it is a relation and what relation it is. However, it does not designate whether it is real or rationate. Note, however, that in saying that it does not include this relationship to existence, we are not saying that it excludes a relationship to existence. Rather, we are saying, "it can indifferently exist in a real or un-real manner."

To conceive and express this, we need a second concept that itself attains relation as a real mode of its subject, as making it exist in a particular manner, that is, precisely in a manner that is relative to something other than itself. By contrast, the concept that expresses a quality, can express that quality only as a substance's particular mode of being. Thus, we conceive by one, single concept what a given quality is, as well as the fact it is the quality of a substance.

The first concept, which only indicates what a relation is (i.e., its essence), is designated by the term *ad*, for the essence of relation consists in this ordering to a terminus. Another concept is needed in order to say that this ordination *really* affects a subject (a supposit, a substance), and this is designated by *in*. In fact, in the domain of our experience, if a relation is real, it can only subsist *in alio*, as an accident in a substance.

What distinguishes a real relation from a rationate relation is not the *ad*, which they both have. They differ as regards the *in*, which is lacking in the rationate relation.[12]

---

12. N.B., The *ad* and the *in* of a relation are two aspects of a real relation. They are only conceptually distinct. They are not two parts of the real relation. They pertain to the real relation itself, considered from two different perspectives. Indeed, the relation itself is what is real, and the *in* expresses that the *ad* has the character of being real (in the case of a real relation). However, these two concepts are not reducible to one another. I cannot

2. It Is Not Contradictory for a Relation to Be Subsistent

{97} We have seen that only relative opposition can explain the distinction of Those "Being God" who are consubstantial. However, for this to be so, we must be able to find real relations in God. Now, no accident can be found in God, for the accident ever is (indeed, by definition) distinct from the subject that it modifies and, moreover, ever brings to it a complement of existence. We must exclude every composition from God, as well as every super-added actualization. Therefore, if there are real relations in God, they cannot be accidental. Therefore, they must be subsistent. That is, they themselves must subsist *in se*. But is this conceivable?

a) Relation, of Itself, Does Not Need to Be an Accident

{98} Substance and accident are the members of the very first division of real being. Every real being necessarily subsists *in se* or *in alio*. However, this holds only as long as one remembers the following capital precision. Being is an analogue that is said fully only of substance. It is said of accidents only by analogy, in a diminished fashion. Thus, accidents are necessarily limited and deficient from the perspective of being and therefore cannot be found in God. In short, the substance-accident division is of value only for participated being.

We have seen that relation had this singular characteristic, namely, the fact that, of itself and in virtue of its proper requirements, its essence is not ordered to existence. That is, of its essence, it is not ordered to being real. The first conclusion drawn from this fact is that it can indifferently be a real being or a rationate being.

However, another, even more surprising conclusion follows. Relation, of itself and in virtue of its proper requirements, is not ordered to being realized as subsisting *in alio*. In fact, it is not defined

---

have only one concept of it, only one notion of it, to attain the relation simultaneously in what it is (its essence, the *ad*) and as real (in its ordination to real existence, its *in*).

as a particular mode of substance. Therefore, *in its very definition*, it abstracts from a substance that would be its subject. Thus, the condition of being an accident is not essential to it.

b) The Abolition of *in alio* Does Not Lead to the Abolition of *ad*

{99} The same reasoning can be expressed in another manner. What is contradictory is that one simultaneously deny the same thing that one affirms. The notion of a subsistent relation obviously includes the denial of the *in alio*. If the *in alio* were included necessarily in the *ad* (as it is included necessarily in the definition of quality, for example), the very notion of *subsistent relation* would be intrinsically contradictory. Indeed, in saying "relation," I would posit the *ad*, and in saying "subsistent," I would deny this same *ad* by denying the *in alio*, which would be included in it. However, as we have seen, this is not the case here for relation. The *in alio* is not included in the *ad*, and this is why it can be made explicit only by a concept that is distinct from that which expresses the *ad*.

Thus, the notion of a "subsistent relation" is not contradictory.

c) Subsistent Relation Is Not a Substance

{100} Everything that is real subsists either *in se* or *in alio*. Now, given that, in the domain of our experience, only substance subsists *in se*, we are led to identify, purely and simply, substance with that which is subsistent.

The notion of a subsistent relation requires us to reflect on this point, for *relation* and *substance* are and remain essentially different. Substance is what the being under consideration is in itself. Relation is only its connection to others. Therefore, if a relation is subsistent, it will remain a relation and not become a substance.

Already in the domain of our experience, the *in alio* inserts relation into the absolute. The *in alio* is a mode of the substance's being. For example, to be a father qualifies the very man who is a father, all the while designating only his connection to others and not what he is in himself. By its essence, a relation is *extrinsecus affixa*, that is, wholly externalizing. However, by its existence, it is interior to the subject. It is part of it.

Likewise, though more paradoxically still, a subsistent relation, inasmuch as it is a relation, is externalized, wholly turned toward the correlate. However, inasmuch as it is subsistent, it is constitutive of the very being thus referred (i.e., of itself). It is therefore an Absolute-Relative; a relative endowed with an absolute being (*esse*).[13]

C. The Multiplication of Subsistent Relations in God

1. The Transposition of This "Perfection," Relation, to God

a) This Transposition Is Not Impossible

{101} As a general rule, every perfection or ontological value that is found in the beings we experience can be transposed to God by way of the three classic and indispensable rules: *causality, negation,* and *eminence.* If certain, so-called "mixed perfections" do not allow themselves to be transposed in this manner, this is precisely on account of what these rules require. Indeed, the rule of negation, com-

13. The scholastic notion of *transcendental relation*, a notion that is classic but whose Thomist sources and intrinsic value have been contested, not without reason, nor without exaggeration as well, would be a *Relative-Absolute*, a being that is simultaneously an *in self* and a *towards the other*: "Certain entities are intermediaries between those that are only absolutes and those that are only relatives" (Cajetan, *In ST* I, q. 77, a. 3, no. 4); See Anton Krempel, *La doctrine de la relation chez Saint Thomas, exposé historique et systéma-tique* (Paris: Vrin, 1952); Benoît Montagnes, "Compte-rendu de Krempel, A., La doctrine de la relation chez Saint Thomas, exposé historique et systématique," *Revue Thomiste* 54 (1954): 200-204; Adriaan Pattin, "Contribution à l'histoire de la relation transcenden-tale," in *L'homme et son destin d'après les penseurs du Moyen-Age, Acts of the First Interna-tional Congress of Medieval Philosophy* (Louvain: Nauwelaerts, 1960).

However, this notion, even if one were to accept it, could not serve as our intro-duction to the notion of a "subsistent relation," for we would there be dealing with an *Absolute* (substance or accident) that, in addition, would be relative. In this case, rela-tive opposition would produce (or indicate [*décèlerait*]) an alterity in the absolute itself. This absolute, thus coated with relativity, would differ from the absolute to which it is referred. A subsistent relation, on the contrary, refers only itself. Hence, we have the fol-lowing expressions: *Absolute-Relative*, in one case (that is, a Relative endowed with an absolute *existence*), and *Relative-Absolute*, in the other (the Absolute being endowed with a relative *in* its *very essence*).

bined with that of eminence, requires the denial of the limited mode of the realization of the "perfection" in question, without abolishing this perfection itself, in such a way that it can be pushed to infinity without bursting.[14] A "mixed" perfection is a one whose limited mode of realization is essential to it and is not merely something befalling the conditions in which that perfection is realized. For example, *velocity* is a mixed perfection because it includes corporeity and, therefore, a limitation of the perfection of existence [être] by the material component.

Every accident is, as such, a mixed perfection, for it is essential to accidents that they subsist *in alio*, that is, that they exist imperfectly. Consequently, every perfection that can be realized only as an accident is a mixed perfection and cannot be transposed to God—for example, quality.

We have seen that this is not the case for relation, since it is not opposed to being realized as subsisting in itself. It is not non-transposable.

Still, let us note that such reasoning does not lead to pure and simple possibility but leads, rather, to non-impossibility. Indeed, everything that we said earlier concerning subsistent relation leads only to this assertion: this notion is not contradictory and therefore is not, *of itself* and through its essential requirements, unrealizable (as is, for example, the notion of a square circle). However, nothing proves that for existential reasons, not directly essential ones, it would not, in fact, be unrealizable, for we find nothing similar to it in our experience. Moreover, what we find in our experience would seem to exclude such a possibility. Indeed, we could say that given that relation is not essentially ordered to being an accident, this enables us to conclude, as we first did, that it can be "rationate" (i.e., "unreal"). However, if it is real, it can exist only as an accident. In any case, neither is this proven, nor provable, but it does make the notion of subsistent relation problematic and, thus too, the transposi-

14. See Jean-Hervé Nicolas, *Dieu connue comme inconnu* (Paris: Desclée de Brouwer, 1966), 142–48.

tion of the relative perfection to God. All that we can say is that such a transposition is not rationally objectionable and that such a transposition does not violate the principle of non-contradiction.

b) This Transposition Is Imposed upon Us by Faith

{102} As we have seen, relative opposition is the only means that our reason has at its disposal for giving an intelligible meaning to faith's affirmation that there are three, really distinct "Being God" that are consubstantial in the Godhead, that is, Three who are not distinct from each other according to their substance, Three who have the same identical substance. Now, in order for there to be a relative opposition, obviously there must be relations within the Godhead.

One can connect this requirement of faith to the question of the divine processions. What is directly a matter held on faith is that there are real processions in God—a really begotten Son, and a really "spirated" Spirit. Now, if every real procession includes a real distinction of what proceeds in relation to that from which it originates, this distinction is what relative opposition brings about, for of itself, the former alone is absolutely required by the procession. If a son is not his father, this is, in the first place, because formally, on account of generation, he is relative to his father, and his father to him.... As was seen from the beginning of theological speculation on this matter, Father and Son (and also, though less clearly, Spirit) are relative terms.

c) The Identification and Distinction between the Subsistent Relations and the Divine Substance

{103} The way of eminence makes us aware of the fact that the perfections that are limited and manifold in creatures are found in God at the summit of their ontological value, united in a super-eminent and infinitely simple perfection, the *Deity*, which is simultaneously, pushed to infinity, everything that is positive in each of the created perfections of which it is the Exemplar:

The formal notion of wisdom and the formal notion of justice transcend their own, proper limits so as to be merged in a single notion that exceeds them, the formal notion of the Deity, so that, in God they are one and the same formal notion in which they are both eminently included.[15]

Given that all the perfections that are "forms" in creatures are subsistent in God, all the perfections thus coalesce in the Divine Substance.[16] The "Deitas" is the perfect, infinite, simple substance in which all ontological perfections are eminently realized, in an infinite manner.

However, as we have seen, relation, even at infinity, does not become substance. From the moment it is clear that not only substance but also relation is subsistent in God, we must recognize these two subsistent perfections, which themselves are infinite, namely, infinite substance and the relation (or, rather, those [*les*] relations): "And it is for this reason that it is said that one finds in God only two predicaments."*

Nonetheless, one cannot think that these two absolutes co-exist as really distinct in God. God is Pure Act, *Ipsum Esse subsistens*. The subsistence of the infinite substance and the subsistences of the infinite relations coalesce in this subsistence of *Esse*. However, just as

---

15. Cajetan, *In ST* I, q. 13, a. 5, no. 7; Nicolas, *Dieu connue comme inconnu*, 94–100; Cornelio Fabro, *Participation et causalité selon Saint Thomas d'Aquin* (Paris: Vrin, 1961), 344–62.

16. See St. Thomas, *ST* I, q. 3, a. 3.

* [Tr. note: No citation is provided. It is an odd comment to make, for a text such as *ST* I q. 3, a. 5, ad. 1 shows that the predicament of substance (that to which it belongs not to exist in another) implies a distinction of essence and existence (and hence cannot be applied to God). Likewise, according to the Thomistic theory of relation, which Fr. Nicolas himself explains, precisely *as a predicament*, relation involves inherence in a substance (*in-esse*), although precisely *as a relation*, it only involves *ad-esse*. It is only the latter that is involved in the case of the Three Divine Persons. For a discussion of this question by Fr. Nicolas, see J.-H. Nicolas, *Synthèse Dogmatique: complément, de l'Univers à la Trinité* (Fribourg, CH: Éditions Universitaires, 1997), 127n22: "To say that only two predicaments remain attributable to *Self-Subsistent Existence* is to say that among the divine attributes, there are some that are attributable after the manner of substance (all those which are related to what God is in Himself) and others after the manner of relation (all those which are related to the 'propria Personarum')" (my translation). He then cites this section of *Synthèse dogmatique*.]

thought, love, goodness, and wisdom coalesce in the Divine Substance without, for all that, thought becoming love or wisdom becoming goodness or power (though, each is lost in this *ratio formalis Deitatis* which includes all of them by surpassing them), so too the infinite substance and the infinite relations coalesce in a superior *ratio formalis*, without being lost in one another and are identified without being confused (by the partial identification of each to something that exceeds them both, namely the *Res Divina*):

Note well that, as the transcendent Divine Reality is one, neither purely absolute, nor purely relative, nor moreover is it mixed, composed of both of them, nor resulting from their confluence, but including in its perfect unity everything that there is of reality in relation (moreover, in several relations), and everything that there is of reality in the absolute, so too, on the level of formal notions, one and the same formal notion corresponds in God to this Reality, not for us,[17] but in itself.[18] It is a unique formal notion, which is neither absolute, nor relative, which is simultaneously—from two different perspectives—communicable and incommunicable, containing in itself everything that absolute perfection demands and everything that a Trinity of relatives requires.[19]

Thus, the subsistent relations in God must be identical with the Divine Substance and therefore with each other, at least inasmuch as they are Absolute. Indeed, from this perspective, they are, along with the substance, the Divine Absolute, which is one and simple. Nonetheless, they are distinguished from it according to a conceptual, non-arbitrary distinction, called a "minor virtual distinction." (It is so-called because it is founded, not on a composition in the subject itself in which they are realized, namely, God, but rather, on the creatures from which we draw the concepts that enable us to attain, in this complex manner, the Divine Being in its infinite simplicity.)[20]

---

17. For we are incapable of conceiving such a formal notion, whose amplitude is infinite, and moreover, cannot embrace it within our finite mind. (Fr. Nicolas's note.)

18. Indeed, this transcendent formal notion is identical with the Divine Essence, which is simultaneously the Supreme Reality and the Supreme Intelligible. (Fr. Nicolas's note.)

19. Cajetan, *In ST* I, q. 39, a. 1, no. 7.

20. See Nicolas, *Dieu connue comme inconnu*, 137–42.

2. The Multiplication of Subsistent Relations and the
Unity of the Divine Being

{104} We now arrive at the final point of our reflection on this matter. It is an inviolable rule that when we transpose to God the ontological values discovered in creatures that, whatever may be the modifications that they must undergo in order to pass from the created order to the uncreated order (here, relation must pass from the condition of "subsisting *in alio*" as an accident to that of "subsisting *in se*"), the proper notion, the *ratio analogata*, must be discovered in each of the analogates. Failing this, obviously, the transposition would be purely verbal, the same word designating in God a wholly different *ratio* than in the creature. Now, as we have seen, the formal notion of relation includes the alterity of the referred vis-à-vis that to which it is referred. In the case of rationate relations, it is a purely conceptual alterity. However, in the case of real relations, the alterity is real. Now, what is transposed to God is [the notion of a] real relation. Rationate relations only exist in the created intellect, not in God. However, since we here are concerned with subsistent relations (i.e., of relations that refer to each other), we are in the presence of relations that are opposed to one another and that are really distinct on account of this opposition.

This is a purely relative opposition, the notion of which we attempted to articulate in our prior discussions. Such an opposition introduces no alterity into the substance itself, for it does not pertain to the substance. The Divine Relations are identical with the substance on account of the *in* that bestows upon them their absolute character. They are opposed and distinguished on account of the *ad*[:]

We must grant the fact that when two absolute realities (*esse in*) are identical with a third, they are also identical with one another. For in the case of absolute realities there is no reason why they should differ when their whole reality and intelligibility is, as absolute (as not-relative), identical with a third.

The case is different, however, when two opposed relations are given. In this event, they must be really distinct from one another. They possess also a content (an intelligibility) which does not let them *simply and altogether* (*re et ratione*) coincide with the absolute reality with which they are supposed really (*re*) to be identical. In this event, the relations are not distinct by what they posit "absolutely" each for itself, but through their opposition as such. That which is absolute possesses, as it were, its content in itself, whereas that which is relative is constituted by its relatedness to another, and in the case of real relative opposition by its necessary distinction from the opposed relation to which it refers. Hence, despite its real identity with an absolute, an identity which is presupposed, a relative reality possesses a content through which it is distinct from the other, opposed relations. Hence in our case we presuppose that two opposed relations can be really identical with something absolute. Such a presupposition cannot be positively verified in the empirical domain of finite reality, nor can it be shown to be positively contradictory, unless one already admits that the basic difficulty is insuperable.

Now if we accept the above presupposition, then the "principle of compared identity" cannot provide a *peremptory* argument *against* the doctrine of the Trinity. For this principle derives its meaning and its strength from the principle of the *formal* identity or from the principle of contradiction. Only if an absolute reality would posit two other absolute contents, which are really identical with it, will these two contents ultimately be formally identical with each other. It would not be possible for them to be really distinct from each other, without clashing with the formal principle of contradiction. On the other hand, when an absolute is really identical with two opposed relatives, this real identity does not yet imply a formal identity of the two opposed relatives. Their real identity cannot be apodictically demonstrated from the formal principle of contradiction.[21]

How can a mere conceptual distinction justify a real distinction? It does so because, in itself, this real distinction evades us. We can only look in its direction and aim at it. The conceptual distinction does not "represent" the real distinction which exists in God. It serves

21. Karl Rahner, "Dieu Trinité fondement transcendant de l'histoire du salut," in *Mysterium Salutis. Dogmatique de l'histoire du salut*, vol. 6 (Paris: Cerf, 1971), 82–83. [Tr. note: Translation taken from Karl Rahner, *The Trinity* (London: Burns and Oates, 1970), 71–72.]

as our noetic instrument for reaching the real distinction situated above every representation within the mystery of God, doing so in a groping manner and obscurely, though with a certitude affirmed by faith: "How this is—this is what we must seek to understand, guided by what the holy doctors have said, although reason cannot fully succeed at doing so."[22]

This is also found, although in a less difficult manner to grasp (because it no longer directly concerns the Divine Being) in other points concerning the knowledge of God. Thus, I must really distinguish the infinity of possible beings from the real beings that constitute the really existing universe and therefore have really been created by God. How? Their distinction comes from the fact that, among all the possible beings that He knows, God has freely chosen, by His will, those that exist by virtue of this willing. I can posit only a conceptual distinction between the divine will and His thought, and nevertheless, although all [possible] beings have been thought of, only real beings have been willed. Obviously, this fact is what really distinguishes these latter from the former. Thus, although in the subsistent relations the distinction between the absolute (the *in*) and the relative (the *ad*) is only conceptual, they are really distinct from each other according to the *ad* and not according to the *in*.[23]

3. The Number of Divine Relations

{105} Given that the divine relations are founded on the processions, and given that each procession gives rise to two opposed relations (the relation of the originating to the proceeding, and the opposed relation of the proceeding to the originating), there are four subsistent relations in God. On the one hand, there is paternity and filiation and, on the other, active and passive spiration. What are the termini of the second pair of relations? On one side, the terminus is the Holy Spirit, indeed. On the opposed side, according to Ortho-

22. *De pot.*, q. 8, a. 1.
23. For everything discussed in this chapter, read and meditate upon *ST* I, q. 28, a. 3; *De pot.*, q. 8, a. 2.

dox theology, the terminus is the Father alone. According to the doctrine of Catholic theology, the terminus is the Father and the Son together. Here, merely note that we are not asserting something that would be unintelligible from the perspective of logic, namely, that the two spirations (active and passive) involve three termini: the Father and the Son on the one side, the Spirit on the other. Instead, we mean that the Father and the Son constitute a single terminus facing toward the Holy Spirit who proceeds from them. We will speak about this matter in due time.

III. CONCLUSION

{106} Having arrived at the end of this quite laborious undertaking, we could be deceived by the slenderness of the results we have obtained. What proportion is there between what these living and life-giving realities—the Father, the Son, and the Holy Spirit—represent in Christian faith and in salvation history, and these relations, which are realities that are so poor, so purely formal, and so devoid of life and of goodness? It could well seem that we have worked in vain!

However, this is not the case! We have not sought and found the answer to the question, "In what do the Three 'Being God' consist?" Instead, the question underlying our discussions has been, "How are they distinguished? How can we understand the fact that they are three, all the while being the one, unique God?" We now must consider them in themselves and ask ourselves what they are.

The Greek tradition calls them *hypostases*. The Latin tradition refers to them using the term and notion of *persons*. We will ask ourselves whether these designations are justified and what they provide for us in our attempt to understand what the Father, the Son, and the Holy Spirit are in themselves.

6

The Divine Persons

I. THE THREE "BEING GOD" ARE THREE DISTINCT PERSONS

A. Statement of the Problem

1. Arguments against the Utilization of the Notion of Person in This Domain

a) Difficulty Involved in Attributing the Notion of Person to God

{107} In the nineteenth century, under the influence of Hegel, the idea of God as a personal Being was systematically combatted. He is, in fact, *Absolute Spirit*, and the person, precisely speaking, is a particular manifestation of spirit, its limited and necessarily accidental individualization. The classical analogical process of freeing the notion of personality from the limitations in which it is realized within the domain of our experience comes to be radically contested:

The concept of personality cannot be taken up by a finite spirit in such a way as to be abstracted thereby from the moment of finitude. Personality is rather the specific form of the subsistence of the human spirit as finite ... This notion [of God's personality] is, however, to be lifted by strict thought into the pure concept of the absolute spirit that is alone adequate for God, which presupposes no finite existence in God Himself, but which is in His being in Himself the absolute presupposition for the totality of all finite existence.[1]

---

1. Karl Barth, *Dogmatique* (Genève: Labor et Fides, 1953–1970), II, 36. [Tr. note:

On the other hand, the person increasingly tended to be defined in terms of self-awareness, and, in fact, it was asserted that a human person becomes self-aware only by being opposed to other persons. Whence it is said:

As persons we know and feel ourselves only in our difference from other similar persons outside of ourselves, from whom we differentiate ourselves, that is, as finite; in this realm of finitude, and fashioned for it, the concept of personality logically seems to lose every meaning apart from this, and a nature which has no other like itself outside itself seems unable to be a person.[2]

In our own days, we find the same sort of objection in Henry Duméry:

When the notion of person is submitted to analysis, it breaks down into an empirical self and an intelligible singularity. Now, it turns out that that the *I*, in the psycho-social sense, is expressible and expressed only on the level of the latter. Hence, to attribute it to God is not to honor Him. Even worse, to say that God is a person is to openly express an equivocation. He cannot be a person like us.[3]

b) Difficulties Involved with the Multiplication of Personality in God

Even for those very people who hold that we can and must attribute personality to God, great difficulties arise when it is a question of multiplying it by making it into an attribute of Those "Being God."

{108} *First difficulty.* The term "person" can only designate the individual, which is an absolute, a "substance." Therefore, if, as we have seen, multiplication in God can occur only according to relative op-

---

Taken from Barth, *Church Dogmatics*, vol. 2.1, 289. Fr. Nicolas does not explicitly note the fact, but this is a quote from A. E. Biedermann's *Church Dogmatics*. The text in brackets is Fr. Nicolas's.]

2. Barth, *Dogmatique*, II, 36. Here Barth is citing D. F. Strauss. [Tr. note: Taken from Barth, *Church Dogmatics*, vol. 2.1, 288–89.]

3. Henri Duméry, *Critique et religion* (Paris: Sedes, 1957), 58n2. N.B. We must note the ambiguity of this last assertion. If Duméry means that God is a person but not like us, we can only agree with him (adding, however, that God is not *a* person but, rather, three Persons). However, in that case, it is not at all clear how the conclusion is derived from what precedes. If he means (as seems more likely) that God is not, as we are, a person, he rejoins the Hegelian denial of personality in God.

position (and not according to substance), it is inconceivable that personality would be multiplied in God.

St. Augustine was brought to a halt at length by this difficulty, without successfully overcoming it in a satisfying manner, as much for himself as for his readers.[4] While he resigned himself to employing the term "Persons" for designating the three distinct "realities" [*les trois distincts*] that are the one God,[5] he did so on account of the impossibility of finding another term.[6]

Going to the heart of the matter, we find that the difficulty at hand is that of applying to the plurality of those "Being God" the general law holding that multiplicity is always reduced to unity (for pure multiplicity is unthinkable and impossible, given that unity is a property of being insofar as it is being). This does not mean that God is a "case" of a metaphysical law. Instead, it means that I cannot conceive the Divine Reality other than by means of my concepts and above all by means of the concept of being and of the first principles. If faith requires me to say, "A Plurality exists in God, but His substance is not what is multiplied and plural," I cannot prevent the question from arising: "What, then, is multiplied?" To put it another way: "What is the 'one' that is multiplied?" Now, what is common precisely to the "three," namely the Divine Substance, itself remains numerically one and is not multiplied. The Father, the Son, and the Holy Spirit are God. However, they are not three gods. Must we not similarly say: "The Father, the Son, and the Holy Spirit are a 'Person' but they are not three Persons?" But then, what is "three"?[7]

{109} *Second difficulty.* This second difficulty is what Karl Barth vigorously raises against the use of the term "Person" for designating the Father, the Son, and the Holy Spirit. For him, the biblical notion of God is this: *God is He who loves.* And this alone is what the notion

---

4. See St. Augustine, *La Trinité*, Books I–VII, OESA 15, trans. and ed. Marcellin Mellet and Pierre-Thomas Camelot, introduction by Ephraem Hendrickx (Paris: Desclée de Brouwer, 1955), VII, 7–11.

5. See Augustine, *La Trinité*, VII, 12.

6. See Augustine, *La Trinité*, VII, 9; 2, XV, 5.

7. See Augustine, *La Trinité*, VII, 7.

of personality expresses when it is attributed to God. However, the one who loves man is God the Father, the Son, and the Holy Spirit: "But it is as who He is and therefore as the One who loves that He is this. The concept of personality as such is too colorless to form a necessary basis for our description of this absolutely indispensable moment in the nature of God."[8]

Thus, if we limit ourselves to knowing God in His relations with us, what He is for us, will we not be speaking of three gods when we speak of three persons? Note that this indirectly brings us back to the question of how the "Economic Trinity" is related to the "Immanent Trinity," as well as how *Deus unus* is related to "*Deus trinus.*"

{110} *Third difficulty.* If the person is defined as a center of consciousness, is it not contradictory to speak of three Persons in God, since there is only one center of consciousness in God (one thought, one love, and one freedom)?[9]

2. Reasons for the Utilization of the Notion of Person[10]

a) The Tradition

{111} Tertullian is the one who introduced the word "persona" into Latin Trinitarian terminology.[11] He himself seems to have translated it from the Greek term *prosopon*, which was used for the first time by Hippolytus. In the two cases, the sense is more "ontological" than "psychological." Against modalism, which held that there was one unique *prosopon* in God having three different names, Hippolytus affirmed that there are three *prosopa* in God, that is, three distinct individualities. His concern was to affirm that there are three Divine "individuals." Doubtlessly, in the background of this affirmation there is a reference to three individual humans in whom the same

---

8. Barth, *Dogmatique*, II, 35–45. [Tr. note: Taken from Barth, *Church Dogmatics*, vol. 2.1, 296.]

9. See Rahner, "Quelques remarques sur le traité dogmatique 'De Trinitate,'" in *Ecrits théologiques* VIII (Paris: Desclée de Brouwer, 1967), 138–39.

10. Joseph Ratzinger, *La foi chrétienne hier et aujourd'hui* (Paris: Mame, 1969), 64–122.

11. See Tertullian, *Traité du baptême*, ed. and trans. François Refoulé and Maurice Drouzy, SC 35 (Paris: Cerf, 1953).

"substance" is realized, making all three be men. However, in the application made to God, care is taken to specify that the *substantia*, the *ousia*, is one and the same for the three and not only similar.[12]

The term comes into common usage only in the middle of the fourth century, concurrently with the term "hypostasis." At first, the latter does not have the same sense as the former. It was introduced by Origen in order to say that the Father and the Son are two distinct "realities."[13] In classical usage, this term was practically synonymous with *ousia* and for some time was subject to looseness in usage. "A hypostasis" was commonly said in Alexandria in the sense that we say, "a substance." At the Synod of Alexandria (362), the two expressions were brought into confrontation, and this led to an agreement concerning the meaning, which St. Athanasius reported in his *Tome to the Antiochians*.[14]

We have seen how St. Basil definitively introduced the formula, which became dogmatic, "One substance, three hypostases," in which the term "hypostasis" is equivalent to that of "person" in the formula, "One essence in three Persons."[15]

Thus, the term "person" became classic and was accepted by the Greeks as well as by the Latins and seems to have been understood in a very different sense than that which it evokes for us, namely as designating a reality of the moral and spiritual order. However, we must not be deceived by this. Long before these terms had become classic, the moral and spiritual reality that they designate was already contained and signified by the scriptural terms Father, Son, and Spirit. It is to express the real distinction of these "three who are the One God" that words were sought out for expressing their distinct reality, their "individuality." However, it was clear to all that this individuality was that of three intelligent, loving, and free beings—of "persons" in the sense given greater emphasis by the modern meaning of the

12. See George Leonard Prestige, *Dieu dans la pensée patristique* (Paris: Aubier, 1955), 142–146.
13. See Prestige, *Dieu dans la pensée patristique*, 158.
14. See Athanasius, PG 24, 800–804.
15. See §43 above.

term. To deny that the "three" are "persons" in the modern sense of
the word would by that very fact be a denial that they are "persons"
in the ancient sense, for they cannot be three "divine individuals"
without thereby being three "Persons," as three human individuals
are necessarily three persons.

b) The Manifestations of the Three "Being God" Are
Manifestations of Persons

{112} Since we know the "Three" only through Their manifestations, it is through these manifestations that we can know something about what They are. Now, it is clear that They manifest Themselves as persons. The Son manifested Himself as a human person
and simultaneously manifested the Father as a Person: the Father
has sent Him; He loves the world, and so forth. The Holy Spirit also
is a *Someone*, who proposes the truth, who sustains, gives testimony,
spreads His gifts as He wishes, and so forth.[16]

16. N.B., It is often said that the term "person" is not found in Scripture for designating what the Father, Son, and Spirit are. This is true. But what can we conclude
from this remark? Prior to every definition for what a person is, even before one would
have dreamt of thus designating the human "subject," there is a vague but sure intuition
of what the word "person" expresses—namely, a being that is responsible for its acts,
capable of taking his destiny in hand, and, on account of this, a being that neither can
nor should be "manipulated" like a thing, likewise having rights and duties. The phenomenological analyses and ontological explanations are posterior to this intuition but
are ruled and provoked by it. By applying this term, "person," to the Three "Being God"
and attributing to Them the results of these analyses and these explanations, nothing has
been added to Scripture. In so doing, what Scripture says has only been made clearer, being expressed in terms that are clearer and more explicit for reason. Moreover, this is how
things are for all the "dogmatic formulas" in relation to Scripture. In the present case, the
Three "Being God" manifest Themselves, according to Scripture, as intelligent, responsible forces who are masters of Their acts, not blind forces like the powers of nature. This
reality, which is expressed in Scripture, is what we express by the word "person."
    If we believe, as we must, that what is thus manifested to men are three distinct
beings, we cannot truly contest that these are three Persons, since a typically personal
conduct is attributed to each one. One could propose this counter-proof: if the "Wisdom," the "Word" [*Parole*], or "Spirit of Yahweh" in the Old Testimony did not designate,
at least openly, "persons," this is not because the personal conduct that is attributed to
them would be that of impersonal forces. No indeed! These texts manifestly express the
idea that it is a person who is acting. However, what was not clear was that there would
be several distinct persons in God. The novelty of the New Testament's revelation of the

c) Responding to the Question: "Three" What?

{113} We have seen that St. Augustine posed this problem to himself in this form. This is not only a question of language, which can be completely resolved simply by naming the three the Father, the Son, and the Holy Spirit (or, again, as we have done up to this point by means of a methodological scruple, by saying, "the Three 'Being God'"). This is also what St. Athanasius did. However, if this is legitimate on the level of faith, the question cannot fail to be posed by the theologian. Moreover, the very affirmation of faith is emptied of its meaning if one refuses to respond to it and above all if one says that it does not have a response.

Now, what response could be given other than the traditional one? If the Father, the Son, and the Holy Spirit are not Persons, what will They be? "Things"? "Anonymous forces"? However, in addition to the fact that these denominations are unworthy of God and absolutely do not correspond to Scripture's way of speaking, they would necessarily lead to a division of the substance. Karl Barth has proposed saying "modes of being" (*Seinweisen*) instead of "persons."[17] However, this expression either returns us to modalism—against which Barth defends himself energetically—or, as Barth says, if it is a question of a distinction within the Divine Essence, leaves open the question of knowing what this "one" (which is called a "mode of being") is and what is multiplied by the three.

Conclusion

We will simply accept the term and the notion of person for designating the Three "Being God" and for expressing what They are and what is multiplied in God. Our effort will be exerted in showing how this notion, obviously constructed on the basis of our expe-

_____

Trinity is not found in the personal character of God but, rather, in the affirmation of the three distinct "individuals" [*les trois distincts*] who possess and exercise God's personality. These can only be three Persons.

17. See Barth, *Dogmatique*, 51; criticism in Vincent Taylor, *La personne du Christ dans le Nouveau Testament* (Paris: Cerf, 1969), 247–49.

rience, can be validly applied to the "Three." We will likewise strive
to show how it enables us to know Them in their distinction and
singularity. Also, we will strive to show how the term designates
something that is common to the Three. Naturally, in doing this, our
methodology will make use of analogy.

B. From Created Personality to the Personality of the Three "Being God"

1. Created Personality

a) Boethius's Definition

{114} In the fifth century, thus providing content for a lacuna
found in Augustine, Boethius gave, in relation to the mystery of the
Incarnation, a definition of person. Scholastic theologians made use
of this definition in their attempts at resolving the problem concerning the persons in God: *rationalis naturae individua substantia,* "an individuated substance of a rational nature."[18]

Several scholastics, Abelard in particular (though his Trinitarian theology ended up in modalism), judged that it was unusable.
The fundamental critique registered against it is that of Richard of
St. Victor, in short: is not the Divine Substance, common to the
three, an *"individua substantia"*?[19] Other critiques, which are easi-
er to overcome, are concerned with the term *rationalis,* which is not
appropriate for God, given that "reason" is proper to man. Further
critiques wish to exclude from God the very idea of individuation,
given that matter is the principle of individuation. Or, they wish to
exclude the idea of "substance," which includes a relationship to accidents (*substare accidentibus*). The first objection alone goes to the
heart of the matter.

All the while aware of the difficulty involved, St. Thomas pre-

18. See Boethius, *Liber de persona et de duabus naturis Christi,* PL 64, 1343; Martial
Bergeron, "La structure du concept latin de personne," in Études d'histoire littéraire
et doctrinale du XIIIe siècle, 21–161 (Paris-Ottawa: J. Vrin-Institut d'études médiévales
d'Ottawa, 1932); Maurice Nédoncelle, "Les variations de Boèce sur la personne," *Recherches des sciences religieuses* (1955): 202–39.
19. See Richard of St. Victor, *La Trinté,* SC 63 (Paris: Cerf, 1959), IV, 21.

serves Boethius's definition and preferred to purify it by subjecting it to a rigorous analogical analysis.

1° *"Person" Designates a Reality Belonging to the Extra-Mental Universe*

The extra-mental universe is made up of *real beings* that exist and act. The intra-mental universe is made up of *intentional beings* (*intentiones*), which are these same beings present to the mind according to their intelligibility in order to be known. *Real beings* are concrete, singular ("particular" according to St. Thomas's terminology in a. 1),* and individuated. *Intentional beings* (in the human, intramental universe), on the contrary, are *universal*. That is, they present to the mind an intelligible form that is found realized (or realizable) in a host of real beings. The term "person" designates a real being precisely as such.

2° *"Person" Designates a Subsistent Reality: A Primary Substance*

In the extra-mental universe, we must distinguish: *entia* properly speaking and *entia per attributionem*. The former exist through themselves and exercise the act of existence in their own right. They are substances. The latter do not exist by themselves but instead exist through the substance that they qualify and determine and that gives them real being. They are accidents.

Persons are not, ontologically speaking, accidents. They are real and subsistent beings, primary substances, beings that exist and act.

3° *"Person" Designates a Prominent Subsistent Reality, One Exercising Self-Possession*

What characterizes substance in the extra-mental universe is the fact that it exists and acts. However, some substances are distinguished by the fact that they are masters of their acts and are free. This freedom, which gives them mastery over their acts, is rooted in a property that is even more profound, namely, knowledge. They

---

* [Tr. note: That is, in *ST* I, q. 29, a. 1.]

Persons 209

know themselves and thereby are not only, in some manner, doubled but moreover, exist in such a way that their existence, even though it is totally received, belongs to them. They possess themselves, and this is why they have the power of self-determination. In this, we are faced with another, superior manner of subsisting. In order to distinguish these substances from others, the general term *suppositum* or "subsistent," which designates substances in the extra-mental world, was replaced by the special term "person."

St. Thomas accepts the ordinarily received etymology, namely, that *person* designated the mask with which a theater actor covered himself, both to make his voice resonate and to designate the persona that he represented.[20] This leads to an equivocation when the term is applied to God. The term brought to mind the actor who changes a mask in the course of the performance, as though one meant that God, remaining one in Himself, only manifested Himself to men with different visages. Left to itself, such terminology would express a form of modalism. In reality, going beyond this original idea of the mask, one passes on simply to the idea of dignity, the mask overlaying the actor with the "personality" of the represented persona. Therefore, philosophically, the word "person" came to designate the excellent manner of subsisting that belongs to substances endowed with consciousness and freedom.

4 ° Terminological Precisions[21]

We first must distinguish *secondary substance* from *primary substance*.[22]

Secondary substance is universal "substance." Therefore, it belongs to the intra-mental universe. It is a "universal," which encompasses all substantial beings within it its generality. In this sense, it is a synonym for "essence." *Primary substance* is, in the extra-mental uni-

---

20. See *ST* I, q. 29, a. 3, ad. 2.
21. See *ST* I, q. 29, a. 2.
22. See Aristotle, *Organon*, vol. 1, trans. Jules Tricot (Paris: Vrin, 1946), Cat. 5; *Metaphysics*, Δ, 8.

verse, the substantial (or, subsistent) being. It is that which exists and acts.

However, this primary substance can be considered from two different perspectives. Indeed, it lies at the junction point of the intra-mental and extra-mental universes, being the realization, in the latter, of the intelligible form that belongs to the former. Therefore, it can be considered either as the ultimate determination of the intentional being, the point where the *intentio* touches the terminus toward which it tends or, on the other hand, as the real terminus that the *intention* aims at, that by which and in which the extra-mental universe is distinguished from the intra-mental universe and is contrasted to it.

According to the first consideration, it is the ultimate determination of the intelligible form, of the essence. From the universal of the greatest scope (the supreme genus), one arrives, through increasingly precise determinations, at the most restricted universal (the specific essence). The extension of the concept diminishes to the degree that its comprehension increases.*

Between the specific essence and the individual, there are (for material beings) individuating principles, whose source is matter. They add nothing to the comprehension of the concept and therefore add nothing to the "intelligible value" that is the essence. (In other words, there is no more intelligible value—and therefore no more ontological value—in the individual than in the specific essence, which, on the contrary, is realized in the individual in a partial and limited manner.) However, they make the essence realizable, for the universal as such is not realizable. Therefore, it is not correct to speak of an individual essence. Instead, one should speak of an essence realized in an individual. Nevertheless, the individuating principles are part of the essence such as it is realized in a given individual, so that: "Individualized matter cannot enter into the definition of man as such, but it is part of the definition of Socrates (this human

---

* [Tr. note: That is, the intelligible notes included within the concept. Logically speaking, extension and comprehension bear an inverse relationship to each other.]

individual), if it were possible to define Socrates."[23] Therefore, the singular, the primary substance, can also be considered as being the ultimate determination of the essence, and this is what is expressed by the term "individual," which is a "logical term."[24] The same holds for the term *suppositum.*

According to the second consideration, primary substance designates real being as real. In this case, it can be designated in three ways. First, there is *subsistentia* (a word fabricated in the wake of Boethius), that is, as "subsisting," as that which is and acts. Second, there is, *res naturae,* that is, a "realized (universal) nature," having become "concrete." Finally, there is *hypostasis* or *substantia,* which emphasizes the realized substance's character as the subject of accidents (which indicates its existential complexity in contrast to the abstract purity that it has in the mind).

Indeed! The term "person" designates what these three terms designate for an ordinary substance. However, it does so for those special substances that are endowed with consciousness and freedom.

5 ˚ Objection: Is It Not Contradictory to Define a Primary Substance, and Therefore, a Person?

Now, if a person is a primary substance, and if the latter is the real being as such (i.e., inasmuch as it belongs to the extra-mental universe), it is paradoxical to claim to define it, that is, a kind of translation into the intra-mental register. This represents a grave problem, and the resolution of the Trinitarian problem encountered earlier depends on its resolution. If "person" is a predicate that is common to the Three Persons, it designates something that is one in God and that consequently cannot be multiplied.[25]

St. Thomas responds to the objection, first with regard to the no-

---

23. *De ente et essentia,* 11.7. [Tr. note: Fr. Nicolas appears to be citing the twenty-third paragraph of the first chapter of the text.]

24. See *De pot.,* q. 9, aa. 1 and 2; *ST* I, q. 29, a. 1, ad. 2 and ad. 3.

25. See Rahner, "Quelques remarques," 125–26.

tion of the person in general,[26] then directly in relation to this Trinitarian problem.[27]

The response can be summarized as follows. "Person" does not designate an intelligible form common to several "beings." The term designates a given being (or, rather, a particular kind of being, namely that in which a rational nature is realized), not according to the form that it possesses in common with others (i.e., the nature), nor in what it holds as its own (i.e., its individuation), but rather, in the universally shared fact that it possesses its common nature in the mode of singularity, its being a singular existent thing.

This mode of singularity consists in ontological incommunicability: this given being has being for itself and in itself, such that it is distinguished from all other beings and cannot become or be common to several things. Beings that are distinct and incommunicable as regards their being can indeed commune with each other through action and love, but this is a communication in the good, not in being.

Ontologically, the person is characterized by this incommunicability in being, which makes it a being that is distinct from all others. Strictly speaking, this is not a definition but, instead, a designation.

b) From Person as a Hypostasis to Person as a Center-of-Consciousness

{115} Boethius's definition is "ontological." That is, it designates the person as a being among beings. Hence, it stands in contrast with the modern conceptions of personality, which envision the person first of all as a "center of consciousness" that is set in opposition to all other beings as a subject to an object, as a someone to a something.

However, note that Boethius inserts the notion "rational nature" into his definition. As we have seen, this introduces consciousness and freedom into it.

The modern conception of the person is phenomenological. It designates the person by how he emerges in experience, namely, in

26. See *ST* I, q. 29, a. 1, ad. 1.
27. See *ST* I, q. 30, a. 4.

self-awareness or in others' awareness. And it is true in what it affirms. However, it would be false if it claimed to represent the denial of the ontological definition of personality, which, in reality, is presupposed by the phenomenological conception.

For all that, from a phenomenological perspective, one can say that the person is a subject, that he is the center of spiritual relations with other subjects, that he is, of himself, independent, the master of himself and of his destiny, etc. Yet, all this first presupposes that *he is*. And this is what Boethius's definition says: the person *exists* as an individuated substance (*substantia prima*) in which a rational nature is realized, from which, precisely speaking, he derives the fact that he is a center of consciousness who is independent and possesses self-mastery.

Far from being opposed to the ontological conception, this phenomenological conception presupposes it and prolongs it. Moreover, one finds a sketch of it in the ancients—indeed, more than a sketch. Thus, we can read in Richard of St. Victor:

> From what has been said, one can sufficiently understand, I believe, that the term "person" does not designate something but, rather, designates someone. What, in fact, does the word "person" suggest if not a someone taken apart, separated from every other thing through what he has that is proper to himself?[28]

And St. Thomas, to situate the "spiritual creature" in relation to Divine Providence, emphasizes that on account of its intellect, the spiritual creature is capable of conceiving the "project" of its destiny in general, of such or such a series of actions in particular, and of freely realizing it. Whence the spiritual creature is *provisa propter seipsam*. That is, God has a project for him in his singularity and does not make use of him purely and simply like a pawn placed upon the chessboard of the universe.[29] This singular, "personal" relation with God is what founds everything that can be said about the person's independence, his right to freely fulfill its destiny, his

28. Richard of St. Victor, *La trinité*, IV, 7.
29. See *De ver.*, q. 5, a. 5ff.

"dialogic structure" (a dialogue with God and with others), and so forth.

The paradox of the created person is that he receives this characteristic independence, this "self-possession," from God through creation, so that, inasmuch as he is a person, he is wholly dependent upon God. One must not say, "He is a person, though he is also a created being." Instead, one must say, "Inasmuch as he is a person, he is a created being." And this again is what Boethius's definition expresses, for this rational nature (whence he comes to be a person) is received from God.

2. Personality in God

a) Transposition of the Notion of Person to God

{116} In order to establish that God is "personal" and that the "notion" of person is indeed realized in Him, St. Thomas, with his customary rigor, makes use of analogical reasoning. The person is that which is most perfect in nature. Every perfection must be attributed to God. Therefore, the perfection of personal being must be attributed to Him. However, as is ever the case when one passes from the created realization of a perfection to its uncreated realization, it can be found in God only in a transcendent form.[30]

In opposition to this reasoning, we first of all find ourselves faced with Karl Barth's radical methodological critique, namely, his rejection of analogy. However, here, this rejection is based on a false interpretation of the process of transposition. [It seems that for Barth] it would be a question of "[conceiving] God as the content of the highest human values."[31] On the other hand, the opposite process, which Karl Barth recommends, is hardly satisfying for the mind:

If anyone had suddenly taken seriously the matter with which at bottom Lotze and Siebeck only played, if anyone had once begun to think of God and to speak of God to the effect that God as such was the true, speaking,

30. See *ST* I, q. 29, a. 3.
31. Barth, *Dogmatique*, II, 34–35 [*sic*]. [Tr. note: Taken from Barth, *Church Dogmatics*, vol. 2.1, 291.]

acting person, if anyone had done this (and it could not happen otherwise), not on the basis of speculative considerations, but on the basis that God is actually present in His revelation.[32]

Indeed, one wonders how we could recognize that God acts like a personal being without first having some sort of idea of what a person is. Whence would it come if not from our knowledge of the human person?

In reality, let us repeat that the use of analogy consists in taking a perfection that is found in the domain of our experience, though in a limited way, and freeing it from the conditions that it undergoes there, thus attributing it to God only by carrying it to infinity. The difficulty obviously consists in the discernment one must undertake, distinguishing the *ratio perfectionis* (i.e., what it is essentially) from the limits of its realization. This difficulty is not insurmountable, for in the case of pure and simple perfections, there is a difference between what this perfection is in itself and the limitations that prevent it from deploying all its ontological values.

As regards our particular issue here, the "formal notion" of person (i.e., that on account of which a *being* is said to be a person) is, as we have seen, that power which it has on account of its nature, namely its power of self-possession by means of consciousness and, consequently, its self-possession of its own activity [*opération*] and destiny through freedom. Now, it is indeed clear that in man (who is the only *being* who is a person within the domain of our experience) both of these interconnected powers are highly limited. His self-awareness is progressive and highly obscure, and moreover, is vexed by passions and the imagination. His freedom is extremely conditioned, both by external circumstances and by the aforementioned obscurity, as well as by the internal movement of the passions that ceaselessly incline him toward what he would not like to choose and to do. In contrast to this, freedom is unconditioned in God. Indeed, we cannot say that freedom would be conditioned by

32. Barth, *Dogmatique*, II, 41. [Tr. note: Taken from Barth, *Church Dogmatics*, vol. 2.1, 293.]

the requirements of His nature, for this Divine Nature is the Absolute Good, and if it is the rule of freedom, it is as the good rule of the will of which it is the object. Indeed, freedom is always and essentially the power of choosing the good, so that the good does not condition freedom, but, on the contrary, is constitutive of the free act. (Far from affirming his freedom, the person who chooses what is evil inasmuch as the chosen object is evil, brings about the failure of freedom in himself.) Moreover, if nature and freedom are virtually distinct in God, they are really identical in Him.

Now the other objection, which we also encountered earlier, consists in denying that personhood would involve a pure and simple perfection. The limitations involved in its existential realization within the domain of our experience would be essential to it, thus meaning that ontological finitude would be of the essence of what it means to be a person.

This must be denied. If, as we have seen, "person" designates a superior manner of subsisting (with self-possession through consciousness and freedom), a being is a person on account of what it positively is and not on account of its ontological limitations (i.e., on account of what it is not). Indeed, "to subsist" is a property of *being* as such, that is, arising simply from the fact that it is a *being*, not from the fact that it is this kind of *being*. Now, *being* as such holds all that it has from its *esse* by which it is a being. Therefore, along with its actuality, *esse* brings subsistence to a given being as well. Thus, that *esse* which is not received into a being (i.e., pure *esse*) can only be subsistent: *Ipsum Esse subsistens*. Just as all the other perfections of limited beings are realized in unlimited *Esse* in an infinite manner (and first of all intellectuality, love, and freedom), *Ipsum Esse subsistens* infinitely realizes the perfection of personality, namely, to subsist in an intellectual and free nature. It can only be personal, indeed infinitely personal.

Naturally, in the course of this transposition, Boethius's definition must be adjusted. Where we see, "rational nature," we must understand this as meaning, "intellectual nature," for it is proper to man that his intellect be rational.* Likewise, when "individual substance" is said, we must exclude the transition from the universal to the particular that we described (as though God were a universal essence realized in one or more individuals). God is a primary substance but is in no way a secondary substance. He is His Godhead.

b) Going beyond the Limits: Several Subsistents in a Unique (Primary) Substance

{117} *In creatures*, it is obvious that primary substance is identical with the subsistent. In other words, a primary substance constitutes one subsistent and one alone. The substance is the *quod* that has the concretely realized nature, which is this or that nature (animal, plant, mineral, and so forth). It is by this nature that it acts in this or that manner (as an animal, a plant, a mineral, and so forth). However, at the same time, it is constituted by it.

The mystery of God requires us to ask ourselves if this is necessary. Indeed, as we have seen, this mystery includes several "Being God," several who have the Divine Nature, which nevertheless is and can only be concrete, a primary substance.

We have tried to see how this plurality could be conceived. It remains that it requires a disjunction from us: these three are distinct from each other and, nonetheless, each is constituted by the same concrete, identically same, Divine Nature.

Where is the "primary substance" here? Inasmuch as it is a substance, it is one with regard to being: it is the Divine Substance, one and the same, common to the three. Inasmuch as it is "primary," that is, in as much as it is "subsistent," it is multiplied into three distinct subsistents. The same must be said about this other expression for what a person is: *res naturae*. The concrete, real nature is one, but there are three *res naturae*, three distinct realities [*trois distincts*] in which this unique nature is realized. The same holds for the expression "hypostasis," which, moreover, is practically identical with "sub-

* [Tr. note: That is, discursive in nature.]

sistent" when we are speaking about God, for substance in God does not have the character that it has in the created order (namely, that of being the subject of accidents, from which the term "substance" or "hypostasis" was derived in order to describe it in the created order).

Therefore if, as we have seen, "person" designates the primary substance, the *res naturae*, when the nature realized in the singular is an intellectual nature, we must say that Those "Being God" are three Persons, even though the nature realized in each—and with which each is identical—is perfectly one.

c) Going beyond the Limits: Several Persons and One,
Unique Center of Consciousness

{118} We have seen the objection: if the person is defined as being a center of consciousness, how can we conceive that the persons would be multiplied without the centers of consciousness being multiplied by this same fact? Nevertheless, one must deny that there is such a multiplication of centers of consciousness. In fact, given that consciousness is the focal point of every intellectual activity, situated at the very heart of the intellect, at the very root of the mind [*esprit*], common to the intellect and to the will (and in God identified purely and simply with thought and love), this would entail that the Divine Intellect and His Will (in short, the Divine Nature) would be multiplied, which would be a form of tritheism. Thence, "in all honesty, one must ask oneself with some embarrassment at the end what right one has to call the surviving remnant of the triune 'personality' in God a person, if one has had to eliminate from these three persons what one began by thinking of as a person."[33]

The response is that "a center of consciousness" need not be introduced into the very definition of personality. To be "a center of consciousness" is a property of personality, rooted in the "rational (intellectual) nature" that constitutes the person as such. Therefore,

33. Rahner, "Quelques remarques," 138. [Tr. note: Taken from Karl Rahner, "Remarks on the Dogmatic Treatise 'De Trinitate,'" in *Theological Investigations*, vol. 4 (More Recent Writings), trans. Kevin Smyth (Baltimore: Helicon, 1966), 101.]

if, in the mystery of God, one and the same rational nature is realized in three *res naturae* (in three subsistents, in three hypostases), that nature will not be multiplied into three centers of consciousness. Instead, this will mean that these three are together the same center of consciousness.

Therefore, by applying the idea of person to the Three "Being God," one has not removed from it what one had first placed under this idea. Each Divine Person is indeed a center of consciousness. What remains a mystery is the fact that this center of consciousness is the same, while the Three Persons are, nonetheless, distinct from each other.

As most often happens when one attempts to reflect deeply on the mysteries, although the infinite realization of a created perfection at first seems bewildering for reason (and indeed remains so), it nonetheless illuminates this perfection with a new light, all the while itself remaining in obscurity. Indeed, created personality is characterized by its openness to the other. It is not admissible to say that it is constituted by its relations with other persons, for it is the subject of these relations, and except in God, every relation presupposes its already-constituted subject. However, there can be no doubt that these relations have their root in it and that they are necessary for it so that it may develop itself, bring itself to completion, and flourish. Now these interpersonal relations tend toward identification in distinction: persons who love each other, to the degree that they love each other, are "one," all the while remaining several persons: "one" according to the good, several according to being. The unity of the center of consciousness held in common by the Divine Persons realizes at infinity, indeed vertiginously, this characteristic of interpersonal relations. Here, we are faced with a single mind, a single heart, a single will, and Three who are, each, a distinct person [*un distinct*] who thinks by this mind, who loves by this heart, who wills by this will. In short, in the Trinity, there are Three who are conscious and free through this one consciousness and freedom.

3. The Formal Constitutive of Divine Personality

In general, the person is "constituted" (not in the phenomenological sense of "to give a meaning to" but in the ontological sense, "to establish it in being, to make it be what it is") by the substance or nature of which, as a primary substance, it is the realization, a *res naturae*. However, here, the realized substance is numerically one, and yet it has three subsistents. Therefore, we must ask, "What constitutes each of these subsistents in His distinction from the others?"

a) Errors to Be Avoided

{119} *The first sort of error* would consist in conceiving of the Divine Substance as though it were the common subject of distinct relations. Thus, each Person would be the Divine Substance distinguished (and, as it were, "individualized") by the relation proper to each Person. This error is "obvious" on account of the difficulty of truly admitting (and the impossibility of conceiving) a relation without a subject. Historically, it seems that this was the conception expressed by Gilbert de la Porrée (d. 1154), retracted at the Council of Reims (1148), as recounted by St. Thomas.[34]

What was said in the preceding section suffices for denouncing this error. When relation is an accident, it affects its subject. The subject is what is referred. Hence, if, *of itself*, relative opposition in creatures determines only a distinction of relations, it *in fact* entails a distinction of referred subjects. It is a contradiction in terms for one and the same "being" to be the subject of two opposed relations.

From the perspective of Trinitarian doctrine, this error leads one to consider the Divine Persons as being, in some manner, external to the Divine Substance, *extrinsecus affixae*. One could find in this outlook the metaphysical root of certain deviations of so-called mystics "of the essence," holding that we would need to seek out the depth

---

34. See *ST* I, q. 28, a. 2; André Hayen, "Le concile de Reims et l'erreur théologique de Gilbert de la Porrée," *Archives d'histoire doctrinale et littéraire du Moyen Age* 10 (1935/ 1936): 29ff.

of the Godhead, not only beyond the attributes and the modes but even beyond the Persons.

The second error, running in the opposite direction, would consist in conceiving the Persons as being the subject of relations and, therefore, as being constituted independent of them. Such was the outlook expressed by Vladimir Lossky, who writes, "Note that here the relations solely serve to express the hypostatic diversity of the Three and not to found them. The absolute diversity of the three hypostases is what determines the different relations, not vice-versa."[35] In the preceding chapter, we established that only relative opposition can distinguish those "Being God" without dividing the substance. Therefore, they cannot be conceived as being constituted in their distinction prior to the relative opposition, despite Lossky's words of rejection: "The very principle of opposed relations is unacceptable for Orthodox triadology."[36]

b) The Principle of the Solution: Subsistent Relation

{120} We have seen that, from the beginning of theological speculation, the reason for the distinction of the Persons has been sought after in the notion of relation. The great difficulty that reflection encounters when, logically, it wishes to make the Persons be constituted by relations that alone are really distinct in God, is the apparent antinomy between, on the one hand, the concept of relation, which designates what the relative is for another and not what the relative in itself is, and, on the other hand, the concept of personality, which as we have seen designates an intrinsic mode of being. This difficulty, which troubled St. Augustine, finds its resolution only in the concept of a *subsistent relation*, namely, the concept of a relation that, while being its own subject, simultaneously is relative to another thing, thus being a principle of a real distinction as well as something in itself: an *absolute-relative*.

35. Vladimir Lossky, "La procession du Saint-Esprit dans la doctrine trinitaire orthodoxe," in *A l'image et à la resemblance de Dieu* (Paris: Aubier, 1967), 75.

36. Lossky, "La procession du Saint-Esprit dans la doctrine trinitaire orthodoxe," 74.

Although this notion is found in the profession of faith promul-
gated by the Council of Reims (1148), "the realities that they are,
relations, properties ... cannot be said to belong to God if they are
not God," it was truly elaborated only by high scholasticism—first
in Albert the Great in his commentary on "The Divine Names" of
[Ps.-]Dionysius and then, in a more rigorously elaborated way, in St.
Thomas who brought about a definitive form of progress in Trinitarian theology on this point.[37]

Inasmuch as it is subsistent, a relation can constitute the Person.
Inasmuch as there are several subsistent relations (on account of a
relative opposition), there can thus be several Persons.

The Solution Itself

{121} In general, a person is that which exists in an incommunicable manner in a given rational nature. By this, he is distinguished
from every other thing that exists in this same nature.

A Divine Person is constituted in the Divine Nature by the relation *inasmuch as He is identical with this nature.* That is, He is constituted by the relation inasmuch as it is subsistent.

He is distinguished from the other Persons in this same nature
by the same relation inasmuch as it is a relation, inasmuch as it is ad.

Therefore, what thus constitutes the Divine Person is the *ad* inasmuch as it is subsistent, that is, inasmuch as He is identical with the
Divine Nature. There are several *ads* which, being distinct from each
other, are identical with the same Divine Nature. Therefore, they are
directly constituted by the *ad* and indirectly by the nature or the essence—*per relationem in recto, per essentiam in obliquo.*

Consequently, a Divine Person is not a pure and empty *ad* but,
instead, is the whole Divine Nature, with its infinite riches of life,
intelligence, and of love. A Divine Person is the Divine Nature in
which the *ad* subsists, not as in a subject distinct from Him, but by

37. See Francis Ruello, "Une source probable de la théologie trinitaire de Saint
Thomas," *Recherches des sciences religieuses* 43 (1955): 112–13.

an identification of this subject that He is (the *in se,** a subsistent relation) with this nature.

The Trinity

1° Four Relations, Three Persons

{122} How is one to oppose the two, the Father and the Son, when it would be necessary to find an impossible opposition for human logic, the opposition of three so as to truly express the mystery of a personal God?[38]

We already encountered this objection in the preceding chapter. There can be no doubt that with three relations the problem would indeed remain insoluble. Above all, given that the relations are opposed two by two, there must be four of them, founded on the two processions.

Nevertheless, if there are only three Persons, this is because, for one of these relations, the Persons thus referred are already constituted as persons. Therefore, it is not a constitutive relation but, instead, is a relation *conceived of as* though it were subjected in the already-constituted Persons. We will see that this is only a manner of speaking. In reality, this relation is not subjected in the preceding ones which would be distinct from it but instead is identical with them.

Thus, the Father and the Son, already constituted as distinct Persons by the subsistent relations of paternity and filiation, are conceived of as being the sole subject of the relation of active spiration, which is therefore not constitutive of a fourth person. We will encounter this again as regards the Third Person.

2° What Is Proper to Each Person

{123} Each Person is an absolute-relative. However, the absolute that constitutes It is common with the other Persons. It is the nature

* [Tr. note: Reading "*in se*" for "*inse.*"]
38. Vladimir Lossky, "L'apophase et la théologie trinitaire," in *A l'image et à la resemblance de Dieu* (Paris: Aubier, 1967), 22.

or divine essence. Therefore, what is proper to each Person and what distinguishes Him from the others is purely relative. That is, He is relative to the other Persons.

Therefore, we will look in vain for an absolute property for a Divine Person, as though such a property would enable Him to be independent from His relation to the other Persons.

Whence the adage, which cannot suffer any exception: *In Deo omnia sunt unum et idem ubi non obviat relationis oppositio.*[39]

3° The Trinitarian Notions

The use of the term "notion" in Trinitarian theology comes from St. Augustine: "The notion by means of which one understands the first Person as the begetter is different from that which makes Him known as unbegotten."[40]

The term "notion" is used for the concepts that express what is proper and distinct to a Divine Person in relation to the others.

Granted, these concepts express this property "in an abstract manner, as a form." It cannot be otherwise, and nevertheless the Divine Person is a pure subject. However, we can know a subject only by attributing a form to it, even if we otherwise know that the subject and the form are identical—God is good, though in the sense that He is His own goodness. Nonetheless, I can know God as good only by attributing to Him the form "goodness" as though He had it [after the manner of a form], even though He *is* His Goodness. Likewise, the Divine Person is obviously identical with the form that expresses His notion. The Father is His paternity. However, I can express what is proper to Him only by conceptually breaking Him down into two concepts, one which is concrete, "Father," the other which is abstract, "paternity."

What makes this even more difficult is that, in fact, I often need several concepts to express what is proper to a person. I have not said everything that revelation has made known to me about the Fa-

39. See §52 above.
40. St. Augustine, *La trinité*, V, 6.

ther when I have attributed paternity to Him, for He also is the principle of the Holy Spirit. Therefore, we also must attribute spiration to Him.

All these characteristics are present as relations, since they only pertain to the relations that are proper to the Persons. Thus the question arises: "If, as we have said, the relation is constitutive of the Divine Person, how can one and the same Person be 'composed' of two relations?"

When two relations must be attributed to one and the same Divine Person—as in the case of paternity (or filiation) and active spiration—we must say that they come together, beyond all concepts, in one relation, one *ad* that embraces within its eminent unity the *ad Filium*, which is paternity, and the *ad Spiritum Sanctum*, which is spiration. Since these two relations are not opposed, they are not distinct from each other. Therefore, they are only virtually (or, conceptually) distinct.

Among the notions that express what is proper to a person, one of them is called "personal."[41] This personal notion expresses what is constitutive of the Person. The other notion (or notions) expresses the characteristics of the Person, conceived of as though derivative. (However, in reality, as was said earlier, the Person in His distinction is infinitely simple. Nonetheless, just as I can conceive of will in God only as though it derived from His intellectuality, all the while knowing very well that they are identical, so too I can conceive of active spiration in the First Person only as something derived from the paternity, all the while knowing that they are not really distinct.)

4° The Notional Acts

{125} The term "notional acts" is used for divine actions attributed to one or two Persons distinctly, through which the other Persons proceed—that is, generation, which is an act of the Father, and active spiration, which is an act of the Father and the Son together.

---

41. See *In I Sent.*, d. 26, q. 2, a. 3.

In reality, these acts also are reduced to the relations.[42] Just as the creative action is reduced to the relation of the Creator to the creature [in this case, a rationate relation], so too the act of "producing" a Divine Person is reduced, in the originating Person, to His relation to the proceeding Person.

Here again, on the level of action, we are faced with the problem arising from the fact that the Divine Substance is not distinct from the relations, which nevertheless are themselves inter-distinguished. If the *saying* really distinguishes the *sayer* from the *said* despite the fact that they are identical with the *intelligere* which is common to the *sayer* and the *said*, this is because the *intelligere* is not reduced to the relation [*of saying* and of *being said*]. The same holds for the *loving*, understood as designating the (notional) act of spirating the Holy Spirit.

We must always come back to the adage: "In God everything that is absolute, in the order of action or in the order of substance (recalling, moreover, that in God there is no distinction between action and substance) is one and common to the three; everything that properly and distinctly pertains to one of the Persons is purely relative."

4. Divine Personality and Subsistence

{126} Given that the Divine Person is "that which subsists in the Divine Nature," it seems to go without saying that subsistence belongs among the Person's characteristics. It is what the Person has inasmuch as He is a Person and what the Divine Nature has on account of it. Nevertheless, is it not the case that subsistence is an absolute attribute? Does not the Divine Nature subsist through itself, the Deity being a form that is its own proper subject?[43] On the other hand, when we say, "God," are we not speaking about the entire Trinity? (For example, in St. John Chrysostom's treatise *On the Incom-*

42. See *ST* I, q. 41, a. 1, ad. 2.
43. See *ST* I, q. 3, a.3.

prehensibility of God[44] or in St. Gregory of Nyssa's *The Life of Moses.*[45] Or, one may even consider what is said in Vladimir Lossky's *The Vision of God,* which is concerned with the impossibility of seeing the divine essence immediately—as distant as his position may be from the interpretation that I have proposed.)[46]

Now, "God" is a concrete term, designating a subsistent being, a Someone. Must we not envision a particular moment in our knowledge of God wherein He is attained as a Someone, as a personal being, without three personalities yet being distinguished in Him?

This represents the famous question concerning God's absolute subsistence, a question we already encountered on the level of the revelation of the mystery.[47] The theory that there is an absolute subsistence in God, prior (in the order of our knowledge) to the distinction of Persons, is attributed to Cajetan.[48] In reality, this position is expressly that of St. Thomas, and Cajetan merely formulated it and placed it in relief.[49] A great number of theologians today, following De Régnon, rise up vigorously against this outlook.[50]

What is objected against the position could be summarized thus: it represents an intolerable minimization of the Trinitarian mystery. [On such a hypothesis, such objectors say that] the true God, the God who is uncreated and who saves, would be He whom reason already was able to discover as the First Principle of the world. Revelation indeed tells us that He is one in three Persons. We confess this and, in our theology courses, we dedicate a treatise (a quite difficult one!) to this truth. However, it does not, in reality, matter much to

44. See St. John Chrysostom, *Sur l'incompréhensibilité de Dieu, Introduction de Ferdinand Cavalera and Jean Daniélou,* trans. Robert Flacelière, SC 28 (Paris: Cerf, 1951).

45. See St. Gregory of Nyssa, *La vie de Moïse,* ed. and trans. Jean Daniélou, SC 1bis (Paris: Cerf, 1955).

46. See Vladimir Lossky, *Vision de Dieu* (Neuchâtel, CH: Delachaux et Niestlé, 1962).

47. See §§26–28 above.

48. See Cajetan, *In ST* I, q. 3, a. 3, nos. 2 and 3; I, q. 39, a. 4, nos. 8 and 9; III, q. 3, a. 4, no. 10.

49. See *ST* I, q. 39, a. 4; *In I Sent.,* d. 4, q. 1, a. 2.

50. See Rahner, "Dieu dans le Nouveau Testament," in *Ecrits théologiques* I (Paris: Desclée de Brouwer, 1959), 90ff.

us, and "if the doctrine of the Trinity were to be erased as false, most religious literature could be preserved almost unchanged throughout the process."[51]

In this, a fundamental misunderstanding must be denounced. It is not asserted that the term "God" designates a personal being who is distinct from the Three Persons and is in no way affected by this mysterious characteristic of existing in three Persons. God is Father, Son, and Spirit. However, can I not know Him as personal, as a Someone, without knowing that He is the Father, the Son, and Holy Spirit, or even, when I do indeed know the latter, without making this knowledge explicit?

The so-called Cajetanian thesis is established in a rigorous manner as follows. As we have seen, the transcendent *res divina* includes, in its eminent simplicity, all the reality of substance (pushed to the infinity of substantial perfection) and all the reality of relation (equally pushed to infinity, and multiplied on account of the requirements of very notion [*raison même*] of relation).[52] The perfection of substance pushed to infinity gives us *Ipsum Esse subsistens*, absolute subsistence. The perfection of relation pushed to infinity gives us the *subsistent relations*. Therefore, for the Divine Persons, constituted (as we have said) by the subsistent relations, there are two (virtually) distinct reasons for subsisting. On the one hand, They subsist on account of the substance that is common to Them. This is the absolute Divine Subsistence, belonging, by identity, one and the same, to each of the Persons. On the other hand, They each subsist through the proper subsistence of Their constitutive relations.

However, just as the Divine Nature does not exist separately from the Persons, given that each Person in His distinction is God by this nature, so too the absolute subsistence is not separable from the relative substances. Each Person, in His (relative) distinction, subsists from the absolute subsistence of the Divine Being.

51. See Rahner, "Quelques remarques," 110. [Tr. note: Taken from Rahner, *Theological Investigations*, vol. 4, 79.]
52. See §103 above.

When I say that God is known and considered as being personal before I know that He is tri-personal (or, also, when I choose not to make this knowledge explicit when I, in fact, am aware of it), this does not mean that I recognize in Him a kind of personality prior to the distinction of the Persons. The divine manner of being personal is to be Triune, to exist in three Persons.

What is opposed against this explication is the so-called "monarchical" conception, which would be that of Orthodox theology.[53] Today, many Catholic theologians incline in this direction as well. It holds that the primordial Divine Personality is the Father's personality. The personality of the Son and of the Holy Spirit would arise from it, through the processions that communicate the Divine Nature to them:

In relation to the Father, causality expresses the idea that He is a God-Person inasmuch as He is the cause of the other Divine Persons and also the idea that He cannot fully and absolutely be a person except to the degree that the Son and the Holy Spirit are equal to Him in the possession of the same nature and are this same nature.[54]

Now, how does the Father communicate the Divine Personality to the Son and to the Holy Spirit? This cannot be His own personality, for His personality is precisely the only thing that He does not communicate to Them. It is that by which He remains distinct from Them. Therefore, He can only do so by what He has in common with Them, namely the Divine Nature itself. Thus, must we not say that this nature suffices in itself to furnish personality to those who possess it (by identification)? And here again we find ourselves faced with the idea of absolute subsistence, that is, the idea of a subsistence belonging to the Divine Nature as such, which, for this reason, is common to the Three Persons.

Nevertheless, there is a radical difference between a community of subsistence and that of substance. This latter is common in the

53. See Lossky, "La procession du Saint-Esprit dans la doctrine trinitaire orthodoxe," 76ff.

54. Lossky, "La procession du Saint-Esprit dans la doctrine trinitaire orthodoxe," 79.

sense that it is not multiplied in any manner. Each person is identical with the Divine Substance, one and the same with it. On the other hand, there is something profoundly mysterious about [this] subsistence. Indeed, it is the very revealed mystery of the Holy Trinity. The mystery lies in the fact that, instead of being realized in a unique subsistent, as is ever the case in our experience, in the case of God, subsistence is realized in three distinct subsistents. Inasmuch as it is a property of the Divine Substance, which is the *Ipsum Esse subsistens*, it is one and identical in the three. Inasmuch as it is realized distinctly in each of the Three Persons, it is multiplied in three relative subsistences. It is sometimes said (though, it is a poor way of expressing the matter), that in God there is one absolute subsistence and three relative subsistences. It is better to say that the Three Persons distinctly subsist from the unique Divine Subsistence, just as They are God through the One, Unique Godhead. Nevertheless, They are not three gods, although They are three subsistents (Three "Being God"). To explain how this is so, we must return to the key notion of "subsistent relation." As we have seen, in the Divine Person, the *ad* is what subsists, but it subsists on account of the *in*.[55] Now, the Divine Persons are distinct from each other according to the *ad* and thus are three distinct subsistents, whereas They are identical with the unique Divine Substance and, consequently, are identical to each other according to the *in*. Therefore, They subsist distinctly, though in virtue of a single subsistence.

Nothing prevents us from here using Karl Barth's terminology, saying that it is a question of recognizing three distinct modes of existing in God. However, we cannot do away with the notion of person, for what thus exist, in God, are three Persons.

{127} N.B., However, Cajetan's exposition can deservedly be critiqued, and one is justified in thinking that he is somewhat responsible for the misunderstanding noted above. Indeed, he distinguishes (by means of a conceptual distinction, obviously):

---

55. See §120 above.

Natura divina ut forma seu deitas: Essentia
Suppositum naturae divinae: Persona
Singulare, seu habens deitatem: Hic Deus

Indeed, it is clearly unfortunate that he used the term *"Hic Deus"*
in this way for the Divine Nature inasmuch as it is subsistent. It suggests a distinction, in God, between the individual and the Persons,
these latter thus seeming external and super-added (which obviously
was not how Cajetan conceived the matter).

Instead, one must say:

Natura divina = essentia communis tribus per seipsam subsistens.
[The Divine Nature = the essence common to the three, sub-
    sisting through itself.]
Personae = tres distincti in quibus subsistit ista essentia per seipsam
    subsistens.
[The Persons = three distinct ("realities") in whom that es-
    sence, subsisting through itself, subsists.]*

II. THE FIRST PERSON

We now come to our consideration of each of the Persons in
what is proper to Him, that is, in His distinction from the others.
We will study the relations of each Person with creatures (especially
their role in salvation history) in the fourth section of this volume.

A. The Problem concerning the Constitution
of the First Person

{128} According to Scripture, the First Person is characterized by
the fact that He is "the Father." Certainly, He is the Father of men,
and this poses particular problems that will be considered elsewhere.
However, He is, first of all and eternally, the Father of the Son (or
the Word).

* [Tr. note: This was originally small text. It was not moved to a footnote, however,
given that this remark is the whole of this section of text in no. 127.]

According to everything that we have said, it seems that this Person is constituted by the relation of paternity. Indeed, the relations that distinguish and constitute the Persons are founded on the processions. They are born of the procession between the originating Person and proceeding Person. In the case of the first procession, the relations in question are those found between the begetting Father and the begotten Son, who is born of the generation.

However, an immense difficulty arises when one wishes to apply this reasoning to the Person of the Father. Indeed, one can "understand" easily enough that the Son is constituted by the relation of filiation, since He is the terminus of the begetting and therefore "thought of" after the generation. But can we, without absurdity, "conceive" of the Father as being constituted by the relation arising from the notional act of generation, even though this act is conceivable only as proceeding from Him and therefore as already presupposing that He has been constituted? If we consider the very formulation of the first procession, when it is said that "in knowing Himself perfectly, God produces a Word, who is consubstantial with Him," it seems that we must admit that "God" in this proposition designates the First Person, designating Him as already constituted in Himself, "before" begetting and in order to beget.

If this difficulty cannot be resolved, the entire theory of the distinction of the Divine Persons through the opposition of relations is brought to an impasse. Nonetheless, we have shown that we have no other means for conceiving the distinction of Persons within the consubstantiality.

The examination of this difficulty makes us rejoin a traditional datum which is accorded the greatest of importance by Greek Trinitarian theology, which accuses Latin theology of having inadvertently forgotten it. This dictum asserts the Father's role as the unifying principle of the Trinity, the two processions setting out from Him and returning to Him by the relations of origin. It seems that He cannot play this role if He Himself is constituted by the processions.

It goes without saying that we are here concerned with conceptual distinctions. The Three Persons are co-eternal, and we do not dream of imagining that there would have been an instant in eternity wherein the Father would have been alone, after which He would have begotten. Such a conception cannot fail to lead to subordinationism, which ultimately would represent a form of Arianism. However, the difficulty is not abolished for all that, for if the First Person were not constituted by the very relation that opposes Him to the second (i.e., by the relation of paternity) He would need to be distinguished from the second in an absolute manner, and this is what leads to the difficulty at hand.

B. The Outlook Holding That the First Person Is Constituted by Innascibility

1. St. Bonaventure's Position

{129} St. Bonaventure has a clearly determined intention in this matter.[56] For him, it is a question of knowing which of the two concepts (namely, paternity or generation) is the reason for the other—*quae istarum sit ratio intelligendi alteram*? And he specifies the question: Is the First Person the Father because He begets the Son, or does He beget because He is the Father?

His response is that He is the Father because He begets but that this presupposes that He already exists (or, rather, that one conceives Him as already existing) as a distinct Person before conceiving that He is the Father. How is this so? I can conceive of generation only in a person who is capable of begetting, that is, in a person who is fruitful. This fruitful person, indeed with this divine fecundity (which, as we have seen, represents the "key" for understanding the Trinitarian mystery),[57] is the First Person. The term "innascibility" is connected to the first, characteristic note of this Person in or-

---

56. See St. Bonaventure, *In* I *Sent.* dist. 27, pt. 1, q. 2, ad. 2; H. F. Dondaine, *Saint Thomas d'Aquin. Somme théologique, La Trinité*, vol. 2 (Paris: Cerf), 354–56. [Tr. note: The Bonaventure citation incorrectly reads "q. 11." The citation of Dodaine also incorrectly cites another entry in the bibliography originally found in Fr. Nicolas's work.]

57. See §68 above.

der to express His "primacy," this term ("innascibility") signifying, by means of a negative concept, the *fontalis plenitudo* of the First Person (just as we express God's fullness of being by means of the negative term "infinite").

In this way, indeed quite consciously, St. Bonaventure joins himself to the venerable outlook of the Greek Fathers, who held that the Father is the Godhead-source, He from whom the other Persons receive their divine being (in consubstantiality).[58]

Quite logically, St. Bonaventure then comes to say (though, now in contrast to the traditional view holding that the Persons are inseparable, not only in reality, but also for thought) that the First Person can be perfectly considered in Himself, without reference to the other two:

Just as nothing prevents the hypostasis of the Father and that of the Son from being known without that of the Holy Spirit being known, so too the hypostasis of the Father can be perfectly known apart from the other two and before they are known. In this case, the hypostasis of the Father would be known without the paternity being known.[59]

2. Criticism of This Position

{130} At first glance, this position is satisfying for the mind, and if it cannot be called traditional (given that the problem was posed by the Fathers neither in this form, nor with this rigor), it seems to do justice to the traditional datum which we discussed and explained earlier.

58. See Lossky, "La procession du Saint-Esprit dans la doctrine trinitaire orthodoxe," 77–78.
59. Bonaventure, 471. N.B., This position was already held by Alexander of Hales, on whom St. Bonaventure depends, all the while developing and elaborating his thought more rigorously. However, it is also very close to the outlook of someone like Richard of St. Victor, who "explains" the generation of the Son by the impossibility of admitting that "God" would have wished to remain alone in the Godhead. (See Richard of St. Victor, *La Trinté*, III, 4.) For him this personal God, conceived of prior to the Son and the Holy Spirit, is the First Person.
Also, note that Karl Rahner's views concerning the identification of the Person of God (indeterminately conceived) with the First Person (See §27 above) are altogether situated in this line of thought.

However, upon reflection, it does not seem tenable. Indeed, according to this conception, the Person of the Father would be posited absolutely, independent of the two other Persons. He would therefore be *the Person* of God, the Person in whom the Divine Nature is realized. Only by a second step, in virtue of the communication of this Nature made by the First Person to the two others, would the latter also exist as Divine Persons. However, is this communication conceivable? What characterizes a person is that he exists in an incommunicable manner in a concrete intellectual nature—to be *the person* of this nature, as the nature is *the nature* of this person. Therefore, it seems that by admitting the possibility of knowing the First Person as though He were alone, without yet knowing that there are other Persons in God (*nulla alia persona intellecta*), St. Bonaventure makes this passage to the second unintelligible, namely the communication of the Divine Nature to the Son through generation, then the third step as well, namely the communication of the same and identical nature to the Holy Spirit through spiration. Indeed, if the First Person is initially posited as being absolute, it seems that the Divine Nature is realized solely in the First Person. Hence, He would be the *Only* Divine Person, not the *First* Person.

On the other hand, how could we think that the "divine fecundity" would be a property of one Person? As we have seen, this fecundity can be conceived of only as being a characteristic of the divine thought and of the divine love. [60] (Recall too that thought and love belong to the Divine Nature, which is common to the Three Persons who are this nature that the Father communicates to the Son and, with the latter, to the Holy Spirit.)

Nonetheless, is it not true that fecundity is proper to the Father since the communication of the Divine Nature is made to the two other persons through Him? A distinction is required here, one that St. Thomas elaborated and carried out with exceptional rigor.[61] Fecundity is the power that a living being has for communicating to

60. See §§ 68 and 80 above.
61. See *ST* I, q. 41, a. 6.

another living being the form by which it lives (i.e., its nature). This power is exercised by the living being itself (i.e., the hypostasis, the person, when the living being is a personal being). However, this power comes to it from its nature. For example, just as someone is a man on account of the human nature that is realized in him, even though he is the one who is this man, so too he is fruitful on account of this very nature which has fecundity as a property, even though he is the one who is fruitful. Now, what he communicates to the other living being who proceeds from him is precisely the nature by which he himself lives, and he communicates it all the more completely as life more perfectly exists in him (i.e., to the degree that it is interiorized in him).[62] As we have seen, in God, the communication is so perfect that one and the same, identical Divine Nature by which the Father is God is equally the nature of the Son and that of the Holy Spirit. By this Nature, they are God with the Father, the One God. Fecundity is a property of the Divine Nature and thus is common to the Three Persons, though it is exercised by the Father alone (and also, in a derived manner, by the Son with Him for the communication of the Divine Nature to the Third Person). This is so, precisely speaking, because the constitutive relations of both the Originating Person and of the Originated (or, Proceeding) Persons arise through the exercise of this fecundity. They hold the infinitely fruitful Divine Nature from the Father. However, as hypostases, they are the fruits of this fecundity.

Therefore, we cannot admit that the First Person would be constituted as a Divine Person other than by His relation to the Son. He is not a Divine Person who (according to our manner of conceiving) "becomes" first when a second appears on account of the generation. He is a Divine Person only by being the first, the Father of the second and the Spirator of the third. That is, He is constituted as a Person by the relation of Paternity.

62. See SCG, bk. 4, ch. 11.

3. The Importance of the Notion of "Innascibility"

{131} Nonetheless, we must not "let everything slip away from the secret that presses upon St. Bonaventure."[63] This "secret," which comes from the remotest and most certain tradition, is that the First Person is characterized by the fact that He is "the first," He from whom the other two proceed. There is an "order" among the Divine Persons, and their places are not interchangeable. Thus, let us note that the Latin image of the triangle used to represent the Trinitarian mystery is gravely deficient from this perspective. Certainly, every image is necessarily deficient, but we must take care not to be too tightly bound to this one in particular. The Divine Persons are equal and co-eternal, each wholly relative to the two others. For this reason, They are presented to the believer's mind together. No Divine Person has a "priority" over the others. Nonetheless, there is an "order of nature," which is precisely what the traditional notion of "innascibility," "principle without principle," intends to express.[64] The image of the triangle obscures this order and tends to represent the Persons as though They were interchangeable.

C. The Outlook Holding That the First Person Is Constituted by the Paternity Itself

This outlook is situated rigorously in line with the theory of the oppositions of relations. It asserts that the First Person exists as a distinct Person in God only in His relative opposition to the second. However, in order to extricate ourselves from the impasse indicated earlier, we must resolve the problem that was raised: How can I conceive of a begetting in God without *first* conceiving of a person who is capable of begetting and who begets?

---

63. See Dondaine, *Saint Thomas d'Aquin. Somme théologique, La Trinité*, 310.
64. See *ST* I, q. 42, a. 3.

1. Paternity and Begetting in God

{132} The Father exists as a distinct Person only through His relative opposition to the Son. It is clear that the Son exists as a distinct Person only through the begetting by which the Divine Nature is communicated to Him. Therefore, we must rigorously state that the Father Himself exists as a distinct Person only by begetting. This means that the unique notional act of begetting (or the "speaking" [of the Word]) simultaneously posits (from all eternity, without any movement or "becoming") its principle (i.e., the begetting Person, the Father) and its terminus (i.e., the begotten Person, the Son).

How is this not contradictory? In a very difficult text, which has given rise to divergent interpretations,[65] St. Thomas strives to avoid the contradiction.[66] He introduces a conceptual distinction in the very relation that constitutes the First Person. As "subsistent," this relation constitutes the Person and makes Him the principle of the notional act (begetting). As a pure relation, it distinguishes this Person from the second, and on this account, it is, like it and with it, the consequence of the notional act.

Obviously, this is useful only as a conceptual distinction, and only if we recall that the notional act is not a new act in relation to the essential act. (That is, the *dicere* is not an act differing from the divine *intelligere*.) Therefore, what is needed is a final effort exercised by the mind in order to conceive of this kind of "dehiscence" produced between the "sayer" and the "said," from all eternity, within the infinitely simple divine thought. The "saying" is what posits the "sayer" in His distinction, and simultaneously, the "sayer" is the principle of the "saying," all this being included in the eternal and infinitely simple relation of "paternity." Below, when we come to discuss the Holy Spirit, we will speak about how we can then "conceive" that the same Person (though, with the second) is the principle of a second notional act (i.e., spiration), through which the Third Per-

---

65. See Dodaine, *Saint Thomas d'Aquin. Somme théologique, La Trinité*, 310.
66. See *ST* I, q. 40, a. 4.

son is constituted. It is immediately clear that the difficulty raised in connection with the first notional act, begetting, no longer exists, for the first two Persons are already constituted by the begetting when They are considered as being the principle of this second notional act. In other words, because They are the Father and the Son, They are, together, the Spirator of the Spirit. Granted, specific difficulties remain pertaining to the second procession. We will examine them in due course.

2. Paternity and Innascibility

{133} This does not mean that the characteristic of being "unbegotten" would lose its importance. Much to the contrary, St. Thomas critiques St. Bonaventure (who identified this characteristic with the *"fontalis plenitudo"* of the Father) for not having sufficiently distinguished it from paternity, thus not doing justice to the light that it brings to our knowledge concerning the First Person.[67]

What the notion "innascibility," or "unbegotten," expresses is the First Person's characteristic of being the first in the Trinity, and therefore His characteristic of being the principle of the Trinitarian order. Just as "God"—i.e., the entire Trinity, the Three Persons together inasmuch as they are the One God—is the principle of order for the universe because all creatures come from Him and return to Him, so too, since we must recognize a multiplicity within the Godhead, we must discern a first principle in this multiplicity. The notion of innascibility expresses and makes known this characteristic of being the first principle in the Trinity. Without it, the First Person would not be entirely known. Similarly, without it, the Three Divine Persons would be conceived as though They were interchangeable, which is simultaneously unthinkable and religiously offensive because the notion of personality is precisely characterized by the fact of being unique and irreplaceable.

The notion of innascibility expresses this in a negative form. It

---

67. See *ST* I, q. 33, a. 4. [Tr. note: The original incorrectly uses an ibid to refer back two notes to the prior citation of *ST* I.]

does so by a negation of what characterizes the Son (i.e., to proceed from the Father) and the Holy Spirit (i.e., to proceed from Father and from the Son). However, what is attained by way of this negation is a positive characteristic that cannot be grasped directly.

What, therefore, is the difference between this outlook and that of St. Bonaventure? An enormous one! Indeed, this positive characteristic is no longer conceived of as though it were something "absolute." As we have seen, this is impossible, given that everything absolute in God is common to the Three Persons. Instead, it is conceived of as being reductively relative. It is the negation of a relation to another Person from whom He would proceed. Such a negation of a relation cannot constitute a Person, nor distinguish Him. However, it is a characteristic or a property of the Person constituted by the relation of paternity. It is a distinct property of the paternity itself (for paternity, *of itself*, does not exclude the possibility that the same person would be the son of another person). However, in God, it is necessarily connected with paternity, as we saw earlier when we studied the first procession.

3. The "Monarchy" of the Father

{134} The one nature in the Three is God. As regards the union, it is the Father, from whom the others proceed and to whom they return without being confused, though coexisting with Him, without being separated by time, will, or power.[68]

This perfect expression of the "monarchy" of the Father can be fully accepted by Latin theology, on the condition that is interpreted along the lines that we find in Vladimir Lossky (without a doubt in complete fidelity to the thought of the Greek Fathers):

The expression "Godhead-source" or "source of the Godhead" does not mean that the Divine Essence would be submitted to the Person of the Father. Instead, it means that the Person of the Father gives rise to the common possession of the Essence because He is not identified with the Essence, not being the unique Person of the Godhead. In some sense, one

68. Gregory Nazianzen, *Orationes*, Or. 42; PG 36, 476B.

can say that the Father is this possession of the Essence in common with the Son and the Holy Spirit, and the Father would not be a Divine Person if He were only a monad. He would be identified with the essence.[69]

Yes, the Father is not and cannot be conceived of in His distinction except in reference to the Son and the Spirit who proceed from Him. However, in this eternal network of references, He is the Principle of existence and of unity.

4. Summary

We have posed the problem concerning the [formal] constitutive of the First Person on the basis of the formulation of the first procession, *Deus intelligendo se profert Verbum*, and we have asked ourselves, "What does the term '*Deus*' designate (*pro quo supponit*) in this double proposition?"[70] We must respond that "*Deus*" in the first proposition ("*Deus intelligit se*") designates God, abstracting from the distinction of Persons ("*Deus unus*," according to the explanation that we proposed),[71] as well as His act of intellection, which is identical with His intellect and with His substance.[72] In the second proposition, there is a shift in the supposition. Having recognized that the *dictio* exists in the heart of the Divine Intellection, the term "profert" distinguishes "*Deus proferens*" (the subject of the proposition) from "*Deus prolatus*," that is, the *Verbum*.

D. The Beloved Son

{135} From all that we have said, it could seem that the Divine Processions take place in a quasi-mechanical, automatic, and "impersonal" fashion in God. This is the criticism registered against Lat-

---

69. Lossky, "La procession du Saint-Esprit dans la doctrine trinitaire orthodoxe," 78–79. N.B. In this text from Lossky, one must understand the expressions, "the Person of the Father . . . is not identified with the essence," "He would be identified with the essence," as being related to a virtual distinction. As we have seen, *in re*, the Person of the Father, like that of the Son and that of the Holy Spirit, is identical to the [divine] essence, though They are virtually distinct from it. See §103 above.

70. See §128 above.

71. See §126 above.

72. See *ST* I, q. 14, aa. 1–4.

in thinkers by Lossky. This represents one of the gravest criticisms registered against the theology that invokes the opposition of relations, and for many, it constitutes an insurmountable barrier to acceptance.[73]

1. Ontological Relations and Interpersonal Relations in God

{136} Obviously, the first response to the objection is that even though the divine processions are necessary, they are always accompanied by consciousness and willing. From all eternity, God knows and wills the processions.[74]

However, this response is not sufficient. Consciousness and willing, even if perfectly concomitant, would remain, in this explanation, a kind of duplication (or, reflection) of the processions, which would occur only in the nature. Thus, even if the persons would take up the processions and make them their own, the processions in themselves would remain purely "natural" and not "personal."

Thus, we must recall that consciousness and love in God are not merely simultaneous with His Being and with His Nature. Instead, they are identical with It, meaning that since the Trinitarian relations are ontological, they are also and simultaneously intentional relations of consciousness and of love.

To say, as we have,[75] that the divine processions are not voluntary, does not deny their intentional character in any way. Once again, the concern here is to establish the proper conceptual order, without which our knowledge of the Divine Reality would be distorted, even though we know and affirm that what these concepts express is one in this Divine Reality.

In the Divine Reality, the processions are at once natural and voluntary. However, I can conceive of them as being voluntary only after having conceived of them as being natural. Indeed, if I simply

---

73. See Henri Barré, *Trinité que j'adore* (Paris: Lethielleux, 1965); Jean-Hervé Nicolas, *Les profondeurs de la grâce* (Paris: Beauchesne, 1969).

74. See *ST* I, q. 40, a. 2.

75. See §69 above.

said that they are voluntary, this would mean that they depend on the divine willing for their being. It would therefore mean that they are contingent and that if they exist, this fact is not on account of an internal necessity of the Divine Being. By that very fact, they would tumble down into the created order. God necessarily wills Himself and everything that He could choose not to will—that is, everything that is contingent—differs from Him and is a creature.

The reverse is not true. To say that the processions are natural does not at all preclude that they be voluntary, on account of the identification of will and being in God. The necessity of God's willing with regard to Himself is not a determinism that is suffered but instead is the supreme form of freedom. That is, it is the source from whence freedom flows forth, for in willing Himself and loving Himself infinitely and necessarily, God freely wills and loves everything that it pleases Him to will and love external to Himself.

While maintaining, against the Arians, that the eternal generation is necessary, St. Thomas explains the intervention of the divine will in the eternal generation by saying that the Father begets the Son *with* an infinite love, if not *by* love, thus purifying the assertion that the eternal generation is necessary from every hint of constraint.[76]

2. Paternal Love as Constitutive of the Person of the Father

{137} Thus, the Trinitarian relations are relations of love. Therefore, one can and must integrate into the Trinitarian theology of relative oppositions the beautiful theology of Richard of St. Victor, the source and guide of every Trinitarian theology that would like to use the sociological schema of a society of several persons living together. Richard is more interested in the "why" (that is, in the *raison d'être*) of the processions than in the "how" of the distinct existence of the Three Persons. So long as one understands well that it is not a question of looking for finality in God Himself (for the divine

76. See *In* I *Sent.*, d. 4, a. 1; SCG, bk. 3, ch. 11; *De pot.*, q. 2, a. 3; *ST* I, q. 41, a. 2.

244 Those "Being God" in the One God

processions are "uncaused" both in the order of finality and in that of efficiency), but of enriching our knowledge of the Trinity by attempting to extricate the "meaning" of the Divine Nature's mysterious characteristic of existing in three Persons, this outlook presents a precious contribution that nothing in the rigor of the Thomistic explanation requires us to neglect, much less to reject.

In what pertains to the Person of the Father, this effort can be undertaken in the following way. We know through revelation that the divine love is also paternal. We know that everything that is found in paternal love (i.e., generosity, the joy of giving to another, abiding in the other, and so forth) can be transposed to God. However, love can be paternal only in relation to a son. If love is an essential act, it can be paternal only by being relative, that is, by being "notional." The person of the Father adds nothing to the divine love, which is identical with the Divine Nature and common to the Three Persons. Thus, we cannot admit the least distinction into this love, even a modal one, inasmuch as it is the nature of the Father, the Son, or the Spirit. Therefore, the note "paternal" is not a modality of the divine love as it is found in the First Person. However, the relation that constitutes the First Person places Him in the condition of being the Father in relation to the second, and this is how the divine love is paternal in Him.

Thus, the relation that constitutes the Father is the paternal love as such. That is, it is the relation of the First Person's love for the second. Inasmuch as this relation is subsistent, it is identical with the divine love which is God's very nature. However, inasmuch as it is a pure relation to the Son, it is the paternal love and is proper to the First Person. Just as the Father and the Son (and also the Holy Spirit) together produce the same intellection, though, at the heart of this infinite intellection, only the Father is He who "says" and the Son is He who "is said," so too at the heart of the infinite love that is common to them, the Father is subsistent paternal love and the Son subsistent filial love.

This does not add a new property to the Person of the Father but, instead, only makes explicit the relation of paternity that constitutes Him.

{138} N.B., It is sometimes said today, following the discoveries of Freud and Jung, that paternity no longer can be attributed to God, given that filial love has not survived their analysis. Just the same, we cannot repudiate revelation! God reveals Himself as a Father: first as the Father of men, and on the basis of that first revelation, in a very mysterious manner, He reveals Himself as the Father of the Son within the Godhead. This Father's love for this Son has been revealed to us in Jesus Christ. On the other hand, it is not out of scorn for psychoanalysis that we persist in thinking that sentiments as fundamental and universal as paternal (or maternal) love and filial love remain, even under the more or less grave aberrations that such analysis has discovered.[77]

3. The First Person's Paternal Love for Creatures

{139} In Trinitarian theology, God's paternal love for creatures poses particular problems that we will study in the fourth section of this volume.

We will see that this love is the manifestation and revelation of this paternal characteristic of God's love. We will also see that this characteristic gives the first procession its meaning and is what characterizes the Person of the Father inasmuch as He is, together with the two others, subsistent love in God. Therefore, continuity is found between the Father's love for the Son and God's love for creatures.[78]

III. THE SECOND PERSON

The Second Person has been revealed to us as "the Son," the "Only-begotten." As we have seen, the mystery of the Trinity was re-

---

77. [Tr. note: This was originally small text. It was not moved to a footnote, however, given that this remark is the whole of this section of text in no. 138.]

78. See ST I, q. 33, a. 2 and q. 45, a. 6.

vealed to us in and through Jesus Christ.[79] In the Incarnation, the Second Person is made manifest in the world as the Son of the Father, who thus has revealed the First Person to us as the Father. He also revealed the Third Person to us by promising to send Him "from the Father." Thus, everything that we can know about the Second Person is related to this fundamental, "constitutive" characteristic of being the "Son of the Father."

A. The Divine Filiation

There is no need to return to what we already said in our study concerning generation in God. This must be presupposed here, as well as what we said concerning the constitution of the Divine Persons in Their distinction.

1. The Constitutive "Proprium" of the Second Person

{140} Therefore, the Second Person is properly constituted by the relation founded on generation *passive sumpta* [passively considered] (cf. *ST* I, q. 40, a. 4), that is, upon "nativity." However, this relation is constitutive only because it is subsistent and, as such, is identical with the Divine Nature. Generation *active sumpta* [actively considered] is the communication of the one and indivisible Divine Nature by the Father to the Son.

The nature is not what is begotten. Nor is it the essence, which is "unbegotten." Instead, what is begotten is He who has (or, more exactly, who is) this Nature *as holding it from Him who does not hold it from anyone*:

Hence, He who is begotten in God indeed receives being from Him who begets Him without it being, on that account, received in a matter or in a subject, for such reception is opposed to the subsistence of the Divine Being. It is said to be "received" because the proceeding terminus holds the Divine Being from another and not because He is distinct from this Divine Being.[80]

79. See §§20 and 33 above.
80. *ST* I, q. 27, a. 2, ad. 3.

Pushed to its limit, this is the process of generation which, *of itself,* does not consist in producing the nature, but instead, in making a new individual exist in the pre-existing nature, although, in all the cases with which we are familiar through experience, the nature is, *in fact,* produced according to its individuation.

We must guard ourselves against the idea, one that is seductive at first glance, that each Person would have His own manner of possessing the Divine Nature and therefore His own manner of being God: "Although the substance and activity are common to the three persons, the possession of the substance is particular to each of them."[81] Implied in this outlook we find a kind of imagining of the Divine Nature itself being individualized, different in each person, in some way similar to the individualization of human nature, which is different in each man. However, in this case, the Divine Nature would need to be produced in the Son (then, in the Holy Spirit) thus individuated, and this would not be the Divine Nature (for the Divine Nature is "uncreated" and "not produced"). In other words, the Son would not be God. The Three Persons *do not possess* the Divine Nature. Each of them *is* one and the same Divine Nature and are distinguished from each other only by the opposition of relations.

Therefore, the Son, distinct from the Father by the opposition of relations founded on the eternal generation, is God from all eternity by the same, identical and simple, indivisible Godhead by which the Father is God: "Christ who is above all, God eternally blessed."[82] What is proper to His person is purely relative to the Father (and, as we will see later, relative also to the Holy Spirit).

2. *The Filial Love of the Second Person*

{141} Above, we were led to consider that the First Person was constituted by paternal love—not as a second constitutive princi-

---

81. Matthias Joseph Scheeben, *Les mystères du christianisme* (Paris: Desclée de Brouwer, 1947), 174; likewise, see Émile Bailleux, "Le Christ et son Esprit," *Revue thomiste* 73 (1973): 397.

82. Rom 9:5 (my translation); see §25 above.

ple but as another "grasp" by the mind upon the unique constitutive principle, namely the relation of paternity, which is at once ontological and intentional.[83] In the same way, we must say that the Second Person is constituted by filial love.

Here again, note well that we are not speaking of a kind of "nuance" in the divine love, inasmuch as it is exercised by the Son. One and the same love, the infinite love, is what is filial by the relation of the Son to the Father, just as it is paternal in the First Person by the relation of the Father to the Son. One thus returns to Richard of St. Victor's profound intuition: by rights, infinite love should be a form of friendship.[84]

Nonetheless, in our experience, paternal love and filial love involve characteristic "nuances," and for this reason are distinguished as kinds of love, paternal love having the characteristics of generosity and "authority," and filial love having recognition, deference, and submission as its characteristics. We can have access to knowledge of the paternal love and the filial love in God only on the basis of these experiential data, eliminating at the limit what cannot be found in God, namely the difference in the love itself and the subordination just mentioned.

For this transposition, the Incarnation of the Son doubtlessly brings us indispensable assistance. The Son manifests Himself to us in a human form, as the man whom He has really become, without ceasing to be the Son. In His human heart, filial love takes on forms that are familiar to us. Without this love, it would be nearly impossible for us to recognize it. Correlatively, paternal love is presented to us in its familiar form. This does not enable us to attain, in themselves and in their proper form, the paternal love and the filial love that are constitutive of the Father and the Son. However, it manifests them to us in a way that is proportioned to our understanding. The divine way of loving each other as a Father loves His Son and as a Son loves His Father evades us. However, Their love is in

83. See §137 above.
84. See Richard of St. Victor, *La trinité*, III.

line, though infinitely and asymptotically, with the way in which, in our experience, a father and a son love each other ... when they love each other, of course!

B. Son and Word

1. The Word of the Father

{142} The Word is another name for the Son that expresses the proper character of generation in God. This generation is an intelligible emanation, the production of a "concept" within the intimate depths of the Godhead, one that is identical with the Divine Essence, being distinguished only from Him who "conceives" it. However, the divine knowledge itself, in which this conception is produced, is common to both and is identical with the [Divine] Essence.[85]

Therefore, we find again for the Word what was said about the Son. He is distinguished from the "sayer" only by the opposition of relations, indeed the same opposition and the same relations.

Therefore, we must absolutely avoid the temptation of considering the Word as being the Divine Nature inasmuch as it is intelligible (a temptation which Blondel did not avoid).[86] The Divine Nature is intelligible by itself and therefore is intelligible just as much for the nature of the Father and that of the Holy Spirit as for that of the Son. The Word is distinguished from the Father solely as the "said" from the "sayer." Only the Father "speaks," whereas the knowledge is common to the Three Persons. Only the Word is "spoken," whereas the "being known" is common to the three.

2. The Divine Knowledge "In Verbo"

{143} Nevertheless, one often speaks of the knowledge of things in Verbo, and this is connected to revelation itself, which presents us

85. See §84 above.
86. See Maurice Blondel, *La pensée*, vol. 2 (Paris: Aubier, 1934), 342; Blaise Romeyer, *La philosophie religieuse de M. Blondel* (Paris: Aubier, 1943), 204–7; Barré, *Trinité que j'adore*, 72–89.

with the idea that all things are contained in advance in the Son and were made by His intermediacy.[87] This is also connected to the important idea that the revelation of God has been made to us through Jesus Christ, the Incarnate Word. It is an idea that many of the Fathers of the Church, especially the great Antiochenes, extended to the condition of man in the hereafter.[88]

How should this be understood? As the supreme intelligibility (the absolute idea that, at this [ontological] summit, is identical to the Absolute Being), the Divine Essence contains within its transcendent unity the "ideas" of all real and possible things. This is common to the Three Persons, who have (and each of whom are) this essence in a pure act of intelligibility. What is proper to the Second Person is to proceed from the First as the expression of the divine knowledge. The Divine Essence with the constitutive relation of the Word is the infinite "concept" wherein the divine knowledge is expressed. Correlatively, the same Divine Essence, with the constitutive relation of *dicens*, is the Person who expresses this common knowledge through the Word.

Everything that is attained by this knowledge—God, One and Triune, all possible things, and all real things—is thus expressed in the Word. In this sense, it can be said to be "known" in the Word. This does not mean that the Word would be first known and that the rest would be known through Him. (How could the Word be known without the Divine Essence and all that it "contains" being simultaneously known since He is, by identity, this Essence?) Instead, it means that He is, properly speaking, the perfect expression of this shared knowledge:

"To know" solely indicates the lived relation of the knowing subject to the known thing. No origin is evoked in this but only a kind of informing of our intellect, for our knowledge needs to be placed into act by the form of the object to be known. In God, "to know" will call to mind a total identity, since, in God, the knower and the known are absolutely one.

---

87. See Jn 1:1–8; Col 1:15–18; Heb 1:2–4.
88. See Vladimir Lossky, *Vision de Dieu*, 77ff.

By contrast, "to say" is related first to the conceived word, since to say is to emit a word; but by the intermediary of the word, he is related then to the known thing, manifested to the subject by this word that he emits. Therefore, in God, only the Person who *speaks* is He who utters the Word, although each of the persons knows and is known, and consequently is *spoken* in the Word.[89]

On the basis of this, we can interpret this *theologoumenon* stating that God made all things *through His Word*. All creation is the realization of what God has thought and willed, the realization of the creative knowledge [*science*] expressed in the Word. The creative knowledge itself is common to the Three Persons, but the Word is the Creative Idea, and the eternal uttering [*prolation*] of the Word is at the principle of the creative action, as (according to the ancient analogy) the conception of the work in the mind of the architect is at the principle of his activity undertaken to bring it about.[90]

The illuminative role of the Word in relation to men can be understood in the same way. He is "Begotten Wisdom." The Father is Wisdom as well, as is the Spirit, like the other two Persons, for God is Pure Wisdom. However, only the Word is Wisdom as expressed. Therefore, He is the principle of revelation, which is precisely the expression of God's Wisdom for men. (The reader should consider the admirable pages of St. Augustine on this subject.)[91]

C. Son and Image

{144} Another revealed attribute of the Second Person is that He is the image of God. Actually, this attribute is said to belong to Christ, the Incarnate Word,[92] even, according to certain exegetes, in the famous text: "He is the image of the invisible God."[93] However, if Christ is the image of the Invisible God, He holds this on account of His character as *The Son of God*. Therefore, the theologian

---

89. *ST* I, q. 34, a. 1, ad. 3.
90. See *ST* I, q. 34, a. 3.
91. See St. Augustine, *De trin.* VII, cc. 1–4.
92. See 2 Cor 4:4; Heb 1:4.
93. Col 1:15 (RSV).

is, in any case, justified in saying that He has not become an "image" by being made man, but rather, on the contrary, that He has communicated to man His eternal character as the image of God. Through the Incarnation, this image has become visible, and it has also become the principle for the reformation of God's primitive image in man: "For those whom he foreknew he also predestined to be conformed to the image of his Son, in order that he might be the first-born among many brethren."[94] The *Traduction Oecuménique de la Bible* comments:

Christ is the perfect image of the Father. The Father reproduces the image of His Son in all those who participate in His filiation. This conformity to the image of the Son is brought about through an interior and progressive transformation and will be full and complete only at the Parousia.[95]

How are we to understand that the Son is the "Image of God" already in the "Immanent" Trinity?

The Son is identical with God Himself, with the very Godhead of the Father, of whom He is the image. If likeness consists in community according to form, here we have a case of perfect unity. The same, identical form is common to the image and to that of which it is the image. Nevertheless, if the very "notion" of likeness and of an image is not abolished by thus arriving at the limit, this is because, even at this limit, they are two distinct "ones" [*deux distincts*] having this form and because the one proceeds from the other, receiving from Him the fact that He exists according to this form. Consequently, here again, the image is constituted by the form of the Godhead, common to the three, with the relation of filiation proper to the Second Person.

Nevertheless, important Patristic texts hold that the Holy Spirit has this same character as an image—either of the Father, or of the Father and of the Son, or specifically of the Son: "The image of the Father is the Son, and the image of the Son is the Holy Spirit, by

94. Rom 8:29 (RSV).
95. In loco, no. v. See André Feuillet, *Christologie paulinienne et tradition biblique* (Paris: Desclée de Brouwer, 1973), 30–47.

whom Christ living in man makes the latter be the image of God."[96] Moreover, it seems that the same theological reasoning should be carried out regarding the Holy Spirit. Given that He is really distinct from the Father and the Son, though consubstantial with them and holding from them one and the same form of the Godhead, it would seem that He should also be the perfect image of the Son (and of the Father).

Nonetheless, it seems that we should hold that being an image is something proper to the Second Person. This is so first of all because He is the only one so designated by Scripture. Moreover, it corresponds to His proper role in the economy of salvation. Therefore, we will reason as we did earlier in explaining that the Holy Spirit is not the Son even though He proceeds according to a perfect likeness to His originating source.[97] The mode of procession according to love does not, of itself, include this perfect likeness in nature. This perfect likeness in nature—which, like that of the Son, goes all the way to consubstantiality—comes not from the procession of love as such, but from the fact that this procession is divine.

Thus, the quality of being an image is intimately connected with the [Divine] Filiation. "Image" does not reveal to us some new characteristic of the Second Person. Instead, it only specifies what is contained in the idea of "Son."

For this reason, "Word" or "Image" are not distinct Trinitarian notions. They only enable us to penetrate further into knowledge of the Second Person by making explicit the intelligible riches of the notion of the Son.

D. The Son in the Immanent Trinity and the Son in the Economic Trinity

{145} According to Karl Rahner, it is on account of what is hypostatically proper to Him [*sa propriété hypostatique*] that the Son was incarnate, not in the sense that the Incarnation would be necessary

---

96. St. John Damascene, *De fide orthodoxa*, PG 94, p. 856.
97. See §80 above.

(as it *is* obviously necessary that the Second Person exists and that He be the Son), but rather, in the sense that if God determines that the Incarnation is to occur, it belongs exclusively to Him who is the Son in the Trinity to be incarnated:

Only the Logos can, in virtue of His immanent relation to the three (?) Divine Persons be He who is capable of hypostatically assuming a created reality and thus of being the essential and irreplaceable revealer of the Father.[98]

His fundamental reason is that Christ, so to speak, fulfills in the order of the Economic Trinity the same function proper to the Logos in the Immanent Trinity. Just as the Son is not the Father, so too God made man can be neither the Father nor the Holy Spirit. However, this rests on a [prior] "metaphysical" conception:

In God, what we call a "hypostasis" is exactly that by which each of the Three Persons is distinct from the two others, in a manner that is unique in each case, and nothing other than that. Therefore, on the basis of what one hypostasis can do in God, one can in no manner conclude that this would be possible for another hypostasis.[99]

Here again, we encounter the problem examined earlier, concerning the meaning that must be admitted for the term common to the three who are God: "three what?"[100] According to Rahner, it seems that the term "hypostasis" must be understood in an equivocal sense, designating in each case only what is proper and distinct to each of the "three." Is this conceivable? In any case, it is not expressible (for, as we have seen, "three" calls for a substantive, indeed one that designates precisely what is multiplied).

The problem is at once Christological and Trinitarian. From the Christological perspective, Rahner is certainly correct. Christ's mission in the world is to manifest the Revealing Word, the Son and Image to whom men are called to be conformed. Thus, we will see

---

98. Karl Rahner, "Dieu dans le Nouveau Testament," 101. [Tr. note: This and the next citation are translated directly from the French, as this seems to be incorrectly cited.]

99. Rahner, "Dieu dans le Nouveau Testament," 101.

100. See §113 above.

that, from the perspective of the Incarnation's meaning, only the Son could be incarnated, for when in the case of God, in whom wisdom is identical to power and to goodness, unsuitability is the same as impossibility, pure and simple.[101] Nevertheless, unsuitability differs from impossibility in that the latter comes from the fact that the thing considered is intrinsically contradictory, which is not the case for the Hypostatic Incarnation of a different Person than the Son.

Therefore, it is from the perspective of Trinitarian theology that it seems impossible to follow Rahner's reasoning. Indeed, we have seen that while each Divine Person subsists distinctly in the Divine Nature, the mode of subsisting is common to the three. It is that of a subsistent relation. The relations are distinct from each other by being opposed inasmuch as they are relations. They are identical with the Divine Essence and identical with each other inasmuch as they are subsistent. And it is inasmuch as He is subsistent that a Divine Hypostasis can make the assumed human nature subsist. In this sense, and in this sense alone, one can say that each of the three hypostases could do that.

IV. THE THIRD PERSON

Obviously, we cannot here ignore the grave debate that arose between the Greeks and the Latins on account of the unilateral introduction of the formula "*qui a Patre* Filioque *procedit*" into the hitherto common symbol of faith (i.e., the Niceno-Constantinopolitan Creed). This debate still stands, constituting an important obstacle to the rapprochement of two sister Churches, who both call themselves *catholic* and *orthodox* (and who doubtlessly are such, as eminent theologians hold). However, for the sake of greater clarity, we will first explain how the Latins conceive of the procession of the Holy Spirit and strive to resolve the difficult problems that are connected with it. Then, we will present the conflict over the *Filio-*

---

101. See §230 below and §312 in the second part of this course.

que and will ask ourselves if an ecumenical conclusion could not be found, one that would enable each Church to preserve its position in what is essential and "non-negotiable" to it without, for all that, forbidding the other Church from preserving what it believes cannot be abandoned in its own position.

The question could be divided into three parts: a study of the procession (however, this was already undertaken earlier); a study of the *originating terminus* of this procession and of the corresponding relation; a study of the *proceeding terminus* and of the corresponding relation.

A. Presentation of the Latin Position

1. The Originating Terminus of the Second Procession

a) Why Must the Third Person Also Proceed from the Second?

{146} Through [the influence of] St. Augustine, this position became common among Latin Christians, not only in theology but also in decisions of the Magisterium. It was something novel, at least in its formulation ("the Holy Spirit proceeds from the Son"), and gradually in the other direction, the opposite doctrine was constituted among the Greeks, namely, "the Holy Spirit proceeds from *the Father alone*." The Latin position was defined at the Councils of Lyon (1274) and of Florence (1442), whereas, after the separation, various eastern councils defined the "orthodox" formula.

In St. Thomas, we find a more rigorous theological demonstration of the procession *a Filio* than is found in St. Augustine or even in St. Anselm. This demonstration is found in a condensed form in *ST* I, q. 36, a. 2, but is completed by the considerations that are found in the responses to the objections* and that are more developed in *De potentia*, q. 10, aa. 2ff.

What is essential to the demonstration amounts to the following. The Divine Persons are distinguished from each other by relative opposition, and the opposed relations are founded upon the pro-

---

* [Tr. note: Fr. Nicolas writes "R / R".]

cessions. They are established between the originating terminus and the proceeding terminus. Therefore, if, in the second procession, the Second Person is not an originating terminus, His real distinction from the proceeding terminus is unintelligible and unthinkable, and thus we find ourselves forced to identify the terminus proceeding by the first procession with the terminus proceeding by the second. The "triad" is reduced to a "dyad," which is contrary to the faith.

The Greeks reject this argument because they reject its premises. As we have seen, they reject the idea that the Persons are distinguished from each other only by relative opposition. But how can we avoid contradiction if we say that the Three Persons are only One God and that nevertheless their distinction is absolute?

Within Latin theology, St. Thomas's rigor, which was novel, was not universally accepted. Scotus will come to reject it, taking up the arguments of St. Bonaventure and Alexander of Hales, which St. Thomas had already refuted in the *De potentia*. They consist in saying that what distinguishes the persons are, first of all, the "processions," the "origins." Because the Second Person proceeds by way of generation and the third by way of spiration, they are distinct, even without needing to appeal to relative opposition.

St. Thomas's response can be broken down as follows. First, it is impossible that the processions would distinguish the proceeding termini because through one as through the other, the same, identical nature is what is communicated (indeed, wholly).[102] What distinguishes them is the fact that this nature is communicated to two distinct Persons. Therefore, the distinction of proceeding Persons is what explains the distinction of the processions, not vice-versa. And the Persons can be distinguished, in perfect consubstantiality, only by relative opposition, which presupposes, as is shown in the principal argument, that the one proceeds from the other. One must admit that it is inconceivable to say that the same Person would receive one and the same Divine Nature two times, by two distinct processions. How-

102. See *De pot.*, q. 10, a. 2; *ST* I, q. 36, a. 2, ad. 7.

ever, what this means is that the second procession is unintelligible if the terminus proceeding from the first is not its originating terminus.

Then, he adds the argument that opens the way to an agreement, although it is not accepted by the Greeks.[103] Through the first procession, the Father communicates to the Son everything that He has, except His paternity. Therefore, He also communicates His "spirative power," which is not constitutive of His paternity.

From this twofold argumentation, it follows that what characterizes the second procession is the presupposition of the first. It does not merely come after it (which moreover would be meaningless, for all this is simultaneous and eternal). It is consequent upon it. This order is what St. Thomas places in relief in two other arguments in the *Summa theologiae*.

St. Thomas admits the expression *"per Filium,"* which can be found in the Greeks (though contemporary Greek theologians think that it holds only for the "economy" and not for the eternal processions). He explains it within the framework of his Trinitarian doctrine simply by the ordering of the two processions: the Son possesses with the Father indistinctly the power to spirate, as a property common to both, but He holds it from the Father through the first procession. Thus, He is conceived of as an intermediary between the Father and the Holy Spirit, the second procession presupposing the first by which the Son is constituted in His proper, singular, personality and receives a communication of the spirative power that is common to Him and the Father.

b) Unus Spirator

{147} Another aspect of the Latin doctrine, which also comes to him from St. Augustine and which St. Thomas only elaborated more rigorously, opens the way for a possible agreement with the Greeks, and in any case, ought to be better understood by them when they critique the Latin position.

Indeed, the great scandal they find in this Latin theory is the

103. See *ST* I, q. 36, a. 4.

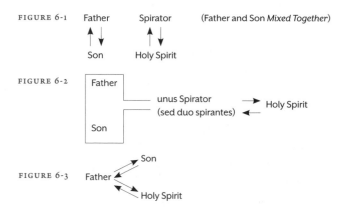

FIGURE 6-1   Father   Spirator   (Father and Son *Mixed Together*)

Son   Holy Spirit

FIGURE 6-2   Father

unus Spirator   → Holy Spirit
(sed duo spirantes)   ←—

Son

FIGURE 6-3   Father   Son

Holy Spirit

fact that it seems, to them, to withdraw from the Father His hypo-static property of being the "principle" [of the Trinitarian order], as though the Son were, next to the Father, another principle of the Holy Spirit. Indeed, this would be unacceptable if it was what the Latins assert. However, it does not correspond to the true Latin position. Indeed, according to the latter, the Father and the Son communicate in the possession of the "property" of active spiration. In other words, *together they are one, single principle of the Holy Spirit*.

At least in St. Thomas, this relies essentially on the rigorous application of the Trinitarian adage, "In God all is one where relative opposition does not intervene." The Father and the Son are relatively opposed as Father and Son, not as God [and God]. This is why, while being personally distinct, they are only one God. Likewise, they are not relatively opposed as "spirator" [and "spirator"], and this is why they are together one unique Spirator. And just as they are Two "Being God," they are Two "Being Spirator," which is expressed, "*duo spirantes*."[104]

The Greeks accuse us of dividing the "triad" into two dyads [as shown in figure 6-1]. In truth, according to the Latin conception, the triad remains undivided [as in figure 6-2]. Rather, it is in the Greek conception that it would be divided [as in figure 6-3].

104. See *ST* I, q. 36, a. 4.

c) The Mutual Love of the Father and the Son

{148} A debate exists within scholasticism, indeed even within Thomism, one that was raised by Penido.[105]

The question is whether the love from which the Third Person proceeds is the *essential love* (that is, the love of God for Himself, conceived anteriorly to every consideration of Distinct Persons, such as it is spoken of in the *"De deo uno"*)[106] or the *notional love*, that is, the divine love considered formally as an exchange, a friendship, between the Father and the Son. This debate, which can seem very abstract, in reality engages our understanding of Latin Trinitarian theology. Does it merit the criticism registered against it by Lossky, namely that of giving the Persons an impersonal origin, "having as a real foundation the one essence, differentiated by its internal relations"?[107]

Richard of St. Victor, without a doubt, explains the second procession by the mutual love of the Father and of the Son.[108] St. Anselm, by contrast, does not dream of doing so and speaks only of the Love of God for Himself (what Richard of St. Victor names *amor privatus*, which he opposes to *caritas*, friendship). According to Penido, St. Anselm would in this sense justly stand St. Augustine's intellectual lineage. St. Thomas himself, having at the start of his career leaned in the direction of the Ricardian solution, would gradually distance himself from it starting with the *Summa contra gentiles* and definitively in the *Summa theologiae*.[109]

In what concerns St. Augustine, let us note that Peter Lombard interpreted him in the same sense as did Richard of St. Victor, that

105. See Karl Rahner, "Dieu dans le Nouveau Testament," 13–111; Dondaine, "Notes doctrinales thomistes," in *Saint Thomas d'Aquin. Somme théologique, La Trinité*, vol. 2, 393–401.
106. See *ST* I, q. 19.
107. Vladimir Lossky, *Théologie mystique de l'Église d'Orient* (Paris: Aubier, 1944), 72–73.
108. See Richard of St. Victor, *La trinité* III, 11ff.
109. See SCG, bk. 4, ch. 19.

is, as teaching that the Holy Spirit proceeds from the mutual love,[110] and this interpretation appears to be justified:[111] "And if the love with which the Father loves the Son and with which the Son loves the Father shows beyond all words their intimate communion, nothing is more appropriate than to properly call 'Love' the Spirit who is common to both of them."[112]

In what concerns St. Thomas, Penido's thesis is formally contradicted by texts in the *Summa theologiae* itself, where the question of mutual love is openly discussed.[113] In reality, this thesis rests principally on the explanation of the second procession found in question 27.[114] In this explanation, the question at hand is in no way that of the mutual love of the Father and the Son. However, there we are still at the threshold of the treatise, and the personal character of the "begetting" terminus and of the "begotten" terminus have not yet been established. Proof that this first explanation of the second procession seemed insufficient to St. Thomas is found in the fact that he takes it up in a much more developed manner in question 37 where he speaks clearly about the Father and Son's mutual love.[115]

Penido seems to have set off on the wrong track, namely, the supposed opposition between "God's self-love" and "the mutual love of the Father and the Son." St. Thomas never posited this opposition. Indeed, the two explanations are found in one text, namely that of *De potentia*, where in the body of the article he is concerned with God's self-love, although in the responses to the objections the mutual love is clearly mentioned.[116] In this, Penido curiously adopts the problematic of Richard of St. Victor holding that an *amor privatus* in God would be opposed to *caritas*. (However, though he bases him-

110. Peter Lombard, *Sentences* I, 10, 1; 32, 1.

111. See St. Augustine, *La Trinité, Books VIII–XV*, OESA 16, trans. P. Agaèsse (Paris: Desclée de Brouwer, 1955), XV, cc. XXVIIff.

112. St. Augustine, *La Trinité*, XV, no. 37.

113. See *ST* I, q. 36, a. 4, ad. 1; q. 37, a. 1, ad. 3 and a. 2, ad. 1.

114. See *ST* I, q. 27, aa. 3–4.

115. See *ST* I, q. 37, a. 1c and also ad. 2 and ad. 3.

116. See *De pot.*, q. 9, a. 9.

self on this Victorine problematic, he ends, for his part, at a contrary conclusion, which he claims is St. Thomas's own conclusion.)

In reality, God's love for Himself, such as it can be discovered in natural theology, is the unique love of God *imperfectly known*. He who does not yet know (or who methodologically ignores) that God is a Trinity can think of God's love for Himself only as a form of self-love, the Supreme Being's sovereign attachment to His own goodness. However, the revelation of the Trinitarian mystery teaches us that this self-love in God is an infinite friendship between the three distinct Persons who constitute the One God.

Here, we must recall a primordial rule of theological epistemology, namely, even though everything is one in God (except the opposed relations), we can know the infinitely simple Divine Reality only through a number of concepts that are distinct from each other and *ordered* (thus meaning that they are not interchangeable). Thus, the "essential" concepts, which express what God is according to His Essence (and what is common to the Three Persons), are presupposed for the "notional" concepts that express what each person has properly and distinctly in relation to the others. The latter can be reached only by passing by way of the former, which, given the successive character of the process of reasoning, implies that at one moment of this process God is known through the "essential" concepts without being yet conceived through the "notional" concepts.

Thus, to conceive of the first procession, I pass from the essential concept of *intelligere* to the "notional" concept of *dicere*, and to conceive of the second, I pass from the "essential" concept of *diligere* to the "notional" concept of *spirare*. But here, we are confronted with an important difference. In the case of the first procession, the passage from the "essential" concept to the "notional" one is brought about immediately, so that the Person of the Father is known in His distinction only simultaneously with the Person of the Son and not in a first moment when He would be known on His own. This is not the case for the second procession, which, as we have seen, presupposes the first. That is, it can be conceived of only after the first.

Therefore, at this moment of the rational process addressing the second procession, we already know that there are a Father and a Son, who together are the one God. Hence, the expression, *"Deus diligit se,"* is naturally understood of the mutual love of this Father and this Son, God's self-love being an infinite love, exercised by these two persons together. Thus, in what concerns the second procession and its terminus, the passage from the essential concept (*diligere*) to the notional concept (*spirare*) is brought about through the mediation of notional concepts that were elaborated by reflection on the first procession.

Both the predicate *"Se [diligit]"* and the subject *"Deus"* include the two distinct persons. In fact, friendship is not "ecstatic" love, meaning that it would exclude self-love. (Without a doubt, this is contrary to Richard of St. Victor's conception of the matter.) It is based on self-love and does not cease to include it, extending to the beloved precisely as another self.[117] Thus, the Father loves Himself with the infinite love with which He loves the Son:

As the Father loves both Himself and the Son with a single love and as the same holds for the Son's love, the mutual relation between the Father and the Son, a relation of lover to beloved, is included in the Holy Spirit, inasmuch as He is Love.[118]

d) Infinite Friendship

{149} However, does this mean either that the Holy Spirit would be excluded from friendship in God or at least that in this friendship of the Three Persons a special connection would exist, a kind of "aside" between the Father and the Son? Here anew, we find, on the level of love, the accusation of dividing the triad into two "dyads."

We must compare the two processions anew. In the first, the *intelligere* is common to the Three Persons, whereas the *dicere* is proper to the Father, [relationally] opposing Him to the Son, who is the

---

117. See *ST* II-II, q. 25, a. 4; Jean-Hervé Nicolas, "Amour de soi, amour de Dieu, amour des autres," *Revue thomiste* 56 (1956): 5–42.

118. *ST* I, q. 37, a. 1, ad. 3.

Word spoken, the Father being He who "speaks," an opposition that is established at the heart of the *intelligere*. In the second, *Diligere essentialiter* (the very act of love) is common to the Three Persons, and this love is a friendship only because it is exercised by three distinct Persons, each of whom is simultaneously God loving and God beloved, whereas *Diligere notionaliter* (*spirare*) opposes and distinguishes the Father and the Son on one side, and the Holy Spirit on the other, an opposition that is established at the heart of the common *Diligere*. Therefore, the Holy Spirit is no more excluded nor precluded from the Infinite Love than He and the Son are excluded or precluded from the Infinite Knowledge.

2. The Proceeding Terminus of the Second Procession

a) Personified Love

{150} In what sense should we understand that "Love" designates the (distinct) hypostatic property of the Third Person? This is a problem that greatly preoccupied St. Augustine,[119] one that St. Thomas[120] strove to resolve through the rigorous application of the principles of his Trinitarian theology. The Holy Spirit in God is, properly speaking, Love, in the sense whereby "love" designates not the act of loving but, rather, the beloved being inasmuch as he is rendered present to the intimate depths of the lover through the very act of loving.

A particular difficulty arises from what was said earlier concerning the first two Persons, namely that the Father can be said to be constituted by the relation of paternal love and the Son by the relation of filial love. What is uniquely asserted when one says that the Third Person is also constituted by the relation of love?

In reality, love as such is not what [relationally] opposes and distinguishes the Father and the Son. On the contrary, it is because they are personally distinct that the infinite love is paternal in one and filial in the other. It is in a completely different sense that the Holy Spirit must be said to be constituted by the relation of love. He is the

119. See Augustine, *La trinté*, XV, no. 37.
120. See *ST* I, q. 37.

(affective) expression of the infinite friendship, as the Word is the intelligible expression of the infinite knowledge:

Without a doubt, we believe and understand that charity is not the privilege of the Holy Spirit alone in the Trinity, but also that it is not without foundation that one attributes the name of charity to Him properly. We have said why this is so.... Given that He is common to the Father and to the Son, He properly receives the names that are common to both of them.[121]

And St. Thomas:

In this way, just as the Father speaks Himself and speaks all of creation through the Word whom He has begotten (because the begotten Word perfectly expresses the Father and all creatures), so too He loves Himself through the Holy Spirit because the Holy Spirit proceeds (from Him) as the love of the first Goodness, a love by which the Father loves Himself and all creatures.[122]

The Holy Spirit is "Personified Love" in the same sense as one can say that the Son is "Personified Wisdom."

b) The Divine Gift

{151} According to a very beautiful insight expressed by St. Augustine, one that dominated the whole of [Latin] medieval thought on these matters, "*Donum*" is a name that expresses what is hypostatically proper [*la propriété hypostatique*] to the Third Person.[123]

This does not pass without difficulty, for it seems that the concept of "Gift" implies a relation to those to whom the Gift is given. This would seem to imply that the Holy Spirit exists in what is hypostatically proper to Himself only in function of creatures, which would be the same as making His "hypostatic existence" depend on the divine willing of creation, which is free. Therefore, He would not be a Divine Person. St. Augustine resolved the difficulty, though a bit

121. Augustine, *La Trinité*, no. 37.
122. *ST* I, q. 37, a. 2, ad. 3. N.B., Earlier, he had written, "The Father does not only love the Son, but also loves Himself and us as well through the Holy Spirit."
123. See Gonzales J Gutierrez, *Génesis de la doctrina sobre el Espiritu Santo-Don, desde Anselmo de Laon hasta Guillermo d'Auxerre* (Mexico: Progreso, 1966).

too rapidly, by distinguishing *"Donum"* from *"donatum"*: "One must distinguish the designation of *gift* and that of *given*. The *gift* preexists the *giving*, but the latter is necessary so that the thing that is the *gift* may be *given*."[124]

St. Thomas gives precision to the response.[125] In the *"Donum,"* he distinguishes the good communicated and the reason for communicating it. What formally characterizes the *"Donum"* is its gratuity. The good is communicated to the other without any self-serving intention (therefore, *by love*). Thus, what the term *"Donum"* essentially expresses is love inasmuch as it aims to be expressed by the effective communication of the good.

According to this outlook, to say that the Holy Spirit proceeds as *"Donum"* is only to make explicit one aspect of what was already said, though implicitly, when we said that the Holy Spirit proceeds according to Love, that He is Love. Consequently, from all eternity, and by what is hypostatically proper to Him, the Holy Spirit is He who will be given if there are beings susceptible to receiving the Gift of God (i.e., rational creatures). But what does "will be given" signify? Does this mean that He will be given separately from the Father and the Son? We will encounter this problem when we come to discuss the divine missions. Here, let us merely note, along with St. Thomas, that the notion of *"Donum"* inseparably includes an "essential" element (namely, the Divine Good) and a "notional" element (namely, the Person who is personified Love), for the love that is the reason for the giving is obviously implied in the act of giving, and what is given by this act can only be the Divine Good:

The fact that the notion of *Gift* includes a relation to the creature does not suffice to make it into an *essential* attribute. Instead, this only indicates that an essential attribute is included in this notion, as the Divine essence is included in the notion of [a Divine] Person.[126]

---

124. Augustine, *La trinité*, V, ch. 16, no. 16; 2, XV, no. 36. Gutierrez-Gonzalez, *Génesis de la doctrina sobre el Espiritu Santo-Don*, 8ff.
125. See *ST* I, q. 38, a. 2.
126. *ST* I, q. 38, a. 1, ad. 4.

According to the Greek Fathers, the Holy Spirit brings about the connection between the Trinity and man: through the Spirit, men discover the Son, and the Son manifests the Father to them.[127] These analyses concerning the notion of *"Donum"* enable us to retrieve the same insight in Latin theologians, and this could be a middle ground. Indeed, in His hypostatic quality as *Gift*, the Holy Spirit appears as being situated at the hinge of the Immanent Trinity and the Economic Trinity.

B. The Filioque Conflict

1. Historical Circumstances of the Conflict

{152} The reader can refer to texts on ecclesiastical history for the historical circumstances surrounding this conflict. [The basic narrative could be briskly summarized as follows:] the introduction of the *Filioque* into the Creed in Spain after (or during) the 3rd Council of Toledo (589), a very rapid adoption of the Creed thus occurring in the various Latin countries, then the first conflicts on this subject and the explosion of the latent doctrinal conflict on the occasion of the Photian crisis.

From its very beginnings, Latin triadology [*sic*] was spontaneously oriented toward the *Filioque*. In Tertullian, the *per Filium* clearly has this meaning:

Everything that arises from another is clearly second in relation to that from which it arises, without however being separated from it. Indeed, God uttered the Word, as the Paraclete also teaches, as the root the stem, the source the stream, and the sun the ray. For these kinds of processions are of the same substance as those from which they arise. On the other hand, where there is a second, there are two, and where there is a third, there are three. The Spirit is third after the Father and the Son, as the fruit is third, coming forth from the root and in coming out from the stem ... Thus, the Trinity deriving from the Father according to a continuous and coherent order alters the Monarchy in nothing and safeguards the status of the Economy.[128]

127. Marie-Joseph Le Guillou, "Réflexions sur la théologie des Pères grecs en rapport avec le Filioque," in *L'Esprit Saint et l'Église*, 220–34 (Paris: Fayard, 1969).

128. Tertullian, *Traité du baptême*, ed. and trans. François Refoulé and Maurice Drouzy, SC 35 (Paris: Cerf, 1953), VIII, 5–7.

The central idea is that of the intra-Trinitarian order, which assures the permanence of the monarchy (that is, the permanence of God's unity), because the communication is made on the basis of the first. Earlier, he said: "The Spirit is not otherwise than from the Father through the Son."[129]

The *Filioque* is found explicitly for the first time in St. Ambrose: "When the Holy Spirit proceeds from the Father and the Son, He too is not separated from the Father, nor from the Son."[130]

Therefore, St. Augustine was not an innovator in this matter but only synthesized the various elements that he found in the earlier Latin tradition concerning the procession of the Holy Spirit. Thus, it is not surprising that the formulas of St. Ambrose, taken up by St. Augustine, passed into the Western Churches' [*sic*] confession of faith. It is found in a letter by St. Leo in 447 against the Priscillians (modalists) aiming to affirm the proper and distinct personality of the Holy Spirit.[131]

What is certain is that throughout the centuries the two theological expressions peacefully coexisted. Only Eastern Christians were present at the First Council of Constantinople, and the Latins ignored the additions made then to Nicaean Creed up to Chalcedon. There, the Latins heard "*a Patre procedit*" without seeing an opposition being expressed by that. (The addition of the *Filioque* [to the Creed] had not yet taken place in the West.) On the other hand, the Greeks did not dream of protesting or of being scandalized by the Latin formulas that they were well aware of. As the Russian theologian Bolotov noted in 1898: "During this era, in accord with an unfathomable decree of Providence, the Eastern Church did not register any protestation against the Western position proposed by St. Augustine."[132] Perhaps this was so because it corresponded to anoth-

---

129. Tertullian, *Traité du baptême*, IV, 1.

130. St. Ambrose, *De spiritu sancto ad gratianum augustum*, PL 16, 762–63.

131. St. Leo, *Epistolae*, PL 54, 681.

132. [Collective work,] "Orient et Occident. La procession du Saint-Esprit" *Istina* (1972 3 / 4), 288.

er approach to the mystery, rather than being opposed to the position of the Greek Fathers of this era.

2. The Formation of the Orthodox Position

{153} It is clear that the Orthodox position is in no way a Photian creation (contrary to a now-outdated interpretation that was once classic among Catholics).[133] Instead, its roots sink down into the Trinitarian doctrine of the great Greek doctors of the fourth and fifth centuries.[134]

The Latin formula is congruous with their theological approach to the mystery of the Trinity, which first of all considers the communication of the divine nature to the Persons, beginning with the Father, according to the order: Father => Son => Holy Spirit. The Greeks were themselves more preoccupied with considering the Father as being the principle of the hypostatic existence of the Persons. For them, what is hypostatically proper to the Father (i.e., *what distinguishes Him*) is the fact that He is the principle. The Latins have only one word, *procedere*, for designating both, on the one hand, what is common in the communication of the Divine Nature to the Son and to the Holy Spirit and, on the other, the derivation of the personality of the Holy Spirit from the Father's personality. By contrast, the Greeks have two words: *proienai* and *ekporeusthai*. The first is found in John 8:42 with regard to the Son: "I come from the Father."* The second in John 15:26 is precisely in regard to the Holy Spirit. The two words are translated in the most ancient Latin translations, then in the Vulgate, by *procedere*. The cause of profound misunderstandings is found here in this difference of vocabularies.

Did the Greeks admit the "procession" of the Holy Spirit from

133. See Martin Jugie, *De processione Spiritus Sancti ex fontibus revelationis et secundum orientales dissidentes* (Roma: Lateran, 1936).

134. See Le Guillou, "Réflexions sur la théologie des Pères grecs en rapport avec le Filioque," 220–34.

* My translation (Minerd).

the Son in the sense of *proienai*? Le Guillou[135] and Garrigues[136] cite texts that are violently contested by Orthodox theologians today. By contrast, the denial of the procession *a Filio* is found, indeed with a clearly polemical intention, in Theodoret of Cyrus, whose principal argument is that, in these mysteries it is inappropriate to claim to say more about them than what Scripture says. As Le Guillou notes:

> On account of the formulas employed by a great biblicist and adversary of this development, Theodoret of Cyrus, we would be tempted to believe that a fairly important current of Greek theological thought would have gradually come to admit that the Holy Spirit holds His being from the Son (existence from [du] the Son, or through [par] the Son).[137]

Still, according to Le Guillou, this vigorous intervention of the great Antiochene would have stopped the movement toward a further study of the second procession and of His relation to the first: "Nobody will any longer dare to say that the Holy Spirit receives His being from the Son, and the formula 'through the Son' will be preserved for the communication of the Holy Spirit to the faithful."[138] As, on the contrary, this development was pursued in the West with St. Augustine and his successors, "Photius simply unveiled a latent conflict whose importance had not been grasped, one that is situated at the very point where faith and theological reflection come into contact."[139]

Must we follow the conclusions drawn by Garrigues? He claims:

> It remains the case that the Greek and Latin traditions have deepened each of the irreducible but inseparable aspects of the abyss of the Father. On the one hand, in the Greek tradition, there is the incommunicable as-

135. See Le Guillou, "Réflexions sur la théologie des Pères grecs en rapport avec le Filioque," 220–34.

136. Juan-Miguel Garrigues, "Procession et ekporèse du Saint-Esprit," *Istina* 17 (1972): 348.

137. Le Guillou, "Réflexions sur la théologie des Pères grecs en rapport avec le Filioque," 216.

138. Le Guillou, "Réflexions sur la théologie des Pères grecs en rapport avec le Filioque," 217.

139. Le Guillou, "Réflexions sur la théologie des Pères grecs en rapport avec le Filioque," 219.

pect of the Monarchy conceived as the incommunicable character of the Father, the unique origin (*archè*) of the Son and of the Spirit. On the other hand, in the Latin tradition, there is the communicable aspect of the Monarchy inasmuch as the Father is the source of the substantial communion and principle of the Trinitarian order.[140]

Nothing is less sure! For precisely in communicating the indivisible nature to another (then again to another, though He can be a third precisely only by receiving this communication also from the second), the Father is constituted in His singularity and simultaneously constitutes each of the two others in His hypostatic distinction.

3. *The Debate*

The Greek Arguments against the Latins

The Greek arguments against the Latins can be reduced them to the three following heads.

{154} 1° The rejection of the pretension of "rationalizing" the mystery, as though reason claimed to impose its law upon God Himself.

As we have seen, this includes the rejection of the explanation of the Persons by relative opposition. The claim is that the relations manifest the distinction but do not bring it about. Above all, they do not constitute the Persons.

This argument is supplemented by the concern to say nothing that goes beyond, even to the slightest degree, what Scripture says about so elevated a mystery.

2° In a more precise manner, perhaps, the Latins are critiqued, in consequence of this rationalizing pretense, for absorbing the Trinitarian mystery into their overriding concern for the [Divine] unity and, because of this, allowing the Persons to dissolve into the anonymity of the Essence.

We have seen that many Latin theologians today, following De Régnon, are extremely sensitive to this reproach. In what concerns

---

140. Garrigues, "Procession et ekporèse du Saint-Esprit," 360.

the *Filioque*, this position of the Latins would lead to this result precisely on account of what we ourselves believe is a point of contact, namely that the Father and the Son are not distinguished from each other inasmuch as they are the principle of the Holy Spirit. [For those who are thus concerned,] this would mean that the Father and the Son would thus constitute "an anonymous principle of the Holy Spirit."[141]

3° Finally the *Filioque* would undermine the "monarchy" of the Father, which "conditions the personal diversity of the Three at the same time that it expresses their essential unity."

Fecundity is a hypostatic property of the Father, according to which He is the "Principle" of the hypostatic existence of the two other Persons.[142] A similar attribution of fecundity to the Son as well would ultimately make the recapitulation of the Trinity in unity impossible.

a) Responses of Latin Theology

{155} 1° Language is largely responsible for this general reproach, though perhaps (but not necessarily), certain theologians' language also entails conceptualizations that also play a role in the disagreement. A principle of theological epistemology holds that when one is concerned with the knowledge of God, there is an inversion of the real order and of the noetic order. Before all things and all thoughts, before every reasoning and every revelation, God is. He is the Trinity, with the processions and relations and what is hypostatically proper to the Persons. Therefore, it is not at all a question of imagining in any way the rational laws to which the Trinity must be "fitted" so as to be viable! However, in the order of our knowledge, our grasp of the Trinity is not achieved at the end of a process of reasoning. Rather, it lies beyond every rational process, in the Beatific Vision,

---

141. Lossky, "La procession du Saint-Esprit dans la doctrine trinitaire orthodoxe," 72–73 and 81–82.

142. Paul Evdokimov, *L'Esprit Saint dans la Tradition orthodoxe* (Paris: Cerf, 1969), 57. Collection, *L'Esprit Saint et l'Église* (Paris: Fayard, 1969), 231.

after death. Consequently, we *noetically* "construct" the Trinity, and it is here that "rational laws" play their role. However, it is in no way a question of imposing them on God. Nonetheless, they rule our rational processes, and we must be faithful to them in order to avoid being led astray. An expression like, "The Persons cannot be distinguished from each other except by pure relative opposition, on pain of being led either to modalism or to tri-theism," or indeed, "The Holy Spirit could not be distinguished from the Son if He did not proceed from Him," does not signify any pretense of ruling the Divine Life itself but, instead, indicates to reason the straightway [*sic*] enabling it to access the transcendent Trinitarian mystery.

Thus, understanding things this way, we cannot accept the following outlook: the negative attitude that, placing our thought before the insitial antinomy of the absolute identity and of the no less absolute diversity in God, does not seek to suppress this antinomy but, rather, seeks to express it properly so that the mystery of the Trinity may enable us to transcend the philosophical mode of thinking so that the Truth may free us from our human limitations by transforming our means of intellection.[143]

What is initial is not the "antinomy" indicated here, which is of the noetic order. What is initial, instead, is the very mystery of the Trinity. And if this "antinomy" is unacceptable, it is because it is, in reality, a "contradiction." Now, according to Gregory Palamas himself, "antinomic theology" excludes contradiction (thus rendering it totally different from "dialectic theology"): "It is proper to every theology that wishes to respect piety to affirm as much one thing as another when the two affirmations are true. To contradict oneself in one's affirmations is suitable only for men who are completely deprived of intelligence."[144] Indeed, to simultaneously affirm the absolute diversity of the Divine Hypostases and the absolute unity of God is to contradict oneself. On the contrary, to seek, by means of

143. Lossky, "La procession du Saint-Esprit dans la doctrine trinitaire orthodoxe," 75–76.

144. St. Gregory Palamas, "La théologie de la lumière chez S. Grégoire Palamas," cited by Lossky, in *A l'image et à la resemblance de Dieu* (Paris: Aubier, 1967), 45.

analysis and an analogical transposition of the notion of relation, a real distinction which is not absolute and which, consequently, is not incompatible with an absolute unity, is to open for reason a way to understand the primordial affirmation of faith: "Three distinct realities [*trois distincts*], the Father, the Son, and the Holy Spirit, who are one God," or, "one substance in three hypostases."

Therefore, the reasoning which starts with the real distinction of the Second Person from the Third in order to come to the affirmation that the Holy Spirit necessarily proceeds from the Son (by passing through the middle term of relative opposition) will in no way "transpose revelation onto the level of philosophy,"[145] but in fact, will enable intellection to "increasingly open itself to the mysteries of revelation."[146]

2° The second objection brings out the danger of a rationalist interpretation of the position of Latin theologians like that offered by Penido.[147] An Anglican theologian, perhaps under the influence of these interpreters of St. Thomas, takes care to oppose, in the Latin and medieval tradition, the line of Richard of St. Victor (where the Reformers were situated) to that of "Boethius and St. Thomas."[148] We have seen that this supposed opposition involves a false interpretation. A great commentator on St. Thomas, John of St. Thomas, marvelously cast light on the fact that "notional love" (i.e., love as "producing" the Holy Spirit) of its very nature is the mutual love of two persons, the Father and the Son.[149] Thus, it is false to say that Latin theology holds that the *Spirator* would be "anonymous" (at least according to an interpretation that is certainly St. Thomas's and that alone should be retained). The *Spirator* is not the Father and the Son mixed together but, instead, is the Father and the Son perfectly united in love in order to constitute together the one, unique *Spirator*—just as the word "God" does not mix the Persons together but,

---

145. Lossky, "La procession du Saint-Esprit dans la doctrine trinitaire orthodoxe," 76.
146. Lossky, "La procession du Saint-Esprit dans la doctrine trinitaire orthodoxe," 76.
147. See §119 above.
148. See *L'Esprit Saint et l'Église* (Paris: Fayard, 1969), 222 [*sic*].
149. John of St. Thomas, *Cursus theologicus*, IV, disp. 35, a. 4.

instead, designates the three distinct "ones" [*Trois distincts*] that are the One God.

3° Here again, a deepening of the Latins' "theologoumenon," (i.e., "The Father and the Son together are the unique principle of the Holy Spirit") would enable one to show that Latin theology is perfectly able to do justice to the hypostatic function of the Father as the unifying principle in the Trinity. St. Thomas does this in his treatment of the notion of "innascibility."[150] Le Guillou firmly professes: "I truly believe that the Father is the origin, in the sense of *fons, origo*. We affirm the monarchy [of the Father] as much as the ancients do."[151] We must be very clear: the Father loses nothing of what He communicates to the Son, and what continues to distinguish Him from the Son, in this very thing that is common to them, is the fact that He is the originating principle of the Son. Therefore, the Father is the *origo* and *fons* because the Son holds from Him the very thing that is common to the two of them, namely being the principle of the Holy Spirit. Here, we could perhaps draw an analogy with the communication of causality to creatures: just as God loses none of His prerogative as the First and Universal Cause of all that is when He communicates the reality and dignity of causality to creatures, so too the Father loses none of His prerogative as the principle of the existence of the other hypostases in God by communicating to the Son the reality and dignity of being the principle of the Holy Spirit along with the Father.

b) Seeking A Way for Reconciliation

{156} Le Guillou asks,[152]

If the Western Church during all this time (between the formation of Latin Trinitarian theology in St. Augustine and the schism) indeed pushed onward in this direction (of the *Filioque*), we perhaps must admit that the *Filioque* was accepted by both sides, eastern and western, at least for a peri-

---

150. *ST* I, q. 34, a. 4.
151. *L'Esprit Saint et l'Église*, 231.
152. *L'Esprit Saint et l'Église*, 230.

od of time. The right to develop itself in this direction was admitted for the Western Church for several centuries. Fr. Bulgakov observed this forcefully. Why would it be impossible for the dialogue to be resumed on this level?

An indispensable aspect of such dialogue would first of all require both sides to seek to be understood and to listen to the response to the other side's objections.

Are we faced with an insurmountable obstacle in the fact that the two Churches have "defined" their respective positions? Might it not be sufficient that each Church respect the position of the other and accept the fact that its own position does not bind the faith of the other Church—at least such as it can be understood by it. (In any case, each Church's position cannot be understood without certain presuppositions and outside a given theological context, into which the other Church need not enter into in order for unity of faith to exist.)

Indeed, one must not forget that there is an essential point of agreement in this matter: the Greeks admit, as much as the Latins do, that in the "economy," the Father sends the Spirit "through the Son." We will see that, for the Latins, this implies that the Holy Spirit eternally proceeds from the Son (or, "through the Son") as well, and one is right to think that the way the Greeks distinguish "theology" from the "economy" is infelicitous here.[153] However, this agreement concerning the "economy" itself entails a fundamental agreement concerning "theology," which it is not essential [*indispensable*] to render clear and explicit.

V. PERICHORESIS

The Greek term *perichoresis* became a technical term for designating the Divine Persons' essential characteristic of including the other two: they are not external to one another. Its scriptural foun-

153. *L'Esprit Saint et l'Église*, 229, 234.

dation is found the Gospel expression: "I am in the Father and the Father in me"[154]

A. History of the Term and the Notion

{157} Originally, *perichoresis*[155] was a Christological term. In the verbal form *perichoreo*, it was first employed by St. Gregory of Nazianzen to indicate the interpenetration of the two natures, without confusion, in the unique Person of the Incarnate Word. It was later taken up, though in a substantive form, by Maximus the Confessor, for indicating the inseparable union of the two natures in action.

An unknown author called Pseudo-Cyril[156] is responsible for the term passing from the Christological register to the Trinitarian register.[157] He uses the word first to designate, in sum, the "communication of idioms." What I say of one of the two natures taken concretely (i.e., God, Man) can be said reciprocally of the other, itself taken concretely: e.g., this man, Christ, is the Creator of all things; God, Christ, was born of the Virgin Mary. This wholly new meaning of the expression led this author to extend it to the Trinitarian domain, so as to express the union of the Three Persons in God and their interpenetration. Thanks to this interpenetration, the multiplicity of the Persons is itself reduced to unity, not only to the unity of the *ousia*, nor only to the concrete unity of the Persons (the Father), but also to the concrete unity of each Person. Each Person is the Unique and Indivisible God.

Though the term is missing in St. Augustine, its reality is not.[158] After him, the great doctors of the Middle Ages used a term modeled on the Greek, "*circumincessio*," which preserves the dynamic character of the original term. However, the word can be found in the form "*circuminsessio*" (from *sedere*), which has a static note, namely, "to be within the other."

154. Jn 14:10 (RSV).

155. See Prestige, *Dieu dans la pensée patristique*, ch. 14.

156. See PG 77, 1117–74.

157. See Julian Stead, "Perichoresis in the Christological Chapters of the 'De Trinitate' of Pseudo Cyril of Alexandria," *Dominican Studies* 6 (1963): 12–20.

158. See Augustine, *La trinité*, VI, ch. 8, no. 9

B. Meaning of the Notion in Trinitarian
Theology: Ontological Interpretation

{158} St. Thomas's interpretation is not solely static. He also appeals to the processions, that is, to the relations of origin.[159] His concern is to show that while the One God includes the Three Persons, each Person is Totally God. If one so dares to speak, there is no more divinity in the Three Persons than in One. There is no perfection in one that would be lacking in another for being all that which God is. It is only the case that the one is not the other.

The notion of circumincession (the word itself is not found in St. Thomas) expresses this by signifying that the other two Persons are found in each of the Persons. None of Them is (and none of Them can be conceived) except in His relation to the two others. Or again, the notional envelopment designated by the term "Person" (three *Persons*) is not an abstract term realized in three individuals who are external to one another. Rather it is a concrete envelopment: each person concretely includes the two others.

Finally, tritheism is avoided thanks to this, without the distinction of the Persons being sacrificed. The Three Persons are, each and together, the One, Concrete God. This enables us to find, once again, from another perspective, the absolute substance.[160]

C. Intentional Interpretation

Astonishment and lamentation have been expressed regarding the fact that St. Thomas bound himself to this ontological interpretation of the Divine Persons, whereas Scripture above all invites us to affirm the interiority and "spiritual" interpenetration of the Persons united through thought and love.[161] Earlier, we noted that the ontological relations in God were *by themselves* interpersonal relations, for there is no distinction in God, *even a virtual one*, between

159. See *ST* I, q. 42; *In* XVI *Jn.*, no. 2161.
160. See §126 above.
161. See Barré, *Trinité que j'adore*, 123ff.

Esse and *Intelligere*, nor between *Esse* and *Diligere*.[162] There is a virtual distinction between *Intelligere* and *Diligere*, for these are perfections that are irreducible to one another on the level of our conceptual representation, whereas the distinction between *Esse* and *Intelligere* (or between *Esse* and *Diligere*) can be conceived of only as the distinction between first act (the Intelligent Being, capable of loving) and second act (this same Being in the act of knowing or of loving), meaning that these are not two perfections but, rather, two states of the same perfection, a duality that the very notion of Pure Act abolishes.

Thus, it is not difficult to enlarge, without thereby doing violence to it, the ontological conception of perichoresis proposed by St. Thomas, so that we may see in it the *koinonia* that Barré justly insists upon. For this reason, we spoke earlier about the infinite friendship of the Divine Persons. There is no need to contest the request that Latin Trinitarian theology, in particular that of St. Thomas, should be opened up in this direction. It suffices that this opening be not only possible but, in reality, called for by the very principles of this theology.[163]

The opposite is not true. A *koinonia* that is not rooted in an ontological perichoresis or circumincession would lead the mind, as well as the heart, toward the practical tritheism that Karl Rahner rightly denounced.[164]

162. See §136 above.

163. See Bernard Lonergan, *Conceptio analogica divinarum Personarum* (Romae: Apud Aedes Universitatis Gregorianae, 1967), 165ff.

164. See Rahner, "Quelques remarques," 137–138.

PART 3

——— : ———

Critical Reflection on Our Knowledge of God

7

Reason, Revelation, and Theology in Our Knowledge of the Mystery

I. THE IMPOSSIBILITY OF DISCOVERING THE MYSTERY OF THE DIVINE LIFE BY REASON ALONE

A. The Possibility of Knowing God in a Partial Manner

{160} The "mirror of creatures" is situated between the human intellect (which divides up reality and is progressive in character) and the infinitely simple Divine Reality. The multiplicity of our concepts is not an arbitrary activity, unrelated to the Divine Reality. This multiplicity corresponds to the multiplication of the infinite and simple Divine Perfection, a multiplicity found in creatures which, on account of the creative act, represent that Perfection in a deficient but real manner.[1]

This leads to the possibility of knowing God *truly* but partially, even though God does not have parts, for He is really (that is, in extra-mental reality) represented in a partial manner by creatures.[2]

Likewise and for the same reason, our knowledge of the Divine

---

1. *In* I *Sent.*, d. 2, q. 1, a. 3; Jean-Hervé Nicolas, *Dieu connue comme inconnu* (Paris: Desclée de Brouwer, 1966), ch. 2.

2. See *In Boetium de Trinitate*, q. 1, a. 4, ad. 10.

Reality is progressive, passing from the general to the ever more determined (let us say, "more essential," even though in God, Pure Act, we do not encounter the determining and the determined, nor species and genus). The addition of new forms of knowledge enables the mind to penetrate further into our knowledge of God, and in this sense, one can legitimately speak of penetrating into the "depths of God," although the Divine Reality obviously does not include the successive layers of perfections suggested by this image.

Having recalled these epistemological principles, we can see how the problem is now set before us. On the basis of [our knowledge of] creatures, making use of the threefold way of causality, negation, and eminence, we can rise up to God the Creator. That is, reason is led to affirm the existence of God, the Uncaused Being and Cause of all beings. Through revelation, we know that this God is triune. However, can reason, on the basis of [our knowledge of] creatures and in virtue of the requirements of the principle of causality, know and say that He is triune?

B. God Created and Moves the Universe Inasmuch as He Is One. This Can Be Shown in Two Ways

1. The Shared Forma Agendi

{161} In the treatise on creation, we see that the common and universal effect according to which all beings of the universe appeal to a Transcendent Cause, situated beyond the universe, is being. That is, this Cause can respond to this exigency only by being Absolute Being, *Ipsum Esse subsistens*.

Now, *Esse subsistens* is the very essence of God, which the Father communicates to the Son, and the Father and the Son to the Holy Spirit, without any division, each of Them being this one, concrete, and identical essence.

Therefore, the Father, Son, and Holy Spirit create and act in the world inasmuch as They are the One God. This does not mean that the abstract essence would act. No abstract essence acts, and the Divine Essence is not abstract. Likewise, this does not mean that

"God" who acts would be distinct from the Three Persons, for He is the Trinity. Instead it means that the distinction of Persons does not affect the numerically one *forma agendi* according to which They act in order to make and govern the world. The Creator is the Father, the Son, and the Holy Spirit together, manifesting Themselves, not according to the "properties" that distinguish Them, but according to the *forma agendi* that is common to Them.

Consequently, rising upward from creatures to the affirmation of God the Creator, reason cannot go beyond the One God to such a degree that, by itself, it would discover and affirm the distinction of Persons in Him.

2. The Shared Creative Action

{162} For the same reason, the creative action is perfectly simple. Certainly, the Father, the Son, and the Holy Spirit create and act in the world. However, just as They exist through the same, identically one *Esse*, so too do They act through the same, identically one Action. For this reason, They constitute only one Agent, and this unique Agent is what reason discovers in its search for the explanatory Principle of the universe. Here again, the distinction of Persons is noetically situated beyond the point where reason leads one in its ascent, setting forth from effects and scaling upwards to the creative action, for this action is not divided by the distinction of Persons.

C. The Ontological Necessity of the Trinitarian Mystery

1. The Absolute Necessity of the Divine Being

{163} The Divine Being is necessary. This first of all means that existence belongs to Him by identity (but so too does everything else that belongs to Him), meaning that He cannot be something other than what He is or exist in some qualitatively different manner [*soit autre ou autrement*].

Through revelation, we know that He is one in three Persons. This means that, at its summit, being includes this marvelous fecundity that we strove to understand in our earlier discussions. Likewise, it means that intellection, at its summit, includes the generation of a Word that is consubstantial with, though distinct from, its generative principle. It means that love, at its summit, is an outpouring of a consubstantial and distinct terminus. In short, it means that these two latter termini, along with the first, constitute Three Distinct Persons who are the One God. This is absolutely necessary *in itself*. Intellection and love, at infinity, include the processions of persons who are distinct from each other and consubstantial.

The Trinitarian mystery is the very depth and ultimate secret of the Divine Being. This mystery is indeed this *Ipsum Esse subsistens* which reason discovers, on the basis of [its knowledge of] creatures, without reason being able to know the mystery in itself.

Nevertheless, reason can know (and ordinarily does know) that its knowledge of God is incomplete. Reason knows Him only as the transcendent exemplar of creatures (and therefore knows Him only to the degree that creatures reflect Him) and can justly know that He is transcendent. Thus informed, reason naturally must conclude that an inaccessible mystery exists in Him, that His own manner of being, thinking, and loving is beyond what reason can conceive. Moreover, if it is true that reason is made for knowing being, it cannot, at least in certain existential conditions ([e.g.,] of the development of research, of fidelity to itself and its aspirations for knowing, and so forth) fail to experience a kind of yearning to grasp the supreme intelligible, something that is sovereignly desirable and yet impossible. This is the famous "natural desire to see God," the "intelligible fascination of the mystery of God" revealing the human mind's kinship with God and its opening to the revelation of what it cannot know by itself.[3]

---

3. See Nicolas, *Dieu connue comme inconnu*, 190–93.

2. The Temptation of the Ontological Argument

{164} If the Trinity is "necessary," why is it impossible for it to be demonstratively deduced on the basis of the intrinsic exigencies of Being, Thought, and Love when they are pushed to infinity?

Without going that far, many theologians and Christian philosophers have thought that this necessity can become clear to the believer's mind and that he can make it clear (even in order to convince the nonbeliever, or at the very least, interest him) as soon as he knows the mystery by faith. Such thinkers have held this because when man of knows this mystery, he can know it only as something necessary.

Someone like Richard of St. Victor is an illustrious representative of this second attitude in the Middle Ages.[4]

This represents a transposition of the "ontological argument" into the domain of the mystery. It consists in passing unduly from ontological necessity to logical necessity. In order for me to be able to demonstrate such a property of such a subject, it does not suffice that it belong to it necessarily. Beyond this, I must be able to know the reason for this necessity. This requires the possession of the quidditative definition of this subject, from which I could deduce the property or at the very least demonstrate that once the subject is posited it must have this property on account of its constitutive principles. Such a definition is wholly precluded for our knowledge of God. We only make judgments of existence concerning God, concerning His existence or the existence of this or that property in Him.[5] When these judgments of existence are concerned with the attributes that must be recognized as belonging to God as soon as we recognize Him as the Cause of all beings, such attributes are affirmed of Him as necessarily belonging to such a cause. As St. Thomas observes:

---

4. See Gaston Salet, "Introduction," in *Richard de Saint-Victor, La Trinité,* SC 63 (Paris: Cerf, 1959), 33–45.

5. See Nicolas, *Dieu connue comme inconnu,* 18–29; 116, n.5.

However, because such effects depend totally on their cause, on the basis of them we can first be led to know that God exists. Moreover, we are led to know that He has all the attributes that He cannot not have, since He is the first cause of everything that exists, a cause that transcends all His effects.[6]

When it comes to attributes that belong to Him on account of what, in His being, is a mystery inaccessible to human reason ([i.e.,] the distinction and the "propria" of the Persons), such things can be affirmed of Him only by the act of faith or by an act of reason in dependence on the act of faith (i.e., a theological judgment). They are absolutely necessary, but the judgment by which we affirm them of God is not necessary.

3. The Double Meaning of the Term "Divine Essence"

{165} *In reality*, the absolutely simple *res divina* includes the relations, processions, and Persons. The *propria Personarum* are not super-added to the essence, which is itself identical with the [Divine] *Esse*. Therefore, the term "Divine Essence" designates this transcendent reality, which is at once absolute and relative, one and triune. It designates the reality of our God.[7]

From the perspective of our knowledge, there are multiple concepts, along with an interrelated order among them. We saw above that the concept that expresses the Divine Being, such as He is affirmed on the basis of creatures, affirming Him as their First Cause, is anterior to the concepts by which we know the distinctions and *propria* of the Persons. When these *propria Personarum* are revealed to us, we conceive the Divine Being (i.e., the Divine Nature by which God is God) as being undividedly communicated by the Father to the Son, by the Father and the Son to the Holy Spirit, and possessed by the three together in consubstantiality. This gives us another meaning for the term "Divine Essence." It then designates the Divine Absolute, common to the Three Persons and conceptually distinct from them.

6. See *ST* I, q. 12, a. 12.
7. See §103 above.

Although this conceptual distinction arises from the abstractive character [*pouvoir*] of our intellect, the Divine Essence in this second sense is not "abstract." Instead, it is conceived of as subsisting through itself.[8] The reason for this is rooted in the particular conditions of our knowledge of God. God is not present to our mind as a reality having only one part considered by means of abstraction, leaving the rest of Him out of our consideration (*abstrahere*). We strive, rather, to reach the Divine Reality by penetrating ever more profoundly into the general concepts (e.g., being, intellectuality, love) in order to attempt to discover what He is, He who is the Being in whom all the intelligible perfection contained in these concepts finds its infinite realization. We affirm this Being as existing, as concrete, and as the real and actual Cause of beings. Thus, this "essence" that we attribute to Him is *esse* itself, unreceived and subsistent. And we see that the distinct relations, constitutive of the Persons, which, instructed by revelation, we attribute to Him, are in no way the ultimate determination of this essence, as though they gave it the character of subsisting. Instead, we see that they are identical with it in one common substance, which mysteriously leaves room for three relative, really distinct subsistences—not by being added to them but, rather, in its own intimate depths.

II. THE POSSIBILITY THAT REASON COULD RECEIVE THE REVELATION OF THE TRINITARIAN MYSTERY

A. The Trinitarian Mystery and Being

{166} In saying that, solely on the basis of the requirements of the notion of being and of the transcendentals, reason cannot grasp the intrinsic necessity of the Trinitarian mystery, we are not saying that the Trinitarian mystery is beyond being and the transcendentals. Something purely and simply "beyond being" is unthinkable

---

8. See *ST* I, q. 3, a. 3.

and impossible. I can think of nothing except by means of the concept of being, and the latter compels me to judge it to be impossible that something would both be and not be.

Instead, we mean something completely different, namely that He is beyond *esse commune* (i.e., being as realized in the beings given to our experience). However, in order to be intelligible, these very beings appeal to a principle situated beyond them, in which we find the perfect realization of everything included in the notion of being. In short, *Ipsum Esse subsistens* is not "beyond being." Much to the contrary, it is the Perfect Being, and all other beings are "below being."

Thus, the divine processions and personal relations are, so to speak, in the domain of being [*sont de l'être*]. For this reason, it is not impossible for the human intellect to know them using the notions of being and the transcendentals.

B. The Revelation of the Trinitarian Mystery

{167} This kind of knowledge requires revelation. Indeed, since reason can know it neither *a posteriori* on the basis of [our knowledge of] creatures, nor *a priori* on the basis of the Divine Essence, this knowledge must be communicated to it by God: "No one has ever seen God; the only Son, who is in the bosom of the Father, he has made him known."[9] Concerning the topic of revelation, as well as the problems posed by it, the reader should refer to a course on Fundamental Theology.[10]

In short, because the Trinitarian mystery is the supreme realization of the "perfection of being," of the *actus essendi*, it is expressible, of itself, in terms of being. The concepts elaborated by man on the basis of his experience, concepts that are directly related to the values of being realized in the created universe (the only thing offered to our experience), are fundamentally apt to being extended to the point of designating and expressing, by means of analogy, the perfect

9. Jn 1:18 (RSV).
10. Also see Nicolas, *Dieu connue comme inconnu*, 193ff.

realization of these values in God. However, this analogical "extension" of a concept can be brought about only by means of judgment, the act by which the mind returns to reality, affirming of it what the concept expresses, and, at the same stroke, expanding the concept to the point of designating the unique way it holds true for this transcendent subject, God.[11]

For attributes that reason can discover and recognize in Him on the basis of [its knowledge of] creatures, the domain of such a judgment is the primordial affirmation of God, itself founded on the principle of causality. God is affirmed, indeed, as the Transcendent Cause whom creatures necessarily posit. However, in the case of the *propria Personarum*, the analogical judgment by which they are affirmed of God can be only an affirmation of faith, founded on revelation. Indeed, it is one thing to understand the theological concept of *divine generation* or of *consubstantiality* (i.e., what Christians mean when they say that God is Father and that He is Son, and that the Father and the Son are consubstantial), but it is another thing to know and affirm that God the Father begets the Son eternally, and that the Father and the Son are consubstantial. It is only at this point that the analogical transposition is accomplished and that the concept becomes an analogue in act, the means for attaining God in His mystery. Up to that point, not only is its analogical value virtual (as is the case for all concepts that serve for the knowledge of God), but it is also hidden, imperceptible, and contestable. By itself, reason cannot know, nor, above all, ensure, that the concept of *generation* is transposable to God and that the concept of *consubstantiality* is not illusory.

This judgment, in which the act of faith consists, presupposes revelation, which furnishes the analogical concepts (through the superanalogy of faith). However, given that it is an act of the believer's intellect, it also requires an intrinsic super-elevation of this intellect by a gift of grace, the supernatural *habitus* of faith, as is discussed in the treatise on faith.

11. See Nicolas, *Dieu connue comme inconnu*, 104–7.

In this way, we thus reconcile the two antinomic aspects of our human knowledge of the mystery. On the one hand, it is *supra-rational*, having for its object truths that reason can neither discover nor verify (even by objectively constraining reasoning, the wholly interior form of verification that makes clear the necessary reason for the truth of what I affirm). On the other hand, it is *rational* in the sense that it is an act of reason. (Man believes by means of his intellect, which is reason [i.e., subject to discursivity].) In order for it to be an act of reason, the truths thus believed must be an object for reason. That is, they must be expressible in concepts elaborated by reason.

III. THEOLOGICAL INVESTIGATIONS: REASONING IN FAITH

{168} In this way, theological investigations, which represent a methodical and rational reflection on believed truths, are wholly dependent on the act of faith not only at their outset, but throughout the entire course of their progress. They presuppose it. They do not terminate in it. They do not abolish faith at their terminus, as though, after having believed at the beginning we would arrive at a rational verification of the truths that we believe. On the one hand, these truths are discovered as being inserted into the believer's intellectual universe. On the other hand, they are organized among themselves so that they may be illuminated by one another. Now, the act of understanding is always brought about by means of a reduction of an organized ensemble of truths to unity, for the object of the intellect is being, which itself is *one*.[12]

In what concerns the Trinitarian mystery, theological investigations strive to situate within man's intellectual universe the knowledge that the believer has concerning it through revelation, showing how the mysterious affirmations of faith are not contradictory and

---

12. See Jean-Hervé Nicolas, "La théologie," in *L'université et l'intégration du savoir*, ed. Norbert A. Luyten (Fribourg: Éditions Universitaires 1970), 37–53.

how reason, using these concepts, can assimilate these affirmations without, for all that, emptying them of their mystery. Such investigations also situate the Trinitarian mystery within the ensemble of the truths of faith organized by theology, showing that this mystery is the principle and terminus of the whole of salvation history.

Here, we find ourselves faced with a question: What intellectual universe are we speaking about? Does not the intellectual universe of each person depend on his era, his cultural milieu, and his personal formation? Does this not mean that theological investigations must find themselves deeply conditioned by this diversity?

This vast and difficult problem cannot be given a full treatment here. Let us merely observe that its resolution profoundly depends on what one holds concerning the nature of knowledge: is knowledge "realistic" or idealistic? In the former case, it is wholly ordered to grasping reality, ruled by being, finding its truth—and therefore its admissibility—in its conformity to reality. In the latter case, it is interiorly ruled by the subject. It would essentially express the idea that one forms concerning oneself and concerning the world in function of oneself.[13]

Certainly, even from the realist's perspective, a considerable amount of "personal coefficient" (and therefore a subjective coefficient) remains in the determination of truth. Reality is not a "brute datum." Rather, it reveals itself in different ways, depending on the angle from which it is approached. The analysis of the expressions of knowledge in function of such a coefficient falls to hermeneutics, and this represents an indispensable task. However, it remains the case that, if the intellect is fundamentally ordered to being, various "intellectual universes" have a common foundation to which their multiplicity can be reduced. Moreover, it would be easy to show that this alone can make intellectual dialogue possible, despite the diversity of the interlocutors' cultural milieus. Also, this alone renders

13. See Étienne Gilson, *Le réalisme méthodique* (Paris: Téqui, 1935), 90: "The greatest difference between the realist and the idealist is that the idealist thinks, whereas the realist knows."

hermeneutics itself possible. Indeed, if hermeneutics were wholly affixed to the intellectual universe of the interpreter in his unique particularity [*sa différance*], the very enterprise of interpreting the expressions used in a different intellectual universe would be futile.

This common foundation is what assures that theological investigations may possibly attain the reality of the mysteries and that their results may hold with universality.

Contemporary theologians are increasingly concerned with ascertaining what dogmas have to say to contemporary men and, to this end, with reexamining the Church's dogmas and doctrine in function of the lived context of men in their own era. Certainly, we must understand and participate in this concern. However, we cannot do so without critiquing it. There can be no doubt that revelation is made for men. Likewise, there can be no doubt that God promised Himself by revealing Himself and begins already here below to give Himself to the believer. Therefore, in the dogmas themselves, as well as in theology, there is a relation to the intellect and to the hearts of the men to whom these dogmas are addressed, *and this relation is essential to those dogmas*. But, first of all, who are these men? The expression "contemporary men" is used, not taking care to note that diversity cuts across groups of contemporary men just as much as it does among men from different ages. Moreover, when these diversities are indeed taken into consideration, enough care is not given to recognizing the fundamental unity of man and of the human intellect, a point we took care to note earlier. Likewise, thinkers fail to acknowledge the fact that the mysteries are ontologically independent of the human intellect (both the mysteries of "theology," that is, the intimate and eternal life of God, as well as those of the "economy," that is, concerning God's eternal design and its slow realization in time and history). God offers Himself to man by revealing Himself, through words and the events of history. Nonetheless, both the God who offers Himself, as well as the act through which He offers Himself, are what they are from all eternity, not what man's changing consciousness would make them be through the course

of time. To believe is to accept revelation. It is to hold as being true
what God says about Himself and about His designs. To the degree
that man believes, he discovers the meaning that revealed truth has
for him, for his generation, and for the whole of humanity. Revealed
truth is not modified in accord with the meaning that he claims to
give it. Therefore, dogmas are not what change. Instead, what changes is man's total comprehension of them (i.e., as truths and as principles of life). It is from the perspective of this comprehension that the
variations of intellectual universes and of living contexts play their
roles. However, they do so while being based on the common foundation shared by all men, thus constituting an at once unique and
diversified interlocutor before God.

IV. BEYOND THEOLOGY: CONTEMPLATION
OF THE MYSTERY IN FAITH

{169} The servitudes of analogy (i.e., the impossibility of verify-
ing both its points of departure as well as its points of arrival) place
reason in a very difficult situation as it investigates into the *intellectus fidei*. On the one hand, of itself, it is unable to shed a complete
light on the object of its investigations. Therefore, it must submit itself to a norm that is external to itself, the Word of God. Certainly, it
can submit itself to this norm without abdicating its rights. However,
given that it is presented in human language and by a human authority, this norm "mortifies" reason. On the other hand, the only means
that it has for knowing this transcendent reality are those which are
adapted to the realities of experience and elaborated on the basis of
them. In short, it only has at its disposal concepts that are radically
inadequate for representing that which is beyond every representation.

This infirmity of theology is felt most keenly in the treatise on
the Trinity. Here, we are concerned with knowing and expressing
the most concrete reality that there is, in which everything is pure
subsistence, where nothing, consequently, gives rise to distinction

between the abstract and the concrete: the Divine Persons. However, given that this reality is vertiginously elevated above every sensible experience, the concepts that must be used to grasp it, at least to some degree, necessarily must be carried to the highest degree of abstraction, and this is the level of abstraction where theological reasoning moves about in its reasoning and judgments. Of course, by means of judgment, it ceaselessly strives to rejoin the concrete reality at which it aims, affirming God as the Pure Subsistent in Three Distinct Persons. Nonetheless, this very affirmation, and all those that surround it, necessarily make use of abstract concepts.

Experience is the only remedy for these limitations. This is not the place to show that an experience of God would be really possible. Nor is this the place to look into the conditions for such an experience. Let us merely recall that it is brought about by means of love, God being attained as the loving and beloved being, communicating Himself and desired, present with a presence at once ontological (i.e., His presence of immensity) and spiritual (i.e., a presence of knowledge and love).[14] Let us also recall that this experience is wholly dependent on faith, itself being an act of faith, though of faith that is impregnated with love and inspired. In this experience, God is attained obscurely, beyond formulas, though not outside of them. The knowledge we have through faith (and thus the notional theology that prolongs our faith) furnishes this experience with the noetic content without which it would not be a form of knowledge but, instead, a mere subjective exaltation without any bearing on reality and, consequently, incapable of attaining God truly, for God is eminently real and not a self-projection.[15]

In this mystical experience, the believer—beyond all the formulas that awkwardly attempt to express the distinction of the Divine Persons as well as what each has distinctly and singularly—"knows" in the most experiential sense of the term, each of the Persons in His distinction. (The Father is not the Son, and the Holy Spirit is nei-

14. See Jean-Hervé Nicolas, *Les profondeurs de la grâce* (Paris: Beauchesne, 1969), 437.
15. See Nicolas, *Les profondeurs de la grâce*, ch. VI; also §207 below.

ther the Father nor the Son. However, how is one to say, and how is one to express to oneself, what each Divine Person Himself is in distinction from the two others?) Properly speaking, such an experience is "ineffable," for on the basis of his own experience, the mystic runs into the same difficulties as does the theologian in his attempts to express it. He experiences the inadequacy of concepts, images, and words, and if he is not a theologian, in attempting to express the mystery that he has in some manner "touched," he falls into using the inadequate formulas that he has drawn from theologians, not always making use of the most exact ones. However, through what he does communicate concerning this experience, the mystic makes known to others that he has experienced a loftier form of knowledge, and he invites all believers to similarly stretch themselves beyond formulas, toward such an experience even though it is quite clear that only God can give it to whomever He wishes. However, it is good to know that such an experience exists.[16]

V. BEYOND FAITH: FACE-TO-FACE VISION

A. The Consummation of Faith in Vision

1. The Promises of Scripture

{170} Scripture, which ceaselessly requires that faith be man's fundamental attitude as well as the free act necessary for his salvation, equally presents faith to him as a transitory phase of salvation history. Faith must lead to the revelation of the Son of Man in glory.[17]

The two essential texts where this promise is expressed are 1 Corinthians 13:12 and 1 John 3:1–2. There also is Revelation 22:4. In the latter, it is not only a question of the Son of Man's coming "in glory," or of the "revelation of the glory" of Yahweh, but also is a question of "seeing the Face of God."

---

16. See Jean-Hervé Nicolas, *Contemplation et vie contemplative en christianisme* (Fribourg-Paris: Éditions universitaires, Beauchesne, 1980), chs. 2 and 5.

17. See Mt 24:30; Mk 13:26; Lk 21:27.

2. The Plea Expressed by Theological Reason

{170²} Earlier, we discussed the profoundly unsatisfying character of faith. Moreover, mystical experience, with its obscure and "ineffable" character (even for him who is the beneficiary of it), only
provides an imperfect remedy for this unsatisfying character. This
lack of satisfaction is a sign that faith, even if it is pushed to its highest point of perfection, cannot be the definitive state of saved man. If
God gives Himself in revealing Himself, it is impossible that this gift
of Himself through the human words of revelation be the last word
concerning His love. Faith is the reception of God only by being the
promise of a complete and fulfilling knowledge. If the mere "hun-
ger to know and understand" that is born in the depths of the intellect is already a more or less perceived yearning for this complete
knowledge of God, how much more will faith and mystical experience bore into the believer's mind the impatient and painful desire
for a perfect knowledge that they can anticipate without procuring
it?[18] [In the words of St. John of the Cross:]

¡Ay, quién podrá sanarme!—¡Acaba de entregarte ya de vero;—no quieras
enviarme—de hoy más ya mensajero—que no saben decirme to que quie-
ro!: Ah, who has the power to heal me?—Now wholly surrender your-
self! Do not send me—any more messengers;—they cannot tell me what
I must hear.[19]

Faith can only be understood as being an expectation of an adequate
knowledge of the mystery of God. This represents true knowledge
concerning this mystery—but how deficient it is! Imperfect revelation (through words, images, and the concepts expressed in imperfect human language) can only be conceived of only as being the
preparation for a perfect revelation.

---

18. See §163 above.
19. St. John of the Cross, Spiritual Canticle, str. 6. [Tr. note: Taken from St. John of
the Cross, "The Spiritual Canticle" in The Collected Works of Saint John of the Cross, rev.
ed., trans. Kieran Kavanaugh and Otilio Rodriguez (Washington, D.C.: ICS Publications,
1991), 45.]

However, the only thing that such a revelation could be is immediate vision. God, who is beyond all concepts, cannot be directly represented by any concept. Since He is perfectly concrete and infinitely simple, He can be experienced directly only by being seen without an intermediary. And, indeed, this unmediated vision is what is promised to the believer: "For now we see in a mirror dimly, but then face to face. Now I know in part; then I shall understand fully, even as I have been fully understood."[20]

3. The Misgivings of Theological Reason

{171} However, reason recoils before such prospects. Indeed, does it suffice to say that God lies beyond all concepts? Is He not also beyond all direct knowledge, at least beyond all creaturely knowledge? If to know is to be equal to what one knows, is not the hope of knowing God Himself, in Himself, a sacrilegious pretension that we must reject?

The same Scripture that in certain texts encourages this hope, in many other texts discourages it, proclaiming, in a seemingly absolute manner, that "Nobody has ever seen God."[21]

On this point, a notable divergence exists between Orthodox and Latin theology. There is even, as for the *Filioque*, a notable divergence between the profession of faith of the Catholic Church and that of the Orthodox Church [*sic*]. Indeed, in the Catholic Church in 1336, face-to-face vision was solemnly declared by Pope Benedict XII to be part of the ordinary teaching of the Church and was defined at the Council of Florence in the *Decretum pro graecis*.[22]

As we did for the *Filioque*, we will first explain the Latin thesis, such as it was elaborated by St. Thomas. Then, we will confront it with the thesis of Orthodox theologians and will see if there is a way to bring about a reconciliation between the two perspectives.

20. 1 Cor 13:12 (RSV).

21. See 1 Tm 6:16; Jn 1:18; 1 Jn 4:12; Vladimir Lossky, *Vision de Dieu* (Neuchâtel: Delachaux et Niestlé, 1962), 21–27.

22. See D.-Sch., 1000 and 1305.

B. The Knowability and
Unknowability of God

{172} It is a fundamental truth of Christian soteriology that, here below, God is inaccessible in Himself to man's knowledge and that He can be known only in and through Christ, being revealed by Him. All Christians are in agreement on this point: "No one has ever seen God; the only Son, who is in the bosom of the Father, he has made him known,"[23] and "no one knows the Father except the Son and any one to whom the Son chooses to reveal him."[24]

However, does this hold true universally? Is not the Son, the Logos-made-man, the required intermediary for the creature's knowledge of God? Many of the Greek Fathers thought so:[25]

The affirmation that knowledge of the Divine Essence is above man's natural powers is a commonplace affirmation in them* (in the first Christian theologians). However, they instead place the accent on the fact that God, who is inaccessible to human powers, is made known by grace in Jesus Christ. In particular, this is the teaching of Irenaeus and of Origen.[26]

This constitutes a profound insight of faith. Following the Cappadocians, John Chrysostom reacts vigorously against the outrageous rationalism of the Anhomoians [or, Eunomians], represented for him by Eunomius, who reduced the mystery of God to the level of reason. Eunomius teaches:

God does not know His being more than we do. His being is not clearer for Him than it is for us. He knows, in an equal manner, everything that we know about Him, and everything that He knows about Himself, we find it easily in ourselves without any difference.[27]

23. Jn 1:18 (RSV).
24. Mt 11:27 (RSV).
25. See Lossky, *Vision de Dieu*; Paul Evdokimov, *La connaisance de Dieu selon la tradition orientale* (Lyon: Mappus, 1967).
* [Tr. note: there is a closing double quote right here with no correlative.]
26. Jean Daniélou and Ferdinand Cavallera, "Introduction," in Saint John Chrysostom, *Sur l'incompréhensibilité de Dieu*, SC 28 (Paris: Cerf, 1951), 16.
27. Daniélou and Cavallera, "Introduction," 12–13.

What Eunomius is lacking is an adequate metaphysical sense of God's transcendence.

However, we have seen that the believer is promised "face-to-face vision." The Orthodox tradition wishes to do complete justice to the texts that contain this promise, without abandoning God's absolute transcendence in relation to every created intellect, as well as the necessary mediation of the Transfigured Christ, of His deified humanity, which, like a "torch of glass" will make "the ineffable splendor of the one nature in three hypostases"[28] burst forth.

1. The Position of Orthodox Theology

{173} This position was elaborated in the fourteenth century by St. Gregory Palamas and was sanctioned by the so-called "Palamite" councils from 1340 to 1360 ("councils whose dogmatic importance and magisterial authority for the whole Orthodox Church are in no way inferior to the authority and importance of the councils we call 'ecumenical'"[29]). The sources of this explanation must be sought much earlier, in the Cappadocians and in [Ps.-]Dionysius. It consists in distinguishing God's essence from His natural energies ([through] "an ineffable distinction").[30] The Divine Nature is participable in Its energies, not in Itself. The grace that divinizes us is a divine energy, and this is what leads to the rejection of the Latin notion of "created grace."[*]

Palamas's adversaries (gathered around the monk Barlaam) accused him of undermining the divine simplicity.[31] However, "the essence and energies are not, for Palamas, two parts of God, as some modern critics still imagine them to be. Instead, they are two different modes of God's existence, in His nature and outside of His

---

28. Evdokimov, *La connaisance de Dieu selon la tradition orientale*, 72.

29. Lossky, *Vision de Dieu*, 129.

30. See John Meyendorff, *Introduction à l'étude de Grégoire Palamas* (Paris: Seuill, 1959), 279–310; Vladimir Lossky, "La théologie de la lumière chez S. Grégoire Palamas," in *A l'image et à la resemblance de Dieu* (Paris: Aubier, 1967), 39–65.

* [Tr note: Reading "grâce créée" for "grâce incréée."]

31. See Meyendorff, *Introduction à l'étude de Grégoire Palamas*, 65–94.

nature, the same God remaining totally inaccessible through His essence and communicating Himself totally through grace."[32] Curiously, Palamas expresses this distinction between God's "energies" (or, "attributes") and His essence—a distinction that he claims is found *within God's unity*—in terms that are akin to what the Trinitarian mystery compels us to say concerning the three *distinct* hypostases.

This distinction between the imparticipable Divine Essence and the participable energies is not limited to God's relations to the created world: "If the world had not been created, God would ever have existed, not only in His inaccessible essence, but also, outside of His essence, in the energies that are the effluences of the essence."[33] And once again, we find this quite surprising comparison with the Trinitarian processions: "The essence must be called superior to the energies in the same sense that the Father, who is the source of the whole Godhead, is said to be superior to the Son and to the Holy Spirit."[34] In reality, we certainly must say that the Father is not superior to the Son and to the Holy Spirit!

In what concerns the precise problem of the Vision of God, all of this leads to the conclusion:

After many centuries, we find ourselves before the same vision of the Transfigured Christ, by which the Father communicates in the Holy Spirit the light of His inaccessible nature, a vision of God that we encountered at the beginning of our study, in St. Irenaeus, this Father of the Christian tradition, disciple of St. Polycarp, disciple of St. John, who said: "No one has ever seen God; the only Son, who is in the bosom of the Father, he has made him known" (RSV).[35]

2. The Position of Catholic Theology

{174} This distinction between the Divine Essence and uncreated* energies, understood as a distinction that is both real and that

32. Lossky, *Vision de Dieu*, 130.
33. Lossky, "La théologie de la lumière chez S. Grégoire Palamas," 49.
34. Lossky, "La théologie de la lumière chez S. Grégoire Palamas," 50.
35. Lossky, *Vision de Dieu*, 140.
* [Tr. note: Reading "incréées" for "créée."]

does not divide God's unity, is not only foreign to the "categories" of the Latins. It is contradictory in itself, as we saw earlier with regard to the rejection of relative opposition:[36] "We do not think that it is intelligible to say a real distinction exists within the Godhead, however diminished such a distinction might be."[37]

Nevertheless, the problem for which it intends to be the solution persists and is not foreign to Latin theology. In His distinctive propriety, in His "essence," God absolutely transcends every creature. If the creature can participate in this transcendent perfection, it cannot do so by itself, immediately. Rather, it can do so only by means of a gift coming from God who divinizes [the creature]. On the other hand, by definition, this participation cannot be total. In the very gift that He makes of Himself to the spiritual creature, God remains transcendent, the "Wholly-other."

In what concerns the necessary mediation, the difference between the Greeks and Latin [believers] could be summarized as follows. *For the Greeks*, this mediation is assured by something properly divine, something of God, His "uncreated energies." Now, this position has the aforementioned drawback, namely that it thus requires us to posit within the unity of the Divine Being a real (and unintelligible) distinction between the Inaccessible Essence and the participable energies. *For Latin* [*theology*], this mediation is assured by a gift from God, a gift *that is created*, transforming the created spirit, elevating its intellectual faculty to the level of the transcendent divine object, namely, *the light of glory*. It is an infused *habitus*, produced in the created mind [*esprit*] by God's action, rendering the creature capable of "seeing God."[38] It assures a "subjective mediation," without which the created mind, left to itself, would remain infinitely distant from the divine object. What the [beatific] "vision" excludes is every "objective mediation," meaning that there is no intermediary between the created mind [*esprit*] that (intellectually) sees the Divine

36. See §155, 1˚ above.
37. Michel Labourdette, "Mystique et apophase," *Revue thomiste* 70 (1970): 637.
38. Nicolas, *Les profondeurs de la grâce*, 134–41.

Essence and this Transcendent Essence. God is seen immediately. Moreover, He can be seen only in an immediate manner, as the metaphor of sight precisely suggests. Therefore, "immediacy" here signifies the exclusion of every intermediary concept. (In other words, every kind of objective intermediary is excluded.) Indeed, God cannot be conceived in any created concept produced by the created mind. His infinitely transparent essence is "made to be seen" by God Himself informing the created intellect in a pure act of intelligibility.[39] For the Greeks, by contrast, an "objective mediation" does exist, namely, Christ's humanity, through which the uncreated light of the Divine Essence passes, enabling us to see the latter while leaving it in itself in its transcendent unknowability. In short, what the Latins call the "light of glory" is a perfecting of the intellectual faculty rendering it capable of seeing God. (Thus, the imagery of light is transposed. The "light of glory" does not illuminate the object, for the latter is infinitely luminous of itself. Instead, it renders the created intellect capable of seeing this object, which is too luminous for it.) For the Greeks, the light is what is emitted from the Divine Essence, illuminating Christ's face in which the blessed thus can see God. However, how can we thus explain the fact that the "impure mind [*esprit*]" does not see Him? How is one to explain that during His life, Christ did not allow the light of His divinity to be perceptibly transparent to all (except during the Transfiguration when, according to the Greeks, the eyes of the apostles were opened to see the light of Christ's divinity which was always there)? In any case, it is indeed necessary to admit that the created mind is itself changed so that it can see by grace what it cannot see by itself. However ineluctable this necessity may be, it is what the Greeks refuse to take openly into consideration.

The Greeks vigorously perceived the need to safeguard God's transcendence even in relation to the creature whom He enables to see Him. However, St. Thomas also recognized this need, which he assured by means of the distinction between *videre Deum* (to see

39. See *ST* I, q. 12, a. 2; SCG, bk. 3, ch. 51.

God) and *comprehendere essentiam divinam* (to comprehend the Divine Essence in one's mind).[40] The creatures who see God do not "comprehend" Him (meaning by "comprehension" the embracing of an object, leaving none of it outside the intellect's grasp). To explain this fact, he relies on the identity, at infinity, between being and knowing. The created act of knowledge, which is necessarily finite as an act, cannot be equal to this infinite object and thus cannot know it to the degree it is knowable. It can only be "proportioned" to it.

St. Thomas takes care to say that this does not mean that God would not be seen entirely, for God does not have parts within Himself. In the Beatific Vision, He informs the created intellect according to His being, without the mediation of concepts and without the mediation of creatures: "If we say that it is impossible for the created mind to *comprehend* God, this does not mean that some part of Him would not be seen but, rather, that He is not seen as perfectly as He is visible in Himself."[41] Admittedly, this distinction is very difficult to understand. St. Thomas makes use of a comparison that in itself is quite illuminating, though it must be understood aright from the start: one and the same truth can be attained by two minds at different depths of comprehension. A human truth—even a scientific one (in the modern sense of the word) and, even more, a philosophical truth—in itself is richer than however much it enriches a given mind that grasps it. This mind could progress not only by accumulating particular truths but, more importantly, by deepening a formerly grasped truth, unveiling its riches, which were first perceived in a vague manner. Although human knowledge cannot reach the perfect simplicity and absolute unity of the Truth Itself, it is nonetheless the case that that even the most insignificant of the partial truths that it attains is mysteriously dependent upon this fundamental Truth and refers to it. Thus, there is forever more to be found in such a truth than what we now know to be in it. For all the more reason is this the case for the Primordial Truth Itself, which is one, simple, and in-

---

40. See *ST* I, q. 12, a. 7.
41. *ST* I, q. 12, a. 7, ad. 2.

finite. Only the one, simple, and infinite Mind [*Esprit*]—i.e., God—
can penetrate into its furthest depths.

Karl Rahner proposed his own interpretation of this outlook. It
certainly is not St. Thomas's and, moreover, is contestable in itself.
According to him, the human mind is defined as being ordered to
mystery. Indeed, he holds that mystery remains, as mystery, in the
Beatific Vision itself: "Grace does not imply the promise and the beginning of the elimination of the mystery, but the radical possibility
of the absolute proximity of the mystery, which is not eliminated by
its proximity, but really presented as mystery."[42] He goes so far as to
say that according to the "biblical data in St. Paul," and in contrast to
scholastic theology, faith must be conceived of as being "something
that abides (in its inmost kernel)."[43] A rigorous analysis must be applied to the proximity which he discusses, thereby claiming to distinguish [the Beatific] [V]ision from faith's knowledge here-below.
When one speaks of "absolute proximity," is one speaking of ontological proximity? If so, it is given from the start and is [God's] presence of immensity. Is it a question of a noetic proximity? In order to
be able to provide a meaning for "absolute proximity" understood in
this second manner, every kind of concept must be excluded [from
such knowledge]. How then would it be different from the immediate vision proposed by "scholastic theology"? If there is no concept,
then there must be an immediate information [of the intellect] by
the divine essence, something that does not hold for faith, for the
latter is knowledge "in a mirror."[44]

3. Ways toward a Reconciliation

{175} Must we hold that [St.] Gregory Palamas (fourteenth century) invented the distinction between essence and energies in God,

42. Rahner, "Le concept du mystère dans la théologie catholique," in *Ecrits
théologiques* VIII (Paris, Desclée de Brouwer, 1967), 79. [Tr. note: Taken from Karl
Rahner, "The Concept of Mystery in Catholic Theology" in *Theological Investigations*,
vol. 4, *More Recent Writings*, trans Kevin Smyth (Crossroad: New York, 1982), 55.]

43. Rahner, "Le concept du mystère dans la théologie catholique," 86. [Tr. note: Tak-
en from Rahner, "The Concept of Mystery in Catholic Theology," 60.]

44. 1 Cor 13:12.

as has been claimed by Catholic theologians, following on the studies of Jugie in the early twentieth century? Or, on the contrary, with modern Orthodox theologians, must we say that Palamas only systematized a very ancient outlook, which can be drawn from Gregory of Nyssa, Basil, and [Ps.-]Dionysius? We cannot treat this very difficult question here. When we refer to the exposition of a supposedly decisive text drawn from [Ps.-]Dionysius, we must say that we find it difficult to find this distinction in the form given to it by Palamas.[45] Indeed, note that the Greek term *energeia* of itself means "activity." When it is translated as "energies," in the very technical sense that Orthodox Palamite theologians give it, does this not already incline one toward a biased exegesis? Above all, when [Ps.-]Dionysius speaks about the Super-essential, imparticipable Essence, which is multiplied in its participations all the while remaining one and unparticipated in itself,[46] and when he says that we know this transcendent Being only through the participations and "by the powers that descend from Him to us in order to deify us,"[47] we first need to have read and approved St. Gregory Palamas (or Lossky) if we are to read these statements as referring to the "uncreated energies" identical to the essence yet flowing forth from it!* In its obvious sense, the text is speaking about the activities by which the "thearchy" produces its participations outside of itself.

We are in the presence of "two different mystical gnoseologies, based on an ontology that would not always be the same for the Byzantine East and the Latin West."[48] However, both sides must realize that the two theologies are equally aware of the same theological problem. A reconciliation in reciprocal understanding would be easy if the Orthodox were willing to hold that the "energies" are the

45. Denys l'Aréopagite, *Des Noms divins*, trans. Maurice de Gandillac in Denys (Paris: Aubier, 1980), ch. 2.

46. Denys l'Aréopagite, *Des Noms divins*, ch. 2, §11.

47. Denys l'Aréopagite, *Des Noms divins*, ch. 2, §7.

* [Tr. note: Before the exclamation point there is a closed quotation mark without a correlative opening one.]

48. Lossky, *Vision de Dieu*, 12.

"incomprehensible" divine essence inasmuch as it is grasped and attained by the clear but imperfect vision of the elect and not distinct realities in God Himself. With this concession, the terminological differences could be preserved. Since they refuse to do so, the debate can be maintained on the level of theological reflection without falling into theological relativism (i.e., while maintaining that their explanation, as such, remains unacceptable). [The level of the debate is properly theological] because, through these divergent theological explanations, both sides aim to maintain the same truth of faith: "The entire theological work of Palamas constitutes a defense of the immediate vision of God."[49]

C. Vision of the Essence, Vision of Persons

{176} Recall what we have said a number of times above. If the term "essence," in our language, invincibly evokes the idea of an "abstract form" (i.e., that by which a concrete being is what it is), in the case of God, we exclude every distinction between form and subject. The Divine Essence is concretely the Father, the Son, and the Holy Spirit.

Thus, it is futile to ask oneself if the blessed see the Divine Essence or the Persons, or, put another way, if they see the Persons *mediante essentia* or the essence *mediantibus Personis*. Given that the mediation of concepts no longer exists in the [beatific] [V]ision, the Divine Essence informing the intellect is this *res divina* about which we have spoken many times, which contains in its vertiginous simplicity the one substance and the Three Persons.

On the other hand, this vision is an "eminently real" form of knowledge, since its principle is the contact of the created intellect with the very reality of God. It is a knowledge from which love flows forth.

Through this knowledge, the elect become the companions of the Three Divine Persons, vitally sharing in their ineffable communion.

49. Lossky, *Vision de Dieu*, 138.

8

Knowledge of the Divine Persons
in Their Singularity

I. THE PROBLEM

{177} If, as we hold on faith, the Divine Persons are really distinct, we must admit that each has His own proper, unique, and irreplaceable personality. Therefore, it is not enough for us to know, in general, how They are distinct from each other. The goal of our investigation must be to know each Person in His singularity, that is, in what is unique to Him. But how can we arrive at such knowledge if the only noetic instruments at our disposal are concepts elaborated on the basis of [our knowledge of] creatures? This seems problematic, for as we have seen, creatures are the work of the Three Persons together, therefore resembling the Persons only in what They have in common, not in what is proper to each.

This represents the grave and difficult problem of *appropriation*, which we still must study.[1]

---

1. See Jean-Hervé Nicolas, *Dieu connue comme inconnu* (Paris: Desclée de Brouwer, 1966), 345–48; Jean-Hervé Nicolas, *Les profondeurs de la grâce* (Paris: Beauchesne, 1969), 110–26; Henri Barré, *Trinité que j'adore* (Paris, Lethielleux, 1965), 81n112. Hyacinthe-François Dondaine, "Notes doctrinales thomistes," *Saint Thomas d'Aquin. Somme théologique, La Trinité*, vol. 2 (Paris: Cerf[, 1946]), 409–23.

A. The Difficulty Involved in
Conceptual Knowledge of the Divine Persons
in Their Singularity

{178} Generally speaking, we do not know a person in his singularity by way of concepts. We know him through experience. However, when we know a human person, beginning with the conceptual knowledge that we can have concerning human nature and also concerning many of its existential conditions (character, psychogenesis, and so forth), and also on the basis of our own self-knowledge, we can translate this experience of the other into a host of concepts that, all the while remaining inadequate in relation to this person's unique singularity, sometimes do indeed discern and express a great deal concerning it.

Is this the case as regards our knowledge of a Divine Person? The perfect experience that the created mind can have of Him is that of the Beatific Vision, wherein the realism of contact and the luminosity of the gaze are conjoined at vertiginous heights—the perfect experience of a perfectly transparent object. It is a fully conscious form of knowledge. However, it also is inexpressible in concepts, for the only "concept" that could express it is the Word, which, of course, the created mind cannot utter. As for mystical experience, we noted earlier the radical disjunction which exists between, on the one hand, this sublime but obscure knowledge experienced in a profoundly felt, though inexpressible, contact, and on the other hand, the verbal, conceptual expression that the mystic gives of it *when he comes forth from his mystical experience*. Certainly, the Divine Persons who are "touched" in this manner are the very same Persons spoken about in the formulas, and these formulas have directed the mystic's mind [*esprit*] to them. However, neither the formulas of faith, nor the theological expressions elaborated on the basis of them, translate the experience itself, for it is beyond them. As for poetic symbols, they evoke the same experience of the mystic without making known the experienced reality in what is proper to it.

Nevertheless, a conceptual knowledge of God is possible, however inadequate it may be. Yes, but when it comes to a Divine Person, such knowledge does not seem possible for the reason given
above, namely, the fact that the concepts we use for knowing God
attain Him through the real representation that creatures furnish
concerning Him, and this representation attains the Persons in what
They have in common, not in Their singularity.[2]

It will be insisted: this is true concerning the representation that
creatures as such present concerning God. However, is it not the
case that the beings and events that make up "salvation history" represent the Persons at work, each in His singularity, in the work of
saving man? This objection plays on the ambiguity of the term (and
of the notion) of "supernatural effects." We will examine this notion
later on, and that is when we will respond to this objection.[3]

B. The Need for a Conceptual
Approach to the Divine Persons
in Their Singularity

{179} Nevertheless, both on the level of faith and on that of theological reflection, the *propria Personarum* must be somehow concep-
tualizable and expressible in words (and even in images), given that
faith is an affirmation concerning the Divine Reality, thus requiring
some sort of conceptualization. Mystical experience cannot replace
it, since, much to the contrary, such mystical experience presupposes
faith (and, therefore, presupposes at least a possible formulation of
faith, an intellectual knowledge of the believed truth).

Certainly, there can be (and without a doubt there are) cases of
mystical experience of the Divine Persons without any formulation
of faith in the Trinitarian mystery. Such is the faith of the "righteous
on the outside" [*justes du dehors*], who, under the action of the Spirit, can surely arrive at the highest summits of mystical experience.
Perhaps this is also the case for the faith of certain *minores* in the

2. See §§161–62 above.
3. See §182 below.

Church when it is born aloft to these very heights by a very lofty and pure charity, despite the paucity of its intellectual content. However, we must be utterly clear in understanding that faith lives in the Church (even, tendentially and inchoately, for the case of the faith of the "righteous on the outside"). Indeed, what is impossible is the idea that the Church, whose mission is to make the revelatory action of the Incarnate Word reach all generations and all men, would not have the full intellectual knowledge of revelation needed for her life and teaching. If the *propria Peronsarum* had not been revealed, they would have remained wholly unknown to men, who then would have had no means for entering into relations with the Divine Persons. In short, the ignorance of some (even if they are, in fact, very numerous) rests on the Church's knowledge, which must itself be conceptual.[4] Moreover, we have already made use of concepts for this knowledge of the Divine Persons. We must now ask how they are formed and what their noetic value is.

C. Principle of the Solution

{180} Given that all of our concepts are drawn from our experience of the universe, the universe itself is where we must seek out the point of departure for elaborating a *proprium*-concept for each Person. Indeed, Scripture makes known to us the "manifestations" (or, missions) of the Divine Persons and speaks to us about each in His singularity, on the basis of such "manifestations." Therefore, in the midst of created realities, we must seek out effects that could be called "supernatural," ones that could enable us to rise to the *propria personarum*. However, how can we understand and discern such effects, given that *opera Trinitatis ad extra sunt indivisa* [the works of the Trinity *ad extra* are undivided]?

It is very tempting to ignore this difficulty on the pretext of sim-

4. N.B., Here, we can draw an analogy with the necessity of natural theology for faith. In order to have an act of faith, each believer does not need to know "natural theology" and hold its truths. However, he does need "natural theology" to be possible and to, in fact, exist in the community of believers, the Church.

ply being submissive to Scripture (and, it is also said, to Tradition), which attributes distinct actions to the Divine Persons—e.g., the Father raised the Son; the Holy Spirit prays for the believer, and so forth. This is to forget that, far from breaking with the great revelation of God's unity, the revelation of the Trinity presupposes it and confirms it. Moreover, this requires one to forget that, according to Scripture's own testimony, this unity is found in the divine activity.[5]

The notion of a "mission" places us in the presence of an antinomy. An antinomy is not resolved by neglecting one of its terms, whether definitively (by simply not taking it into account) or provisionally (by passing alternatively from one term to the other, by a dialectical procedure). One must accept the tension that the antinomy imposes upon the mind and orient oneself toward a comprehensive explanation that fully does justice *to each of the opposed terms*.

II. THE NON-DIVISION OF THE THREE PERSONS IN WORKS "AD EXTRA"

A. The Tradition

{181} It is not contestable (and is contested by no one, at least openly) that the most ancient and unanimous tradition affirms that the Three Divine Persons act in the universe, and that They do so only together and indivisibly, first in the activity of creation and then in the governance of the universe. This means that no effect is produced by one Divine Person acting alone, apart from the others.[6]

Of course, in saying this, *efficient causality* comes to mind (i.e., the kind of causality that makes what does not exist exist or makes that which already exists now exist in a different manner). Hence,

5. See Jn 5:19–24; 1 Cor 12:4–6.
6. See Paul Galtier, *L'habitation en nous de trois Personnes* (Rome: Pontifica Universita Gregoriana, 1950), 15–21; Albert Michel, "La Trinité," *Dictionnaire de théologie catholique*, ed. Alfred Vacant, 1822–26 (Paris: Letouzey & Ané, [1950]), vol. 15.2, sect. 2–5; George Leonard Prestige, *Dieu dans la pensée patristique* (Paris: Aubier, 1955), 216–22; Pangiotis N. Trembelas, *Dogmatique de l'Église orthodoxe catholique*, vol. 1 (Paris: Desclée de Brouwer, 1957), 355–58.

from the start, it has been "felt" that if one were to attribute to a Divine Person a unique and proper action that would not be common with the two others, this would be to make that Person into a separate and distinct God. Obviously, this would represent the destruction of the Christian faith in the Trinity, along with the fundamental affirmation of God's unity, which is held in common by Israel and the Church (and by Islam as well).

On the other hand, we cannot say that the Tradition similarly excludes the idea that a Divine Person could exercise a distinct influence on the believer as an object of his knowledge and love, as the end toward which he tends. Can theology recognize this, and if so, how should it be understood? We still must examine this point. It remains an open question.

B. The Unity of the Divine Being Necessarily Entails the Unity of Action

{182} Earlier, it was demonstrated that, on the basis of [our knowledge of] creatures, the rational process leading us to affirm God's existence as the efficient Principle, Creator, and First Cause of all contingent beings, as well as of the universe constituted by these beings, cannot lead us to know and affirm the Trinitarian mystery. This was because the Three Persons create and save the world through one unique action, that is, as constituting One Unique Agent. *In the noetic order*, the distinction of the Persons is situated beyond the point that is discovered by reason in its process of scrutinizing contingent beings, namely, the relation of radical ontological dependence that those beings have vis-à-vis their principle.

Are matters different for those things pertaining to salvation history? Does it include "supernatural effects" that would themselves be distinctly produced by each of the Persons according to what is respectively proper to each [*selon leur propriété respective*]?

What characterizes "supernatural effects" is the ensemble of new relations that grace establishes between humanity (whether considered in its totality or in each of the persons in it) and God. From this perspective, in what concerns Trinitarian theology, there is a fundamental difference between "natural" and "supernatural" effects. On account of the latter, human persons are placed in relation with each of the Divine Persons in His distinction, although not separately. That is, each Divine Person can be known and loved according to what is hypostatically proper to Him [*sa propriété hypostatique*], though not separately from the two others, given that They are inseparably "in Him" in virtue of perichoresis. This is possible only by revelation and by grace. However, the "natural effects" that are "prior" to revelation (at least according to a priority of nature) do not give birth to such relations, but instead, only place human persons in relation with God considered as one, in the way that we recalled earlier.[7]

But we must account for the fact that these new, "supernatural" relations presuppose a change brought about within the creature by the divine action. Without this, salvation would not be brought about by God. Each person would be saved and freed by giving himself superior objectives and by effectively tending toward them by his effort alone. This would be akin to saying that such a person is freed from debauchery (or from anguish, and so forth) by science, art, love, and so forth. Therefore, we must carefully note the part played by the divine efficiency in the work of salvation, all the while heeding the fact that efficiency alone does not explain what is specific to the work of salvation in relation to the works of the divine power. The salvific events are characterized by the new relations spoken of earlier, interpersonal relations, whose living source is in man (ontological relations, but simultaneously also conscious ones). Such relations include that of the humanity assumed to the Word who made it His own, the spiritual relations of saved man to the Divine Persons, the symbolico-real relations of sacramental actions (and of the actions and words that constitute them) in their identity with Christ's saving acts and with the sanctifying [action of the] Holy

7. See §161 above.

Spirit, and so forth. However, these relations would not have any reality if they were not founded on real, ontological changes caused efficiently by God.

For this effectuation, the principle of the non-division of every Trinitarian action *ad extra* is at play. This principle is universal and necessary: the divine action is one, just as the Divine Being is one. Or, to put it another way, we could say: "The Three Divine Persons are one Unique Agent. Their action is one like Their nature. Just as Their real distinction does not affect the Divine Substance in any way, so too it does not affect the divine action in any way."

Therefore, it is inconceivable that an "effect" in the world, even a "supernatural" one, would be *produced* (that is, realized) by one Divine Person acting apart from the two others or simply acting by an action that would be proper to Him. In this, we are faced with a necessary consequence of the great principle: *In Deo omnia sunt unum et idem ubi non obviat relationis oppositio.*[8]

III. THE DISTINCTION OF PERSONS
IN THE UNITY OF ACTION

{183} Must we therefore forgo giving real content to the biblical concept of [a Divine] "mission"? This is the fundamental criticism registered against every Trinitarian theology founded on the presupposition that the principle of non-division in the [Divine] [A]ction is inviolable: "It is fair to ask whether classical theology sufficiently honors the divine missions."[9]

The remainder of this course must show how unfounded this criticism is. However, it would remain a latent issue if we did not show here how the principle of non-division leaves room for the Divine Persons in the salvific action, consequently leaving room for the manifestation of what is hypostatically proper to Them in this action.

8. See §52 above.
9. Ghislain Lafont, *Peut-on connaître Dieu en Jésus-Christ?* (Paris: Cerf, 1969), 15.

For this, we must extend to Action what we said concerning Being. The Divine Being is not a kind of monolithic substrate on the surface of which (or in the depths of which) the Trinitarian processions would take place, meaning that the *Deus unus* would be distinct from the *Deus trinus*. He is wholly and necessarily one and triune. He is triune because He is God, the One God. If He can be known as being one without being known as triune, this is on account of the imperfect and progressive character of our knowledge of God. However, in His reality, He is not one before being triune. He is triune in Unity, one in the Trinity.

The same holds for [the Divine] Action. The Father, the Son, and the Holy Spirit are a single principle of action, a single action. However, it is essential and necessary that the divine action has the Father, Son, and Holy Spirit as its principle, distinct from each other, each being the principle of this Unique Action along with the two others, though according to what is hypostatically proper to each.

In other words, just as, in general, a person is manifested by his action, so too the Father, the Son, and the Holy Spirit are manifested by this unique divine action, each according to what is hypostatically proper to Himself, all three inseparably but distinctly. (The Father, in fact, is manifested as the Father of this Son and, with Him, the Spirator of the Spirit.)

In short, if the Trinitarian processions do not divide the divine action, they are included in it and, for this reason, are manifested by it.

However, does this hold true for every action of God *ad extra*? It is clear that the creative action, as well as all the actions that are immediately connected to it ([i.e.,] conservation, motion), have the Three Persons as their principle, for the God who created and who moves creatures is the Trinity. Nonetheless, we cannot say that They act distinctly in these actions. Why? "Manifestation" includes a twofold relation, one to the hidden mystery that is manifested and another to the created intellect, capable of allowing itself to be led to the mystery through the effect that manifests it. The first relation is always found in the effects of the divine action since the Trinity is the efficient principle of these effects. The second relation is lacking in "natural effects," which only refer the created intellect to God as one, without placing it in relation with the Persons in Their distinction, as saw above.[10]

Nevertheless, it remains the case that, *of itself*, a natural effect is capable of manifesting the processions and Persons. Therefore, if revelation and faith enable the created intellect to know the mystery of the Divine Persons, by returning to such "natural effects" it will be able to extract their value as manifesting the Trinitarian mystery.

This is what we must now consider.

A. The Divine Processions and Creation

1. The Creator

{184} If the Three Persons together are the One Creator, it is traditional to attribute creation to the Father as to Him who has created, through the Son and in the Holy Spirit. Recall St. Irenaeus's image: the Son and the Holy Spirit are the "hands of God."[11] Also see St. Basil: "In the act of creation, understand the Father as principal cause of all that is made, the Son as the demiurgic cause, and the Spirit as the perfecting cause."[12] What theological interpretation can we provide for this traditional outlook, while maintaining the principle of non-division which we established in the preceding chapter?

a) From the Intra-Trinitarian Processions to the Extra-Trinitarian Procession of Creatures

{185} Basing itself first on the beings of the universe, reason rises to God as to their intelligent and voluntary cause. In this way, following a necessary process of reasoning, it arrives at the twofold affirmation that God exists as the First Cause of everything that exists

---

10. See §§161–62 above.

11. St. Irenaeus of Lyon, *Contre les hérésies*, bk. 3 (SC 34); bk. 4 (SC 100 bis et 100 ter); bk. 5 (SC 152 and 153), V, 1, 3; 5, 1; 28, 1.

12. Basil of Caesarea, *Sur le Saint-Esprit*, trans. and ed. Benoît Pruche, SC 17 bis (Paris: Cerf, 1968), XVI, 37.

outside of Him and that He exercises His causality "through His Intellect and His Will."

What is revealed—or, rather, what the same reason, though believing, discovers in reflecting on the revelation of the Three Divine Persons and processions—is that intellection and will in God respectively include the uttering [*prolation*] of a Word and the spiration of a Spirit, who are consubstantial with their principle and who are Divine Persons like Him and with Him.

Thus, the extra-Trinitarian processions appear to faith-illuminated reason as prolonging and externalizing the intra-Trinitarian processions. Before being at the principle of creation and of the government of creatures, the Divine Intellection and Divine Will are, in God Himself, at the principle of the Word-Son and of the Holy Spirit.

To understand this continuity, we must recall the necessary character of the Trinitarian processions. The uttering [*prolation*] of the Word and the spiration of the Spirit are not accidental to the Divine Intellection and Will. They are identical with them. They constitute the "infinite mode" of the creative intellection and will. Thus, this intellection (including the uttering [*prolation*] of the Word) and this willing (including the spiration of the Spirit) are posited by reason as being at the principle of creation without reason knowing this, for on the basis of [our knowledge of] creatures, our reason cannot discover the nature of the "infinite mode" of the Divine Intellection and Willing.

Therefore, we can and, indeed, must hold two conclusions simultaneously. On the one hand, the procession of creatures is consequent to the intra-Trinitarian processions. On the other, we cannot rise to the intra-Trinitarian processions on the basis of [our knowledge of] the procession of creatures [from God].

b) The Necessity of the Intra-Trinitarian Processions and the
Contingency of Creatures

{186} Nonetheless, an obvious difficulty remains, namely the fact that whereas the intra-Trinitarian processions are necessary, the procession of creatures is contingent. Hence, how is there not a "rupture" between these two types of procession, a rupture that contradicts the continuity that we claimed to recognize above? Ought we not admit that, far from prolonging the intra-Trinitarian processions, the procession of creatures is added to them, as it were, from without and therefore must be thought of independently from them?

The response to this difficulty is found in another aspect of the mystery of God, namely, the freedom of the creative act (and of all the acts that depend on it). Indeed, it is a freedom without a shade of contingency. The contingency is entirely in the objects of this act. Taken all together as well as individually in detail, creatures are contingent *volibilia* (and therefore, also contingent "ideated things" [*idéats*], if one uses the term "ideas" with regard to the divine thought to speak about things that are thought of as real). To say that they are *volibilia contingentia* means that they could have been not willed. They could not be willed if they were not goods (and they are good to the degree that they exist). However, their goodness is not and cannot be thought about except as being consequent to the divine act of willing them ([i.e.,] of loving them). Their goodness is neither prior to nor independent from this.[13]

This divine act is not contingent. It is not a second act, super-added to the act by which God loves Himself and, in loving Himself, spirates the Holy Spirit. It is this same act, considered as related to contingent objects. Thus, from all eternity, God thinks of the created universe *in Verbo* and wills it "in the Spirit" by an act that is necessary in itself but whose object is not necessary. This combination of the necessary and the contingent constitutes the "factual necessity" of creation, which makes it so difficult to think about and express its contingency. Indeed, it can only be expressed by means of the hypothetical mood: "the created universe" (or this or that given being) could have not existed. This hypothetical mood must not be introduced into the very divine act of creating, as though God were really faced with the simple possibility of the universe and then, by

13. See *ST* I, q. 19, a. 3; q. 20, a. 1.

an act of choice, actualized this possibility. This hypothetical mood expresses, in an unreal manner (conjuring up what has not taken place, namely the non-creation of the universe or of this given being), a fundamentally real characteristic of the created being, namely, its contingency.

This represents one of the vertiginous summits involved in our consideration of God, one which makes many minds today doubt the objectivity of such a consideration. In order to avoid giving way to this "vertigo," we must recognize that creatures are what force us to assert that God is real and transcendent. God thus posited as real transcends not only all the beings of our experience but also all our representations. This means that we can in no way "represent" God to ourselves, as well as all that is in God, in particular His free will, which is identical with His necessary willing while nonetheless having a contingent object. Still, we are compelled to affirm this God who is situated above all representations and thus find ourselves compelled, in this sense, "to aim" at Him. However, we are compelled to aim at Him as one aims at an object which has its reality in and through itself and not only in the mind that aims at it.[14]

c) Appropriating to the Divine Persons the Various Aspects of
the Creative Action

{187} Now, what does the diversified attribution of the creative act to the Divine Persons mean, namely: The Father creates through the Word in the Spirit?[15]

As we have seen, the Father, the Son, and the Holy Spirit together are the Agent of the creative act. They create inasmuch as They are one God. However, God creates through His Intellection and His Will. The [Divine] act of intellection and the [Divine] act of willing belong together to the Three Persons, whereas the diction that is included in the infinite divine intellection and the spiration that is included in the infinite willing distinguish the Persons from

14. See Nicolas, *Dieu connue comme inconnu*, 107–12.
15. See St. Thomas, *In I Ioan.*, 1, nos. 75–78.

each other. We will see that, on account of this latter point, all the divine attributes that pertain to the intellect are referred to the Son and those that pertain to the will and love are referred to the Holy Spirit. This reference is not mere wordplay. It is a means of conceptually attaining what is proper to each Person. Thus, inasmuch as the unique creative act proceeds from the Divine Power, it is attributed to the Father. Inasmuch as it proceeds from the [Divine] Intellection, it is attributed to the Son. Finally, inasmuch as it proceeds from the Divine Willing and Love, it is attributed to the Holy Spirit. This does not mean that the persons provide three distinct contributions to it but, rather, that the unique creative act is a means for reaching the three distinct Persons at the source of this unique act.

Creation is attributed in a unique way to the First Person, for although the Son and the Holy Spirit are the one Creator with Him, they hold from Him the undivided Divine Nature according to which They are the Creator. We have seen that we can analogically say that the Holy Spirit proceeds from the Father *per Filium* in the sense that, although the Father and the Son are, together, the One Spirator, the Son holds from the Father, with the Divine Nature, the property on account of which He is the Spirator.[16]

Finally, when Scripture and the creedal expressions of the faith attribute creation to the Father, we there encounter a process that is analogous to what we examined for the attribution of the title "God," *o Theos*, to the Father. The First Person is called "the Creator," just as He is called "God." This does not intend "to confiscate" this title, which, on the contrary, holds true for the Three Divine Persons, as the believer knows through the revelation made in the New Testament. Instead, He is called this because this revelation could occur only by coming from the First Person, the Principle without principle, to whom this title should be given first because He does not hold it from another, though one must immediately say that He communicates it to the other Two through the processions.[17]

16. See §§146 and 156 above.
17. Lafont, *Peut-on connaître Dieu en Jésus-Christ?*, 252–56; Nicolas, *Dieu connue comme inconnu*, ch. 6.

2. The Image of the Trinity in Creatures

a) The Trinity's Seal upon Creatures

{188} If the creative action has the Three Persons in Their distinction as its principle, the terminus of this action (i.e., the creature precisely as such) must be referred to the one and triune God. This is so not only in the line of efficient causality but also in that of formal causality, which depends strictly on efficient causality.[18] The Trinity could not have failed to place Its seal upon creatures.

Consequently, knowledge through revelation concerning the mystery of God reverberates on our knowledge of creatures, enabling us to discover that it has this unsuspected aspect by which it resembles God, not only in the fact that it is a being, good, and one, but also in the fact that it conceals, within its own mystery, the intra-Trinitarian processions.[19] It does so because the intra-Trinitarian mystery is the mystery of being at its infinite point of perfection.

This secret point of resemblance represents the mystery of created beings. Thus, we can say that God, in revealing Himself, reveals to man the universe and, above all, man himself.

b) The Manifestation of the Trinitarian Mystery in Creatures

{189} For the reasons already discussed, without revelation, we cannot know the "seal" of the Trinity upon the created universe, and especially upon man. Therefore, without revelation, this "seal" cannot serve as the point of departure for a rational process that would lead to the discovery of the [Trinitarian] mystery of God. Hence, we can say that in revealing Himself to man, God revealed to him what He Himself is in His depths and what created being is. We can thus ask ourselves, "What interest is there for us in discovering this seal afterwards, that is, after the mystery of the Trinity has been revealed to us in a much more complete manner than it is 'manifested' to us

---

18. See Nicolas, *Dieu connue comme inconnu*, 91ff.
19. See Nicolas, *Dieu connue comme inconnu*, 335–41.

by creatures?" This "interest" is immense, for this resemblance of the Trinity impressed on beings by the creative act is itself the condition for the possibility of revelation. Indeed, if there were no opening upon the Trinitarian mystery in the concepts that we elaborate on the basis of our knowledge of creatures, they could not be of use for revelation, which, nonetheless, can only be made by means of these concepts (and the words that signify them). Thus, it is clear that supernatural revelation is in continuity with the "revelation" (or "manifestation") of God that is creation.[20]

c) Conclusion

{190} Thus, in virtue of the creative act, the Three Persons are present at the intimate depths of created being (and especially those of created spirit). It is a latent presence which cannot enable one to discover the mystery of the Trinitarian processions on the basis of their externalization in creation. However, it renders possible a language that is intelligible for man, in which and by which this mystery will be revealed to him, according to the good pleasure of God.

B. The Conceptual Approach of *Propria Personarum*

1. Appropriation

{191} In Holy Scripture, then in the creedal expressions of the faith, in liturgical formulas, and in tradition, we constantly see certain divine attributes or certain particular works being attributed to one Person in particular. Creation is attributed to the Father, as well as power and glory. The work of salvation is attributed to the Son. (However, this creates less difficulty, for only the Son is incarnate, and salvation is the work of the Incarnate Word. Nonetheless, it is also said of Him that He "sustains the universe by His Word.")[21]

20. See Benoît Montagnes, "Compte-rendu de Krempel, A., La doctrine de la relation chez Saint Thomas, exposé historique et systématique," *Revue Thomiste* 54 (1954): 200–202; Benoît Montagnes, "La Parole de Dieu dans la création," *Revue Thomiste* 54 (1954): 213–41; Émile Bailleux, "La création, oeuvre de la Trinité selon S. Thomas," *Revue thomiste* 62 (1962): 27–50.
21. Heb 1:3 (my translation).

Holiness and sanctification, "deification," are attributed to the Holy Spirit.

Must we hold that these works, as well as the divine attributes to which they lead us, express what is proper and distinct to the Person in question? But, if so, how are we to conceive that power, wisdom, holiness, and so forth, would be proper to one Divine Person, thus holding that the others do not have this attribute?

Historically, this problem was posed in the twelfth century, when Abelard thought (doubtlessly innocently) that he could simply distinguish the Divine Persons in the fact that the first was distinguished by power, the second by wisdom, and the third by goodness. It has been thought that he intended to divide the divine attributes among the Persons, but, in fact, his explanation inclined rather toward a form of neo-modalism. The Father was God inasmuch as He is powerful. The Son was God inasmuch He is wise. The Holy Spirit was God inasmuch as He is good. In any case, Abelard was condemned at the Council of Sens (1140) for having taught that "the Father is full power, the Son a certain power, and the Holy Spirit no power" and "omnipotence pertains to the Father in a proper and special sense because he is from no one else, but not likewise wisdom and goodness."[22] Procedurally, the condemnation is very contestable,[23] and from the doctrinal perspective it was wrong to disregard the traditional character of the process [of naming] that consists in attributing to one Person as proper something that in reality belongs to the Three.[24]

It is a question of a commonplace logical procedure. However, how is it applied to our knowledge of the [Divine] Persons, and what is its value?

---

22. D.-Sch., 721 and 734.

23. See Irénée Vallery-Radot, *Bernard de Fontaines, abbé de Clairvaux, le prophète de l'Occident* (Paris Desclée de Brouwer, 1959), 201–44.

24. See Dondaine, "Notes doctrinales thomistes," vol. 2, 411–13.

a) The Use of Appropriation in Trinitarian Theology

{192} Since all the concepts which we use for knowing God are
related to His essential attributes, which are common to the Three
Persons, we can use them (and first of all, revelation can use them)
for designating (and in some manner expressing) what is proper to a
given Person only by "appropriating" them to that Person, that is, by
applying them to this Person in His singularity in such a manner that
the concept thus attributed becomes "proper" to Him. This is a logical procedure, a designation "by autonomasia" as when we use the
expression, "the Roman orator," for Cicero. In order for this activity to avoid being arbitrary (thus becoming pure wordplay, without
any bearing on reality), it must in some way be founded on the real
property that distinguishes one Person from the two others, His *proprium*. In order to justify the "appropriation" of this property, which
is unknown in itself, and to confer a noetic value upon it, we have a
sufficient indication of this property by the mode of the procession
of the Person to whom the attribution is made (or, in the case of the
First, by the fact that He does not proceed from any other and that
the other two proceed from Him). Thanks to it, while I cannot directly know what is proper to the Person, I can indirectly reach it
by the mediation of the essential attribute used in such a way that
this gives me a kind of obscure knowledge of what each Person is
in His distinction and in such a way that I can express it (although,
very imperfectly). In this way, we attribute to the Father the concepts that designate the divine power, namely His character as the
source of being and of life. We do this on account of the mysterious
resemblance that exists between, on the one hand, this more manifest characteristic [i.e., power] (even though it belongs to the three)
and on the other hand, the Father's personal characteristic as the
principle of the other Persons, the *plenitudo fontalis*. Likewise, all the
concepts that are related to the intellectual attributes are attributed
to the Second Person, not because these attributes would be proper
to Him but, rather, inasmuch as they evoke, by resemblance, the hid-

den character of this Person who proceeds according to intellection. Finally, this is also the case for the Third Person as regards the concepts related to the attributes of goodness, love, and holiness.

One could ask, "Since one of the two termini of this resemblance is unknown (precisely what one seeks to attain through the first), how can we know that such a resemblance exists?" We must respond that we can know it in the same way that we know the processions, namely, through revelation and through theological reflection exerted on it. Through revelation, we can be sure that the First Person is "unbegotten," the principal of the two others. Through theological reflection on revelation, we can be sure that the Second Person proceeds by way of intellection and the Third Person by way of love. But above all, revelation itself, such as the Church has understood and lived it, is what makes these attributions. Here, theology comes forth above all to explain in what sense we can understand such attributes in a way that does justice to what revelation itself affirms with such force, namely that the Three Persons are One God, are one, unique God, and therefore the All-Powerful, Wise, and Holy One.

b) The Rejection of Appropriation

{193} Nevertheless, a strong theological current rises up against the explanation of these attributions by means of appropriation. It finds its source in Pétau who himself thought he was retrieving the doctrine of the Greek Fathers by understanding these attributes as properly belonging to each Person.[25] Orthodox authors agree with him. Thus, Myrrha Lot-Borodine writes: "According to the Greek Fathers, if they are not read through scholastic lenses, hypostatic holiness is the *proprium* of the Giver."[26]

---

25. See Denis Pétau, *Dogmata theologica Dion. Petavii* (Paris: Vivès, 1865), vol. 8, 6; Théodore de Régnon, Études de théologie positive sur la Sainte Trinité, 4 vols. (Paris: Victor Retaux, 1892–1898), XXVII; Karl Rahner, "Pour la notion scolastique de la grâce incréée," *Ecrits théologiques* III (Paris: Desclée de Brouwer, 1963), 35–69; in the opposite direction, see Paul Galtier, *Le Saint Esprit en nous d'après les Pères grecs* (Rome: Pontifica Universita Gregoriana, 1946).

26. Myrrha Lot-Borodine, *La deification de l'homme* (Paris: Cerf, 1970), 225n40.

The principal argument is that appropriation seems to be an artifice essentially destined to divert away from their obvious sense the scriptural and traditional expressions that are related to the Divine Persons. Thus, the result would be to minimize the Trinitarian mystery by diminishing the distinction of the Persons in order to place God's unity in such high relief that the Trinitarian dogma would lose all its importance in salvation history and Christian spirituality.

c) A Defense of Appropriation

{194} In general, Scripture is cited in opposition to the use of appropriation, and it is strongly affirmed that whatever difficulties may exist, it is sovereignly important to respect in their content the scriptural formulas that distinguish the Persons.... But who will dare to sustain to the bitter end that holiness is the *proprium* of the Holy Spirit and Wisdom the *proprium* of the Son? This would mean, in rigorous terms, that only the Spirit is holy—and therefore that the Father and the Son are not holy! It would mean that only the Son is wise—and therefore that the Father and the Holy Spirit are not wise! The Fathers never said this, and it is an untenable position. Nonetheless, terminological agreement is necessary. He who says, "to attribute properly," means "to attribute to a subject (an individual or a class of beings) that which in reality belongs to it and to it alone." If, on the contrary, this characteristic belongs to other subjects and yet is attributed to one of them as though it belonged only to it (e.g., if I say, "the City," in speaking of Rome), then we have a case of appropriation. Most declarations of the anti-appropriationists are contradicted by the fact that they themselves recognize that the [given] divine attribute attributed to one Person also belongs to the two others.

The theological problem of appropriation is not exactly the problem of making the biblical concept of God agree with our reason. Rather, it is that of seeing how the revelation of Jesus Christ does not contradict the revelation made to Moses but instead completes and crowns it. There would be a contradiction if one of the attributes of Yahweh belonged properly to one of the Three Persons.

2. The Noetic Value of Appropriation

{195} However, does appropriation truly accomplish its end, such as we defined it earlier, namely, that of enabling a conceptual approach to the *propria Personarum*? Indeed, in the end, it seems like it is only a linguistic procedure.

One forgets all too readily that the mediation of concepts exists between words (and propositions, formed from words) and reality. Although all the attributes in the Divine Reality are mutually identical in the transcendent Divine Substance, which itself is identical with each Person, nonetheless the concepts by means of which we attain the various attributes (in a very imperfect but true manner) are not identical and interchangeable. On this conceptual level, "resemblance"—or, to express it better, "affinity"—has a role to play here. Thanks to it, we can have access to what is proper to the persons by the means of essential concepts.

We can understand the process of appropriation in the following manner by making use of the parallelism that St. Thomas claims exists between the rational process that ascends from creatures to God (who is thus known according to His essential attributes) and the process of appropriation, which enables us to pass from the essential attributes to the [Trinitarian] "notions" or personal properties.[27]

a) The Passage from Created Perfections to Essential Attributes

{196} On the basis of the created perfections known in and through experience, reason elaborates the analogical concepts that represent these perfections by imperfectly abstracting from the limits imposed upon them by their realization in creatures. By means of an analogical judgment, supported upon the principle of causality and receiving its dynamism from the felt need to have recourse to a First, Transcendent Cause, these concepts are applied to this transcendent Subject, the First Cause. From this moment onward, they transcend all limitations, and beyond all limitations, their dis-

27. See *ST* I, q. 39, a. 7.

tinctions fade away into the Infinitely Simple Reality in which all perfections are realized. However, this reality cannot be conceived and, thus, the concepts used for attaining and knowing it (however imperfectly) remain distinct and ordered among themselves in our intra-mental universe. Thus, God is known through His essential attributes, which we conceive as though they were distinct, all the while affirming that they merge together in the infinitely simple Divine Reality.[28]

Our words express our concepts. Even though these words designate one and the same Divine Reality, they are not synonyms because the distinction, multiplicity, and order of our concepts remains.[29]

b) The Passage from the Essential Attributes to the *Propria Personarum*

{197} The super-analogical judgment of faith (and the theological judgment that relies upon it) makes use of the analogical concept by means of which an essential attribute is known, applying it to one Person in His distinction.

To do this, it is guided by revelation (which first does the same thing). Reason, illuminated by faith, justifies this utilization by appealing to the affinity that it detects between this essential attribute and this Person known by His mode of procession (or of non-procession in the case of the First Person). This concept does not express what is proper and distinct to this Person, just as, moreover, it does not express the essential attribute as though it were distinct from the others, even though it can embrace and designate only one particular perfection, distinct from the others, perfections that are also attributed to God, though by other concepts. However, it orients the mind toward a given mysterious property by which this Person is distinguished from the two others. This represents only a noetic approximation. However, it is a true noetic approximation and not mere wordplay. These attributions are not useless, and their

28. See Nicolas, *Dieu connue comme inconnu*, ch. 3.
29. See *ST* I, q. 13, a. 4.

verbal expressions are in no way interchangeable. (I cannot say, "I believe in the Holy Spirit, the Creator of heaven and of earth," although I believe that, in fact, the Holy Spirit created the heavens and the earth, with the Father and the Son, for this attribution, far from giving me access to the "proper nature" of the Holy Spirit, leads me astray. Likewise, I cannot say, "I believe in the Father, the life-giver and sanctifier," for the same reason.) These expressions are not useless because the foundational affinity between the essential attributes and the *propria Personarum* is *objective*, all the while existing only on the level of concepts.

3. Appropriation and the Believer's Relations to the Divine Persons

{198} One of the most important criticisms registered against appropriation is that it would rule out relations between the believer and each Divine Person in His singularity: "In the unique supernatural state, which comes forth entirely from each Person, we acquire real and distinct relations with the Three really distinct Persons of the One God."[30] The reproach is taken up with insistence by Karl Rahner. For example:

> In *De gratia*, only strictly appropriated relationships are considered between man and the divine persons; objectively, only the efficient causality of the One God is considered; and this is as much as to say soberly but expressly that we ourselves have really nothing to do with the mystery of the Trinity, beyond receiving some revelation "about" it.[31]

Here, we encounter anew the ambiguity of the term "relation." It signifies either an *ontological relation* (founded on efficient causality) or *interpersonal relations* of knowledge and love. Two things must be said about these *ontological relations* between God and creatures. On the one hand, they are rationate reasons* from God's perspective.

---

30. Régnon, vol. 3, 552–553.

31. Rahner, "Quelques remarques sur le traité dogmatique 'De Trinitate,'" in *Ecrits théologiques* VIII (Paris: Desclée de Brouwer, 1967), 113–14. [Taken from Karl Rahner, "Remarks on the Dogmatic Treatise 'De Trinitate,'" in *Theological Investigations*, vol. 4 (More Recent Writings), trans. Kevin Smyth (Baltimore: Helicon, 1966), 82.]

* [Trans. note: *relations de raison = relationes rationis*.]

On the other hand (and this is what is of direct interest for our purposes here), in God the terminus of these relations is God in the unity of His nature. In other words, the terminus is the Three Persons precisely inasmuch as They are one, unique God, and therefore, one unique Creator. The case is completely different for interpersonal relations, whose terminus is obviously the Person, each Divine Person in His singularity. This poses no difficulty, since each Person can be known and loved in His singularity. As we have seen, this knowledge is had by way of mystical knowledge (awaiting the Vision that we will have in the hereafter). But mystical contemplation itself, which is an act of faith, presupposes both revelation, which is the divine teaching, and faith, which is conceptual knowledge of the mystery. Appropriation is the means, indeed the only means, both for the divine teaching (to man) and for human conceptual knowledge [concerning these *propria Personarum*]. It is only a noetic approach, though it is one that opens access to the mystery of each Person, which is experienced in contemplation.[32]

Conclusion: The Trinity of
Persons and Salvation

Salvation consists in the union of the created person with God—his ultimate fulfillment. This union is interpersonal. Therefore, it presupposes and indeed requires that God's Personality first be manifested and then attained by the creature as someone known and loved.

Now, the Divine Personality is triune. This Personality is the Father, the Son, and the Holy Spirit. Prior to the Trinitarian revelation, the Divine Personality was hidden. His works (even by those that inaugurate salvation history in the Old Testament) manifest only the existence of this personality. What that Personality was in itself was not unveiled. The revelation of the Trinity represents the unveiling of this Personality. Because He is Triune, revelation includes the un-

---

32. See Nicolas, *Les profondeurs de la grâce*, 126n52.

veiling of each of the three Personalities of God, the Unique One. Its purpose is to render possible and provoke union with God in the form of the believer's personal union with each Person.

It hardly makes any sense to say "if we learn that God is not a Trinity, nothing would be changed in our thought and in our Christian life," for there is only one God—the Father, the Son, and the Holy Spirit—and we are invited to be united to this One God. There can be no other, and our union with Him can be nothing other than a union with the Three Persons together and with each in particular.

PART 4

The Divine Persons at Work in Salvation History

9

From the Immanent Trinity
to the Economic Trinity

{200} The expression "Economic Trinity" is used for the Trinity at work in the world for the sake of man's salvation, manifesting Himself in the salvific deeds that make up salvation history. We have seen how and why the "Economic Trinity" refers the mind to a consideration of the Immanent Trinity, as that which manifests refers to that which is manifested. For this reason, we dedicated a significant amount of time and rather extensive investigations to the task of acquiring at least some understanding (*intellectus fidei*) of the mystery of the One God in three Persons. We now return to the Economic Trinity, no longer to ask what It manifests to us concerning the Trinitarian mystery, but instead, in order to try to understand, *in light of the Trinitarian mystery*, the salvific work begun by the Three Divine Persons acting in the world, a work involving us.

The legitimacy of this undertaking has been contested.[1] It is said that the "Immanent Trinity" would be the transcendent summit to which the Economy would certainly refer, but It would be a summit from which we could not descend once again. From such a perspective, it is said that we cannot "reflect on creation and on sal-

---

1. See Ghislain Lafont, *Peut-on connaître Dieu en Jésus-Christ?* (Paris: Cerf, 1969).

vation history on the basis [of what we know concerning] God the Trinity.... Having arrived at this contemplation (of the Eternal Trinity), we cannot return in order to give a theological interpretation of the Economy."[2]

This sort of claim seems to express a kind of bias, one based on the utterly just and traditional idea that Jesus Christ is the revealer of God the Father, Son, and Spirit, and that one can know nothing about the mystery of God except in Him and through Him. Indeed, what is meant by saying, "The God-Being is manifested only in the humanity of Jesus," or, "The figure and sacrament of this unity (between the Father and the Son) is given to us in the very history of Jesus"? The notion of "manifesting" is essentially relative to that of "the manifested." In other words, what Jesus manifests in and through His humanity is necessarily something other than His humanity. If this were not the case, the term "manifestation" would become meaningless. To say, following Schillebeeckx, that "it is neither behind, above, nor below the man-Jesus that one must look for His being-God,"[3] is to blur our ideas by introducing spatial metaphors into the definition of God's relations to the creature, for although we cannot completely avoid such metaphors (as when we say that "God is everywhere"), we must avoid using them as explanatory principles. Metaphysical alterity exists between Jesus's humanity and His Divinity. Certainly, we know by faith that [His] being-God and being-man are identical in the Person of the Incarnate Word. However, in order for there to be a being-God, there must be a Divine Nature, and in order for there to be a being-man, there must be a human nature, which must be really distinct from the Divine Nature, all the while being united to it in the identity of the Person. Once again, the distinction and union of these two natures cannot be defined in spatial terms.

2. Bernard Rey, "Théologie trinitaire et revelation biblique," *Revue des sciences philosophiques et théologiques* 54 (1970): 636–53; Bernard Rey, *Le cheminement des premières communautés chrétiennes à la découverte de Dieu* (Paris: Cerf, 1972), ch. 4.

3. Rey, *Le cheminement des premières communautés chrétiennes à la découverte de Dieu,* 130.

In the same way, a "sacrament" refers to a "signified reality" (*res*). Jesus' humanity, which is the sacrament of His Divinity, cannot refer to itself as that on account of which Jesus is God. Thus, to say that Jesus is the Son of God on account of His humanity would represent the abolition of the mystery of the divine filiation (or, to make the same point in a different way, it would empty the expression, "Jesus is the Son of God," of all its meaning), whereas as Bernard Rey shows, in a very suggestive manner, the (pre- and post-Paschal) Apostolic Church discovered and confessed this filiation.[4]

On the other hand, I can conceive of Jesus's humanity as being the "sacrament of the unity of the Father and of the Son" only in light of the signified reality.[5] To claim to concentrate one's gaze upon Jesus' humanity, thus only having knowledge about His human conduct, would be to refrain from grasping Him as the sacrament of the eternal filiation. It is in light of this eternal filiation, to which this humanity refers us (by what Jesus said about Himself, by what He did, and by the faith of the apostles and of the first community) that we can understand what He was and what He is. If He is truly the Son sent by the Father—as the Church believes Him to be, and indeed as we, with her, believe Him to be—two things follow:

1. *On the one hand*, I cannot avoid asking questions about what is meant by this distinction which we have made in God, namely that of a Father and a Son. Indeed, if it were meaningless for us and wholly unknowable, the proposition, "the Father has sent His Son," a proposition coming to us from the apostles and on which the Church herself is founded, would be meaningless.

2. *On the other hand*, Jesus' conduct and words receive another meaning and another intelligible content from this fact. In order to see everything that Rey sees in them, so that they may become for us the principle of personal communion with the Divine Persons,

4. See Rey, *Le cheminement des premières communautés chrétiennes à la découverte de Dieu*, 2 [*sic*].

5. Rey, *Le cheminement des premières communautés chrétiennes à la découverte de Dieu*, 132.

they must be illuminated from on high by faith in the Trinity, by the recognition and theological explanation of the distinction of the Divine Persons.

If the Eternal Trinity is the source of salvation history, how could knowledge of the former not illuminate the latter? Salvation history can be understood only in light of the Trinitarian mystery, for God who saves is the Father, the Son, and the Holy Spirit, and They act to save man, each Person acting according to what is hypostatically proper to Himself [*sa propriété hypostatique*]. Cut off from its transcendent source, the Economy would be only an ensemble of religious phenomena in which man's religious nature and aspirations for salvation would be expressed. However, it would in no way be the authentic Christian experience, that of the apostles and the first Christian community, indeed, that of the whole Church, which affirms: man is really saved, by real events in which he did not have the initiative, events which were provoked and accomplished by the Divine Persons, and he is asked only to participate voluntarily in them through faith, the sacraments, and the "*sequela Christi.*" Thus, just as in the order of reality, the Economy proceeds from the Eternal Trinity (i.e., from the free design conceived and decided within the intimate depths of the Trinity), so too in the noetic order, knowledge of the Economic Trinity of itself follows upon knowledge of the Immanent Trinity. Granted, in the genesis of our knowledge, the Economic Trinity is the first thing known, for It is the manifestation of the Immanent Trinity. However, when the believer's mind, referred by the Economic Trinity to the Immanent Trinity, has been able to "know" the latter (though, very imperfectly!), it is referred anew to the Economic Trinity in order to know It more fully.

This part of Trinitarian theology is the *theology of the divine missions*. It is in no way a mere appendix or a corollary, for it is what definitively explains the meaning of the mystery of the Trinity (that is, what it means *for us*). However, it also is not the principal part of the treatise, making the study of the Trinitarian relations and of the Persons into a mere a corollary to the theology of the divine missions. The missions are the manifestation of the mystery, and through them, the believer is led "to the complete truth" that will be revealed in the definitive contemplation of the mystery, in the [Beatific] [V]ision.

Thus, Trinitarian theology can be described as a movement having four stages (not following each other in a linear fashion, but rather, enveloping one another):

1. First, there is knowledge of the Economic Trinity had through faith, that is, knowledge concerning the action and manifestations of the Divine Persons in salvation history.

2. Then, through this first knowledge, we are referred to the Immanent Trinity. Here, both faith and theological reflection are operative: *faith* in the Trinitarian mystery as expressed in the dogmatic formulations and *theological reflection* on these formulations leading to some knowledge of the Divine Persons in Their distinction and in the unity of the Divine Being.

3. In light of this knowledge of the Immanent Trinity, we return to the Economic Trinity (i.e., the mission of the Word and the mission of the Spirit, both finding their transcendent explanation in the Immanent Trinity).

4. However, the Immanent Trinity is not only the source and explanatory principle of the missions, It is also their ultimate end and terminus: the Son comes forth from the Father and returns to Him, bringing in His wake the men whom the Holy Spirit leads to the whole truth. Knowledge of the Trinity is not brought to its completion in knowledge of the Economic Trinity. Rather, it is brought to completion in the full and complete knowledge of the Immanent Trinity to which the Economic Trinity orders us.[6]

6. N.B., Understood in this way, Trinitarian theology could embrace all theology. In principle, the study of the mission of the Word could embrace all of *Christology*. The study of the mission of the Spirit could embrace *ecclesiology and sacramentology*. The study of the ordering of the missions to the definitive revelation of God would be *eschatology*.

However, this could not avoid being somewhat artificial. It is quite true that the sole "subject" of theology is God the Trinity and that everything in theology is understood in

Also, in this fourth part of the treatise, we will speak about the "missions" as the intra-worldly and intra-historical continuation of the intra-Trinitarian processions, leaving to Christology and pneumatology the study of Word's action in the world through the humanity that He assumed in becoming incarnate and the action of the Spirit through the Church.[7]

---

relation to Him. (See See *ST* I, q. 1, a. 7.) Nonetheless, it is also true that our intellect is discursive in nature and can make progress in knowledge of the subject only by multiplying it into partial objects. From this perspective, the *Treatise on the Trinity* has a distinct and partial object. This is inevitable and legitimate, on the condition that the mind does not rest in this "artificial" division but instead, by means of the dynamic of judgment, ever seeks to surmount it in order to retrieve unity (or at least in order to aim at it).

7. See Michael Schmaus, "Sendung," *Lexikon für Theologie und Kirche*, 2nd ed., vol. 9, Josef Höfer and Karl Rahner (Freiburg im Breisgau, 1957).

10

Mission of a Divine Person

{201} If the Divine Persons act in creation, They always do so inasmuch as They are the One and Triune God. By contrast, in salvation history, the Three Persons are revealed as acting, if not separately, at least distinctly, each playing His role in the common work of man's salvation and sanctification.

The key notion used for this revelation is that of *mission*. The Father *sends* his Son into the world, to men and to His death. The resurrected Son *returns* to the Father having accomplished the work for which He was sent. In turn, He *sends* the Holy Spirit in order to continue and fortify this work, leading it to its head.

Indeed, this biblical notion of "mission" represents the hinge between *Theology* and *the Economy*[, that is, between the "Immanent Trinity" and the "Economic Trinity"]. It must first be analyzed in itself with care, so that after that we can see how it is applied (or not applied) to the Persons in particular.

I. ANALYSIS OF THE NOTION OF THE "MISSION" OF A DIVINE PERSON

A. The Problem

{202} At first glance, it seems that this notion can be understood only in a metaphoric sense. First of all, in its proper sense, the notion of a mission seems to entail the separation of the sent person from the person who sends him. Secondly, it seems necessarily to entail a spatial and temporal change for the sent person, for the sent person is sent in order to be where he was not heretofore. Finally, it seems to entail that the sent person is subordinated to the person who sends him.

However, can we accept the reduction of the notion of "mission" to this metaphoric sense? This would deprive salvation history of all its consistency and reality. Indeed, this expression is the means by which salvation history was revealed to us (at least in its essential and decisive phases, namely, the Redemptive Incarnation and the action of the Holy Spirit), and it is by accepting the reality designated by this expression that man is called to participate in it. In other words, we must recognize this reality, a recognition which can occur only by means of a "proper" concept (i.e., one that can make us attain this reality such as it is, even if we do so only in a very imperfect manner, as is the case for all our theological concepts). Now, to attain and express this reality, we do not have any other concept at our disposal than that of mission.

B. A Theological Examination of the Biblical Notion of "Mission"

1. Determination of the Notion of "Divine Mission" on the Basis of the Notion of Mission Drawn from Experience.

Here again, we find that we must make use of the classical theological process [of analogy, indeed the super-analogy of faith]. Taking the notion drawn from experience, the *ratio analogata* (a notion which we know is applied to God Himself precisely on account of how it is used by revelation), and extricating it from the conditions of limitation that it undergoes in all its created realizations, doing so by means of negation, we then, simultaneously, push it to its extreme point of perfection in order to attribute it to God beyond all its created realizations.

a) The Notion of "Mission"

{203} It seems that this is a "personal" notion in several ways. First of all, it is applied in a proper sense only to a person, for a person is who is sent. Then also, he is sent by another person and is sent to persons. Thus, this concept designates the person to whom it is attributed in a relational manner, in two directions: a relation to the person who sends (or, *the relation of origin*) and a relation to the persons to whom he is sent (or, a *relation of access**).

The *relation of origin* is founded on an act by which the person in question is sent by the other. That is, in some way or another, the one person goes forth from the other. There would not be a mission if this action of sending did not occur.

The *relation of access* is a relation of presence to the persons to whom the given person is sent, a relation itself also founded on this action of sending, which is oriented toward these persons. In sum, we are faced here with the double relation that every action founds: a relation to the agent and a relation to its terminus. What is characteristic here is that the object of this action is a person and that he is the one who thus has new relations with other persons.

How can this hold true for the case of a Divine Person?

b) Analogical Treatment of the Notion of "Mission"

{204} In the universe given to our experience, the action that founds the relations of origin and access is a causal action, namely, moral causality, in the form of an order that is more or less imperative or in the form of counsel. However, it is ever the case that the sent person is in a situation of passivity and subordination in relation to the person who sends him. On the other hand, of itself, the action involves a separation: the sent person departs from the person who sends him.

---

* [Tr. note: The original "relation d'accès" could perhaps also be rendered "relation of entry" or "relation of admission." However, given the awkwardness of all such forms, I have maintained the most literal, which the reader can take as a technical usage.]

If this were part of the *ratio analogata*, this notion could not be attributed to a Divine Person, who cannot be in a situation of subordination and passivity in relation to another. Now, faith informs us about the origination of one Person in relation to another distinct Person in God. However, this origination, as real as it is, includes neither subordination nor passivity. Now, subordination and passivity are not essential requirements for the notion of mission. What is essential is origination, the "going forth" and the "arising from." Therefore, the action of sending, reduced to its pure essence, is found in God, namely, in notional acts by which one Person proceeds from another.

Thus, the aspect of "separation" is eliminated in a single stroke, for the Divine Person who proceeds remains in Him from whom He proceeds. Such is the reality of perichoresis.[1] Now, it is not essential to the mission that the sent person "depart from" the person who sends him. This pertains only to the created conditions of the realization of this notion as we experience it.

The *relation of access* remains. In our experience, it is always founded on a movement of the sent person and, therefore, on a change. This is the aspect by which the action of the sending person becomes a "passion" in the person in question, namely the ["passion" of] "being sent." We have seen that the Trinitarian procession was an "action" of the originating Person, without a passion in the proceeding Person.[2] However, if we exclude this aspect of passivity, will there still be room for the relation of access? In other words, how can we conceive that the sent Person reaches the persons to whom He is sent without Himself undergoing a change? Nonetheless, the Divine Person is absolutely immutable.

Here, we must recall the universal law that governs God's relation to creatures (and therefore the relation of the Divine Persons to them). God is referred to creatures (e.g., the relation as Creator), not on account of any change whatsoever undergone by Him (God did

1. See §§157–59 above.
2. See §83 above.

not "become" the Creator) but, rather, on account of a change having taken place in the creature.[3] It is a "rationate relation,"* for there
is no change in God Himself. However, it is a relation that can really
qualify God. God really is the Creator, even though His relation to
the creature is rationate. Indeed, He is really the terminus of the relation of total dependence from the creature to Him, in which "being created" consists.

The same is true for a Divine Person in His singularity. If it is
true that one can identify a change in the creature, founding a new
relation (i.e., a relation of presence) to the Divine Person, this Person will be rendered present to His creature in a new manner without undergoing any change in Himself. For Him, this presence will
be a "rationate relation," though one that will really qualify Him. It
will be the "relation of access" that we are seeking, one that is necessary so that the notion of "mission" can be attributed properly to
this Divine Person.

The validity of the attribution of the notion of "mission" to a Divine Person completely depends on the possibility of such a change,
that is, on the possibility of a change that establishes a completely
new relation of the created person to one or several of the Divine
Persons in Their singularity.

2. Comparison with the Biblical Notion of "Mission"

{205} At first sight, it could well seem that the analogical treatment thus imposed on the notion of mission empties it of the realism that it has in biblical language: "I came from the Father and
have come into the world";[4] "God sent forth his Son, born of woman, born under the law";[5] "But when the Counselor comes, whom I
shall send to you from the Father";[6] and so forth. But nonetheless,

---

3. See *ST* I, q. 13, a. 7. Jean-Hervé Nicolas, *Dieu connue comme inconnu* (Paris: Desclée de Brouwer, 1966), 131–35.

* [Tr. note: relation de raison = relatio rationis.]

4. Jn 16:28 (RSV).

5. Gal 4:4 (RSV).

6. Jn 15:26 (RSV).

other affirmations say that the sent Son did not depart from His Father and that the Father was always with Him.

In truth, a notion drawn from experience cannot be applied to God without undergoing such an analogical treatment. If such treatment were eschewed, we would be like people who believed that the biblical expression "the Word of God" actually referred merely to sounds in the air. If the analogical treatment respects what this aims at essentially, through the created reality that the biblical expression first designates by means of human language, it does not betray the true meaning of this expression but, instead, uncovers it.

This is the case here. If it is at least conceivable that the Divine Person is rendered present to a created person in a special and new way, then the eternal procession by which He sets forth from the Originating Person without being separated from Him, prolonged by this temporal relation of presence, truly has the essential characteristics of a mission.

3. From Theology to the Economy

{206} The theological notion of a mission that we have elaborated places it in close dependence on the eternal processions and therefore upon the mystery of the Immanent Trinity (or, on Theology [as distinguished from the Economy]).

We have seen that this dependence is contested today. Doubtlessly, the real dependence is not contested. Instead, what is contested is the possibility that our mind can "think about creation and the economy of salvation, doing so on the basis of [our knowledge of] God the Trinity."[7] However, can we even form a conception of the "divine mission" without expressly connecting it to the eternal processions? In reality, without this connection, the notion of the divine missions would be emptied of their meaning. Indeed, what would remain if they were deprived of the relation of the sent Person to the

---

7. Bernard Rey, "Théologie trinitaire et revelation biblique," *Revue des sciences philosophiques et théologiques* 54 (1970): 653.

Person who sent Him? Certainly, God sent to men prophets who were mere men. However, when He did this, He did not bring about a "divine mission," for the person who was sent was not a Divine Person. The mission of a Divine Person can be understood only if one expressly thinks that there are other Divine Persons and that this Person has a relation of origin in relation to one among them. Without this, the notion of a divine mission becomes a mere wordplay.

But how can we think about the economy of salvation, such as it has been revealed to us, other than by the notion of the mission of a Divine Person (in reality, the notion of two missions, respectively concerning the Son and the Holy Spirit)?

It would be incoherent to insist so much on the realism of the divine missions and simultaneously to forbid oneself, and forbid us, the only means that we have for understanding them, namely seeing them as being the temporal prolongation of the eternal processions.

However, we still must examine the other aspect of the [divine] missions, namely, the sent Divine Person's access to the created persons.

C. The Mission and Access of the Divine Person to Created Persons

We are faced with the problem of discovering how a change caused in the human person by the divine action can unite a Divine Person to a human person in such a way that we can say that, through this action, the Divine Person has reached [*accédé*] the human person without Himself undergoing a change.

1. The Divine Person Reaches the Human Person by Becoming,
through the Gift of Grace, an Object That He Knows and Loves

{207} This is the solution proposed by St. Thomas.[8] To understand it, we must recognize that the fact that the Divine Person

---

8. See *ST* I, q. 43, a. 3; Jean-Hervé Nicolas, *Les profondeurs de la grâce* (Paris: Beauchesne, 1969), 437ff.

reaches the created person is not explained solely by the fact that the Divine Person would be *known* by that created person, for mere knowledge of Him is not a real union.

No more is it explained by love alone. Love tends toward real union but itself is not real union. Instead, it is an affective union, and the beloved being can be distant without, by this fact alone, being less beloved.

And nonetheless, this access must take place through an activity in the created person, since one must rule out every form of change in the Divine Person. It is only as an object of activities [*opérations*] that He can be united to the created person, all the while Himself remaining immobile. And, of course, we mean that this is only as an object of spiritual activities.

We must return to knowledge. Of itself, it only establishes an intentional union. However, there is a type of knowledge that *also* includes real union, for the *intention* that is proper to it terminates at the actually existing thing. We are speaking of experiential knowledge.

The paradigm of such knowledge is sensorial perception. However, one finds it also, on that basis, in human intellectual knowledge. It is found first of all in intellectual knowledge of individual things. In this case, intellectual knowledge properly so called is prolonged to the actually present individual thing, making use of sensorial perception. So too (although this is much contested), it occurs in the intuition of being, which is the immediate grasp of being given concretely in the beings thus experienced.[9]

Whatever may be the case for this metaphysical problem concerning the intuition of being, there is, at the terminus and summit of the life of grace, a perfect experience of the Divine Persons in the Beatific Vision, where the most complete intentional union and the most realistic real union are conjoined.[10] Now, the Beatific Vision is the fulfillment of what is already given in faith. Will not this faith

9. See Nicolas, *Dieu connue comme inconnu*, 34–35.
10. See §178 above.

also include an experience of the Divine Persons, at least in an inchoate and very imperfect form?

We discussed this experience earlier.[11] Here, we need not establish its existence (and therefore its possibility) and can take it for
granted. How are we to conceive of it?

For there to be an experience, the known being must first of all
really be present and be known as being present. In other words,
that knowledge must open out on its actual existence. Now, the Divine Persons are actually existent in the created spirit, as in every
creature, through [God's] presence of immensity. They are present as
causing the creature's being. Also, They are there as causing the grace
by which the created spirit is rendered capable of knowing Them
and loving Them. God gives Himself to be known and loved, not by
becoming an object of knowledge and love but, rather, by causing in
the created spirit the ability to see Him:

> If there were a being who was simultaneously the source of the power of
> seeing and the reality seen, we would need to say that he who sees him
> would receive from that being both the power for seeing and the form by
> which the action of seeing is realized (the *impressed species*).[12]

Nonetheless, it is clear that, in order to make knowledge open out
from faith onto the Divine Person thus really present, we cannot appeal to sensorial perception as we do for the case of knowledge of
the singular existent. Nor can we appeal to the idea that the created mind would be informed by the Divine Essence as we do for the
case of the [Beatific] [V]ision. It is here that love intervenes, not to
substitute itself for knowledge but to render the knowledge experiential by penetrating it.

Indeed, love connaturalizes the loving person to the beloved person. Charity connaturalizes the created spirit to God, not by abolishing the infinite ontological distance that separates them but by making the created person communicate with the Divine Person in the
Good (this presupposing the initial kinship of the created spirit with

11. See §169.
12. *ST* I, q. 12, a. 2.

God, in whose image he was made). Hence, in those who believe and love God, self-knowledge is susceptible to becoming an experience of the Divine Persons. It is a mediated experience, in the sense that what is directly experienced is the created spirit himself. However, in and through it, knowledge opens out on the Divine Persons present by Their action, as we have said.[13]

Such a knowledge of the Divine Persons corresponds well to what we are seeking: it is a new presence of the Divine Persons to the created persons. Indeed, it is a real presence, though one involving no change for the Divine Persons, being formally realized by the created person's acts of knowledge and love. It is a presence through the "access" [or "approach"] of the Divine Person to the created person, for God is the one who, by His grace, transforms the created person in such a way that the latter is rendered capable of this experiential knowledge. He is the one who makes him elicit it. It is a presence of each Person in His distinction, for each is distinctly the object of knowledge and love. However, it is also a presence of the three together, for They are inseparable.

This experiential knowledge is what St. Thomas had in view when he wrote: "God is said to be in the rational nature as the known in the knower and as the beloved in the lover."[14] Indeed, He adds a precision, namely, that this is a case of "perception": "Perception designates a kind of experiential knowledge."[15]

2. Mission and Gift

{208} In the aforementioned texts from St. Thomas, the notion of a "gift" of a Divine Person is joined to that of "mission," and in what concerns the relation of the Divine Person to the created person, this notion is treated in the same manner. Grace is the means by which the Divine Person reaches the created person and is given to him.

---

13. See Jean-Hervé Nicolas, *Contemplation et vie contemplative en christianisme* (Fribourg-Paris: Éditions universitaires, Beauchesne, 1980), 48–59.

14. See *ST* I, q. 43, a. 3.

15. *ST* I, q. 43, a. 4, ad. 2.

Indeed, in the language of the New Testament, when the Divine Person is the one who is given, the term "to give" has the same sense as "to send." This is clear in the following parallelism: "For God so loved the world that he gave his only Son,"[16] and, "In this the love of God was made manifest among us, that God sent his only Son into the world, so that we might live through him."[17] The same holds for the Holy Spirit: "And I will pray the Father, and he will give you another Counselor."[18] One may also consult a host of other texts wherein the Holy Spirit is designated as being the Gift of God.[19]

This makes clear an essential aspect of the mission of a Divine Person. If He is sent, this is principally in order for Him to be the riches, good, and joy of those to whom He is sent. He is sent in order "to be with" [the person to whom He is sent]. Certainly, He is also sent in order to accomplish a work. However, as we have seen, this work is not an end in itself that would justify the mission, for every "doing" reveals efficient causality and is explained by the unified action of the Three Persons together. With regard to all "natural effects," the work for which a Divine Person is sent is characterized by the fact that it is essentially performed in order to unite created persons to the Divine Persons in a definitive manner. This is what will determine the relation of the visible missions to the invisible ones.

Equally, the divine action without which there would not be a mission (since the mission cannot be understood without a transformation in the creature, brought about by God) is presupposed for the mission. However, this action does not constitute the mission. In particular, the divine action of causing the gifts of created grace in the soul does not constitute the invisible missions of the Son and of the Spirit. Grace is the means for these missions, but by this means, the very Persons are sent and given.

16. Jn 3:16 (RSV).
17. 1 Jn 4:9 (RSV).
18. Jn 14:16 (RSV).
19. See Acts 2:38, 10:45; 2 Cor 5:5; 1 Thes 4:8; etc.

THE DIVINE MISSIONS AND
THE ASSIMILATION OF THE CREATED
SPIRIT TO DIVINE PERSONS

{209} If the access of the Divine Persons to the created person is brought about by means of the connaturality of love (the creature experiencing the Divine Persons through the experience of the self being connaturalized to Them), when we ask how each person in His distinction reaches the created person, we are thus looking into the nature of the assimilation of the created spirit to each Divine Person in what is proper to Him.

This is what St. Thomas explains in the *Scriptum super Sententiis*, though he does so in a way that is so restrained (in comparison to the *Summa theologiae*, where the presence *sicut cognitum in cognoscente et sicut amatum in amante* is placed in relief) that one is tempted either to oppose the two explanations to each other, or to interpret the one by the other. In reality, these are two aspects of the same relation of access, whose synthesis must be perceived (a synthesis that St. Thomas, in the texts in question, himself proposes clearly enough).[20]

A. How to Understand the
Assimilation of the Created Person by
Grace to the Divine Persons

1. Explanation by the Imprint of the Divine Persons within the Created Spirit

{210} According to this theory, the Divine Persons reach the created person by the very act of producing grace.[21] Grace is thus understood as being an act that does not consist in "making" something but in impressing their resemblance in an actual and continuous

---

20. See St. Thomas, *In I Sent.*, d. 14 and 15; *ST* I, q. 43; Thomas J. Fitzgerald, *De inhabitatione Spiritus Sancti, doctrina Sancti Thomae Aquinatis* (Mundelein: 1949); Jesús Martinez-Castañeda, *Los dones de las misiones divinas según Santo Tomás* (Lima: Renovabis, 1958); Louis Bouyer, *Le Consolateur, Espirit Saint et vie de grâce* (Paris: Cerf, 1980), 270–72.

21. See Paul Galtier, *L'habitation en nous de trois Personnes* (Roma: 1950), 217–19.

manner, as the signet does in marking wax with its imprint, such that
its imprint would disappear if it were to withdraw itself. It is a kind
of irradiation of the Divine Form, configuring the soul to itself solely
by its presence. It seems that it would be conceived of as being a kind
of exemplar cause that would itself bring about its image in the effect
without efficient causality as an intermediary. It would thus assume
the realizing power of efficient causality.

It goes without saying that the Trinity as such is impressed in this
imprint received from the Trinitarian God. In other words, the soul
is made to exist as the image of the Divine Persons together and the
image of each in particular.

Of course, we recognize that grace, which is this imprint of the
Trinity, is also the principle of the acts of knowledge and of love by
which the created person can communicate in the Trinitarian life.
Therefore, we here find the operative and intentional union (*sicut
cognitum in cognoscente ...*) mentioned above. Nonetheless, the difference between the two explanations is great, for in the aforementioned explanation, the union with the Divine Persons was explained
formally through an operative union. In the explanation being considered now, we have an ontological union of the Divine Persons
with the created person, a union prior to every operative union, the
latter being only the consequence of the former.

What should we think about this explanation? This way of attributing an efficient causality to the exemplar cause precisely as such
could be criticized, for the exemplar cause is not, of itself, a productive cause. Instead, it is such only by the intermediary of the efficient
cause that produces the effect according to the form that rules its action. However, even if we set aside this confusion of causalities, as
soon as we admit a "realization," we necessarily have the production
of an effect that is distinct from the cause. Thus, grace is an effect
that is distinct from God, an effect that is caused and created. Therefore, there is not truly an ontological union of God the Trinity with
the soul, for the Creator remains at an infinite ontological distance
from the creature, with the metaphysical distance that is alterity. This

is so even if He is in the soul, at the source of its being, through the presence of His being, through [His] presence of immensity.

This explanation would find its full force only in the Palamite theory of "uncreated energies" which we discussed earlier.[22] According to their explanation, it is explicitly professed that God Himself gives Himself to the spiritual creature through grace according to the mode of existence belonging to His "energies" or "attributes," all the while remaining inaccessible and incommunicable in His Essence. No Latin theologian admits this strange distinction *in God Himself*, which is not intended to be a notional distinction (for then it would affect the knowledge that we have of God but not* the very Being of God), but which nevertheless claims not to introduce any division into the Divine Being (as a real distinction would necessarily do). As we said above, it cannot, in fact, be admitted because it implies a contradiction. In order to go as far as possible down this path concerning God's ontological union with the spiritual creature, it has been imagined that there would be an "informing" of the creature's being by God's Being. Is this compatible with the divine transcendence?

2. Can One Think of a Formal (or, Quasi-Formal) Action Exercised Distinctly in the World by a Divine Person?

This is the idea defended by Karl Rahner.[23]

a) In the Order of Salvation, Can We Admit a Formal Causality Exercised by God in Relation to the Creature?

{211} We must firmly say that this is metaphysically impossible. The formal cause is characterized by the fact that it is partially identical with its effect. It causes by being really united to the "material cause."[24] Now, it is impossible for God, who is Pure Act, to enter into

22. See §173 above.
* [Tr. note: Reading "par" as "pas."]
23. See Karl Rahner, "Pour la notion scolastique de la grâce incréée," in *Ecrits théologiques* III (Paris: Desclée de Brouwer, 1963), 36–39.
24. See Cornelio Fabro, *Participation et causalité selon Saint Thomas d'Aquin* (Paris: Vrin, 1961), 381–412.

composition with a "potency" (for potency limits act),[25] thus becoming a part of a whole (for the part depends on the whole).

It will be said that this is not a true form of dependence, since this can exist only voluntarily on the part of God, arising from His pure initiative. This explanation excludes moral dependence but leaves open the question of ontological dependence. Thus, we must ask whether we can admit that God has freely decided to render Himself ontologically dependent on His creature. Now this is inconceivable, for ontological independence is the very thing that we express when we say that God is Pure Act, so that the renunciation of this independence would entail that God would renounce His divinity. An absurd hypothesis!

Rahner, who wishes to situate his theory within St. Thomas's metaphysical framework, here appeals to the Thomist theory of knowledge. According to Rahner, this theory would require a real and ontological union between the knower and the known at the point of departure of knowledge. Such a union is therefore necessary for explaining the Beatific Vision. However, given that the Beatific Vision is the summit, fulfillment, and consummation of the union of grace, it is also necessary to posit an ontological union at the basis of grace, as a kind of informing of the created spirit by the Godhead, God thus being the formal cause.

The idea of evaluating the union of grace in light of the definitive union of the [Beatific] [V]ision must be fully and appreciatively accepted. However, it is not precise to say that an ontological union between the knower and the known is required (both by St. Thomas and according to the principles of his theory of knowledge) as the foundation of intentional union. In fact, in most cases, such a real union between the knower and the known does not exist. In the case of the [Beatific] [V]ision, there is indeed a kind of real union since, as we have seen, vision excludes every intermediary. However, the informing of the created mind [*esprit*] by the Divine Essence

25. See *ST* I, q. 7, a. 1.

is not ontological (that is, by composition). It is intentional (that is, by way of the identification of the knower to the known according to intelligible being). Indeed, St. Thomas himself expressly excludes this connection, even though his authority is invoked to endorse the idea that a real union between God and His spiritual creature is a necessary prerequisite for the intentional union of Beatific Vision and Love:

> Therefore, it is clear that for the created intellect, the Divine Essence can take on the role of the intelligible representation (*species intelligibilis*) by means of which it knows (*qua intelligit*), and this can be said of no other separate substance. And nevertheless, according to natural existence (in contrast with intentional existence, that is, to the existence by which the intelligible representation *exists* in the intellect)[26] it cannot inform something that differs from itself. Indeed, if this were so, it would follow that it would constitute one single nature with this other thing, whereas the Divine Essence is itself complete in its own nature. The intelligible representation united to the intellect does not constitute a single nature with it, but instead perfects it so as to render it capable of eliciting intellection. This is not incompatible with the perfection of the Divine Essence.[27]

b) Supposing Such a Quasi-Formal Causality, Could We Discern a Hypostatic Activity Proper to Each Person?

{212} Here again, we must respond negatively, for the Divine "Form" is common to the Three Persons. Therefore, if the creature were "informed" by the Godhead, the distinction of the Persons would not divide up this activity any more than it would divide up the Divine Substance.

Therefore, in every instance, the principle *omnia opera Sanctissimae Trinitatis ad extra sunt indivise trium Personarum*, remains inviolable. We cannot conceive of anything brought about by God in the

26. See SCG, bk. 3, ch. 51; Jean-Hervé Nicolas, "L'unité d'être dans le Christ selon S. Thomas d'Aquin," *Revue thomiste* 65 (1965): 248–49.

27. N.B., Rahner uses the expression "quasi-formal," not in order to diminish the reality of this "information" of the created mind by the Godhead, but instead, in order to highlight that it does not entail any ontological dependence on the part of God. But it is contradictory to say that an information is at once real while nonetheless not entailing that the "formal cause" depends on the "matter" that it informs. See SCG, bk. 4, ch. 11.

world as though it were something uniquely proper to one of the Divine Persons.

3. Interpretation by Dynamic Assimilation

{213} In every finite being, we must really distinguish its *being*, by which it is constituted and thus is "a given, determinate being," from the *activity* [*opération*] by means of which it progresses toward its end and attains it, that is, by which it realizes its good.

This distinction does not hold for Infinite Being, *even conceptually*, for being is in potency in relation to its activity and to all the increases that it obtains through it. In Pure Act, the line of being and the line of activity are united to each other and merge. It is Pure Act in the sense of "Subsistent Being" and simultaneously that of "Pure Action" (i.e., "Subsistent Intellection" and of "Subsistent Love"). In other words, in God, the "static" (that is, being, considered as the constitutive act of being, "first act" in potency to activity) is not encountered in any way, even according to a conceptual distinction. In Him, there is only "pure dynamism," an Act that is at once constitutive and operative.

If I consider this act as constitutive, it establishes God at an infinite metaphysical distance from every created being. The creature's resemblance to God according to being can only be distant. Moreover, as we have seen, such resemblance can only pertain to the Divine Essence and not to the personal properties. Also, it is futile to look in the structure of created being for a configuration to the Divine Persons that would be equal to the presence of these very Persons. As we have seen, even where there is, properly speaking, an "image" in the spiritual creature, it is unable to be deciphered without faith. On this static level, grace itself leaves the creature in its difference and infinite distance.

However, grace penetrates and super-elevates the dynamism of the spiritual creature. Now, by its dynamism, the latter is not incapable of crossing distance separating it from God, even though it is infinite. The spiritual creature can have God Himself, in His mystery, as the object of his spiritual actions (knowledge and love) and, thus, can share in the life of the Divine Persons. In short, the spiritual creature can have as his good the good that is properly that of God and thus can find his ultimate fulfillment in God.

Grace brings this about in the spiritual creature. It does not come about through a kind of "creation," for it is him, the created person, in his own, proper being who is transformed by grace without ceasing to be himself. Instead, grace brings this about through a super-elevation of his nature, which already tends toward God as toward an inaccessible and only regulative [*régulateur*] end, and which by grace, is exalted all the way to this very God as toward the object of his knowledge and love.[28]

In this way, we return anew to the results of the preceding investigation, and it seems that we find ourselves in the same place, that is, in the presence of the Divine Persons as an object of knowledge and love. However, this is not the case. For if being is distinguished from activity, it is in potency to it and virtually contains it. I can consider the same being by which a being is constituted in its difference ([i.e.,] essence or substance) as the principle of activities (i.e., as a nature), and thus it already belongs to the dynamic order, where it can rejoin God. Hence, I can understand this elevation of the spiritual being's dynamism through grace as a kind of configuration to God. Two beings that have the same end, operatively communing in the same good, are dynamically similar (whether that good is possessed together or is only pursued and possessed inchoately and tendentially). But here, one of the two Himself is the Absolute Good in whom the encounter and convergence of dynamisms occurs. He is the Perfect Model, the Exemplar to whom the other is increasingly conformed to the degree that his communion with Him is intensified. Hence, it is God *in His reality*, as the infinite Good, who models the creature upon Himself. Thus, in the dynamic order, we again discover this action of God imprinting His image in an actual and

28. See §207 above.

continuous manner upon the spiritual creature, really present in this way through this imprint, something which Fr. Gaultier tries in vain to find in the static order.

It is God (i.e., the Trinity), for through grace the object of created spiritual activities receives the same object as the divine activities of knowledge and love. God gives Himself to be known and loved as He is in Himself, in His mystery.

However, can we speak of an assimilation of the created person to each of the Divine Persons according to what is hypostatically proper to Him? And if so, what is the proper way to explain this?

B. Distinct Assimilation to Each of the Divine Persons

1. Beyond Appropriation

{214} What was said about the dynamic assimilation to God through objective mediation [*par la mediation de l'objet*] can be understood for each Person in His distinction. Indeed, each Person is a distinct object in the divine object (as each is a distinct Being in the unique Divine Being). Assimilated to God dynamically through grace, which renders the creature capable of these activities that have the Divine Persons in their distinction as their objects, the created person finds himself assimilated to each Person of the Trinity, being rendered capable of knowing and loving Him in what is proper to Him.

It is here, in the notions of objective presence and assimilation, that we have achieved a synthesis between the two manners of conceiving the relation of access constitutive of the [divine] mission[s]. Through the love of charity, the soul is connaturalized to each Person, being really configured and assimilated to Him. It is by experiencing himself thus configured (not a natural experience, but rather, a mystical one) that he can attain the Persons in what is proper to each as an object of experience.

This leads us beyond appropriation, for the soul is truly and really assimilated to each Person in a distinct manner. While the noetic

approximation of appropriation cannot be transcended in the line of
conceptual knowledge, it can be transcended in another way, namely
that of mystical experience.

2. Assimilation to the Son and to the Holy Spirit

{215} Grace in itself is one, for it is a participation in the perfectly simple and unified Trinitarian Life. However, it is diversified in
accord with the complexity of the created person upon whom this
participation is bestowed. While knowledge and love are identical in
God, they are two distinct activities in the human person, though increasingly unified to the degree that the participation in the Divine
Life intensifies. It remains the case that, even though the gifts of light
that illuminate this person's intellect and the gifts of love that en-
flame his heart are only aspects of the same grace by which he is conformed to God, they assimilate him distinctly to the Son, the Word,
in whom the Divine Intellection's dazzling brilliance is expressed,
and to the Holy Spirit, Personified Love, who is the eternal outpouring of the Infinite Love.

Here we must cite St. Thomas, specifically the *Summa theologiae* where he explains how grace assimilates the soul to the Son and
to the Spirit. Certainly, his explanation is far more condensed in this
text than it is in the *Scriptum*, but—whatever some have said about
it—it does not sacrifice any of the riches detailed at length in his
earlier work:

Through grace, the soul is conformed to God. Consequently, in order for
one to be able to speak of the sending of a Divine Person to someone
through grace, the latter person must be assimilated to the sent Divine
Person through a gift of grace. As the Holy Spirit is Love, it is by the gift of
charity that the soul is assimilated to the Holy Spirit. Thus, assimilation to
the Holy Spirit must be understood as resulting from the gift of charity. As
regards the Son, He is the Word, certainly, but not indiscriminately in any
manner whatsoever. He is the Word from whom Love proceeds. Therefore, the mission of the Son must not be understood as though it resulted
from any kind of intellectual enrichment without further distinction but,
rather, must be understood to result from an enrichment giving rise to

love's impulse, as is said in Jn. 6:45 (RSV): "Every one who has heard and learned from the Father comes to me."[29]

Further on in this response to the given objection, St. Thomas specifies that the knowledge in question, implied in the mission, is an *experiential knowledge,* one that motivates this passage from experiential knowledge to assimilation, which is emphasized even more strongly in the next response, where he expressly states:

(If, we consider the relation of origin in the mission) the mission of the Son is distinct from that of the Holy Spirit as generation is from procession. However, if we consider (the relation) arising from grace, the two missions have in common the fact that they arise from the same root of grace. However, they are distinct in that they are understood in relation to two distinct effects of grace, namely, illumination and the enkindling of the heart. This makes it clear that they cannot exist without each other, for neither the one nor the other takes place without sanctifying grace, and the Divine Persons are inseparable.[30]

Therefore, he does not hold that the soul is assimilated to the Word by particular gifts of grace and to the Holy Spirit by others. One and the same sanctifying grace brings about the twofold assimilation, one as illuminating, and the other as being set ablaze.

St. Thomas speaks of "the soul" in order to note well that this assimilation is brought about in the depths of the spirit. However, it is the person who is thus divinized through this transformation of his soul by grace expecting it to spill over upon the body itself, fully at the resurrection and inchoately here below.

3. Assimilation to the Father

{216} It is not the case that only the persons of the Son and the Spirit are inseparable. Rather, all three Persons are inseparable. The Father could not be sent, since there is no Divine Person from whom He proceeds in eternity and who could send Him. Nonetheless, He also dwells in the soul through grace no less than do the

29. *ST* I, q. 43, a. 5, ad. 2.
30. *ST* I, q. 43, a. 5, ad. 3.

others, Himself being known distinctly as well.[31] He is known by appropriation, on the level of conceptual knowledge, and through mystical experience on the level of "real" knowledge (known and loved, for here, as well, it is a question of knowing Him as the Father in order to love Him).

Therefore, grace assimilates the soul to the Father as well. It does so inasmuch as it is the vital principle at the source of all spiritual activities, making these activities flow forth from the depths of the person, as acts in which the latter is truly engaged as in his very own acts, inasmuch as grace is the entitative *habitus* in which the *habitus* of faith, hope, and charity are enrooted, through which the intellect's illumination and the heart's enkindling are brought about.

III. TRINITARIAN PRESENCE AND PRESENCE OF THE TRINITY

If, beyond the work to be accomplished in the world by the sent Person, the end and terminus of the missions is the giving of the Divine Persons to the created person in order to make Their abode in him, we are thus naturally faced with the great question of the indwelling of the Trinity in the souls of the just.

A. An Explanation of the Trinitarian Presence

{217} As a matter of fact, the principles of the solution to this great question (one of the major points whereby theological reflection helps to provide a foundation for the spiritual life) have already been proposed.[32] The Divine Persons exist in the intimate depths of the created spirit (as they do in every being on account of the creative action) through the gift of grace, which transforms the created spirit. In this way, They render him capable of attaining Them in Themselves, in Their distinction, in the personal singularity of each, by means of the experiential knowledge that we attempted to

---

31. See *ST* I, q. 43, a. 4.
32. See Nicolas, *Les profondeurs de la grâce*, 429–49.

describe above (a knowledge that includes love as an integral part*). They are thus rendered present to the created person in a completely new way, namely, as a loving and beloved person is present to a person with whom he exists (i.e., first as an object of knowledge and of love but also and consequently as dynamically assimilating him to Them).

This solution presupposes an analysis of the notion of "presence." It is a personal notion, at least in the sense that it expresses the relation of a thing or an object to consciousness, to a person: one is present to someone. The notion is doubly personal if the reality thus present to a person is itself a person. In this way, presence tends toward reciprocity: two persons are present to one another if each is an object for the other's awareness. However, he is present as a particular sort of object, for the person is a "subject." If he is present to the other person's knowledge solely as known, he will only be there as an object and not as a subject.[33] He can be known as a subject only by means of love, which establishes communion between the persons, making each exist within the other. Of itself, such a presence is intentional. However, love tends toward real union, toward "existing together with one another," for *bonum est in rebus*, the good is in things. Under the internal pressure of love, the lover desires and seeks the real possession of the beloved and likewise seeks to be really possessed by him. However, love alone does not make the union real. In the case of human persons, this real union is conditioned by spatio-temporal co-existence, which we can call the beloved's "there-being" [être-là]. Such mere "there-being" is not presence if spiritual intimacy is lacking (as well as psychological intimacy in the case of human persons). However, this intimacy, for its part, is not a real and complete presence, if the "there-being" is lacking. The conjunction of the two are necessary.

The "there-being" of the divine Persons is assured by the creative

* [Tr. note: That is, a part needed for the full perfection of the reality in question. See *ST* II-II, q. 48, a. 1c.]

33. See Jacques Maritain, "L'existant," in *Court traité de l'existence et de l'existant* (Paris: Hartmann, 1947), 110–11.

act, and grace makes it a true presence. In this way, we find knotted together, on the one hand, ontological there-being (without which one person is not really present to another) and on the other, inter-personal relations (without which this "there-being" is not a true form of presence). It is a fully supernatural knowledge, a kind of experience of the Divine Persons already present at the source of being, at the very source of the believer's knowledge and love, and this explains how grace makes the Three Persons really and personally present to the created person.

B. Objections against This Explication

Two objections are registered against this explanation. They merit being taken into consideration, and after examining them, we will need to express important precisions regarding what we have said.

1. Is the Trinitarian Presence Reserved to Mystics?

{218} Justification, including divinization (and therefore the missions of the Word and of the Spirit as well as the indwelling of the Three Persons), begins with the infusion of grace. Mystical experience begins only after a time in the life of grace, often a very long time. Moreover, in many people, for various reasons that are not reduced to a fault committed by them—far from it!—it is not produced here below or is barely produced, in a fleeting manner. In the mystic himself, it has a discontinuous character, which is contrary to the very idea, itself biblical, of indwelling and "abiding."[34] Thus, for many, this explanation seems unacceptable.

We must respond that although the very act of mystical experience is not given immediately and is not continuous in any of the righteous here below, what is given to all both immediately and in a continuous manner (apart from interruptions caused by sin) is, with grace and the theological virtues, the *real power* to produce the act of mystical experience. It is a power of producing such experience

34. See Donatien Mollat, "Saint Jean l'évangéliste," in *Dictionnaire de spiritualité as-cétique et mystique, doctrine et histoire*, vol. 8 (Paris: Beauchesne, 1974), 235–37.

when the required conditions are existentially posited, each time that the Holy Spirit wishes to intervene. However, with grace, the Holy Spirit is given and disposed to intervene at an opportune moment:

> In order for there to be a mission, actual knowledge of the Person in question is not required. Habitual knowledge suffices, provided that in the gift conferred, the *habitus*, what is proper to the Divine Person is represented as in a likeness. This is why one says that to be sent is to be known in the manner of a representation as coming from another: as one says that someone is manifested or is made known by being rendered present through his likeness. However, given the resemblance between natural acts and meritorious acts, I cannot know with certitude that I have in myself the actual gift in which the Divine Person is given. Despite this fact, I can conjecture about its existence by way of given signs. Only a revelation could give me certitude, for we cannot know with certitude if we have sanctifying grace, through which the advent of the Divine Person occurs. And nevertheless, of itself, the very gift that we perceive is capable of leading to knowledge of the Person who comes.[35]

This response seems futile to many who do grasp the distinction between the real power for acting that the *habitus* gives and the simple possibility of knowing and loving God that every created spirit has because of its ontological structure. An example can serve to make this difference clear. An infant in his cradle is as incapable of an act of intelligence and of freedom as a small animal is. Nevertheless, the infant belongs to the world of civilization and culture, for he has in himself, in a completely latent state, the faculties that will produce acts of knowledge and of freedom once they arrive at a sufficient degree of development. Through such acts, man transcends all animals. He is already a living being having a human life, even though he only produces acts of animal life. Thus, the baptized infant belongs to the world of the children of God, the world of the Church. He is a temple of the Trinity because he has within himself the real power to one day produce acts of knowledge and love by which he will render himself present to the Divine Persons and by

35. St. Thomas, *In I Sent.*, d. 15, q. 4, a. 1, ad. 1.

which They will be present to him. As regards adults, if we think of those who authentically live according to the grace they have, even those who have not entered here below into what is called the mystical life (and who perhaps never will enter into it), they certainly undergo acts of mystical experience, at least in a transitory manner, however imperfectly. When it comes to those who, without living in sin, have very little interest in the Divine Life that is in them and thus experience the bare minimum of the existential conditions required for the realization of mystical experience, without insulting them, we can say that such people are underdeveloped from the perspective of this divine life, as uncultured men are underdeveloped from the perspective of intellectual life. Nonetheless, as long as they persevere in grace, they retain this real potency for such a mystical experience, in virtue of which the Divine Persons abide in them. However, we must indeed acknowledge that they do not actually enjoy this presence!

2. Does the Trinity Come to the Believer or the Believer to the Trinity?

{219} The second objection is that, in this solution, the Trinitarian presence seems to be the fruit of a created activity. By his activities, the believing person renders the Divine Persons present by discovering Them in himself and by uniting himself to Them. Now, the mystery of the indwelling is, in fact, the mystery of the "coming" of the Persons into the believer.

We respond by saying that at the foundation of these created activities, there is the grace by which the created spirit is transformed and rendered capable of knowing and loving God in the mystery of His Triune personality. What is first is the activity of God by which the created spirit is thus transformed and elevated. The created activity by which the creature receives the Divine Persons into himself in order to enjoy Them is secondary and is aroused by the first. The Divine Persons are the ones giving of Themselves and ones being sent. They do so by elevating the believer's spirit to Themselves through the supernaturalizing action of grace.

Thus, the question arises, "Is (created) grace caused by the presence of the Trinity within the soul, or conversely, is the presence of the Trinity in the soul the effect of created grace?" Many Catholic theologians resolutely opt for the first branch of the dilemma.[36] However, in that case, what use does created grace serve? What does it come to do? What can it add to the presence of the Trinity? Should we not resolutely reject it, as do Orthodox theologians? The only thing that seems to prevent Catholics from expressing such a rejection are the formal definitions of the Council of Trent [concerning the role of created grace in justification]. If we opt for the second option noted above, we find ourselves being accused on two heads: first, we will be said to substitute a created gift for the gift of the Divine Persons, which is promised in Scripture; second, we will be said to substitute the accession of the created person to the Divine Person by his own acts, in place of the "coming of the Divine Persons," which is formally promised to us. Certainly, such acts would be informed by grace, but they would represent a human undertaking. In reality, this is a false dilemma. The Trinity's presence in the soul is the effect of the eternal love by which God loves His rational creature in order to make him His child in Christ and in order to make him partake in the Trinitarian Life (the love of communion). However, as we have seen, the Divine Persons are given to the created spirit as an object of knowledge and love (and cannot be given in any other manner), and in being given in this manner, they are really given. For God, *to cause grace* (along with the *habitus* of the theological virtues) is *to be thus given to be known and to be loved*. He does not do this by rendering Himself knowable and loveable in Himself. (From all eternity, the Trinity is infinitely knowable and loveable, and man exists only as fundamentally ordered to this knowledge and this love.) Instead, God does so by rendering His creature capable of knowing Him and of loving Him such as He is, in the mystery of the Trinitarian Life. He renders the creature capable of "reaching

36. See Rahner, "Pour la notion scolastique de la grâce incréée," 65–69.

God Himself." In this way, He comes to meet and be with His creature. Here, we have a case of reciprocal causality. Created grace is the
means by which the Divine Persons give Themselves, whereas grace
itself is an effect of the infinite love by which God loves His creature,
a love that is an extension of the Trinitarian friendship to the creature. This is what St. Thomas expresses in two dense and beautiful
texts, which in no way contradict those in which he affirms that the
presence of the Trinity consists in the fact that the Trinity is made to
be an object of knowledge and love: "We receive the Holy Spirit in
priority and His gifts as a consequence, for it is through His love that
the Son has given us all things."[37] And "his love" is the Holy Spirit.
And again: "Grace is caused in man by virtue of the presence of the
Godhead, as light in the atmosphere is caused by virtue of the presence of the sun."[38]

IV. VISIBLE MISSION AND
INVISIBLE MISSION

{220} In what has been said up to this point, the "access" of the
Divine Person to the human is wholly "interior." The created effect,
namely the changing of the creature by the divine action, is wholly
spiritual and invisible and is related only to the individual person.
(As we have seen, such effects are necessary in order to provide real
content for this notion of access, though without introducing any
mutability whatsoever into the Divine Persons themselves.) Now,
the biblical concept of "mission" includes, as a priority, it seems,
manifestations and external works. Moreover, the Divine Person is
sent to an individual person. He is sent "to the world." Therefore, we
must either renounce our notion of mission or must adjust it in a
way that integrates this visible aspect into it.

---

37. Aquinas, *In I Sent*, d. 14, q. 1, sol. 1.
38. *ST* III, q. 7, a. 13.

A. The Mission of the Divine Persons
Is Also (and First) Visible

{221} The "access" of which we have spoken exists only in and through faith, since the means for it is mystical experience, which is "an act of faith."[39] Now, faith presupposes God's revelation of His mystery. Without this revelation, the Divine Persons are unknowable as distinct Persons.

Revelation can only take place (and only does take place) through signs. In general, man receives his knowledge of another spirit by means of signs, and signs are necessary so that the prophet may be believable and so that the hearer may be able to make himself attentive to God's speech taking place through the mediation of human speech.

Of themselves, these signs do not constitute a mission of a Divine Person. The prophet can be a mere human person, and the signs that render him worthy of belief can be only a work of God's power, in which the Three Persons are not distinguished.

However, the end and terminus of revelation is God's own personal self-gift to the human person. Its paradigm is the Beatific Vision, in which the Three are given simultaneously in an existential and intentional manner, as an object of knowledge and love. Revelation made here below under the veil of images and concepts is a sketch of this full revelation and can be conceived of only in function of it.[40] Also, with regard to this imperfect and inchoate revelation, we must say already that for God to reveal Himself means that He gives Himself.

Indeed, this explains why revelation is brought about through the mission of the Son and that of the Spirit. However, since the very act through which God reveals Himself, of itself, precedes faith (without which the missions of the Divine Persons do not reach the

---

39. See Nicolas, *Dieu connue comme inconnu*, 394–395; *Contemplation et vie contemplative en christianisme*, 57–59.

40. See Nicolas, *Dieu connue comme inconnu*, 198–200.

created person in his intimate depths), the manifestation of the Divine Persons first needed to be realized by external effects.

Thus, absolutely speaking, the visible mission is presupposed by the invisible mission and precedes it.

B. The Visible Mission Is for the Sake of the Invisible Mission

{222} From everything that we have said, it is clear enough that the visible mission cannot be the ultimate goal of the mission. The Divine Person is sent in order to give Himself interiorly and to give the other two Persons along with Himself to the human person in his intimate depths.

Moreover, without this ordering to union with the human person, it would not be a true mission. Indeed, without this, the external effect would be only a work of power, by which we would not be faced with a new approach [*accès*] of a Divine Person in His distinction. The relation of access can only be interpersonal.

C. The Visible Mission Can Exist without the Invisible Mission

{223} However, this does not mean that there is not a visible mission when man does not welcome the sent Person. The visible mission precedes the invisible mission and is ordered to it. This means that, in the intention of the Divine Persons (those who are sent and those who send), the invisible mission must follow [of necessity]. However, it can be prevented by a rejection on the part of the human person to whom the mission is addressed.

In manifesting themselves, the Divine Persons offer themselves to man's freedom, and the visible mission is found there. However, the power of saying, "Yes," includes the power of saying, "No," and if man so refuses, the invisible mission is not realized. The visible mission remains, for this relation of access to man, which is one of its components, is also maintained, [though] as being "hollowed out" by man's "no."

And this can help us understand the public character of the visible mission. The Son and the Spirit are sent to the world (i.e., to men) and to each man inasmuch as he is part of this world. The invisible mission is personal, including the acceptance expressed by each person to whom it is made.

D. Can the Invisible Mission Exist without the Visible Mission?

{224} The anteriority of the visible mission to the invisible mission is a law of salvation history as a whole, that is, inasmuch as it concerns the whole of humanity.

This anteriority is also the ordinary rule for each person's salvation, in the sense that, normally, it is through and in the Church that each man is called to welcome the Divine Persons into himself and to be saved by Them. However, we here find ourselves faced with the existential conflict between individual necessities and the universal order. The whole of humanity stretches throughout an immense expanse of space and time, whereas a human person is enclosed within strict spatial and temporal limits, let alone the human limits that enclose each person. Now, while God wills the salvation of the whole of humanity as a whole, He also wills the salvation of each person within this whole. Substitutes exist in those cases where the ordinary conditions of salvation are not found to be realized within the limitations imposed upon a given person's earthly destiny.[41]

In many cases, although the visible mission has taken place for the entire world, it does not touch the person or the human groups under consideration. In those places where substitutes play a role (on account of the interior acceptance by man), the invisible mission takes place for this man without having been prepared by a visible mission.

However, it obviously does not take place independent of the visible missions. The "righteous person on the outside" obscurely

41. See the third main section in this Dogmatic Synthesis, devoted to ecclesiology and the sacraments.

clings to Christ, without knowing His name. He receives, with the same obscurity, the Spirit of Pentecost.

V. CONCLUSION TO THIS CHAPTER

{225} Thus, there are not, in reality, two missions, one visible and the other invisible. The mission of the Divine Persons is visible and invisible, as is suited to man's twofold existence as a spiritual-bodily being.[42] Studying the relation of access, which is constitutive of the mission, we noted that although this access is defined in function of mystical experience, it starts as soon as grace renders man capable of this experience, even when it is, existentially, very remote (as the infant is capable, through his spiritual soul, intellect, and heart, of participating in the cultural and social life of humanity, without yet being existentially able to perform the acts of this cultural life). In reality, we must push the beginning of this "access" of the Divine Person to the human person even further back. Sufficient for constituting the "mission," it begins as soon as the Divine Person, through His visible mission, manifests Himself to the world and offers Himself to all men.

42. See *ST* I, q. 43, a. 7.

11

The Mission of the Word and of the Spirit

I. MISSION OF THE WORD

A. The Incarnation Considered as the "Visible Mission" of the Word

1. Through the Incarnation, the Word Was "Sent" by the Father to Men

{226} Texts expressing this idea abound. The biblical notion of "mission" is contained in such texts (and in those where the same thing is said about the Spirit). If we compare Christ's "mission" with that of the apostles and the prophets, the following essential difference will become clear: whereas they are men caught up in the world and charged with a particular task, He is "sent into the world" and "given to the world."[1] These texts, which evoke Christ's preexistence, are obviously related to Jesus' human birth and therefore to His presence, then to His action in the world as a man, to His being-man, that is, to the Incarnation: "And the Word became flesh and dwelt among us."*

---

1. See Jn 3:16, 10:36; Gal 4:4; etc.
* Jn 1:14 (RSV).

2. The "Relation of Access" Constitutive of the Visible Mission of the Word

{227} But how can the notion of a "mission," such as we have analyzed it, be applied to the Incarnation? First of all, how can we find a "relation of access" in this case? In seeking earlier to determine the nature of this "relation of access" of a Divine Person to a created person, we were led to speak about a new interpersonal relation, establishing a spiritual presence. However, how can we find such a relation between the Incarnate Word and men merely because of the Incarnation? Indeed, He is not rendered spiritually present to men who do not believe in Him and do not know Him.

However, on further reflection, we see that Christ makes Himself present to all men by becoming incarnate, even to those who do not know Him, solely on account of the fact that He gives Himself to be known and loved in a new way, on account of the fact that He offers His intimacy. He enters into the world of men, that is, into an immense relational universe. Each particular person is a part of this universe merely because he is a man. I am fundamentally present to a given man whom I do not know (and whom I will never know), and he is present to me, because we are both men living at the same time. Virtual interpersonal relations exist between us, relations which an eventual encounter will actualize but will not create. Thus, in becoming man, the Word renders Himself present to all men, *at least to His contemporaries.*

Indeed, pursuing the analysis of this "fundamental presence" of one man to all others, we must specify that it can pertain only to men who are contemporaries. Birth is what makes us enter into the relational human universe, and death removes us from it. In the case of Christ, this raises a question that we will encounter in Christology, namely, the question concerning how His "presence to the world" is extended to all generations after His coming. In a word, here, we hold that this extension must be explained first through the resurrection and then through the Church, which is "His body."

This relation of access of the Word to men, founded on the Incarnation inasmuch as the Word's visible presence to all men is assured by it, constitutes His "visible mission."

3. The Relation of Sending

{228} From what we have said, it follows that the second constitutive relation of the Word's mission (i.e., the relation of sending) can only be the eternal relation of the Son to the Father who begets Him. However, this raises a difficulty. The Incarnation was not willed by an act of will (i.e., by a love) proper to the Father. The [Divine] willing and love are common to the Three Persons.

This is true. But if I say that the willing of the Incarnation is common to the Three Persons, I do not, for all that, preclude that it could be a willing by each Person considered in what is hypostatically proper to each [en sa propriété hypostatique]. Now, as regards the present issue, this common willing is "the willing to send" only inasmuch as it is considered to be the Father's willing. Indeed, what constitutes the Father mittens [sending], in relation to the Son missus [sent], is the eternal relation of the Father to the Son—prolonged by the temporal relation of access to men, which the Son "receives" from this common willing. In short, the Three Persons will the Incarnation by one and the same willing, but, of the three, only the Father is mittens, on account of what is hypostatically proper to Him.

Therefore, the Incarnation is the effect of the whole Trinity's willing and love for men. However, inasmuch as it is the "mission of the Son," it is especially the testimony of the Father's love.

B. Christ, the Revealer of the Father
and of the Holy Spirit

{229} The Incarnation is the manifestation of the Person who becomes incarnate, namely, the Word. Simultaneously, it is the manifestation of the Father, for the Son refers back to the Father: "He who has seen me has seen the Father.... I am in the Father and the Father in me."[2]

2. Jn 14:9–10 (RSV).

It is also the manifestation of the Holy Spirit, who is sent by the Son and must prolong His mission: "If I do not go away, the Counselor will not come to you; but if I go, I will send him to you."[3] As we have already seen, the mystery of the Trinity was revealed through and in Jesus Christ.[4]

This is closely connected to what is hypostatically proper to the Word, namely, the fact that He is God expressed, God "manifested," or at least, God "manifestable."

If we were to say that the Father is manifested through and in the Word while remaining inaccessible in Himself, we would thus forget that the Father's nature is the same nature as the Son, which is neither more, nor less, inaccessible in the one than in the other.[5] This is true of the [Divine] Nature, which is common to the Three and made manifest to men through the Incarnation—manifested and veiled. Moreover, as we will see, this manifestation can be seen as being a kind of temporal realization of what is hypostatically proper to the Word in eternity [*la propriété hypostatique éternelle du Verbe*].

C. Could Another Person than the Word Have Become Incarnate?

{230} We can now take up, in its rightful place, a question we encountered earlier, though at that time we only indicated how it is to be resolved.[6]

This question was raised several times by Karl Rahner.[7] According to the eminent theologian, *to be incarnated*, that is, *to be the person in whom the assumed human nature subsists*, is part of what is hypostatically proper to the Word. This would mean that one can

---

3. Jn 16:7 (RSV).
4. See §14 above.
5. See §172 above.
6. See §145 above.
7. See Karl Rahner, "Le concept du mystère dans la théologie catholique," in *Ecrits théologiques* VIII (Paris, Desclée de Brouwer, 1967) 101; Karl Rahner, "Quelques remarques sur le traité dogmatique 'De Trinitate,'" in *Ecrits théologiques* VIII (Paris: Desclée de Brouwer, 1967), 125–126.

know Christ only on the basis of this hypostatic property and, conversely, that this property cannot be known without it at least including this aptitude for the Incarnation.

In this claim, Rahner expressly opposes the teaching coming from St. Augustine, which, however, found its first expression, it seems, in St. Anselm and then was taken up and developed by St. Thomas, namely, the claim that any of the Divine Persons (and even two together, or all three together) could have become incarnate. Rahner interprets this theory as meaning that the Incarnation is indifferent to whether the union is brought about in this or that Divine Person.

Rahner's interpretation of St. Thomas is much too rigid here. It is true that he defends the thesis holding that any of the Divine Persons whatsoever could have become incarnate.[8] However, to do this he appeals to the *virtus divina*. Therefore, the possibility in question is considered in comparison with the divine power: it is not impossible in itself. And there, he expressly uses the principle that Rahner contests, namely, that what one divine hypostasis can do, another can also do it.

However, in article eight, he develops three weighty reasons why, according him, it was *convenientissimum* [most suitable] that it be the Word and not the Father or the Spirit who is incarnated. What is misleading here is an insufficient estimation of the nature of arguments from suitability. Spontaneously, it is thought to be a weak argument, one that cannot express a proof in a true manner. In reality, however, it is an "argument" and therefore intends to appeal to necessity, though appealing to necessity taken from the final cause. The argument from suitability asserts that, in order to obtain a given end, this given means is the only one (rigorous necessity) or at least, the most suitable means (a looser necessity). Moreover, such necessity is conditional in all the cases wherein the willing of the end depends on a free willing: *if* I *will* this end, I *must will* this means (i.e.,

8. See *ST* III, q. 3, a. 5.

this means is necessary). However, I am able to not will this end, for this willing is contingent (and the means participate in this contingency).

Now, if we understand arguments from suitability along these lines, we can apply such reasoning to our current problem as follows. Given that the willing of the Incarnation is totally free, everything that it conditions also depends on this free willing and therefore is contingent. However, presupposing this willing of the Incarnation, when we say that it is *convenientissimum*, most suitable, that the Word would be the one who is incarnate, we thus attribute a true necessity to the proposition, "The Word, and not the Father or the Holy Spirit, is the Person who ought to become incarnate," *given the infinite wisdom and goodness of God.*

However, what then does the thesis in article five mean? It means that the Hypostatic Union, considered abstractly (that is, abstraction being made from its insertion into the divine plan and into salvation history, that is, considered solely in its "metaphysical structure," and therefore in relation to God's realizing power) appeals only to the Divine Person's characteristic of being *subsistens in natura divina* and of being able to communicate His subsistence to a created nature, a characteristic that is found in each of the three divine hypostases.

When one refuses, like Karl Rahner, to hold that this characteristic is common in this way to the Three, justifying oneself by saying that only the numerically one Divine Nature is common to the Three, Trinitarian theology finds itself brought to an impasse in virtue of unsound reasoning.[9] Once again, one transfers the characteristics of the absolute unity and simplicity of the Divine Being to the concepts by which we know the Trinity. Of itself, this would lead to the abolition of every Trinitarian theology below the level of the Beatific Vision, for we cannot think without concepts, and as we have often said, no concepts represent the divine simplicity. In truth, to know those three "Being God" to some degree, we take the

9. See §114, °5 above.

concept of personhood from our experience and, by means of purification and sublimation, render it apt for designating each of those
"Being God" in the fact that He is a subsistence in the Divine Nature. Certainly, in order to attain each of Them in His distinction, we
would need a further refinement of the concept, which we have seen
is impossible.[10] Also, this concept of personhood still attains those
"Being God" only in an "abstract" manner, not going all the way to
Their ultimate concreteness. (This is also already true on the level of
our natural experience, given that the concept of personhood designates the ensemble of persons in a trait that is common to them
without going all the way to the ultimate personal being of each particular person.) However, it truly attains them. In short, to Rahner's
objection, we must respond that this characteristic of being a *subsistens in natura divina* is *notionally* common to the Three Persons,
whereas the Divine Nature is *really* common to Them. However, this
common notion enables us to know something real in each, abstracting only from the unique form that this common something takes
on in each.

Now, what St. Thomas says (and what is not really contestable)
is that, in the Hypostatic Union, the Word exercises the function of
making the assumed nature subsist on account of this common characteristic that He shares with the two others.

However, it is on account of what is hypostatically proper to Him
that the Word, in becoming incarnate, can realize the goal of the Incarnation, and we must concur with Rahner on two heads. First, we
must agree that the assumed humanity, of itself, manifests the Eternal Son, meaning that it would not manifest another Divine Person
(or would do so very imperfectly). Second, we must concur that the
Son, inasmuch as He is the Word, is naturally designated for realizing, in and through this humanity, the goal of the Incarnation, namely, to reveal the Father to man (and with Him the Son and the Spirit
coming forth from Him), not only so that man may know Them, but

10. See §178 above.

moreover, so that he may be able to enter into Their communion by means of full knowledge and the love that flows forth from it. The aptitude to fulfill the essential intentions of the Incarnation is part of what is hypostatically proper to the Word, in the same way that the aptitude to be "given" is part of what is hypostatically proper to the Holy Spirit.[11] In this way, the Incarnation manifests what the Word is within the Immanent Trinity.

Naturally, we must not say that such conclusions are those of St. Thomas himself. However, they do not truly contradict the line of his thought on this point and therefore can be easily integrated into it.

D. The Invisible Mission of the Son

{231} If what we have said about the invisible mission is true, the mission of the Son cannot be reduced to the fact that the Word has become man, however great and marvelous this mystery may be.[12] Indeed, the Incarnation obviously adds nothing, by itself, to the Word and to the Trinity. It cannot be conceived as though it were an acquisition for God, as though it were a fulfillment of the Godhead. On the other hand, inasmuch as Christ remains external to me and inasmuch as He exists only in human history (through the events of His life and death, through His miracles, and even through the influence of His teaching or His examples upon world history), that is, inasmuch as He does not exist *for me*, the Incarnation brings me nothing either, except a proposition and an appeal. If He was sent into the world in a visible form, He did so in order to dwell in intimacy with men, to give Himself to them, to transform them, and to fill them with His presence. In short, here again, despite the radiance and grandeur of the visible mission, it is ordered to something else which gives it its meaning, namely, *the invisible mission*. More precisely, it is brought to its completion only by the invisible mission, which moreover would not exist without it.

This is indeed what is expressed by so many of St. Paul's strong

11. See §151 above.
12. See §222 above.

and impressive declarations.[13] Likewise, it is expressed in the great Johannine theme that Christ is the Life.[14]

In the treatise on the Trinity, St. Thomas explains the Son's invisible mission solely by the presence of the Word in the soul.[15] This is insufficient, for if the mission of the Word consists in the Incarnation, the Incarnation itself is what must include an invisible face, interior to the created person. And, indeed, Scripture speaks to us about a presence and an indwelling of Jesus Christ, the Incarnate Word, in the believer's spirit. (Moreover, St. Thomas obviously neither overlooks nor neglects this consideration. However, he sets it aside for Christology, and this fact confers a very schematic character on his "treatise" on the divine missions.)

How should we understand this "access" of the Incarnate Word to the intimate depths of the created person? The Word is the "Logos," the Infinite and Eternal Word [*Parole*] wherein the whole mystery of the Godhead and of the created universe is expressed, including the mystery of man. In becoming man, He not only rendered possible and realized the translation and fragmentation of this Eternal Word [*parole*] into concepts, images, and human words (as we will see, in particular, in Christology when we consider Christ's knowledge [*science*] and His character as a prophet). He Himself is, in His existence as man, the Incarnate Divine Word [*Parole*]. Now, the Word [*Parole*] of God is not only the proclamation of the gift that God wishes to make of Himself, God's appeal to accept this gift. The Word of God is itself God giving Himself. God gives Himself in revealing Himself. Thus, the Trinity is given to the person who believes in Christ.

Jesus' visible humanity is the symbol of His divinity, His per-

---

13. See Lucien Cerfaux, *Le Christ dans la théologie de saint Paul* (Paris: Cerf, 1954), 242–258.

14. See François-Marie Braun, *Jean le théologien*, vols. I, II, III/1, and III/2 (Paris: Gabalda, 1959–1972), vol. III, 99–118; Donatien Mollat, "Saint Jean l'évangéliste," *Dictionnaire de spiritualité ascétique et mystique, doctrine et histoire*, vol. 8, 192–247 (Paris: Beauchesne, 1974).

15. See *ST* I, q. 43, a. 5.

sonality, and also of the Persons of the Father and the Holy Spirit who are in Him. It is a symbol that does not refer to an external and distant symbolized thing but, rather, carries the reality of the symbolized thing within itself. To believe in Christ—according to all the full meaning of this term—is to bring this reality, in its intimate depths, into oneself, with the symbol that presents it to the mind and to the heart.

Moreover, in a way that we will study in the Christological part of this dogmatic synthesis, Christ is the cause of the interior grace that is, as we have seen, the means by which the Divine Persons become interiorly present to those who receive it.

Through the Eucharist, the Incarnate Word gains access to the intimate depths of the believer, becoming invisibly present to the person who believes and sacramentally participates in Him. He is present and active, precisely in order to cause this grace whereby the Divine Persons reach [accèdent] the believer.

II. THE MISSION OF THE HOLY SPIRIT

What we have said in general about the divine missions applies to the Holy Spirit in such a manner that it would seem that, in the end, He alone is sent, at least to the intimate depths of the created person, and we have seen that a mission that would not lead to an interior presence would not be a true mission. For this reason, we have attempted to place the specificity of the Son's mission in relief.

With regard to the mission of the Holy Spirit, there is no need to repeat what has been said about His entry [accès] to the intimate depths of the person by grace. Instead, we will need to speak about His visible mission, which risks seeming unnecessary. But before this, we must ask how we should theologically interpret the profound idea that the Holy Spirit is the cause of sanctification, an idea coming to us from the most ancient of tradition [sic].

A. The Sanctifying Spirit

1. The Spirit and Holiness in God

{232} The notion of holiness has two meanings.[16] It can designate "holiness of being" or "holiness of action."

In God, holiness of being is His Majesty, His Transcendence—rather, it would be appropriated to the First Person, like the notions of Creator and Sovereign.

As a rule, holiness of action is its rectitude, its ordination to the good. Just as love gives free action its ordination, love is also what makes an action holy. When speaking about creatures, this is not any love whatsoever but, rather, is right love, that is, love of God. In God, it is His love, which is righteousness itself. Therefore, God's holiness is first and foremost the infinite friendship which is the very life of the Trinity. Then, as an extension of it, it is the love that brings all things back to Him, especially the love that calls spiritual creatures to partake in His friendship.

To the same degree and in the same sense that we can say that the Third Person is Personified Love, we can say that He is Personified Holiness, not that He alone would be holy (just as He is not the only one who loves), but in the sense that He is the expression of the divine holiness. Although what is hypostatically proper to Him remains unknown to us, it is in the line of holiness, and the concept of holiness orients our mind toward it. It is a concept "appropriated" to the Third Person, one that enables us to "suspect" what is proper and distinct to Him in a way that is approximate but true.[17]

2. The Spirit, Principle of Created Holiness

{233} There is a great debate concerning this point. First of all, there is a debate between Orthodox theology and Latin theology in general. The former holds that the Spirit, according to what is hy-

---

16. See "Heilige, das Heilige," in *Lexikon für Theologie und Kirche*, 2nd ed., vol. 5, ed. Josef Höfer and Karl Rahner, 84–92 (Freiburg im Breisgau, 1957ff).

17. See §§191–98 above.

postatically proper to Himself, immediately communicates the divine holiness to the believer, thus divinizing him. By contrast, Latin theology holds that the principle of divinization is a "created grace." However, a controversy exists within Latin theology as well. First, there is a general controversy concerning the relation between the two graces. On the one hand, certain thinkers hold that created grace is the means by which the Trinitarian presence is assured. On the other hand, other theologians, whose position we have already discussed, hold that created grace results from the Trinity present in the soul, so that divinization or sanctification (they mean the same thing) would be formally produced by immediate union with God.[18] However, there is a second controversy concerning uncreated grace itself. Struck by the Greek Fathers' insistence that the Holy Spirit is the sanctifier, Pétau introduced the idea that holiness would formally consist in the union of the created person with the Holy Spirit in His distinction. It would be a mysterious union, which would have some resemblance to the Hypostatic Union. (According to this conception, in the Hypostatic Union, the human nature of Jesus and, by means of it, all men, are united to the Second Person of the Trinity in what is hypostatically proper to Him. We will discuss this in the next volume, on Christology.) This idea was taken up afterwards by a great number of theologians. (This discussion is intimately connected to our earlier discussion concerning the assimilation of the soul to the Divine Persons through grace).[19]

Here, we are in the presence of a troubling opposition (at least an apparent one) between theological principles that seem quite certain (the inseparability of the Divine Persons in every work *ad extra* and therefore in sanctification) and an affirmation that plunges its roots through the Patristic centuries all the way down into Scripture, namely that the Holy Spirit is sent to the Church to bring about the

---

18. See Jean-Hervé Nicolas, *Les profondeurs de la grâce* (Paris: Beauchesne, 1969), 150–60.

19. See §§214–16; Jean-Hervé Nicolas, *Contemplation et vie contemplative en christianisme* (Fribourg-Paris: Éditions universitaires-Beauchesne, 1980).

sanctification of men.[20] Appropriation is an insufficient response, for as we have seen, appropriation is the *knowledge* that we can (conceptually) elaborate concerning what is proper to the Persons in Themselves and concerning the assimilation of the created spirit to Them. Here, we are concerned with the very reality of the sanctifying work, what it is in itself and not the knowledge that we can have concerning it.

In order to inventory the questions before us, let us first envision the divine efficacy in sanctification. In whatever way we conceptualize the role of grace, we must admit that a real change is brought about in the created person when he is "justified," when he passes from the shadow of sin into the light of holiness. Such a change can be brought about only by the divine action, in which the Three Persons concur undividedly.

The real problem is the one related to formal or quasi-formal causality. Can the union of the created person to the Holy Spirit (in which holiness consists) be so compared to the union of Jesus' humanity with the Word? The contradiction is immediately clear: the second union envisioned is "hypostatic." In other words, it excludes personality from the united terminus (i.e., human nature) and requires that personality be found wholly at the terminus of the union, in the uniting terminus. By contrast, the union with God in which sanctity consists is characterized by the created person being united to the Divine Persons while remaining distinct. In other words, sanctification does not abolish the saint's personality but, on the contrary, exalts and fulfills it.

On the other hand, can holiness be understood solely as being a union with the Holy Spirit? Obviously not. The same tradition and the same Scripture present it to us as a "communal sharing [*société*] with the Father and the Son," and as "remaining in Jesus Christ and Jesus Christ remaining in the believer." Holiness is a form of union with the Three Persons.

20. See Louis Bouyer, *Le Fils éternel* (Paris: Cerf, 1974), 306–15; Louis Bouyer, *Le Consolateur, Esprit Saint et vie de grâce* (Paris: Cerf, 1980), 273–98.

Within these strict limits, how can we understand the Holy Spirit's proper role? Let us return to what we said earlier about the assimilation of the created spirit to the Trinity by grace. Grace is a gift that is simultaneously unified and complex. Following St. Thomas and St. Augustine, we discerned each Divine Person's "points of access" in this complexity. As the internal, participated source of Divine Life, making the believer be "one who lives by the Divine Life," grace assimilates us to the Father. In its illuminative character, it assimilates us to the Son. As including the ensemble of the gifts of love, it assimilates us to the Holy Spirit. Nonetheless, grace is indivisible. Where it exists, it gives all this together (at least in germ), although distinctly, as when the Trinity is given, the Three Persons are given together, although distinctly.

In assimilating us to the Holy Spirit through a dynamic assimilation, grace unites us to Him, not to the exclusion of the others, but as He is the personified mutual Love of the Father and the Son, personified Trinitarian Love, Him in whom the Father and the Son give themselves and give Him. Participated sanctity consists in this gift.

By recognizing this singular union with the Holy Spirit, do we not again find something of Pétau's intuition in his attempt to understand the believer's union with the Holy Spirit in a way that is similar to the Hypostatic Union? We could pursue the reflection as follows. Of itself and first of all, the Hypostatic Union is ontological, making the Word be man. Therefore, it necessarily includes the abolition of every personality proper to the assumed nature. Union with the Holy Spirit is intentional and affective. What it includes is the intentional fusion, through love (*amor facit unum de duobus*), of the ontological duality of the two persons who love each other. Therefore, we cannot speak about the saint experiencing a Hypostatic Union with the Holy Spirit, for this term, consecrated by immemorial theological usage, irresistibly calls to mind the exclusion of every created personality. However, we can perhaps (?) speak of a personal union according to love.

3. The Relationship between the Mission of the Son and that of the Holy Spirit

{234} In this same line of reflection, we can better "understand" the relationship that Scripture incontestably establishes between the mission of the Son and that of the Spirit: the Spirit is given in fullness to Christ and communicated by Him to the apostles and to "all those who believe on their word."

As we have seen, the gifts of knowledge by which the created spirit is "assimilated" to the Word are inseparable from those of love.[21] However, an internal order is found within this gift of grace, which includes the two together: love flows forth from knowledge. This makes clear the internal order of the two missions, representing on the temporal level the internal order of the eternal processions—an internal order that is manifested by their external order, that is, by the order of the visible missions.[22]

However, the mission of the Holy Spirit is not the ultimate terminus. The Spirit leads the believer "to the whole truth," that is, to the Father through the Son, for the Holy Spirit is the "bond" between the Father and the Son.

B. The Visible Mission of the Holy Spirit

1. The Visible Signs of the Gift of the Spirit

{235} There is no doubt that the sending of the Spirit, which Jesus had announced, was accompanied by brilliant signs at the beginning of the Church's life, and the first Christian community held that these signs were of great importance.[23]

It seems that soon enough there was a process of "devaluation" concerning the importance and role of these signs. This occurred for two reasons. On the one hand, they were devalued because of their

21. See §215 above.
22. See §131 and 146 above.
23. See Lucien Cerfaux, *Le chétien dans la theologie de saint Paul* (Paris: Cerf, 1962), 222–39; Nicolas, *Les profondeurs de la grâce*, 161–77; Heinz Schürmann, "Les charismes spirituels," in *L'Eglise de Vatican II* (Paris: Cerf, 1966), 572–73.

rarity, which seemed to contrast with their abundance in the primitive Church. On the other hand, this devaluation occurred due to how they very quickly came to be abused ([e.g.,] the crisis of Montanism in the second century), an abuse that will recur often in the Church's history, leading certain "charismatics" to claim that one can set the institutional Church and the "Church of the Spirit" in opposition to each other. Thus, the visible manifestations of the Spirit tended to be confined to the domain of the ascetical and mystical life, and even there, in Western spirituality, a current of defiance with regard to extraordinary phenomena came to be formed. St. Thomas's texts expressly dedicated to the visible mission of the Holy Spirit clearly imply this kind of devaluation.[24] Nonetheless, note that St. Thomas admits that the gift of prophecy permanently remains in the Church.[25]

Now, in our own era, the charismatic movement attracts attention anew to the role and importance of the manifestations of the Holy Spirit's presence and action in the Church's life.[26] We cannot ignore the importance and meaning of this movement, even if it poses problems of discernment. The Holy Spirit is manifesting Himself in our era in the Church in a new manner, and this should draw our attention to two things. First, it should draw our attention to the fact that He never ceased to manifest Himself throughout the course of the Church's history. Moreover, it should draw our attention to the need to undertake a more serious study concerning the question of the connection between the visible mission and the invisible mission of the Holy Spirit, whereas for the reasons already stated, there has been a unfortunate tendency to dismiss the visible mission as something outdated or wholly marginal, in order to focus only on the invisible mission.

24. See *ST* I, q. 43, a. 7; *In* I *Sent.*, d. 16, q. 1, a. 2, especially ad. 3.

25. See *ST* II-II, q. 45, a. 5 and q. 174, a. 6, ad. 3; I-II, q. 111, a. 1; SCG bk. 1, ch. 50 and bk. 1, ch. 54.

26. See Yves-Marie Congar, *Je crois en l'Esprit Saint*, vols. 1–3 (Paris: Cerf, 1980–1982), 187–255.

2. The Invisible Mission and the Visible Mission of the Spirit

{236} In reality, the Spirit's visible mission is permanent and necessary. The Holy Spirit was given to the Church. He is her Soul, and she cannot live without Him. However, the Church is visible as well, and her personality needs to be externalized (a point that holds in general for man, as an embodied person). Indeed, the body is not only the ontological support for the soul, nor its instrument. The body is, first of all, the expression of the soul.

This externalization can take on many forms. The spectacular character of the Spirit's manifestations at the beginning of the Church's history is rare (and even then, they were doubtlessly less frequent than spontaneously comes to mind when reading the relevant texts, for the narratives concentrate these miracles, placing them in relief in a somewhat artificial manner). This is because, ordinarily, God intervenes in the world—even in salvation history—only under the cover of second causes and human wills, mysteriously directing human freedoms toward the good. Nonetheless, all of these interventions, taking place within the world history, in social life, and in private life, manifest the Church's holiness. They are manifestations of the Holy Spirit living in the Church, animating her, and leading her.

Such signs are ambiguous, for one and the same external manifestation can be related to man's spirit—sometimes to man's evil spirit—or to the Spirit of God. For this reason, the Church developed the art of "the discernment of spirits," which finds its first sketch in Scripture itself: "Do not quench the Spirit, do not despise prophesying, but test everything; hold fast what is good,"[27] and: "Beloved, do not believe every spirit, but test the spirits to see whether they are of God; for many false prophets have gone out into the world. By this you know the Spirit of God: every spirit which confesses that Jesus Christ has come in the flesh is of God, and every spirit which does not confess Jesus is not of God."[28]

27. 1 Thes 5:19–21 (RSV).
28. 1 Jn 4:1–3 (RSV).

Thus, it will be asked, "What is the use of these signs?" We have seen that, in general, the visible mission precedes and prepares for the invisible mission. Now, here, we seem to witness a reversal: the Spirit, invisibly present in man's spirit, enables him to judge and discern the externally manifested Spirit. This is not truly the case. The sending of the Spirit to the Church (and, through her, to the world) was first of all visible. It is Christ's resurrection, a brilliant manifestation of God's power and love: "designated Son of God in power according to the Spirit of holiness by his resurrection from the dead," and, "If the Spirit of him who raised Jesus from the dead dwells in you, he who raised Christ Jesus from the dead will give life to your mortal bodies also through his Spirit which dwells in you."[29] Next, it is Pentecost, the veritable creation of the Church, in which we see the two aspects of the Holy Spirit—His visible and invisible aspects—tightly and indissolubly woven together. All the other manifestations of the Spirit are prolongations of these two central manifestations. Certain ones are "guaranteed," namely those that have the Church as such as their subject, as was the case for Christ's Resurrection and Pentecost. Likewise, such guaranteed manifestations include the charisms of truth and governance assured to the Church. Other manifestations, which do not have this guarantee, need to be "discerned" and are, in the end, discerned by the Church herself.[30]

3. Charisms and the Holiness of the Charismatic

{237} Already in St. Paul, we find that manifestations of the Spirit, even authentic ones, can be found in someone who does not have charity and therefore who does not have grace and the Holy Spirit in himself.[31] St. Thomas interprets this fact as follows. When these manifestations are authentic, they are always a sign of the Holy Spirit given to the Church, dwelling in the Church. Of themselves, they also signify the Holy Spirit dwelling in those in whom or by whom

29. Rom 1:4 (RSV) and 8:11 (RSV).
30. All this will be examined in the third volume in the section on ecclesiology.
31. See 1 Cor 13:1–3.

they are produced, for the Holy Spirit dwells in the Church by dwelling in the believers who are part of the Church and who are her members. However, it can happen that a believer personally places an obstacle before this communication of the Spirit. In this case, he testifies to the Holy Spirit's activity and presence in the Church but not to His presence in himself:

> To say something "in the Holy Spirit," can be understood in two ways. On the one hand, it can happen "in the Holy Spirit," acting on man but not dwelling in him. Indeed, it does happen that the Holy Spirit makes men speak, even though He does not dwell in them ... or it can happen "in the Holy Spirit," acting on someone in whom He also dwells.[32]

Thus, extraordinary manifestations of the Spirit do not always bear witness to the personal holiness of the person in whom they are produced. This is the reason why the "process of canonization" begins with the examination of the virtues and fruits of holiness that are the acts of the holy life. However, we must avoid the contrary excess that would consist, if not in considering them to be counter-signs, at least in denying that they have any relation to holiness. If the latter is established by other means, extraordinary manifestations also signify the personal holiness of the beneficiary and exalt him, at least when those manifestations are authentically of a supernatural origin.[33]

C. There Was No Spirit Yet

{238} "Now this he said about the Spirit, which those who believed in him were to receive; for as yet the Spirit had not been given, because Jesus was not yet glorified."[34]

---

32. St. Thomas, *In XII 1 Cor.*, 12:11.

33. Benedict XIV, *De servorum Dei beatificatione et canonizatione* (Prato: 1840), III, 42.

34. Jn 7:39 (RSV); see Marie-Émile Boismard, "De son ventre couleront des fleuves d'eau vive," *Revue biblique* 65 (Paris, 1958): 523–546; François-Marie Braun, "L'eau et l'Esprit," *Revue thomiste* 49 (1949): 5–30; Braun, *Jean le théologien*, vols. I, II, III/1, and III/2 (Paris: Gabalda, 1959–1972) III/2, 50–56; André Feuillet, "Les fleuves d'eau vive de Jn VIII, 38," in *Parole de Dieu et sacerdoce*, ed. Louis Bouyer and Eugène Fischer (Tournai-Paris: Desclée et Cie, 1962), 107–120; Pierre Grelot, "De son ventre couleront des sources d'eau vive," *Revue biblique* 66 (Paris, 1959): 271–378.

This text poses a difficulty for the theologian, for while the missions of the Divine Persons must be defined by their entry [accès] into the created person by means of grace, it seems that wherever there is grace, there is a mission of both the Word and of the Holy Spirit. This is St. Thomas's position, which led him to an excessive disjunction between the invisible and visible missions, thus minimizing the role of the latter.[35] Nevertheless, there can be no doubt that Scripture connects the sending of the Holy Spirit to Jesus' glorification and departure, as well as to faith in Him and to adherence to Him through the sacraments.

Would this require us to call into question the definition we provided for what a divine mission is? No. However, it means that we must be conscious of the intimate connection between the visible mission and the invisible mission, as we noted above. The mission of the Holy Spirit is neither exclusively the Holy Spirit's entry [accès] into the created spirit through grace, nor His external manifestations, if these two elements are considered separately. Instead, such a mission consists in the conjunction of these two elements. The Holy Spirit can be sent to a particular person only after He is sent to the Church and to the world through her—a sending that occurred by means of brilliant manifestations. Nobody receives the Holy Spirit except in and through the Church, by means of the sacraments, which are another external manifestation of the Spirit. Through them the believer is placed in close conjunction with Christ's resurrection and with Pentecost, which are the great manifestations of the Spirit. In order to extract the authentic meaning of the so-called "charismatic movement," the theologian's study of these matters must place the Spirit's manifestations within this ecclesial context.[36]

35. See ST I, q. 43, a. 6c and ad. 1.
36. See Jean-Hervé Nicolas, "Le Saint-Esprit est donné à l'Église et à chacun dans l'Église," Nova et Vetera 51 (1976): 188–209.

III. CONCLUSION TO THE FIRST PART (BOOK 1)

{239} Here, we must draw our theological study of the Trinitarian mystery to its close. The fourth stage of the process that was described earlier—the return to the Immanent Trinity on the basis of the Economic Trinity ordering the believer to it, wherein the Economy comes to its consummation—has been sketched out in these pages dedicated to the invisible missions of the Son and the Spirit. In a sense, it must be continued by the whole second section of this work. It is dedicated to Christ, since He is our way of return and of access to the Father, and it is comes to its completion with Eschatology. This final stage will equally be pursued throughout this synthesis's third main section, dedicated to "the Church and the Sacraments," that is, to the continuation, up to the Parousia, of the redemptive and sanctifying action of Christ by the Holy Spirit, whom He sends to the Church from the Father in order to announce the Gospel to men and to lead them to the Father.

Therefore, having concluded the "treatise on the Trinity," we are in no way turning the page and passing on to something else. The richer and more precise knowledge that we have been able to acquire concerning the Three Divine Persons must illuminate from on high all the investigations that remain to be undertaken, so that the realities of salvation may be known more profoundly, for salvation is the work of the Father, through the Son, in the Spirit.

We are well aware that there is room for a host of deeper investigations in the study of the Trinitarian mystery itself—either in the biblical domain, in the domain of tradition, or moreover, at the level of theological reflection. Still, it is our hope that this synthetic presentation of multiple aspects of the mystery will perhaps not be useless for those who wish to pursue such further investigations. Indeed, as necessary as it may be to concentrate such considerations on a given particular point, they will be truly fruitful for theology, and even valuable, only if they constantly refer back to the mystery considered in its entirety.

Bibliography

—————:—————

Ambrose, St. *De spiritu sancto ad gratianum augustum.* PL 16.

Anselm, St. *De processione Spiritus Sancti.* PL 158.

——. *Pourquoi Dieu s'est fait homme.* Edited and translated by René Roques. SC 91. Paris: Cerf, 1963.

Aristotle. *La métaphysique.* Edited by Jules Tricot. 2 vols. Paris: Vrin, 1953.

——. *Organon.* Vol. 1. Translated by Jules Tricot. Paris: Vrin, 1946.

Athanasius, St. *Epistola de Decretis Nicaenae Synodis.* PG 25.

——. *Tomus ad Antiochenos.* PG 26.

Augustine, St. *La Trinité, Books I–VII.* Oeuvres de Saint Augustin (OESA) 15. Translated and edited by Marcellin Mellet and Pierre-Thomas Camelot. Introduction by Ephraem Hendrickx. Paris: Desclée de Brouwer, 1955.

——. *La Trinité, Books VIII–XV.* OESA 16. Translated by Paul Agaësse. Paris: Desclée de Brouwer, 1955.

——. *La Cité de Dieu.* OESA 33–37. Paris: Desclée de Brouwer, 1959–1960.

——. *De Natura et Gratia,* OESA 21, 222–412. Paris: Desclée de Brouwer, 1966.

——. *De peccatorum meritis et remissione.* PL 44.

Bailleux, Émile. "La création, oeuvre de la Trinité selon S. Thomas." *Revue thomiste* 62 (1962): 27–50.

——. "Chronique. La dogmatique de la Trinité." *Mélanges de science religieuse* (Lillle) 29 (1972): 101–8.

——. "Le Christ et son Esprit." *Revue thomiste* 73 (1973): 373–400.

Bardy, Gustav. "La Trinité. La révélation du mystère: Écriture et Tradition." In *Dictionnaire de théologie catholique,* edited by A. Vacant et al., vol. 15, 1580–1702. Paris: Letouzey & Ané, [1950].

Barnard, Leslie William. "The Logos Theology of St. Justin Martyr." *Downside Review* 89 (1971): 132–41.

Barré, Henri. *Trinité que j'adore.* Paris: Lethielleux, 1965.

Barth, Karl. *Dogmatique.* Genève: Labor et Fides, 1953–1970.

Basil of Caesarea. *Sur le Saint-Esprit.* Translated and edited by Benoît Pruche. SC 17 bis. Paris: Cerf, 1968.

Benoît, Pierre. "Les origines du symbole des apôtres." In *Exégèse et Théologie*, vol. 2, 193–211. Paris: Cerf, 1961.

―――. "Préexistence et incarnation." *Revue biblique* (Paris) 77 (1970): 5–29.

Benedict XIV. *De servorum Dei beatificatione et canonisatione*. Prato: 1840.

Bergeron, Martial. "La structure du concept latin de personne." In Études d'histoire littéraire et doctrinale du XIIIe siècle, 21–161. Paris-Ottawa: J. Vrin-Institut d'études médiévales d'Ottawa, 1932.

Birault, Henri. "De l'être, du divin et des dieux chez Heidegger." In *L'existence de Dieu*, 49–76. Paris / Tournai: Casterman, 1961.

Boismard, Marie-Émile. *Le prologue de S. Jean*. Paris: Cerf, 1953.

―――. "De son ventre couleront des fleuves d'eau vive." *Revue biblique* (Paris) 65 (1958): 523–46.

Blondel, Maurice. *La pensée*, vols. 1 and 2. Paris: Aubier, 1934.

Boethius. *Liber de persona et de duabus naturis Christi*. PL 64.

Bonaventure, St. *Commentarium in Ium librum Sententiarum*. *Opera omnia*, vol. 1. Quaracchi: 1882.

Bouillard, Henri. *Karl Barth*, vols. 1, 2, and 3. Paris: Aubier, 1957.

―――. "Le refus de la théologie naturelle dans la théologie protestante contemporaine." In *L'existence de Dieu*, 95–108. Paris / Tournai: Casterman, 1961.

Boularand, Éphrem. *L'hérésie d'Arius et la foi de Nicée*, vols. 1–2. Paris: Letouzey, 1972–1973.

Bouyer, Louis. *Le Fils éternel*. Paris: Cerf, 1974.

―――. *Le Consolateur, Esprit Saint et vie de grâce*. Paris: Cerf, 1980.

Braun, François-Marie. "L'eau et l'Esprit." *Revue thomiste* 49 (1949): 5–30.

―――. *La Mère des fidèles*. Paris / Tournai: Casterman, 1954.

―――. *Jean le théologien*, vols. I, II, III / 1 and III / 2. Paris: Gabalda, 1959–1972.

Camelot, Pierre-Thomas. "Le dogme de la Trinité. Origine et formation des formules dogmatiques." *Lumière et Vie* 30 (1956): 9–48.

Cazelles, Henri. "Le Dieu d'Abraham." In *Les Quatre Fleuves. Cahiers de la recherce et de réflexion religieuses* 6 (1976): 5–17.

Cerfaux, Lucien. *Le Christ dans la théologie de saint Paul*. Paris: Cerf, 1954.

―――. *Le chétien dans la theologie de saint Paul*. Paris: Cerf, 1962.

―――. *La théologie de l'Église suivant saint Paul*. Paris: Cerf, 1965.

―――. *Jésus aux origines de la Tradition*. Paris: Desclée de Brouwer, 1968.

Chavannes, Henry. *L'analogie entre Dieu et le monde selon saint Thomas d'Aquin et selon K. Barth*. Paris: Cerf, 1969.

Chevalier, Irénée. *Saint Augustin et la pensée grecque. Les relations trinitaires*. Fribourg: Librairie de l'Université, 1940.

Clavel, Maurice. "Heilige, das Heilige." In *Lexikon für Theologie und Kirche*, second edition, vol. 5, edited by Josef Höfer and Karl Rahner, 84–92. Freiburg im Breisgau, 1957ff.

―――. "Orient et Occident. La procession du Saint-Esprit." *Istina* 17, nos. 3 and 4 (1972).

———. *Ce qu je crois*. Paris: Grasset, 1975.

Congar, Yves-Marie. "Théologie." In *Dictionnaire de théologie catholique*, edited by Alfred Vacant et al., vol. 15, 341–502. Paris: Letouzey & Ané, [1950].

———. *Le mystère du Temple* Paris: Cerf, 1957.

———. "Le moment économique et le moment ontologique dans la Sacra Doctrina: Révélation, Théologie, Somme théologique." In *Mélanges Chenu*, 135–187. Paris: Vrin, 1967.

———. *Je crois en l'Esprit Saint*, vols. 1–3. Paris: Cerf, 1980–1982.

Corvez, Maurice. "Le problème de dieu." *Revue Thomiste* 67 (1967): 65–104.

Cottier, Georges. "Difficultés d'une théologie de la liberation." In *Les Quatre Fleuves. Cahiers de la recherche et de réflexion religieuses*, vol. 2, 64–81. Paris: Seuil, 1974.

Cullmann, Oscar. *Christologie du Nouveau Testament*. Neuchâtel, CH: Delachaux et Niestlé, 1966.

Cyril of Alexandria, St. *Deux dialogues christologiques*. Edited and translated by Georges-Matthieu de Durand. SC 97. Paris: Cerf, 1964.

Daniélou, Jean and Ferdinand Cavallera, "Introduction." In Saint John Chrysostom, *Sur l'incompréhensibilité de Dieu*, SC 28. Paris: Cerf, 1951.

Daniélou, Jean. "Bulletin de théologie sacramentaire." *Recherches des sciences religieuses* 34 (1947): 369–384.

———. *Essai sur le mystère de l'histoire*. Paris: Seuil, 1952.

———. *Théologie du Judéo-christianisme*. Paris: Desclée, 1958.

———. *Les évangiles de l'enfance*. Paris: Seuil, 1967.

Deissler Alfons. "La revelation de Dieu dans l'Ancien Testament." In *Mysterium Salutis. Dogmatique de l'histoire du salut*, vol. 5, 303–371. Paris: Cerf, 1970.

Denys l'Aréopagite. *Des Noms divins*. Translated by Maurice de Gandillac. Paris: Aubier, 1980.

Denzinger, Heinrich. *Enchiridion Symbolorum: A Compendium of Creeds, Definitions and Declarations of the Catholic Faith*. Edited by Peter Hünermann, Robert Fastiggi, et al. San Francisco: Ignatious Press, 2021.

Dominique, De Petter. "Le caractère métaphysique de la preuve de l'existence de Dieu et la pensée contemporaine." In *L'existence de Dieu*, 167–80. Paris / Tournai: Casterman, 1961.

Dondaine, Hyacinthe-François. "Qualifications dogmatiques de la théorie de l'*Assumptus Homo* dans les oeuvres de Saint Thomas." *Revue des sciences philosophiques et théologiques* 30 (1941–1945): 163–68.

———. "Notes doctrinales thomistes." In *Saint Thomas d'Aquin. Somme théologique, La Trinité*, vol. 1, pp. 214–58; vol. 2, pp. 383–453. Paris: Cerf, [1946].

———. "Bulletin de théologie dogmatique." *Revue des sciences philosophiques et théologiques* 35 (1951): 609–13.

Dumiege, Gervais, ed. and trans. *La foi catholique: textes doctrinaux du magistre de l'église*. Paris: Editions de l'Orante, 1961.

Duméry, Henri. *Critique et religion*. Paris: Sedes, 1957.

──────. *Le problème de Dieu en philosophie de la religion*. Paris: Desclée de Brouwer, 1957.

Durand, Georges-Matthieu de. "Sa generation qui la racontera? Is. 53,8B: l'exégèse des Pères." *Revue des sciences philosophiques et théologiques* 53 (1969): 638–57.

Evdokimov, Paul. *La femme et le salut du monde*. Paris / Tournai: Casterman, 1958.

──────. *La connaisance de Dieu selon la tradition orientale*. Lyon: Mappus, 1967.

──────. *L'Esprit Saint dans la Tradition orthodoxe*. Paris: Cerf, 1969.

Fabro, Cornelio. *Participation et causalité selon Saint Thomas d'Aquin*. Paris: Vrin, 1961.

Fitzgerald, Thomas J. *De inhabitatione Spiritus Sancti, doctrina Sancti Thomae Aquinatis*. Mundelein: 1949.

Froidevaux, Léon. "Le symbole de S. Grégoire le Thaumaturge." *Recherches des sciences religieuses* 19 (1929): 193–247.

Feuillet, André. "Les fleuves d'eau vive de Jn VIII, 38." In *Parole de Dieu et sacerdoce*. Edited by Louis Bouyer and Eugène Fischer, 107–20. Tournai-Paris: Desclée et Cie 1962.

──────. *Le Christ Sagesse de Dieu*. Paris: Gabalda, 1966.

──────. *Le mystère de l'amour divin dans la théologie johannique*. Paris: Gabalda, 1972.

──────. *Christologie paulinienne et tradition biblique*. Paris: Desclée de Brouwer, 1973.

Galtier, Paul. *Le Saint-Esprit en nous d'après les Pères grecs*. Rome: Pontifica Universita Gregoriana, 1946.

──────. *L'habitation en nous de trois Personnes*. Rome: Pontifica Universita Gregoriana, 1950.

──────. "La conscience humaine du Christ. A propos de quelques publiations récentes." *Gregorianum* 32 (1951): 525–68.

Gagnebet, Marie-Rosaire. "La nature de la théologie spéculative." *Revue thomiste* 44 (1948): 213–55, 645–74.

Garrigues, Juan-Miguel. "Procession et ekporèse du Saint-Esprit." *Istina* 17 (1972): 345–66.

──────. "La personne composée du Christ d'après S. Maxime le Confesseur." *Revue Thomiste* 74 (1974): 181–204.

Geffré, Claude. "Théologie naturelle et revelation dans la connaissance de Dieu un." In *L'existence de Dieu*, 297–318. Paris / Tournai: Casterman, 1961.

──────. "La mort comme nécessité et comme liberté." *Vie Spirituelle* 492 (1963): 264–80.

──────. "La théologie, science de la foi." In *Encyclopédia Universalis*, vol. 15, 1087–91.

Geiger, Louis Bertrand. "Transcendance et subjectivité." In *Problèmes actuels de la connaissance de Dieu*, edited by Norbert A. Luyten, 73–92. Fribourg: Éditions Universitaires, 1968.

Gilson, Étienne. *Le réalisme méthodique*. Paris: Téqui, 1935.

──────. *Le thomisme, introduction à la philosophie de Saint Thomas d'Aquin*. Fifth edition. Paris: Vrin, 1945.

————. "L'être et Dieu." *Revue Thomiste* 62 (1962): 181–202.

Gregory Nazianzen, St. *Orationes*. PG 35–36.

————. *Lettres théologiques*. Edited and translated by P. Gallay. SC 208. Paris: Cerf, 1974.

————. *Discours 27–31 (Discours théologiques)*. SC 250. Paris: Cerf, 1978.

Grelot, Pierre. "De son ventre couleront des sources d'eau vive." *Revue biblique* 66 (1959): 271–378.

————. *Sens chrétien de l'Ancien Testament Esquisse d'un traité dogmatique*. Paris: Desclée et Cie, 1962.

Guillet, Jacques. "Le titre biblique de Dieu vivant." In *L'homme devant Dieu, Mélanges offerts au P. H. de Lubac*, vol. 1, 11–23. Paris: Aubier, 1963.

Le Gouillou, Marie-Joseph. "Réflexions sur la théologie des Pères grecs en rapport avec le Filioque." In *L'Esprit Saint et l'Église*, 220–34. Paris: Fayard, 1969.

————. "Réflexions sur la théologie trinitaire." *Istina*, (1972): 457–64.

————. *Le mystère du Père*. Paris: Fayard, 1973.

Gutierrez, Gonzales J. *Génesis de la doctrina sobre el Espiritu Santo-Don, desde Anselmo de Laon hasta Guillermo d'Auxerre*. Mexico: Progreso, 1966.

Hadot, Pierre. "Introduction." In Marius Victorinus, *Traités théologiques sur la Trinité*, SC 68, 7–89. Paris: Cerf, 1960.

Hayen, André. "Le concile de Reims et l'erreur théologique de Gilbert de la Porrée." *Archives d'histoire doctrinale et littéraire du Moyen Age* 10 (1935/1936): 29ff.

Hippolytus of Rome, St. *Contre les hérésies: Fragment*. Étude et edition critique par Pierre Nautin. Paris: Cerf, 1949.

————. *La tradition apostolique*. Edited by Bernard Botte. SC 11bis. (Paris: Cerf, 1968).

Irenaeus of Lyon, St. *Adversus Haereses, libri quinquie, Libri I–II*. Edited by Ubaldo Mannucci in *Bibliotheca sanctorum Patrum et scriptorium ecclesiasticorum*. Rome: Ex Officina Typographica Forzani et Socii, 1907.

————. *Contre les hérésies*, bk. 3 (SC 34); bk. 4 (SC 100 bis et 100 ter); bk. 5 (SC 152 and 153).

John Chrysostom, St. *De fide orthodoxa*. PG 94, 784–1228.

————. *De proditiione Judae*. PG 49, 380–89.————. *De Verbis Apostoli*. PG 51, 271–310.

————. *Homélies sur 1 Corinthiens*. PG 61, 9–381.

————. *Homélies sur l'épître aux Hébreux*. PG 63.

————. *Sur l'incompréhensibilité de Dieu, introduction de Ferdinand Cavallera and Jean Daniélou*. Translated by Robert Flacelière. SC 28. Paris: Cerf, 1951.

Jourjon, Maurice. "Introduction." In St. Gregory Nazianzen, *Discours théologiques: Discours 37–31*, edited and translated by Paul Gallay, SC 250, 7–65. Paris: Cerf, 1979.

Jugie, Martin. *De processione Spiritus Sancti ex fontibus revelationis et secundum orientales dissidentes*. Rome: Lateran, 1936.

Krempel, Anton. *La doctrine de la relation chez Saint Thomas, exposé historique et systématique*. Paris: Vrin, 1952.

Kleinknecht, Hermann. "Dieu." In *Dictionnaire biblique*, 7–33 and 125–28. Genève: Labor et Fides, 1968.

———. "Esprit." In *Dictionnaire biblique*, 37–55. Genève: Labor et Fides, 1968.

Labourdette, Michel. "La théologie intelligence de la foi," *Revue thomiste* 46 (1946): 5–44.

———. "Problèmes d'eschatologie." *Revue thomiste* 54 (1954): 658–75.

———. "Problèmes du mariage." *Revue thomiste* 68 (1968): 125–48.

———. "Mystique et apophase." *Revue thomiste* 70 (1970): 629–40.

Lackmann, Max. *Vom Geheimnis der Schöpfung. Die Geschichte der Exegese von Römer 1, 18–23; 2, 14–16 und Acta 14, 15–17; 17, 22–29 vom 2. Jahrhundert bis zum Beginn der Orthodoxie*. Stuttgart: Evangelisches Verlagswerk, 1952.

Lafont, Ghislain. *Structures et méthode dans la Somme théologique de Saint Thomas d'Aquin*. Paris: Desclée de Brouwer, 1961.

———. *Peut-on connaître Dieu en Jésus-Christ?* Paris: Cerf, 1969.

Lamarche, Paul. "Le prologue de S. Jean." *Recherches des sciences religieuses* 52 (1964): 497–537.

La Potterie, Ignace de. *La vérité dans Saint Jean*. Vols I–II. Rome: Biblical Institute Press, 1977.

Larcher, Chrysostome. Études sur le livre de la Sagesse. Paris: Gabalda, 1968.

Leo, St. *Epistolae*, PL 54, 582–1213.

L'Esprit Saint et l'Église: L'Avenir de l'Église et de l'oecuménisme. Paris: Fayard, 1969.

Liébaert, Jacques. *L'incarnation*. Vol. 1. *Des origines à Chalcédoine*. Paris: Cerf, 1968.

Lonergan, Bernard. *De Deo Trino*. Vols. 1 and 2. Rome: Apud Aedes Universitatis Gregorianae, 1964.

———. *La notion de Verbe dans les écrits de Saint Thomas d'Aquin*. Paris: Beauchesne, 1966.

———. *Conceptio analogica divinarum Personarum*. Rome: Apud Aedes Universitatis Gregorianae, 1967.

Lossky, Vladimir. *Théologie mystique de l'Église d'Orient*. Paris: Aubier, 1944.

———. *Théologie negative et connaisance de Dieu chez Maître Eckhart*. Paris: Vrin, 1960.

———. *Vision de Dieu*. Neuchâtel, CH: Delachaux et Niestlé, 1962.

———. "L'apophase et la théologie trinitaire." In *A l'image et à la resemblance de Dieu*, 7–23. Paris: Aubier, 1967.

———. "La procession du Saint-Esprit dans la doctrine trinitaire orthodoxe." In *A l'image et à la resemblance de Dieu*, 67–93. Paris: Aubier, 1967.

———. "La théologie de la lumière chez S. Grégoire Palamas." In *A l'image et à la resemblance de Dieu*, 39–65. Paris: Aubier, 1967.

Lot-Borodine, Myrrha. *La deification de l'homme*. Paris: Cerf, 1970.

Malet, André. *Personne et Amour dans la théologie trinitaire de Saint Thomas d'Aquin*. Paris: Vrin, 1956.

Maritain, Jacques. *Réflexions sur l'intelligence et sur sa vie propre*. Paris: Desclée de Brouwer, 1930.

———. "L'existant." In *Court traité de l'existence et de l'existant*, 103–39. Paris: Hartmann, 1947.

———. *La philosophie bergsonienne*. Paris: Téqui, 1948.

———. *Distinguer pour unir ou Les degrés du savoir*. In *Oeuvres completes*, vol. 4, 259–1110. Fribourg-Paris: Éditions universitaires-Éditions Saint-Paul, 1983.

Martinez-Castañeda, Jesús. *Los dones de las misiones divinas según Santo Tomás*. Lima: Renovabis 1958.

Merleau-Ponty, Maurice. *Eloge de la philosophie*. Paris: Gallimard, 1965.

Meyendorff, John. *Introduction à l'étude de Grégoire Palamas*. Paris: Seuil, 1959.

———. "Note sur l'interprétation orthodoxe de l'eucharistie." *Concilium* 24 (1967): 53–60.

Michaeli, Frank. *Dieu à l'image de l'homme*. Neuchâtel, CH: Delachaux et Niestlé, 1949.

Michel, Albert. "Hypostatique (Union)." In *Dictionnaire de théologie catholique*, edited by A. Vacant et al., vol. 7, 437–78 and 485–86. Paris: Letouzey & Ané, 1922.

———. "La Trinité." In *Dictionnaire de théologie catholique*, edited by A. Vacant et al., vol. 15.2, 1702–1830. Paris: Letouzey & Ané, [1950].

Moingt, Joseph. *La théologie trinitaire de Tertullien*. Paris: Aubier, 1965.

Mollat, Donatien. "Saint Jean l'évangéliste." In *Dictionnaire de spiritualité ascétique et mystique, doctrine et histoire*, vol. 8, 192–247. Paris: Beauchesne, 1974.

Montagnes, Benoît. "Parole de Dieu et parole humaine." *Revue Thomiste* 52 (1952): 209–15.

———. "Compte-rendu de Krempel, A., La doctrine de la relation chez Saint Thomas, exposé historique et systématique." *Revue Thomiste* 54 (1954): 200–204.

———. "La Parole de Dieu dans la création." *Revue Thomiste* 54 (1954): 213–41.

Nédoncelle Maurice. "Les variations de Boèce sur la personne." In *Recherches des sciences religieuses* (1955): 202–39.

———. "Démythisation et conception eschatologique du mal." In *Le mythe de la peine. Colloque Castelli*, 195–222 (Paris: Aubier, 1961).

———. "Le moi du Christ et le moi des hommes à la lumière de la réciprocité des consciences." In *Problèmes actuels de christologie*, edited by Humbert Bouëssé and Jean-Jacques Latour, 201–22. Paris: Desclée de Brouwer, 1965.

Nicolas, Jean-Hervé. "Chronique de théologie dogmatique." In *Revue thomiste* 53 (1953): 415–31.

———. "Amour de soi, amour de Dieu, amour des autres." *Revue thomiste* 56 (1956): 5–42.

———. "La théologie et les théologiens." *Vie Spirituelle* (1960): 279–301.

———. "L'unité d'être dans le Christ selon S. Thomas d'Aquin." *Revue thomiste* 65 (1965): 229–60.

———. *Dieu connue comme inconnu*. Paris: Desclée de Brouwer, 1966.

———. *Les profondeurs de la grâce*. Paris: Beauchesne, 1969.

———. "La théologie." In *L'université et l'intégration du savoir*, edited by Norbert A. Luyten, 37–53. Fribourg: Éditions Universitaires 1970.

———. "Le Saint-Esprit est donné à l'Église et à chacun dans l'Église." *Nova et Vetera* 51 (1976): 188–209.

———. "Universalité de la mediation du Christ et salut de ceux qui ne connaissent pas le Christ." In *Acta del Congressso internazionale Tommaso d'Aquino nel suo settimo centenario*, vol. 4, 261–73. Napoli: 1976.

———. "Maintenir la place priviliégiée de saint Thomas dans un enseignement moderne de la théologie." *Seminarium* 29, no. 3 (1977): 878–97.

———. *Contemplation et vie contemplative en christianisme*, Fribourg-Paris: Éditions Universitaires-Beauchesne, 1980.

———. "Grâce et divinization." In *Studia Universitatis S. Thomae in Urbe*, 35–62. Romae: 1982.

Gregory of Nyssa, St. *La vie de Moïse*. Edited and translated by Jean Daniélou, SC 1bis. Paris: Cerf, 1955.

Ortiz de Urbina, Ignacio. *Nicée et Constantinople, Histoire des Conciles Oecuméniques*. Edited by Gervais Dumeige. Paris: Éditions de l'Orante, 1963.

Paissac, Henri. *Théologie du Verbe. Augustin et Thomas*. Paris: Cerf, 1951.

Parente, Pietro. "Unità ontological e psicologica de l'Uomo-Dio." *Euntes docete* 5 (1952): 337–401.

———. *L'Io di Cristo*. Brescia: Morcelliana, 1955.

Pattin, Adriaan. "Contribution à l'histoire de la relation transcendentale." In *L'homme et son destin d'après les penseurs du Moyen-Age (Acts of the First International Congress of Medieval Philosophy)*, 183–91. Louvain: Nauwelaerts, 1960.

Penido, Maurílio-Teixeira-Leite. "Gloses sur la procession d'amour dans la Trinité." *Ephemerides Theologicae Lovanienses* 14 (1937): 33–68.

———. "Prélude grec à la théorie psychologique de la Trinité." *Revue Thomiste* 45 (1939): 665–74.

Pétau, Denis. *Dogmata theological Dion. Petavii*. Paris: Vivès, 1865.

Prestige, George Leonard. *Dieu dans la pensée patristique*. Paris: Aubier, 1955.

Quasten, Johannes. *Initiation aux Pères de l'Église*. Vols. 1–3. Translated by Jean Laporte. Paris: Cerf, 1955–1962.

Rad, Gerhard von. *Théologie de l'Ancien Testament*. Vols. 1 and 2. Genève: Labor et Fides, 1967.

Rahner, Karl. "Dieu dans le Nouveau Testament." In *Ecrits théologiques* I, 13–111. Paris: Desclée de Brouwer, 1959.

———. "Problèms actuels de christologie." In *Ecrits théologiques*, I, 115–81. Paris: Desclée de Brouwer, 1959.

———. "Essai d'une esquisse de Dogmatique." In *Ecrits théologiques* IV, 9–50. Paris: Desclée de Brouwer, 1963.

———. "Pour la notion scolastique de la grâce incréée." In *Ecrits théologiques* III, 35–69. Paris: Desclée de Brouwer, 1963.

————. "Le concept du mystère dans la théologie catholique." In *Ecrits théologiques* VIII, 51–103. Paris, Desclée de Brouwer, 1967.

————. "Quelques remarques sur le traité dogmatique 'De Trinitate.'" In *Ecrits théologiques* VIII, 107–40. Paris: Desclée de Brouwer, 1967.

————. "Dieu Trinité fondement transcendant de l'histoire du salut." In *Mysterium Salutis. Dogmatique de l'histoire du salut*, vol. 6, 13–135. Paris: Cerf, 1971.

Ratzinger, Joseph. *La foi chrétienne hier et aujourd'hui*. Paris: Mame, 1969.

Régnon, Théodore de. Études de théologie positive sur la Sainte Trinité. 4 vols. Paris: Victor Retaux, 1892–1898.

Rey, Bernard. "Théologie trinitaire et revelation biblique." *Revue des sciences philosophiques et théologiques* 54 (1970): 636–53.

————. *Le cheminement des premières communautés chrétiennes à la découverte de Dieu*. Paris: Cerf, 1972.

Richard of Saint Victor. *La Trinté*, SC 63. Paris: Cerf, 1959.

Rogier, Louis-Jacob, Roger Aubert and David Knowles, eds. *Nouvelle histoire de l'Eglise*. Vol. 1. Paris: Seuil, 1963.

Romeyer, Blaise. *La philosophie religieuse de M. Blondel*. Paris: Aubier, 1943.

Ruello, Francis. "Une source probable de la théologie trinitaire de Saint Thomas." *Recherches des sciences religieuses* 43 (1955): 104–28.

Salet, Gaston. "Introduction" in *Richard de Saint-Victor, La Trinité*. SC 63, 7–48. Paris: Cerf, 1959.

Scheeben, Matthias-Joseph. *Les mystères du christianisme*. Paris: Desclée de Brouwer, 1947.

Schmaus, Michael. "Sendung." In *Lexikon für Theologie und Kirche*, second edition, vol. 9, Josef Höfer and Karl Rahner. Freiburg im Breisgau, 1957ff.

————. "La conception grecque de la Trinité et le mystère de l'Incarnation." In *Théologie du Renouveau*, 171–91. Paris: Cerf, 1968.

Schürmann, Heinz. "Les charismes spirituels." In *L'Eglise de Vatican II*, 541–74. Paris: Cerf, 1966.

Spicq, Ceslas. *L'epître aux Hébreux*. Vols. 1 and 2. Paris: Gabalda, 1952.

————. *AGAPÈ dans le Nouveau Testament, Analyse des textes*. Vols. 1–3. Paris: Gabalda, 1958–1959.

Scheffczyk, Leo. "Die heilsökonomische Trinitätslehre des Rupert von Deutz und ihre dogmatische Bedeutung." In *Festschrift J. R. Geiselmann*, 90–118. Freiburg:1960.

————. "Histoire du dogme de la Trinité," in *Mysterium Salutis. Dogmatique de l'histoire du salut*, vol. 4, 211–302. Paris: Cerf, 1969.

Schierse, Franz Joseph. "La revelation de la Trinité dans le Nouveau Testament." In *Mysterium Salutis. Dogmatique de l'histoire du salut*, vol. 5, 131–84. Paris: Cerf, 1970.

Schillebeeckx, Edward. "En quête du Dieu vivant," in *Approches théologiques 2: Dieu et l'homme*, 21–40. Bruxelles: Éditions du CEP, 1965.

————. "La notion de vérité et la tolerance," in *La liberté religieuse, exigence spirituelle et problème politique*, 113–53. Paris: Centurion, 1965.

Schulte, Raphael. "La preparation de la révélation trinitaire." In *Mysterium Salutis. Dogmatique de l'histoire du salut*, vol. 5, 303–71. Paris: Cerf, 1970.

Schweizer, Eduard. "Esprit." In *Dictionnaire biblique*, 113–242. Genève: Labor et Fides, 1971.

Stead, Julian "Perichoresis in the Christological Chapters of the 'De Trinitate' of Pseudo-Cyril of Alexandria." *Dominican Studies* 6 (1963): 12–20.

Taylor, Vincent. *La personne du Christ dans le Nouveau Testament*. Paris: Cerf, 1969.

Tertullian. *Traité du baptême*. Edited and translated by François Refoulé and Maurice Drouzy. SC 35. Paris: Cerf, 1953.

Trembelas, Pangiotis N. *Dogmatique de l'Église orthodoxe catholique*. Vols. 1, 2, and 3. Paris: Desclée de Brouwer, 1957.

Tresmontant, Claude. *Les idées maîtresses de la métaphysique chrétienne*. Paris: Seuil 1962.

Vanier, Paul. *Théologie trinitaire chez saint Thomas d'Aquin. L'acte notionnel selon Saint Thomas*. Paris: Vrin, 1952.

Vallery-Radot, Irénée. *Bernard de Fontaines, abbé de Clairvaux, le prophète de l'Occident*. Paris: Desclée de Brouwer, 1959.

Vatican Council I. *Dei Filius*. Dogmatic Constitution. April 24, 1870.

Vatican Council II. *Lumen Gentium*. November 21, 1964.

Widmer, Gabriel. "Sens et non-sens des énoncés théologiques." *Revue des sciences philosophiques et théologiques* 51 (1967): 644–65.

———. "Intelligibilité et incompréhensibilité de Dieu." *Revue de théologie et de philosophie* 18 (1968): 145–62.

Index

Abelard, Peter, 174, 207, 325

absolute subsistence of God, 82–84, 226–31

act of nature vs. act of freedom (procession of the Persons in God), 143–46, 160–61, 242–43

Alexandria, Synod of, 204

"all activities of God *ad extra* are performed by all three Persons," 101–102, 284–85, 358; and knowledge of Divine Persons in their distinction, 312–16

analogy: as methodology in theology 24–26, 48–49, 191–92, 291–92; superanalogical judgment of faith, 330

appropriation (logical procedure), 86, 309; need for conceptual knowledge of the Persons in their distinction, 310–12; outline of Thomistic approach, 324–32; transcended in mystical experience, 361–62; ultimately related to connection between Old Testament revelation of God and revelation of Trinity, 328. *See also* essential vs. notional acts/attributes

Arianism, 95–99, 103, 105, 180

Athanasius of Alexandria, 97–100, 204, 206

assimilation of created person to Trinity: continuously present in soul of the righteous, 366–68; through dynamic assimilation, 359–61, 364–66;

to each person in Trinity, 362–64; through quasi-efficient exemplar causality (Galtier and Palamism), 355–56; through quasi-formal causality (Rahner), 356–59

Augustine, 101–3, 116, 117, 121, 122, 124, 143, 148, 158, 160, 173, 202, 206, 207, 221, 224, 255–70, 275, 276, 379, 388

Barth, Karl: on natural theology, 51–53, 56–61; on theological use of notion of person, 201–2, 214

Basil of Caesarea, 99, 100, 103, 204, 317, 318. *See also* "one substance in three hypostases"

biblical theology, 20–21

Blondel, Maurice, 249

Boethius, Anicius Manlius Severinus: notion of person, 207–14

Bolotov, Vasilii: on the non-contestation of the *Filioque*, 268

Cajetan, Thomas de Vio: on the absolute subsistence of God, 226–31; on the super-eminence of the Godhead as one and triune, 193–94

circumincession. *See perichoresis*

co-essentiality and consubstantiality, 136–39

communication of idioms, 76–77, 277

Congar, Yves, 3, 66, 67

"contemporary men": an ambiguous expression often misused, 294–95

creeds: of Chalcedon, 12, 17, 23, 24, 268; of St. Gregory the Thaumaturge, 104; Niceno-Constantinopolitan, 104–6; Quicumque ("Athanasian"), 106
Cullmann, Oscar, 42, 77–81

Daniélou, Jean, 227, 300
"De Deo Uno": and "De Deo Trino," 113–16, 271–73
Didache, 93
Dionysius (pope), 95, 98
Dionysius (Pseudo-), 48, 301, 170, 222, 301, 307
Divine Essence: as absolute and relative, 288–89. See also Cajetan
divine missions: as extension of divine procession, 348–49; general notion of "mission", 345–48; incarnation and visible mission of the Son, 375–82; visible and invisible missions, 371–74; visible mission of the Spirit, 389–90. See also mystical experience
divine presence: immensity vs. presence through knowledge and love, 296

essence and energies of God, 301–2; and Aquinas on videre Deum vs. comprehendere essentiam divinam, 304–5. See also Gregory Palamas
essential vs. notional acts/attributes, 165–68, 218–20, 226, 241, 262–63, 265–66; danger of treating the Word as the Divine Nature inasmuch as it is intelligible, 249; persons do not each possess the Divine Nature in a unique way (contra Scheeben), 247; and process of appropriation, 329–32
Eunomians/Anhomoians: on the knowledge of God ("rationalist"), 300

faith: as form of knowledge, 13. See also mystical experience; theology
Father: attribution of creation to Father uniquely by appropriation, 318, 322; constituted precisely as begetting the Son, 231–41; paternal love of, 243–45. See also innascibility/unbegottenness; monarchy of the Father

Fathers: early formulations concerning the Trinity, 94-95
fecundity: as key Trinitarian notion (related to self-diffusivity of the Good), 168–71
Ferrara-Florence, Council of, 107
Filioque, 198–99, 255–76; importance of "innascibility" for reaching an understanding, 275; proienai vs. ekporeusthai (contrast single term procedere), 261; and termini of the processions, 223, 256–64
first principles of reason, 5

Galtier, Paul, 102, 313, 327, 355
Gagnebet, Marie-Rosaire, 1, 3
generation, 141–43; and notion of procession of intelligible word, 147–50
Gilbert de al Porée, 220
Gilson, Étienne, 48, 53, 293
God: existence and attributes, 45–49; holiness of, 68; omnipotence of, 69; transcendence of, 67–68; wholly other, 25, 57, 181; wisdom and justice of, 69
grace, created vs. uncreated, 301–2, 303; created grace as means for divine missions, 353, 368–70
Gregory Nazianzen, 100–103, 111, 142, 143, 148, 240,
Gregory of Nyssa: psychological explanation for Trinity, 118; and vision of God, 307
Gregory Palamas: and "antinomic" theology (Lossky), 273; on assimilation to Godhead akin to Galtier's theory, 356; and knowledge of God, 301–8. See also grace; essence and energies of God

Hegel, Georg Wilhelm Friedrich, 53, 201–2
Heidegger, Martin, 53, 54
Hilary of Poitiers, 99, 124
Hippolytus of Rome, 96, 203
Holy Spirit: Divine Gift, 265–66; holiness appropriated to, 385; Infinite Friendship of Divine Persons, 263–64; mutual love of Father and Son, 260–63; Personified Love, 264–65; procession

understood by analogy with production of *terminus a quo* in act of willing, 150–60; role in divinization, 385–89; scriptural basis of divine personhood of, 87–89. *See also* essential vs. notional acts; fecundity; love; spiration *per Filium*

homoousios, 98–100

hypostasis, 204

"Image": proper to the Son, 251–53; in relation to the Holy Spirit, 252–53

Incarnation: how it is and is not proper to the Word and to Him alone, 253–55, 378–82

innascibility/unbegottenness, 233–40, 275

Irenaeus of Lyon, 100, 300, 302, 318

Jesus: declared Lord, 77–78; filial awareness, 75–77; pre-existence affirmed, 78–82

John Chrysostom, 71, 226, 227, 300

judgment: act of, 26, 47–49, 291, 296, 329, 242; immediate judgment of principle of non-contradiction as *per se nota*, 177; superanalogical judgment of faith, 330

Jugie, Martin, 269, 307

Justin Martyr, 93

knowledge: fecundity of, 131–33; as presence of the other as other within the knower, 129–31

Labourdette, Michel, 3

Lossky, Vladimir: on apophaticism in theology, 120; on monarchy of the Father, 240–41; on use of relation to articulate mystery of the Trinity, 120, 180, 221, 229, 272–73. *See also* vision of God

love: and production of, within the lover, 151–59. *See also* essential vs. notional acts/attributes

Lot-Borodine, Myrrha, 31, 102, 327

Macedonianism, 100

Maritain, Jacques, 18, 34, 131, 133, 365

mental word: uttering of, as distinct from

but wholly subordinated to knowledge, 131; as applied to knowledge of Word in the Trinity, 134–36. *See also* knowledge

Merleau-Ponty, Maurice, 54

modalism, 95

monarchism, 95, 103, 203, 206, 207, 209, 273, 325

monarchy of the Father, 229, 232–33, 240–41, 267, 268, 271, 272, 275. *See also* innascibility/unbegottenness

monotheism: at first practical and "lived" in character for Israel, 61–62; deepening of awareness by Israel, 63–64

motives of credibility, 3

mystical experience: and the divine missions, 350–52; beyond but not outside formulas of faith, 296; of "righteous on the outside" (of ecclesial communion yet *in voto* desiring baptism) and *minores* in the faith, 313

natural desire to see God, 286–87

natural theology: critiqued by Barth, 51–53, 56–61; truths of faith "objectively" presuppose and imply various truths of reason, 58

notions and notional acts, 224–26

obediential potency, 359–60. *See also* natural desire to see God

"one substance in three hypostases," 97, 100, 101, 103, 164, 204, 219, 274, 301

ontological argument, 287–88

Orange, Second Council of, 112

Origen, 72, 85, 98, 104, 204, 300

patripassianism, 95

Paul of Samosata, 99

perichoresis, 104, 276–79, 315, 346

personality: as applied to God by Israel, 64–65, 83–86; formal perfection of personhood as applied to Trinity, 215–17; modern criticism of its use to articulate those "Being God" in the Godhead, 200–201; ontological and phenomenological-psychological notions of personhood, 212–14;

personality: (*cont.*)
"person" indistinctly applying to each of the Persons of the Trinity, 211–12, 381–82; persons in Godhead having only "minor virtual" distinction from the essence, 194–95, 278–79. *See also* Boethius
personal properties of Persons of the Trinity, 223–24
Pétau, Denis (Dionysius Petavius), 101, 102, 327, 386, 388
philosophy: methodological atheism in contemporary thinkers, 53–54; realistic philosophy required for faith, without rejecting all modern philosophy, 16–20; truths of faith "objectively" presuppose and imply various truths of reason, 58
Photios of Constantinople, 267
prosopon, 203

Rahner, Karl: on assimilation to God through quasi-formal causality, 356–59; on "*De Deo Uno*," 114; on nature of theology, 3, on notion of absolute subsistence of God, 227–28; on relationship between "Immanent" and "Economic" Trinity, 110–13; on revelation of the Trinity in Old Testament, 70, 73; on vision of God, 306; on whether the Word alone could have become incarnate, 253–55, 378
Ratzinger, Joseph, 60, 203
realism (epistemological), 5; in relation to faith and theology, 7, 16–20, 293–95
reason: truths of faith "objectively" presuppose and imply various truths of, 58
Régnon, Théodore de, 101, 102; on notion of absolute subsistence of God, 227–28; rejection of appropriation, 327, 331; on supposed "Greek" and "Latin" conceptions of Trinity, 122–23
Reims, Council of, 220, 222
"reinterpretation of the faith": true and false meanings, 10–12
relation/relative opposition: characterized by *ad esse*, not *in esse*, 185–90; earliest use to articulate Persons of the Trinity, 102–104; foundation of relations, 128; *In Deo omnia sunt unum et idem ubi non obviat relationis oppositio*, 106–8, 173, 224, 316; relative distinction contrasted to other types, 174–81; relative opposition and kinds of alterity, 176–81; relative opposition does not imply the other types, 182–84; sole means for rendering Trinity intelligible, 179–80, 193; subsistent relation, 184–91, 221–22; transcendental relation, 191n13
revelation: mediation of the Son, 84–85; propositional content of, 111–12. *See also* vision of God
Richard of St. Victor, 120, 148, 149, 170, 207, 213, 234, 248, 260, 261, 263, 274

Sabellianism, 95, 175
salvation history: only understandable in light of mystery of Trinity, 340
Scheeben, Matthias Joseph, 102, 103, 247
Schillebeeckx, Edward, 56, 57, 338
Scotus, John Duns: intellection vs. production of mental word, 131
sensus fidelium: not rule of faith, 10
Solzhenitsyn, Aleksandr Isayevich, 33
Spicq, Ceslas, 20, 144
spiration *per Filium*, 258–59, 267, 268, 322; limited to economy of salvation by Orthodox, 270, 276

Tertullian, 96, 98, 118, 124, 203, 267, 268
Theodoret of Cyrus, 270
theology: biblical, 20–21; born of desire to understand the faith, 14–16; doctrinal synthesis aimed at, 26; historical, 21; intrinsically ordered to mystical contemplation and Beatific Vision, 38, 298; limitations accepted for this synthesis, 34–36; notional and mystical, 112; role of interpretation of notions in elaboration of, 5–6; as science, 2–3; and spiritual life, 30–32; subject is God in His inner mystery, 1–3; and temporal problems of mankind, 32–34; theological pluralism, 28; theological relativism, 17

Index

Thomism: as basis of theology in this synthesis, 27–30

Toledo: Third Council of, 267; Eleventh Council of, 106

Trinity: "Economic" and "Immanent," 39, 40, 110–13, 122, 127, 203, 253–55, 267, 337–42, 395; exclusion of processions other than those of Word and Spirit, 162–68; at heart of theology, 37, 341n6, 395; not merely "beyond being," 289–90; not revealed in Old Testament, 71; preparations for revelation of, in Old Testament, 72–73; "psychological" explanation, 116–24, 121–23; schema for dogma in first Christian preaching, 89, 91; treated as a "superadded" concern when dogmatic theology courses treat the Godhead, 38. *See also* essential vs. notional acts/attributes; relation/relative opposition

Vatican I, 50–51, 54

Vatican II, 9

vision of God, 297–308; as at once vision of the Divine Essence and of the Persons, 308; East vs. West on, 300–308; meaning of knowledge *in Verbo*, 249–51; Orthodox (following Antiochenes) holding that this knowledge comes via objective mediation of Christ, 250, 300, 302, 304. *See also* Gregory Palamas; Lossky, Vladimir

Word: sacramentality in relation to incarnation of, 383–84. *See also* essential vs. notional acts/attributes; fecundity; generation; Jesus; knowledge; mental word